The Literature
of Nihilism

THE LITERATURE
OF NIHILISM

Charles I. Glicksberg

Lewisburg
BUCKNELL UNIVERSITY PRESS
London: ASSOCIATED UNIVERSITY PRESSES

Associated University Presses, Inc.
Cranbury, New Jersey 08512

Associated University Presses
108 New Bond Street
London W1Y OQX, England

Library of Congress Cataloging in Publication Data

Glicksberg, Charles Irving, 1901–
   The literature of nihilism.

   Bibliography: p.
   Includes index.
   1. Nihilism in literature. 2. Literature, Modern
—20th century—History and criticism. I. Title.
PN56.N55G58   1975   809'.933'8   74-203
ISBN 0-8387-1520-6

To Margaret M. Bryant

The author wishes to thank Macmillan Publishing Co., Inc. for
permission to quote from Arthur Danto, *Nietzsche as Philosopher*
(Copyright©Macmillan Publishing Co., Inc. 1965).

Contents

Introduction

The decisive point is not only that nihilism asserts the vacuum, the *nihil*, the nothing, but that the assertor himself is oppressed and afflicted by his own nothingness.[1]

Almost all the questions of most interest to speculative minds are such as science cannot answer, and the confident answers of theologians no longer seem so convincing as they did in former centuries. Is the world divided into mind and matter, and, if so, what is mind and what is matter? Is mind subject to matter, or is it possessed of independent powers? Has the universe any unity or purpose? Is it evolving towards some goal? Are there really laws of nature, or do we believe in them only because of our innate love of order? Is man what he seems to the astronomer, a tiny lump of impure carbon and water impotently crawling on a small and unimportant planet? Or is he what he appears to Hamlet? Is he perhaps both at once? Is there a way of living that is noble and another that is base, or are all ways of living merely futile?[2]

The supreme paradox of all thought is the attempt to discover something that thought cannot think.[3]

No one with any insight will still deny today that nihilism is in the most varied and most hidden forms "the normal state" of man.[4]

For, why is the triumph of Nihilism *inevitable* now? Because the very values current amongst us to-day will arrive at their logical conclusion

[1] Helmut Thielicke, *Nihilism,* trans. John W. Doberstein (New York: Harper & Brothers, 1961), p. 54.
[2] Bertrand Russell, *A History of Western Philosophy* (New York: Simon and Schuster, 1945), p. xiii.
[3] Søren Kierkegaard, *Philosophical Fragments,* trans. David Swenson (Princeton, N.J.: Princeton University Press, 1962), p. 46.
[4] Martin Heidegger, *The Question of Being,* trans. William Kluback and Jean T. Wilde (New York: Twayne Publishers, 1958), p. 47.

in Nihilism, because Nihilism is the only possible outcome of our greatest values and ideals, because we must first experience Nihilism before we can realise what the actual worth of these "values" was. . . . Sooner or later we shall be in need of *new values*.[5]

We feel that even when *all possible* scientific questions have been answered, the problems of life remain completely untouched. Of course there are then no questions left, and this itself is the answer.[6]

1. THE PARADOX OF NIHILISM

The aim of this book is to analyze some of the ways in which nihilism makes itself felt, obtrusively or obliquely, in the literature of the modern age. This presents a formidably complex problem of interpretation, for nihilism does not—in literature at least— exist in a pure state. Differently put, the nihilist, both as author and persona, is plagued by internal contradictions; he is rarely, if ever, altogether consistent in his beliefs and behavior. In "Problems of the Theatre," Dürrenmatt takes up the often-heard charge that literature today is nihilistic in content. This is the answer he gives:

Today, of course, there exists a nihilistic art, but not every art that seems nihilistic is so. True nihilistic art does not appear to be nihilistic at all; usually it is considered to be especially humane and supremely worthy of being read by our more mature young people. A man must be a pretty bungling sort of nihilist to be recognized as such by the world at large. People call nihilistic what is merely uncomfortable.[7]

Not that nihilistic writers invariably disguise or conceal their nihilistic outlook. Indeed, some boldly identify themselves as such, yet their writing still bears the marks of conflict and contradiction. For to undertake a work of art, no matter how much it may be infected with the blight of radical pessimism, is in effect to affirm a

[5] Friedrich Nietzsche, *The Complete Works of Friedrich Nietzsche,* ed. Oscar Levy. Vol. 14. *The Will to Power,* trans. Anthony M. Ludovici (Edinburgh and London: T. N. Foulis, 1910), 1 :2.
[6] Quoted in George Pitcher, *The Philosophy of Wittgenstein* (Englewood Cliffs, N. J.: Prentice-Hall, 1964), p. 161.
[7] Friedrich Dürrenmatt, *Four Plays: 1957–62* (London: Jonathan Cape, 1964), p. 39.

value, to live for the sake of the work that is being produced. Even the psychopathological genius of a Céline demands that the truth, no matter how horrible it turns out to be, be told: the truth about the human animal and his homicidal manias, the unflinching truth about his journey to the end of the night. Thiher calls Céline a nihilist by default; Céline's rejection of the destructive powers in life "proclaims a thirst for affirmation and perhaps for transcendence...."[8]

What, then, is generally meant by nihilism? Nihilism is difficult to define because it takes so many different forms, but it is a real enough experience. It is a spiritual crisis through which all thinking men pass at some time in their lives; and very few come through this ordeal unscathed. There is the passive nihilism of the Buddhist variety: life is an empty dream, action is futile, and striving for happiness, fulfillment, or perfection betrays the fact that one is still the slave of illusion.[9] The second type, the nihilism of negativity, is derived from the special brand of nihilism that sprang up in Europe, especially in Russia, in the nineteenth century; it was a nihilism that, despite its professed rejection of all belief, rested its faith in the scientific method.

Then there is a species of nihilism that is active, Dionysian: Nietzsche speaks of ecstatic nihilism. Nietzsche's nihilism is metaphysical rather than ideological. His attitude toward science is

---

[8] Allen Thiher, *Céline: The Novel as Delirium* (New Brunswick, N.J.: Rutgers University Press, 1972), p. 43.

[9] "'Nihilism' connotes negativity and emptiness; in fact, it denotes two bodies of thought that, although distinct from Nietzsche's, nevertheless bear it some partial resemblance. The Nihilism of Emptiness is essentially that of Buddhist or Hindu teaching, both of which hold that the world we live in and seem to know has no ultimate reality, and that our attachment to it is an attachment to an illusion. Reality itself has neither name nor form, and what has name and form is but a painful dreaming from which all reasonable men would wish to escape if they knew the way and knew that their attachment was nothingness. Life is without sense or point, there is a ceaseless alternation of birth and death and birth again, the constantly turning wheel of existence going nowhere eternally; if we wish salvation, it is salvation from life that we must seek." (Arthur C. Donato, *Nietzsche as Philosopher* [New York: The Macmillan Company, 1965], p. 28.) This is the Buddhist outlook that both Schopenhauer and Nietzsche incorporated in their work, but there is a pronounced difference in their attitude toward this type of unmitigated pessimism. Nietzsche fought against its seductive, enervating appeal, searching desperately for an ideal that would affirm and justify life.

therefore not worshipful; science is no more than a body of fictions, a set of conventions; it did not presuppose that it was based on truth. Nietzsche's nihilism was all-inclusive. He perceived no meaning in the world, no ultimate purpose, no sustaining principle of order. Man is saddled with the task of imposing order on a senseless universe.[10] There is also the type of nihilism that is carried to the logical extreme of suicide. Finally, there is the nihilism that promotes and justifies an unconscionable struggle for power. Life on earth is completely amoral in character; categorical imperatives are human constructs; no law exists to prevent the rule of the strong —a doctrine that motivated the Nazi reign of terror.[11]

Webster's New International Dictionary defines nihilism as "a viewpoint that all traditional values and beliefs are unfounded and that all existence is consequently senseless and useless: a denial of intrinsic meaning and value in life." Another definition that this dictionary gives is that nihilism is "a doctrine that denies or is taken as denying any objective or real ground of truth. In a

---

[10] By nihilism Nietzsche "had in mind a thoroughly disillusioned conception of a world which is as hostile to human aspiration as he could imagine it to be. It is hostile, not because it, or anything other than us, has goals of its own, but because it is utterly indifferent to what we either believe or hope. The recognition of this negative fact should not lead us to 'a negation, a no, a will to nothingness.' Rather, he felt, it is an intoxicating fact to know that the world is devoid of form and meaning. . . . To be able to accept and affirm such a view he thought required considerable courage, for it meant that we must abandon hopes and expectations which had comforted man, through religions and philosophies, from the beginning." *Ibid.*, p. 33.

[11] In *Nihilism,* Stanley Rosen directs his attack on the nihilists as the enemies of reason. "Not the least element in the origin of contemporary nihilism is that, when the pride and confidence in the project to master nature evaporated, the light of God was extinguished, and man saw himself altogether in the shadow of the beast." (Stanley Rosen, *Nihilism.* [New Haven and London: Yale University Press, 1969], p. 66). Nihilism, he goes on to say, "is fundamentally an attempt to overcome or to repudiate the past on behalf of an unknown and unknowable yet hoped-for future." (*Ibid.*, p. 140). Such a Promethean ambition entails a disregard, if not downright contempt, for the problematical present. "The nihilist perseveres in the face of despair not because he has a reason for so doing, but because his ostensible comprehension of the worthlessness of all reasons is understood by him as freedom." (*Ibid.*, p. 142). The nihilist "despairs because he is fully enlightened . . . or free from all illusions. His despair is the sign of his enlightenment or freedom, the seal of his integrity." (*Ibid.*)

more specific context this includes the philosophy of moral nihilism, which denies the objective ground of morality."[12]

Literary nihilism manifests itself chiefly in the recurrent effort to break out of this spiritual impasse. Nihilism is universally recognized as a lethal evil that must be resisted and finally overcome if mankind is to survive. It is virtually impossible, the nihilist finds, to endure the pains and perils of life while inwardly convinced that life serves no purpose at all and is therefore not worth living. The nihilist comes to believe that life is a senseless nightmare, a thing of sound and fury signifying nothing, and then struggles desperately to prove that his reasoning or intuition is all wrong. Thus does Professor Teufelsdröckh cry out in anguish when he is in the infernal grip of the Everlasting No: "To me the Universe was void of Life, of Purpose, of Volition, even of Hostility: it was one huge, dead, immeasurable Steam-Engine, rolling on, in its dead indifference, to grind me limb from limb. O, the vast, gloomy, solitary Golgotha, and Mill of Death! Why was the Living banished thither companionless, conscious?"[13] Like Carlyle's hero, the modern nihilist refuses to believe that he is fatherless, outcast, and that the universe belongs to the Devil. On the other hand, he will not allow himself to be deceived by fantasies, religious or metaphysical, of wish-fulfillment. He strives to keep faith with the sorry logic of his position: if all is illusion, then perhaps his anguished crisis of consciousness is also compounded of illusion.

But if the truth that man pursues so eagerly is only a solipsist illusion, then he finds himself trapped in a vicious circle of contradictions. Why speak? Why recommend one illusion as vastly superior to another? If truth is a myth, then all distinctions are

---

[12] "Nietzsche's Nihilism—his idea that there is no order or structure objectively present in the world and antecedent to the form we ourselves give it—has, he believed, the consequence that the men who accept it will have no temptation to disesteem human life by contrasting it with something eternal, inalterable, or intrinsically good. As a metaphysician, he sought to provide a picture of the world as it actually is . . . so that men might have no illusions either about it or about themselves, and, unimpeded by mistaken views, might set about their proper task, which was to make of humankind something more than it had been." Donato, *Nietzsche as Philosopher*, p. 195.

[13] Thomas Carlyle, *Sartor Resartus* (London: J. M. Dent & Sons, 1948), pp. 125–26.

abolished, and one might as well follow the erratic guidance of instinct and feeling instead of the promptings of reason. When the
writer as nihilist exposes the ridiculous limitations of thought
and comes to believe that truth is a will-o'-the-wisp that the mind
vainly chases in a phantasmagoria of locked-in subjectivity, how
can he mobilize the energy to go ahead with his creative effort?
How nerve himself for the enterprise of art? If all things begin
and end in naught, then why strive, why live, why perpetuate the
race?

This is the bind of the absurd from which the nihilist is unable
to extricate himself. We shall examine the different strategies a
number of modern writers employ in order to defeat the nihilism
that afflicts them. Unamuno counteracts the paralyzing constriction of nada by affirming a supernatural faith that assures him of
personal immortality. The Russian writer Leonid Andreyev violently
denounces the God in whom he does not believe for imposing a
cruel and incomprehensible fate on his human victims. In *Breaking-
Point,* Artzybashef ironically hails death as liberator and seems
to recommend the grace of salvation that suicide affords. Kafka,
the most complex and prophetic of the modern nihilists, closely
questions the sphinx of the infinite, but can provide no answer to
its riddle. In France, Sartre describes the demoralizing experience
of Nausea and then attempts to negate the void of Being by af-
filiating himself with the revolutionary movement. Camus rises above
the myth of the absurd by espousing the humanistic ethic of rebellion. Kazantzakis, who frankly proclaims that he is a nihilist,
accepts the challenge posed by a world without divine or ultimate
meaning but remains undaunted and commits himself the more
resolutely to the creative quest.

Though the writers discussed in this book have produced work
that in part or as a whole is steeped in the destructive element of
nihilism, they represent no organized body of thought. Profoundly
influenced as they have been by the disasters of history in their age,
they derive from no common ideological ancestry. The horror born
of the explosion of two world wars has intensified their despair and
accounts in large measure for their nihilistic outlook. As Lewis
Mumford remarks, the cult of nihilism tends swiftly to grow into

a cult of violence and terror on the political scene, "expressing a total contempt for life. . . . In an active or latent state, nihilism is at work throughout our civilization."[14] Important, however, as is the social and historical background in charting the course of literary development, it does not appear that nihilism is the special creation of the twentieth century, this age of crisis and catastrophe. The historical crisis of our time colors and accentuates the dominant motif of doom that crops up, but the nihilist strain has made itself felt in other cultures during the past, though in a less virulent manner. Before the advent of the horrors of the holocaust, there were poets, dramatists, and philosophers, who faced the nihilist dilemma. From Sophocles and Lucretius to Schopenhauer, Nietzsche, Dostoevski, Kierkegaard, and Tolstoy, there is scarcely an important creative figure who has not at some time been stricken with the fever of nihilism. It is always there to be faced—and overcome.[15]

I am assuming that the spiritual conflict that culminates in nihilism, far from being the mark of an unhinged mind or craven temperament or the characteristic but short-lived product of a time of trouble, is an archetypal experience. The writer either passes through the dark night of the soul and beholds finally the glimmer of the light beyond, however ambiguously it shines forth, or he never emerges from the darkness that hems him in. Though the nihilist has presumably abandoned the quest for ultimate meaning, he never actually ceases to question or cry out or seek a solution to the mystery of being. If he did so, he would have to give up entirely his career as a writer. The dialectic of nihilism is charged with unresolvable elements of complexity. It is not the formal expres-

---

[14] Lewis Mumford, *The Conduct of Life* (New York: Harcourt, Brace and Company, 1951), p. 150.
[15] When one considers the hazards of the human condition, it is indeed surprising that the history of world literature affords so few instances of writers overwhelmingly committed to some form of nihilism. Is this failure to find literary champions of the first rank *prima facie* evidence that the nihilistic cause is too restrictive in scope, too starkly negative in its implications, to serve as the vehicle of a universal vision of life, a vision that must include the glory and the triumph as well as anguish of being?

sion of a philosophical position nor is it a logically elaborated system of thought. If it embodies a world vision that is in the end forced to say No to life, it utters this categorical negation with different accents of conviction. The writer as nihilist may, in his work as in his life, be at odds with himself. He believes and disbelieves at the same time. Like Camus, he loves life even in those moments of utter despair when he condemns it as absurd. He may, like Bertolt Brecht, be a nihilist in his youth and then become a man with a cause to support, the founder of the epic theater. He may suspend judgment completely as he conducts an interminable monologue, a debate in which, like Kafka, he espouses both sides of the case without ever arriving at any positive conclusion.

The creative nihilist is thus engaged in a struggle that is never ended. It is hard to envisage a *militant* nihilist. What is there for him, be it a Nietzsche or a Kazantzakis, to be militant about? So long as he writes, he affirms the value of the project to which he is committed, even though he continues to hurl imprecations at a world that fails to conform to the heart's desire. On whatever ground he chooses to conduct his quarrel with God or the universe, he is, as a creative being, celebrating the numinous paradox that is life. He persists in seeking the light that dwells in the heart of darkness, though he cannot silence the suspicion that whatever gods or goals he discovers along the way may be the projections of his own mind. He cannot silence the clamorous voice of doubt. His profession of "faith," whatever form it finally assumes, is instinct with a profound skepticism, but at least this provisional and qualified faith restores him temporarily to life. Only a few nihilists are permanently crucified on the cross of the negative.

The rage of the nihilist against the ineradicable absurdity of existence is an inverted expression of his love of life. Since his life goes on—he rejects, as does Camus, the expedient of suicide—he stops at some point in his career to ask himself: "How am I to live? What is to be done?" In dealing with the torments and tribulations as well as existential contradictions that characterize the nihilistic protagonist, Dostoevski is, like Nietzsche, a prophetic figure. He fights against that which tempts him most: the snares of the Devil, "the destructive element," the blasphemous denial of God's existence. The nihilistic heroes he presents, metaphysical rebels against God, are complex incarnations of his own persona. Dostoevski is Raskolnikov, Smerdyakov, Ivan Karamazov, Stavrogin, Kirillov just as much as he is Alyosha, Zossima, Shatov, Myshkin, and Sonya. If Dostoevski paints with merciless insight the extremes of evil that infect the heart of man, who is capable of the worst enormities, he also portrays the counterpointed craving of the sons of Satan for more and more of life, life everlasting, until the end of eternity. The more violently they rebel against the human condition, the greater the energy with which they love life. Kirillov, the monomaniac who is bent on disproving the existence of God, is a religious mystic.[16]

It is apparent that the nihilist and the humanist share a common body of assumptions. Both believe that man is alone, both reject faith in the supernatural. But whereas the secular humanist then proceeds to declare that man is the measure, the sole source and touchstone of value, the nihilist repudiates all such man-made values as illusions, mere as-if fictions designed to hide from human eyes the emptiness and futility of existence. The nihilist (he may use some other name: Jeffers, for example, called himself aptly an Inhumanist[17]) will not conceal from himself the desolating "truth" of human dereliction. He will proclaim far and wide his discovery that the idea of progress, like the romantic faith in the perfectibility of man, is a spurious myth. He harbors no revolutionary hopes; he does not look forward to the future for the redemption of mankind.

It is at this point of no return that the nihilist reverses his field, as it were, and takes up a position that, in defiance of the canons

---

[16] One critic maintains that it is impossible to answer the question whether Dostoevski was a believer. "He loved his atheists and seemed to cherish their arguments. . . . Certainly Dostoevsky was no firm believer of the naïve and unshaken kind. He had gone through 'a furnace of doubt.' But his oscillations between believing and doubting suggest a wrestling with faith alien to an avowed atheist." William Hubben, *Dostoevsky, Kierkegaard, Nietzsche, and Kafka* (New York: Collier Books, 1962), p. 86.
[17] See "The Ironic Vision of Robinson Jeffers," in Charles I. Glicksberg, *Modern Literary Perspectivism* (Dallas, Tex.: Southern Methodist University Press, 1970), p. 100. See also Mercedes Cunningham Monjian, *Robinson Jeffers: A Study in Inhumanism* (Pittsburgh: University of Pittsburgh Press, 1958).

of logic, brings him to a closer understanding of the intense spiritual battle the religious Existentialist must wage before he can affirm his faith in God. Faced with the ultimate issue of death—his death —as annihilation, the nihilist wants to know how best to live the time of his life. But what is "good," what is "best"? Intellectually he is convinced that he has purged his mind of all religious traces, though his longing for God, as was true in the case of Nietzsche and Kazantzakis, never leaves him. But longing that never goes beyond that stage is not the same thing as the actuality of faith. Like Valéry, the nihilist distrusts the coinages of the mind, the stratagems of the duplicitous self, the abstractions that it creates and then hypostatizes as sacred realities. He applies the same stringent skepticism to his own negative conclusions. He turns to literature as a means of contemplating the universe through a variety of disparate perspectives, realizing as he does so that literature is in itself but a symbolic confrontation of reality that can illuminate but cannot solve his existential conflict.

The literary nihilist nevertheless persists in his search for ultimate meaning, as if to make sure he has made no error in his calculations. Invoking the law of polarity, he shadows forth that which other writers, more modest in their creative aim or less driven by demonic pride to pierce the secret of the universe, deliberately ignore or omit. If Heaven is balanced by Hell and God by the Devil, so the plenitude of being is opposed by the ever-present threat of nothingness. Eros is perpetually in conflict with Thanatos, life is gravitating toward the inorganic state of being. The nihilist suffers excruciatingly from his obsession with the dialectic of nothingness. If he actually believes that nothingness is the ultimate end of existence, then he cannot, like the humanist, be sustained by the constructive role he plays in the historic process or rest his hopes on some radiant consummation in the future order of society.

This encounter with nothingness forms the crux of nihilist literature, just as the experience of the dark night of the soul lies at the heart of Christian mysticism. Most people are sleepwalkers (to use Hermann Broch's expressive term) who take it for granted that life has a meaning beyond the mere living of it. It is this instinctive faith that the nihilist begins by questioning and then finally decides to reject. As soon as he does so, he finds himself trapped in a spiritual cul-de-sac. He is unable either to affirm or to deny. He can neither act nor refrain from acting. How shall he act on his negative beliefs?

This life-negating dementia constitutes a theme that has been pondered by poets, philosophers, mystics, and saints for over two thousand years. It is the archetypal concern of the the tragic vision, the central, though not sole, preoccupation of religion. When human consciousness first arose, man must have formulated the question of questions: Who am I in relation to the cosmos? What am I doing here on earth? What purpose am I supposed to serve? What are the ancient myths but symbolic representations of the unceasing battle man must wage against the demonic powers that each winter threaten the continuity of life.

Nietzsche announced that God was dead and wrestled with the problem of what was to take the place of God. He sought to grasp the truth bearing on the human condition, without regard for the harmful consequences it might have for mankind. The relentless search for the truth at all costs is sustained by a moral principle, but it led Nietzsche to the ultimate of disillusionment. If truth is a myth, then the pursuit of truth must cease, for it leads nowhere. Nothing is to be believed, not even the empirically warranted conclusions of science. The upshot in Nietzsche's case is a nihilism that cannot be borne because it cannot be lived. As Karl Jaspers points out: "Even if his thinking appears as a self-destructive process in which no truth can last, even if the end is always nothingness, Nietzsche's own will is diametrically opposed to this nihilism. In empty space he wants to grasp the positive."[18] He endeavors to formulate a vital faith, a transcendent affirmation that can inspire human life to nobler effort. Hence he glorifies strength, the *élan vital*, the will to power, the ideal of eternal recurrence. This is a far cry, however, from any religious gospel that the general run of mankind can embrace. But the passion of striving, the stubborn

---

[18] Karl Jaspers, *Nietzsche and Christianity*, trans. E. B. Ashton (Chicago: Henry Regnery Company, 1961), p. 84.

hankering after the ideal, is abundantly present in his work; he is not satisfied with the finite, the merely human; he must break out of the nihilistic impasse.

2. THE NIETZSCHEAN INFLUENCE

Nietzsche set the stage for the epic drama of metaphysical despair that was acted out in the twentieth-century mind. Like Heidegger, he cannot reconcile himself to the nihilistic outlook; his struggles to cure himself of this sickness of soul prefigure the metaphysical conflicts that were to bedevil the sons of Nietzsche in the twentieth century. He sounded the cry of spiritual alienation that is the leitmotif of nihilism, but his response to the vision of ultimate nothingness that obsessed him was prophetic in its attempt to go beyond, to affirm life in the face of a skeptical and restive faculty of reason.

Practically the entire history of twentieth-century thought, its transvaluation of the values of the past, its rejection of the gods, is foreshadowed in Nietzsche's work. He predicted the eventual triumph of nihilism. The first section of *The Will to Power,* on "European Nihilism," is a defense of the movement but at the same time an impassioned effort to transcend it. This accounts for the persistent element of paradox in his epigrammatic and oracular utterance; he must show that the experience of nihilism marks the first step in the dialectic of transcendence. Though he savagely attacks Christian doctrine, its ethics grounded in *ressentiment,* and its eschatology, he never rid himself of the insistent need for some viable form of faith. Though couched in iconoclastic rhetoric, the "religious" urge is present in the compulsion to say yes to life, to voice an aesthetic that would glorify instinct and biological health and wholeness. In exalting the will to power, his nihilism announced the glad tidings of the birth of the superman in the future. There we discern the saving, if irrational, contradiction in his outlook: he still believed in the future, in the rise of a race of superior men who will have conquered the nihilism in their own souls. Only when nihilism is lived through, and not before, will it be possible to gratify the need for new values.

Nietzsche insisted that the coming of nihilism was necessary. Nihilism, he argued, is logically the outcome of the values and ideals Western civilization had cherished. The culminating experience of nihilism makes it possible for us to discover the disillusioning truth about these values. Then he added: "We require, sometime, *new values*."[19]

Nietzsche's own life was a series of contradictions that had to be resolved. This self-appointed Antichrist was born of a line of Lutheran pastors. His father and both his grandfathers were ministers. He spent his early years in a parsonage and was brought up, later, in a pious home. As a schoolboy he lost his religious faith and fell into a state of aggressive doubt; he began to question the validity of all religions of the supernatural variety.

While at Bonn he decided to give up the study of theology; he could not subsist on the faith of his fathers. He joined the ranks of the freethinkers of his time, but this did not relieve him of the burden of responsibility for seeking out the truth. If God was only a consolatory fiction, then what was there to lend significance to life? He read David Strauss's *Life of Jesus* and accepted its basic thesis. Once the divinity of Christ was denied, the idea of God would have to be abandoned as well. Nietzsche's intellectual awakening was completed, late in 1865, by his reading of Schopenhauer's *The World as Will and Idea*. Lange's *History of Materialism* turned him into a rigorously consistent materialist; he denied the existence of a world beyond or of things-in-themselves; these are fictions, spooks conjured up by the human mind. Nietzsche had come to the turning of the road: he now perceived that reality was mysterious, inscrutable. All that man can grasp is the phenomenal world; there was no supersensible reality man could be aware of. Nietzsche accepted Darwinism, but detected no directing agency, no teleological drive, at work in evolution. The logical implications were there to be drawn, and Nietzsche did not hesitate to say what these were.[20] Hence he arrived at a nihilistic interpretation

---

[19] Friedrich Nietzsche, *The Will to Power*, trans. Walter Kaufmann and R. J. Hollingdale, ed. Walter Kaufmann (New York: Random House, 1967), p. 4.
[20] Hollingdale sums up what the consequences were: "God, if he existed, was unknowable: he could be no more than an idea in the minds of men. Nothing that

of man's place in the universe. Once he became convinced
that God was dead, he realized "that the universe had ceased to
possess any meaningful reality."[21] From this he drew the heartening
conclusion that man, although surrounded on all sides by chaos,
is entrusted with the task of choosing his own goals.

Nietzsche stresses that the first step to be taken in the conquest
of nihilism is the frank acknowledgment, however reluctantly
made, that the malady exists and that it is spreading. The quest for
ultimate meaning ends in failure, and the result of this aborted
endeavor is the rise of nihilism—the realization that all such
metaphysical ventures are in vain.[22] After suffering the final blow
of nihilistic disillusionment, "one realizes that becoming aims at
nothing and achieves *nothing*" (p. 12). The ontological wound
that nihilism inflicts is not only painful but incurable. Henceforth
man must cease to look upon himself as the hero for whom the
drama of creation was ordained. He must give up, too, the notion
of unity pervading the universe, the belief in a principle of order
informing all of existence, the idea of God and of himself as a
derivative of God. Both these psychological states—the perception
of the absence of all value and the abandonment of the belief
in a presiding unity—are distressing, but there is still a way out—the
postulation of another world as the *true* world; even this last hope,
however, proves illusory. When this happens, nihilism emerges
in its final form; "it includes disbelief in any metaphysical world
and forbids itself any belief in a *true* world" (p. 13). The attempts

existed in the phenomenal world could have come from 'outside': if the universe
were intelligible, it must be intelligible from within. . . . Man was in touch with no
'beyond', and was no different than any other creature. But, as God had been the
meaning of the universe, so man had been the meaning of the earth. Now God and
man, as hitherto understood, no longer existed. The universe and the earth were
without meaning." R. J. Hollingdale, *Nietzsche* (London: Routledge & Kegan Paul,
1965), pp. 89–90.
[21] *Ibid.,* p. 122.
[22] Nietzsche furnishes various definitions of nihilism. This, he says, is what nihilism
means: "*That the highest values devalue themselves.* The aim is lacking; 'why'
finds no answer." (*The Will to Power,* trans. Walter Kaufmann, p. 9). Again, he
defines nihilism as "the conviction of an absolute untenability when it comes to the
highest values one recognizes; plus the realization that we lack the least right to
posit a beyond or an in-itself of things that might be 'divine' or morality incarnate."
(*Ibid.*)

in the past to create a meaningful universe failed; man was guilty of projecting his needs and wishes into the neutral flux of events on the assumption that he was the measure of all things.

Though he knows all this, Nietzsche is not dejected. Nihilism represents a type of decadence, a pathological state that will not last. The nihilistic vision may make possible a surprising richness of life. Nietzsche, as we have seen, distinguishes two kinds of nihilism: the active form, which is a sign of increased spiritual strength, and passive nihilism, which is marked by a depletion of spiritual power. Nietzsche's point is that nihilism can bear witness to the courage and strength of the human spirit; the emancipated man has no further need of the props of faith, the support of illusion. But nihilism can also indicate a falling-off in strength, the inability to create for oneself a goal or a purpose or a living faith. Though Nietzsche accepted an active form of nihilism and affirmed it, sometimes ecstatically, he recognized full well the dangers inherent in nihilism. To ask whether life is worth having is a sure sign of sickness. The question does not make sense. It is madness to ask such unanswerable questions, but the questioning goes on just the same. As Nietzsche puts it: "Nihilism is no cause but merely the logical result of decadence" (p. 27). Once the idea of the existence of God is overthrown, it becomes evident that no absolute moral order is possible. Hence it follows that Nature is amoral, without an aim or ultimate meaning. That is when nihilism takes over: the victim of suffering comes to realize there is no justification for his suffering. Everything seems in vain—a sentiment or state of mind characteristic of nihilism. The logical outcome of nihilism is suicide.

Nietzsche calls himself an immoralist, but he is really an unconventional moralist at heart, a moralist of a new order that celebrates the positive virtues of strength and power. It is Nietzsche the moralist who stands forth most conspicuously in his writings, only it is the wrong, iconoclastic kind of morality—what others condemn as immorality—that he champions. Nihilist though he proclaims himself to be, there is no mistaking the impassioned tone in which he espouses the cause of life, life at all costs, but life in its highest and finest manifestations. He is the intellectual

who realizes all too well the limitations of the intellect, the philosopher who is all the time aware of the ineffectuality of his calling.
He refutes the pretensions of positivism by pointing out that there
are no facts, only "interpretations" (p. 267). The world has to be
interpreted from a multiplicity of perspectives—this is what
Nietzsche calls perspectivism. Truth represents what we accept as
a condition of life for us. Reason is but one idiosyncratic way
of viewing the world. Truth is not a preexisting essence that man
must search out for himself; it is "something that must be created"
(p. 298). The world as it ought to be must be created, too. Hence the
need for vital fictions, viable myths. Those who lack the creative
mythopoeic power become nihilists. Nietzsche defines the nihilist
as one who passes judgment on the world that fails to meet his
conception of the ideal, while recognizing that this ideal world
does not exist. "According to this view, our existence . . . has no
meaning: the pathos of the 'in vain' is the nihilists' *[sic]* pathos . . ."
(p. 318). The free spirit imposes a pattern of meaning on the welter
of phenomena or is capable, by sheer strength of will, of living
without the bread and meat of meaning. As Nietzsche often remarked,
nihilism may be a symptom of vitality and power or of unregenerate
weakness. What happens is that the creative instinct is either
enhanced, and can thus dispense with an overall framework of
justification, or it ceases to function as faith in the possibility of
ultimate meaning declines. Those who have the courage to peer
into the depths behold the specter of meaninglessness. Knowing
that they have created this world that is instinct with values, they
also know "that reverence for truth is already the consequence
of an illusion—and that one should value more than truth the
force that forms, simplifies, shapes, invents" (p. 326). If the world
is our interpretation, then new higher perspectives are possible,
perspectives that will increase our feeling for life. Perspectivism
thus rests on the assumption that "there is no 'truth'" (p. 330).
    Nietzsche declares that it is positively exhilarating to be un-
burdened by a sense of cosmic purpose, a God-controlled system
of rewards and punishments, but he emphatically repudiates
nihilism as the basis of art. Art is the expression of perfection and
plenitude; "art is essentially *affirmation, blessing, deification of*

existence" (p. 434). It follows that a pessimistic art is out of the question. "There is no such thing as pessimistic art" (p. 435). Tragedy induces in the spectator a bracing, tonic effect. Nietzsche speaks of art as "the great stimulant of life" (p. 452). Though as an experimental philosopher he was prepared to face the challenge of a radical nihilism, he saw no reason why nihilism must stop at the pole of negation, since it seeks to transcend this condition and desires to reach "a Dionysian affirmation of the world as it is . . ." (p. 536). At one point in *The Will to Power,* Nietzsche speaks of "an ecstatic nihilism" (p. 544).

In the figure of Dionysus, Nietzsche discerned a dialectical synthesis of seemingly opposed energies, the nay blending with the yea, the destructive and the creative instinct fused. Though Nietzsche stressed the pervasiveness of illusion, he could not escape the knowledge that his most fundamental values were based on illusion. Thought was a disease that brought pain and joy: the pain of entrapment in the coils of cognition and the blinding joy of insight into the human condition. Thus his work was of paradox all compact and the supreme paradox he presented was that of "the intellectual as a protagonist of anti-intellectualism."[23] He warred against excessive reliance on reason and accorded primacy to the voice of instinct, yet he utilized the canons of logic to demonstrate the impotence of logic, though he did not deny the usefulness of logical fictions. Increasingly he came to perceive the value of fictions and myths as liberating perspectives. The search for conceptual truth rests on a lie. It is an elaborate ritual of self-deception connived at by the intellect. The only truth that has merit is the truth born of the Dionysian spirit. "But this truth is nihilistic and suicidal" (p. 105). Nietzsche never resolved this tragic dilemma (p. 110).

The Nihilism that Nietzsche diagnosed in his own time was not caused by flagrant social evils or the growing corruption of mankind. Nihilism arose and was now dominant, Nietzsche maintained, because of the utter collapse of Christianity. If God stands for the symbolic urge to truth, then the revelation must finally come

[23] Peter Heller, *Dialectics and Nihilism.* (Amherst, Mass.: The University of Massachusetts Press, 1967), p. 74.

that Christianity is grounded in a spurious system of morality. Once we give up the moral interpretation of the world, which is completely without foundation, we are compelled to march on the road that "leads to nihilism."[24] Life is then seen as an enigma, a dance of light and shadow, a magnificent if fortuitous play of energy; the heroic man must learn to live with this nihilistic knowledge.

Nietzsche struggled to find a way out of nihilism by resolving to accept life as it is for all eternity, despite the reality of suffering and the misfortunes that fell to his lot. By the concentrated and disciplined power of his will he would rise above the human condition. He would transmute suffering into sheer joy, pain into jubilation. Whatever befell him he would greet with a burst of Dionysian laughter and thus establish his control of life in a problematical and supremely indifferent universe. Hence his euphoric formulation of the doctrine of eternal recurrence, what Sartre calls "the metamorphosis of the most wildly, most bitterly realistic willing into poetry."[25] After his ecstatic vision of the assurance of immortality that this doctrine granted, "he *decided* that the idea was true, without proof, in a burst of enthusiasm. The myth became an article of faith, hence of will."[26] Nietzsche has gone "beyond tragedy"[27] and wills a tragic nihilism.[28]

---

[24] Nietzsche, *The Will to Power,* trans. Walter Kaufmann and R. J. Hollingdale, p. 7.
[25] Jean-Paul Sartre, *Saint Genet,* trans. Bernard Frechtman (New York: George Braziller, 1963), p. 346.
[26] *Ibid.,* p. 348.
[27] Morse Peckham, *Beyond the Tragic Vision* (New York: George Braziller, 1962), p. 368.
[28] Sartre eloquently debunks Nietzsche's total reliance on his deific will: "Nietzsche *wanted to will* his moral solitude, his literary failure, the madness which he felt coming on, his partial blindness and, through his woes, the universe. Vain efforts: his will skidded over the glazed, slippery block of being without getting a hold. What could he do to will, *to have willed,* the clouds that passed over his eyes, the pounding in his head? He was on the lookout for his instinctive repulsions and as soon as he caught himself protesting or begging for mercy, he clenched his fists, scowled and cried out: 'I will it'; he was dancing the ballet of will." (Jean-Paul Sartre, *Saint Genet,* p. 346). Karl Jaspers argues that Nietzsche's attempt to overcome nihilism combines "a speculative mysticism (eternal recurrence) and a metaphysical interpretation of being (will to power) with an inspiring vision of the superman of the future. This is not knowledge of something that exists but the impulse to overcome nihilism, which first will be driven to deduce from the concept of

Nietzsche conceded that nihilism could be rightfully classified as a species of disease. Freud arrived at the same conclusion. And Jung argued that "meaninglessness inhibits fullness of life and is therefore equivalent to illness."[29] Nietzsche sought to cure himself of this metaphysical mania that reduced him at times to a state of absolute despair. It is possible to argue that Nietzsche is no nihilist. A dedicated foe of Christianity, he is at bottom a believer *manqué*. A self-proclaimed immoralist, he ends up by creating his own code of moral values. His will to power is actually a dithyrambic celebration of life.[30]

3. THE LITERATURE OF NIHILISM

There is nothing, to be sure, more familiar than the stock Darwin-Freud-World War I-answer to this question [Why this fascination with the void?]. With the disappearance of God, the rise of science, machine civilizations, and mass culture, the cynical and destructive study of ideologies, and the shattering impact of international conflicts, we have enough social fact—even without the hackneyed, all-purpose atom bomb —to explain much more than a vogue for the void.[31]

We are now prepared to examine the anomalous spectacle of the emergence in literature of the nihilistic temper in an age of revolutionary scientific experimentation and technological exper- tise, an age dedicated to the cult of limitless progress and cyber- netic felicity. The phrase *the literature of nihilism* is actually an oxymoronic coinage, for literature and art, even tragedy, as

incessant becoming the extreme conclusion that the world is without meaning and goal and that all activity is futility. It is this temptation to ultimate negation inhering in this intensified nihilism that will produce the radical turn to the affirmative. . . ." (Karl Jaspers, *Nietzsche,* trans. Charles F. Wallraff and Frederick J. Schmitz (Tucson, Ariz.: The University of Arizona Press, 1965), p. 284).

[29] C. G. Jung, *Memories, Dreams, Reflections.* Rec. and ed. Aniela Jaffé, trans. Richard and Clara Winston (New York: Pantheon Books, 1963), p. 340.

[30] See Appendix A.

[31] Robert Martin Adams, *Nil: Episodes in the Literary Conquest of Void During the Nineteenth Century* (New York: Oxford University Press, 1966), p. 6. *Nil* explores the myth of Nothing that emerged in the past century, the dialectics of a presumed experience that is beyond expression because the experience is, by definition, empty of content. The theme of the void persists in the literature of the twentieth century, notably in the work of Samuel Beckett.

Nietzsche maintained, is intrinsically the negation of the *nihil*. There is, to be sure, a taint of the nihilist, small or large, in practically every tragic writer from Sophocles and Euripides to Malraux, Camus, and Eugene O'Neill; the struggle goes on continually to banish the specter of the absurd, to transform the negative into the affirmative. Whether he acknowledges it or not, the writer, as writer, seeks by virtue of his art to justify his life, and, by implication, he believes in the positive value of his creative work. This study will show that there is no writer who is a thoroughgoing nihilist. The reasons for this must be fairly obvious by this time. To begin with, the writer as nihilist is, like Nietzsche, in conflict with himself. He is not at all happy in his state of absolute negation. He struggles hard to shake off this metaphysical obsession that enfeebles his will to create and insidiously undermines his will to live. Some literary nihilists use their writing as an exercise in the dialectics of exorcism, a form of magic intended to destroy the evil spirit that endeavors to deprive them not only of their love of life but also of their commitment to art. There is no pattern of uniformity, however, in the kind of magic that modern writers employ in their fight against nihilism. Montherlant, a lapsed Catholic, devotes himself to the worship of Venus Naturalis, without the romantic conception of love to distract him. Camus, while still retaining his vision of the absurd, formulates his ethic of rebellion. Sartre rises above the experience of "nausea" by allying himself with the cause of Communism. Malraux seeks out danger and fights in the Spanish Civil War, but he is under no illusion as to the importance of his action when it is viewed in relation to the cosmic scheme of things. A tragic philosopher and poet like Unamuno defeats the paralyzing force of despair that the vision of nada induces, by rejecting the authority of reason and affirming his faith in God, who will grant him personal immortality. Kafka finds the world impenetrable, beyond human understanding, but in his religious need he explores all the answers his imagination can conjure up, without arriving at any conclusion. This accounts for the aura of ambiguity in which his fiction is bathed. But he is powerless to cure himself of his nihilistic obsession.

Though literary nihilism cannot be defined with logical precision, the nihilist, be he author or character, can be identified as the man who is convinced that the human adventurer did not evolve as the result of some operative teleological design. Man is nothing more than a biological sport. He is that because, unlike other species of sentient life, he has developed a consciousness that presumes to question the Being out of which it arose in the remote dawn of time. To ask the why of Being, however, is not only an illegitimate and futile inquiry but a manifestation of illness. The mark of the nihilist, from Schopenhauer and Nietzsche to the literary nihilists of our time, is that he realizes the self-defeating nature of his efforts, through the instrumentality of reason and art, to capture the ultimate meaning of life.

For the literary nihilist is not a philosopher; he is not setting forth a series of propositional statements. What he does, in his imaginative work, is to suspend the element of "truth" or "belief" and create a form that is intentionally left open, unresolved.[32] The writer is free to choose his "action," the level of meaning on which he wishes to operate, so that "the truth" of *Alice in Wonderland* or *The Hunting of the Snark*[33] is as rewarding in its way as "the truth" of *Prometheus Unbound* or *War and Peace.* Each

---

[32] "A structure of tempered and proportioned assertions is not necessarily a structure of literal assertions; in fact, its being a structure almost guarantees that some of its assertions will be determined by structural needs rather than by their relation to a reality outside the poem. But the literary work is uncommitted, one way or the other, with regard to the 'truth' of its assertions, measured by an exterior standard. They may be literally true and literally meant; figuratively, typically, or dramatically true; or outrageously and patently untrue. They may contain several different and perhaps contradictory assertions at once—may even be, in an exterior sense, what we call total nonsense." Robert M. Adams, *Strains of Discord* (Ithaca, N.Y.: Cornell University Press, 1958), p. 3.

[33] It is indeed difficult to pin down the exact "meaning" of *The Hunting of the Snark,* which is a tantalizingly ambiguous and complex poem. What is it about, after all? Is it a symbolic poem, a parable, an allegory, a satire, a fantasy, a metaphysical enigma, a tissue of extravagant nonsense? Each age creates its own method of explication. The latest interpretation of Lewis Carroll's experiment in "nonsense" is the existential gloss provided by Martin Gardner, the editor of *The Annotated Snark.* "In a literal sense, Carroll's Boojum means nothing at all. It is the void, the great blank emptiness out of which we miraculously emerged; by which we will ultimately be devoured; through which the absurd galaxies spiral and drift endlessly on their nonsense voyage from nowhere to nowhere." *The Annotated Snark,* ed. Martin Gardner (New York: Simon and Schuster, 1962), p. 22.

structured perspective is sustained by its own internal logic and communicates the way one mind interprets the world. The open form is "literary form (a structure of meanings, intents, and emphases, *i.e.,* verbal gestures) which includes a major unresolved conflict with the intent of displaying its unresolvedness."[34]

The literary nihilist, a Kafka, a Beckett, finds the open form specially suited to his needs. Everything in his imaginary universe is relative, provisional, held in balance, so that yes and no, darkness and light, life and death, God and Satan, purpose and absence of purpose, meaning and utter lack of meaning, nothingness and plenitude, are involved in a polar dance that seems for a fleeting moment to imply but never actually achieves the harmony of opposites. All he perceives is a world of phenomena that each person interprets in his own way, and these interpretations add up to nothing he can describe with certainty. The mind, which is but a part of Nature, cannot fathom the root-cause of Nature's origin; it can only arrive at the chastening knowledge of its own insurmountable limitations.

Caught in this impasse, the literary nihilist, who is no philosopher by training, wonders uneasily what he will do. What *can* he do? In which direction shall he turn? How can he go on living without a vital purpose to sustain him? He knows now that art offers no answer to these questions. Tolstoy, in his *Confessions,* records how he felt he could not go on living until he had somehow found a valid meaning and purpose in life.

> No matter how often I may be told, "You cannot understand the meaning of life, so do not think about it, but live," I can no longer do it: I have already done it too long. I cannot now help seeing day and night going round and bringing me to death. That is all I see, for that alone is true. All else is false.[35]

As Berdyaev remarks, for many Russian intellectuals in the nineteenth century the quest for the solution to the cosmic mystery was the only thing that mattered. "Belinsky would say, after

---

[34] Adams, *Strains of Discord,* p. 13.
[35] Janko Lavrin, *Tolstoy* (London: W. Collins Sons & Co., 1924), p. 101.

argument had gone on all night: 'We can't go home, we haven't yet decided the question of God.'"[36]

Like Tolstoy, who triumphed over his oppressive doubts by turning to religion, espousing a type of Christianity based on the ideal of brotherly love, the literary nihilist strives to find *the* answer to the riddle of life, even though he suspects beforehand that such a definitive solution is beyond the reach of man. How can the mind search for that which does not exist? To say that there is no ultimate meaning is to imply that the metaphysical search has been made but that it proved fruitless. There is the further implication that the mind of man is capable of recognizing this meaning once it is found. The literary nihilist comes to understand at last that art is not a substitute for religion; it does not pave the road to salvation. He cannot accept Schopenhauer's apocalyptic revelation that art releases man from the bondage of the biological will.

Just when all seems lost, the literary nihilist or his deputized persona does a dramatic turnabout and revises his estimate of the absurd fatality of the human condition. He negates or transcends his nihilism. He will become the maker of history, the protagonist of the secular drama he has himself composed and is directing, the master of whatever destiny he can forge for himself in the contingent sphere of the relative. He silences the Everlasting Nay by defending the finite, human world against the myth of meaninglessness. Unlike the Buddhist who longs and prays for the bliss of Nirvana and who is the only strictly logical (if logic has anything to do with the matter) nihilist, the literary nihilist in Western culture remains active; he persists in striving even though he is fully aware that at the end of time the passion of his quest and the achievement (if he is lucky) of his Promethean project will be swallowed up in oblivion. Like Kazantzakis, he labors at his creative calling even while he preaches that all is illusion.

---

[36] Nicolas Berdyaev, *Dream and Reality*, trans. Katherine Lampert (New York: The Macmillan Company, 1951), p. 165.

4. NIHILISM TRANSCENDED

We shall thus be dealing not with nihilism *per se* but primarily with the literary struggle against it. Many writers pass through this stage, short or long, of nihilistic alienation, but only a few, like Kafka, remain permanently in this condition, and even these few make strenuous efforts to break out of it. The reason for this well-nigh universal desire to repudiate nihilism is not far to seek. The literary nihilist has not escaped the censure and derision of his fellow men. The socially minded critics characterize him as a madman or a neurotic. He is the enemy of life; therefore, down with him! He is the voice of the Devil slyly whispering that idealism is a fraud and that all human aspirations are compounded of illusion. He demystifies the myth of God by exposing it as one of the many crack-brained notions men seriously cherish for the opiate consolation it offers. He is the one who argues that the chief motive of metaphysical speculation is to conceal the unbearable truth that man is an ephemeral, insignificant creature on earth, of no more importance in the economy of the universe than a gnat or a worm.

The writer attempts to break out of the nihilistic trap by regarding consciousness as a disease that runs counter to the demands of instinct;[37] it is consciousness that decides that life is worthless. There is the dilemma on the horns of which the literary nihilist is impaled. From the point of view of instinct, which is not to be denied, the nihilistic interpretation represents the rottenness of decadence, a failure of nerve, a dangerous impairment of the will to live. Knowing this to be so, the writer as nihilist tries to drive out the spirit of negation that has taken possession of him.

Nihilism affords an interesting study in the dynamics of contradiction. The literary nihilist is the first to concede that this is

---

[37] It is the logical pessimist, as Vaihinger calls him, who focuses attention on the ineffectuality of thought; he cannot prove that the world or he himself exists. He looks upon thought as "an extremely defective instrument which falsifies reality, and leads us astray and deceives us." H. Vaihinger, *The Philosophy of 'As if'*, trans. C. K. Ogden (New York: Harcourt, Brace and Company, 1925), pp. 162–63.

so. For life cannot negate life. The nihilist who wrestles creatively with this problem is, in reality, seeking out ways and means to transcend his nihilism. Despite his conviction that nothing can be done to remedy the human condition, despite his inner assurance of the doom that will inevitably befall the human race, he is casting about for some faith that he can affirm without betraying the integrity of his mind. He refuses to be defeated by what Bertrand Russell calls the trampling march of unconscious power. In all his outbursts of defiance or despair, he is endeavoring to throw off the intolerable burden of nihilism. In one form or another he testifies against himself. Instead of brooding bitterly over what will ultimately be the cataclysmic outcome of the human pilgrimage, he carries on with his work. He keeps faith with his self-chosen ideals in the finite domain of history, despite his awareness that these ideals exist only because he fights energetically to keep them alive. Though he devotes himself to the limited task of helping to improve the life of mankind, he has not abandoned his quest for the Absolute. The most sublime and, historically, the most successful myth designed to counter the nihilistic dread induced by the prospect of dying is the myth of the Incarnation and the Resurrection.

The Literature
of Nihilism

PART I:

Religion and the Battle against Nihilism

1

Religion and Nihilism

The Madman—Have you ever heard of the madman who on a bright morning lighted a lantern and ran to the market-place calling un-ceasingly: "I seek God! I seek God!"—As there were many people standing about who did not believe in God, he caused a great deal of amusement ... The insane man jumped into their midst and trans-fixed them with his glances. "Where is God gone?" he called out. "I mean to tell you! We have killed him—you and I! We are all his murderers! ... God is dead! God remains dead! And we have killed him!"[1]

I believe in God, the Holy Nothingness known to mystics of all ages, out of which we have come and to which we shall ultimately return. ... In the final analysis, omnipotent Nothingness is Lord of all creation.[2]

The Hebraic-Christian tradition utilized the cycle of birth, life, death, and rebirth to conquer chaos and disorder, but it made its unique con-tribution to the pattern by giving man the possibility of defeating chaos and disorder by a single, supreme act of human will which could wipe them out at one stroke.[3]

1. RELIGION AS THE CURE FOR DESPAIR

The ritual pattern symbolizes the passage from death to life; it protects the community against the danger of extinction and, in the working out of this process, it saves the individual from the

[1] Friedrich Nietzsche, *Joyful Wisdom,* trans. Thomas Common (New York: Ungar Publishing Co., 1960), pp. 167–68.
[2] Richard L. Rubenstein, *After Auschwitz* (Indianapolis and New York: The Bobbs-Merrill Company, 1966), p. 154.
[3] Herbert Weisinger, *The Agony and the Triumph* (East Lansing, Mich.: Michigan State University Press, 1964), p. 98.

threat of annihilation. Man is brought into harmony with God and Nature. Thus chaos is for the time being overcome, until the next return of the season of death and the menace of nonbeing. But the advent of Christianity brought the ritual mythic pattern to a victorious close; man could himself defeat the forces that threatened to destroy him. Though the original pattern is preserved, it is kept vital by the new element of religious belief that "man can, by himself, transcend the universe."[4]

That belief is no longer the secure possession of twentieth-century man. The essence of nihilism lies in the realization that the human condition sets limits that cannot be transcended. The nihilist denies himself the religious promises that could rescue him from the bottomless pit of despair, but he is comforted by the thought that in confronting an absurd universe with lucidity and courage he ceases to be the hapless victim of illusion.[5] By denying the existence of God, who keeps open the gates of salvation, he resigns himself to existence in the emptiness of space, exposed to the hazards of the lottery of chance, living his brief mortal span under the all-encompassing and ever-imminent threat of Nothingness.

The religious problem, however, cannot be disposed of in this summary fashion. If religion is defined as the perennial quest for ultimate meaning, then it follows that the most extreme skepticism, even the expression of rebellious nihilism, need not alienate the seeker from God. As Paul Tillich states the issue paradoxically:

> The situation of doubt, even doubt about God, need not separate us from God. There is faith in every serious doubt, namely, the faith in the truth as such, even if the only truth we can express is our lack of

[4] *Ibid.,* p. 99.
[5] Ignace Lapp, in *Atheism in Our Time* (trans. Bernard Murchland [New York: The Macmillan Company, 1963]), discusses the career of Claude Mauriac, son of the Catholic novelist François Mauriac, who is utterly without faith. Like Nietzsche, he considers Christianity as the opiate consolation of the weak and cowardly. The superior man has no need for the offices of the supernatural; he shapes his own destiny, without regard for the promise of life everlasting in the hereafter.

truth. But if this is experienced in its depth and as an ultimate concern, the divine is present.[6]

The nihilist literature produced in the twentieth century by the followers of Schopenhauer, Nietzsche, Marx, and Freud is essentially religious in spirit, though it is often not Christian in content. Impelled by a profound urge to discover the underlying meaning of existence, the literary nihilist faces a tragic conflict, which his skeptical spirit provokes. It is the element of exacerbated and intransigent doubt that looms large in nihilistic tragedy. "Tragedy . . . occurs when the accepted order of things is fundamentally questioned only to be the more triumphantly reaffirmed. It cannot exist where there is no faith; conversely, it cannot exist where there is no doubt, it can exist only in an atmosphere of sceptical faith."[7] Tragedy, like nihilism, has been defined in a variety of ways, "but one thing it cannot be and that is a tale signifying nothing."[8]

Had Christianity retained its sovereign hold on mankind, the present epidemic of nihilism might have been averted, but this impressive triumph of faith over the recalcitrance of reality could not be sustained. In a world of absolute and universal faith, the writing of tragedy would be ruled out. As Eliseo Vivas says: "A man who believes in Providence and in immortality knows that the catastrophe the tragic hero suffers is but a fleeting and unreal moment in a pilgrimage towards the real, the eternal. For whom there can be redemption there can be no ultimate doom."[9] Lucien Goldmann, however, in raising the question whether Christianity and, in particular, Pascal's brand of Christianity, is essentially tragic, replies: "Certainly, by its idea of a God who dies but who is immortal, and by the paradox of a God made man, by its idea of mediation and by its insistence upon the folly of the Cross,

[6] Paul Tillich, *The Protestant Era* (Chicago: The University of Chicago Press, 1948), p. xiv.
[7] Herbert Weisinger, *The Agony and the Triumph,* p. 103.
[8] *Ibid.,* p. 112.
[9] Eliseo Vivas, *The Artistic Transaction* (Columbus, Ohio: Ohio State University Press, 1963), p. 132. See also Charles I. Glicksberg, *Literature and Religion* (Dallas, Tex.: Southern Methodist University Press, 1960), p. 152.

Christianity is particularly susceptible to a tragic interpretation."[10]

Pascal is a tragic thinker who uses the language of paradox to suggest the ambiguity of man's relation to God. He prepares the way for the startling religious message of a Kierkegaard. Some literary nihilists found a kindred spirit in Kierkegaard. Kafka, on reading an anthology of his writings in 1913, reported: "He bears me out like a friend."[11] Like Pascal, Kierkegaard gives expression to his conception of religion as paradox. In 1846 he pens this passage in his *Journals,* which sums up his awareness of the absurdity of faith: "Immanently (in the fantastic medium of abstraction) God does not *exist*—God only *exists* for an *exist*ing man *i.e.* he can only exist in faith. . . . When an existing individual has not got faith God *is* not, neither does God *exist,* although understood from an eternal point of view God is eternally."[12] The uncertainty the religious quester harbors within himself is the criterion of faith achieved, "and the certainty without the uncertainty is the criterion for the absence of a God-relationship."[13]

This is the tragic situation into which modern man, when alienated from God, is thrust. In a cultural atmosphere of skeptical faith that is in some quarters not far removed from atheism, he continues his search for God. He still hears the screams of Nietzsche's madman: "God is dead! God remains dead!" And the theologians who head the death-of-God movement assure

[10] Lucien Goldmann, *The Hidden God,* trans. Philip Thody (New York: The Humanities Press, 1964), p. 76. "Since the future is a closed door and the past has been abolished, the tragic mind sees only two possibilities before it, nothingness or eternity." (*Ibid.,* p. 80). The tragic man is constantly in the presence of death, but he lives in hope and never achieves certainty. "This hope, born of the clash between the demand for authentic values and the eternal silence of God and of the world, is, first of all, that the complete reversal of values which his tragic awareness has brought to his soul shall become a reality. Secondly, however, it takes a different and more important form and one which, because of the nature of the tragic experience, is essentially paradoxical. It becomes a confidence in God which can exist only in the form of man's anxiety and concern; and this anxiety is the only form of certainty open to the man who seeks faith. . . ." (*Ibid.,* p. 85).
[11] Franz Kafka, *Diaries of Franz Kafka 1910–1913,* ed. Max Brod, trans. Joseph Kresh (New York: Schocken Books, 1948), p. 298.
[12] Sören Kierkegaard, *The Journals of Sören Kierkegaard,* ed. and trans. Alexander D (London and New York: Oxford University Press, 1951), p. 173.
[13] Sören Kierkegaard, *Concluding Unscientific Postscript,* trans. David F. Swenson (Princeton, N.J.: Princeton University Press, 1941, p. 407.

him that "the proclamation of the death of God is a Christian confession of faith."[14] This abstract gospel of Christian atheism, this attenuated version of a theology that abandons God as a lost cause, attracts no disciples among the literary nihilists.

This surprising transformation of the religious consciousness is not to be taken as an abdication of faith. Tillich contends that "genuine religion without an element of atheism cannot be imagined."[15] The Unconditioned is beyond the reach of man's understanding, and yet, as the Ground of Being, it pervades all of human existence. The affirmation of faith involves an existential risk.[16] God manifests himself in strange ways and in unexpected places: in ritual and sacrament, the ravings of the madman, the fool in Christ, the hairy prophet in the wilderness, the impassioned demand for social justice, the scientist in his pursuit of truth. Though an indwelling spirit of religious yearning runs through much of modern secular and even nihilist literature, it goes masked in the forms of blasphemy and iconoclasm. Those writers who, like Baudelaire and Rimbaud in the nineteenth century, broke away from Christianity, may nevertheless give voice to authentic religious intuitions.[17]

2. SCIENCE AND THE DISPLACEMENT OF FAITH

The realization that nature is utterly indifferent to man has always caused a convulsion of feeling ever since the source of value was transferred from outside the world to inside the world. When people ask,

[14] Thomas J. J. Altizer, *The Gospel of Christian Atheism* (Philadelphia: The Westminster Press, 1966), p. 102.
[15] Paul Tillich, *Theology of Culture* (New York: Oxford University Press, 1959), p. 25.
[16] "The risk of faith is based on the fact that the unconditional element can become a matter of ultimate concern only if it appears in a concrete embodiment." *Ibid.,* pp. 27–28.
[17] Amos Wilder declares that "the custody and future of the Christian tradition has to a considerable degree passed over into the keeping of non-ecclesiastical and even secular groups. The fateful issues of the Christian faith are often wrestled with more profoundly outside the church than within." Amos N. Wilder, *Modern Poetry and the Christian Tradition: A Study in the Relation of Christianity to Culture* (New York: Charles Scribner's Sons, 1952), p. xii.

"What is the purpose of human existence?" they assume they are asking a question that can be answered.[18]

The numinous response that the pronunciamentos of negative theology called forth bore witness to the fact that the Hebraic-Christian tradition lived on, even when, as in the Soviet Union, it had to work underground, but the challenge of science worked havoc in the body of orthodox belief. If God can cause earthquakes, floods, hurricanes, plagues, then he is not in the least concerned about the welfare of mankind. The malignant cruelty of a Nature in which life feeds insanely and insatiably on life "makes God seem a kind of sublime jester; or like the Marquis de Sade, one concludes that God is cruel, that He has arranged the world so that He can enjoy the spectacle of human suffering."[19] Here is the conundrum that appalled poor Job. Why does evil triumph on earth, why is suffering gratuitously imposed on the innocent? Human reason since the Age of the Enlightenment could not solve this tormenting riddle.

The believer in science came to look upon the universe as a meaningless chaos. He felt trapped. He could not recoup his spiritual losses by trying to establish a foothold in the enchanted world of primordial myth. But, as Hugo von Hofmannsthal pointed out, the modern myth that the writers were eagerly trying to create did not exist.[20] Scientific rationalism made a return to the mythological world of primitive man impossible.[21]

[18] Morse Peckham, *Beyond the Tragic Vision* (New York: George Braziller, 1962), p. 81.
[19] *Ibid.*
[20] Hugo von Hofmannsthal, *Selected Prose* (New York: Pantheon Books, 1952), p. xxvi. See "The Mythic Perspective," in Charles I. Glicksberg, *Modern Literary Perspectivism* (Dallas, Tex.: Southern Methodist University Press, 1970), pp. 135–48.
[21] Professor Herbert Weisinger says that such a "return" cannot be made to work, for "the history of myth has been the history of the demythologizing of myth, and any attempts to revive myth as a viable organ of belief, in the same sense in which primitive man believed it, from even the best of motives, seem to me doomed to failure. . . . All of us, believers in gods, myths, and formulae alike, must, in the long run, face up to the fact that despite our blandishments,. bribes, and blusters, the indifferent universe, whatever we may read into it for whatever compelling reasons of our own, remains indifferent." Herbert Weisinger. *The Agony and the Triumph*, p. 209.

The erosion of spiritual and religious values was hastened by the knowledge that Nature was amoral, caring not a whit whether the human race survived or perished in an atomic holocaust. Nature provided no basis for a binding ethical system. Naturalism confidently assumed that man was "as much a part of nature . . . as the humblest weed."[22] T. H. Huxley, the eloquent expounder of the Darwinian outlook to a shocked Victorian age, cited evidence to prove that the theory of evolution had no linkage with the advance of morality. The struggle for existence does not conform to the moral sense of mankind. On the contrary, the cosmos, when "brought before the tribunal of ethics . . . might well seem to stand condemned. The conscience of man revolted against the indifference of Nature. . . ."[23]

But the revolt of conscience was halted by the rise of logical positivism, which held that normative judgments cannot be objectively validated. Logical positivism argued that experience "contains no such qualities of men, events, or things as 'noble,' 'good,' 'evil,' 'beautiful,' 'ugly,' etc."[24] Logical empiricism represented a movement that maintained that scientific observation and testing constituted the sole criterion of truth. Hence all metaphysical statements were to be excluded as meaningless. Ludwig Wittgenstein carried on a vigorous campaign against the pseudo-statements of metaphysics and ethics.[25] Science did not pretend to formulate an answer to the question whether life was meaningful or meaningless.

That is how the anthropomorphic view of the universe was demolished. Jean Rostand, the eminent French biologist, agrees

[22] T. H. Huxley and Julian Huxley, *Touchstone for Ethics* (New York and London: Harper & Brothers, 1947), p. 45.

[23] *Ibid.,* p. 76.

[24] Leszek Kolakowski, *The Alienation of Reason,* trans. Norbert Guterman (Garden City, N.Y.: Doubleday & Company, 1968), p. 7.

[25] For an incisive summing up of Wittgenstein's position up to 1920, see Arne Naess, *Four Modern Philosophers,* trans. Alastair Hannay (Chicago and London: The University of Chicago Press, 1968). Wittgenstein has left his mark on literature as well as logic. A striking example of this influence is furnished by the remark of a character in *Incognito,* by the Rumanian novelist Petru Dumitriu. Erasmus Ionesco, the character in question, dismisses all metaphysical speculations about God, the happiness of mankind, universal brotherhood, a future life, as born of "a misleading and improper use of language." Petru Dumitriu, *Incognito,* trans. Norman Denny (New York: The Macmillan Company, 1964), p. 109.

with Thomas Henry Huxley that man is not the creation of an intelligent will or purpose. As for the delusions of grandeur that buoy up Promethean man because he has conquered Nature, a glance upwards at the starry spaces is enough to put him in his place. "For how could he go on taking himself seriously from any point of view once he had looked on the icy reaches where the spiral nebulae are speeding?"[26] Science can offer no support for the revelations of religion.[27] No theodicy in our time has been able to exorcise the specter of nihilism.[28]

If religious faith has suffered a series of severe setbacks, this did not result in a clear-cut victory of atheism. Such profoundly disturbing spiritual conflicts are not resolved in the popular mind by a kind of intellectual plebiscite. During the past fifty years, many writers who were nonreligious or anti-religious in their outlook, nevertheless portrayed a world that was still steeped in the Judeo-Christian tradition. Some chose to deal with the myth of Christ crucified (D. H. Lawrence, William Faulkner, and Kazantzakis), and their iconoclastic treatment of it highlighted the crucial problem of unbelief in our age. It is the symbol of Prometheus unbound that dominates the literary landscape, not that of Christ crucified and resurrected. Yet the quest for a new, viable faith did not end. The transcendental truths of religion cannot be couched in terms warranted by logical positivism. The language of logical positivism cannot do justice to the *ex-*

[26] Jean Rostand, *The Substance of Man,* trans. Irma Brandeis (Garden City, N.Y.: Doubleday & Company, 1962), p. 60.
[27] Like many of the literary figures in this book who for a time embraced nihilism wholly or in part, Jean Rostand did not support nihilistic conclusions based on scientific findings. In an interview conducted in France, he questioned the validity of the thesis expounded by a fellow biologist, Jacques Monod, in his *Le Hasard et la Necessité,* that the evolutionary process was the result of pure chance. Though he accepts the ethic of science, which is the ethic of truth, he believes that this is not enough. "Personally I miss the dimension of brotherhood, of love of man. I think that may count even more than truth." (*The New York Times,* May 30, 1971). He goes on to say: "I believe in social progress." *(Ibid.)*
[28] Martin E. Marty argues that not all forms of unbelief are nihilistic, "but all nihilism is a form of unbelief from the Christian viewpoint. It denies the possibility of God's positive action in history. . . . It shares with all unbelief and all agonized belief two basic visions: God is not apparent in the universe, and evil is." Martin E. Marty, *Varieties of Unbelief* (New York: Holt, Rinehart and Winston, 1964), p. 112.

perience of faith, which is ineffable.[29] As William Barrett puts it in *Irrational Man:*

> Faith can no more be described to a thoroughly rational mind than the idea of colors can be conveyed to a blind man. . . . Thus vital and indescribable, faith partakes of the mystery of life itself. The opposition between faith and reason is that between the vital and the rational—and stated in these terms, the opposition is a crucial problem today.[30]

This is the very problem that Unamuno grappled with in his fiction, poetry, and philosophical work. This is the dialectic of opposition that emerges in the published writing of a number of literati who were outspoken nonbelievers and nihilists. Camus talks about God, Robinson Jeffers talks about God, and so do Gide, Malraux,

---

[29] For a detailed analysis of the language of religion, which is notoriously imprecise, see Ninian Smart, *Reasons and Faiths* (London: Routledge & Kegan Paul, 1958). "God exists" is not an existential proposition. Man believes, he does not know. He questions but if he questions too deeply his doubts will be intensified, for belief in God transcends the sphere of the natural. "It is not the case that religious propositions are of the same kind as others, except that we have not the facilities (at the moment, in this life) to show them to be true as we might show propositions about moles or men or tomorrow's sunrise to be true." (*Reasons and Faiths,* pp. 170–71). For Tillich, too, God remains unknown and unknowable, hidden, indefinable. "If you start with the question whether God does or does not exist, you can never reach Him; and if you assert that He does exist, you can reach Him even less than if you assert that He does not exist. A God about whose existence or non-existence you can argue is a thing beside others within the universe of existing things. And the question is quite justified whether such a thing does exist, and the answer is equally justified that it does not exist." (Paul Tillich, *Theology of Culture* [New York: Oxford University Press, 1959], pp. 4–5). Walter Kaufmann argues that the meaning of the term "God" is derived from its repeated use in the Bible. "If the universe of discourse is Scripture, Judaism, or Christianity, 'God exists' is true." (Walter Kaufmann, *Critique of Religion and Philosophy* [New York: Harper & Brothers, 1958], p. 126). But in a different context, the question whether God exists is without meaning. "The attempt to salvage religious propositions by admitting their literal falsity while maintaining their truth, provided only that they are interpreted as analogous or symbolic, must fail." (*Ibid.,* p. 131). Kenneth Burke, like Wittgenstein, denies that it is possible to imagine what does not exist. "Since 'God' by definition transcends all symbol-systems, we must begin, like theology, by noting that language is intrinsically unfitted to discuss the 'supernatural' literally. . . . Hence all the words for 'God' must be used analogically. . . ." (Kenneth Burke, *The Rhetoric of Religion* [Boston: Beacon Press, 1961], p. 15.

[30] William Barrett, *Irrational Man* (Garden City, N.Y.: Doubleday & Company, 1958), pp. 81–82.

Bernard Shaw, and Sartre, but their God is stripped of divinity.[31] Like Feuerbach in *The Essence of Christianity,* they believe that God is the creation of man. It is not the God of old they hope to find. They seek God in some other incarnation, "even when His existence seems most doubtful."[32] God is no longer apart from Nature. The two discrete realms, the divine and the natural, are fused, but in this process of fusion

> the God of old has disappeared, leaving man by himself cogitating the mysterious Abstraction that has taken His place; and since man's desire to commune with a Being higher than himself is as fervent as ever, he shows the effects of frustration at being unable to place faith in a personal relationship.[33]

The triumph of naturalism cast doubt, to put it mildly, on the revealed "higher" truths vouched for by the Bible and its devout interpreters, and precipitated a spiritual crisis that culminated in nihilistic disillusionment. There is scarcely a writer of stature in the twentieth century who has not been influenced, for better or worse, by the scientific outlook.[34] Relegating the dream of immortality to the limbo of irrational expectations, modern man is overwhelmed by the obsessive fear of death. Religious images are increasingly secularized, as Frederick J. Hoffman reports in his book *The Mortal No,* and the faith in personal immortality is supplanted by the Marxist vision of social immortality.[35] History becomes the supreme court of justice, the ultimate—and only—

---

[31] One commentator remarks: "If it weren't for the Christian concept of God, the atheists would not know what they ought to deny." William A. Luijpen, *Phenomenology and Atheism* (Pittsburgh: Duquesne University Press, 1964), p. 89.

[32] Sherman H. Eoff, *The Modern Spanish Novel* (New York: New York University Press, 1964), p. 15.

[33] *Ibid.,* p. 16.

[34] In her autobiography, Raissa Maritain relates how she and Jacques Maritain fought from instinct "against a relativism that led nowhere, against a relationship to nothingness, for no absolute was admitted." Raissa Maritain, *We Have Been Friends Together* (New York and London: Longmans, Green and Co., 1942), p. 80.

[35] Frederick J. Hoffman, *The Mortal No* (Princeton, N.J.: Princeton University Press, 1964), p. 6. Ernst Bloch, a Marxist proponent of atheist humanism, maintains that it is "possible to read the Bible with the eyes of the Communist Manifesto." Ernst Bloch, *Atheism in Christianity,* trans. J. T. Swann (New York: Herder and Herder, 1972), p. 69.

ground of redemption in time. Nevertheless, religious overtones continue to resound in the body of modern literature, which is predominantly secular in content. Even the writer who is a non-believer utilizes at times the haunting symbols of vision furnished by the Christian mythos.[36] The heritage of the Judeo-Christian tradition somehow survives, but it survives in a culture that has long since ceased to be theistic. The sense of the numinous is still present but the substance of the traditional Christian faith is largely lacking. In analyzing the reasons for this state of affairs in modern literature, John Killinger remarks:

> The numinous still appears in our literature—some places are freighted with it—but usually where God *isn't*, not where he is! It is in the southern nights . . . in Faulkner; in the "horrorous" darkness and death-facing of Hemingway; in the rotting, stinking jungles of Conrad and Greene; in the nausea of Sartre and the absurdity of Camus. The numinous is there, but the Christian construct is missing. It is a demonic world, without any sense of the Resurrection having ever taken place.[37]

Naturalism is in the saddle and rides mankind. Killinger regards naturalism as a revolt against a morality based on a belief in a providential system of rewards and punishments.[38]

Hemingway in his fiction of the twenties anticipated a number of existential motifs: nada, the myth of nothingness, the shuddering awareness of the threat of death.[39] His heroes are nihilistic hedonists who have pierced the pasteboard mask of life and profess to have outgrown all illusions, knowing that death waits for all men and

[36] See Rebecca West, *The Court and the Castle* (New Haven: Yale University Press, 1957).
[37] John Killinger, *The Failure of Theology in Modern Literature* (New York and Nashville: Abingdon Press, 1963), p. 27.
[38] "It [naturalism] preaches with relentless dogmatism the blindness of justice—and the absence of God." *Ibid.*, p. 51.
[39] In *Hemingway and the Dead Gods,* Killinger critically examines Hemingway's fiction in the light of existentialist thought. "All gods are dead, and man is thrown back upon himself with the responsibility of forging his self out of a private ethics and a private aesthetic. Paradoxically, the only peace in our time is the strenuous no-peace, the continuous striving to mold life, moment-by-moment, from a dreadful nothingness into an ethically and aesthetically authentic form." John Killinger, *Hemingway and the Dead Gods* (Lexington, Ky.: University of Kentucky Press, 1960), p. 81.

that it may strike at any moment. The death-motif pervades practically all of Hemingway's work. His most poignant scenes reveal the estrangement of man in a world that is both hostile and destructive, a demonic world without God.

And in Paris, Sartrean existentialism depicted man as alone in a godless universe. A creature of time, finite and perishable, the twentieth-century writer was often held back from a religious commitment by the suspicion that human existence was utterly without meaning. What troubled Jacques Rivière, for example, was his constant awareness of the aimlessness and emptiness of life. Like a character out of a novel by Dostoevski, he was overcome at times by dark moods when he believed in nothing. The torment of infernal doubt never let up and stood in the way of his religious conversion. He could neither affirm his faith nor reject it. At nineteen he wrote that "perpetually I believe and I doubt; I believe with a gesture of my heart, I doubt with a repulsion of my intelligence. . . ."[40] Karl Jaspers expresses the dominant spirit of his age when he asserts that "God is hidden and every certainty about him is fraught with danger."[41] Man today lives in a culture that has been shaped by relativism and the absence of God.[42]

The Victorian Age bequeathed its legacy of agnosticism to the twentieth century. The publication of Darwin's *Origin of Species* proved a traumatic experience. "Never has any age of history produced such a detailed literature of lost faith, or so many great men of religious temperament standing outside organized religion."[43]

---

[40] Jacques Rivière, *The Ideal Reader,* ed. and trans. Blanche A. Price (New York: Meridian Books, 1960), p. 56.

[41] Paul Arthur Schilpp, ed. *The Philosophy of Karl Jaspers* (New York: Tudor Publishing Co., 1957), p. 784.

[42] *Modern Literature and the Death of God* ends on this note: "If it is madness to live without the theistic conception of God, then the most influential writers of our time are 'mad.' Twentieth-century literature is a haunting threnody that laments, even as it rejoices in, the death of the old God. It is evident . . . that the modern writer, though he hails the new-born freedom of man, is in search of a new 'religious' vision, one that will enable him to affirm his humanity and define his role in the dialogue that always goes on, even in a relativized universe, between the profane and the sacred, between man and God." Charles I. Glicksberg, *Modern Literature and the Death of God* (The Hague: Martinus Nijhoff, 1966), pp. 157–58.

[43] Margaret M. Waidson, *The Victorian Vision* (New York: Sheed & Ward, 1961), p. 211.

Toward the end of the nineteenth century, many writers were driven to despair by their feeling of cosmic alienation. Some began to question if life was worth living and were convinced that it was not. Science was hailed as the new Messiah, but it offered no hope of redemption. It demonstrated that life was without purpose. These Victorian pessimists did not look upon themselves as tragic sufferers who had violated a moral law fixed in the universe. "For the *fin de siècle* there was no moral scheme to be violated; the new despair arose from a world which gave no room for idealism, illusion, or morality whatever."[44] If the nineteenth century was "the period of the death of God in Western Christian civilization,"[45] the twentieth century carried skepticism to a point beyond which men could believe in nothing. Christ, when he appears in the literature of our age, is not only humanized but secularized, like the preacher Casy in *The Grapes of Wrath* or like Christ reborn in the flesh in Lawrence's *The Man Who Died*.[46]

The modern nihilist could not persuade himself to worship a God who was not grounded in truth, and the truth was what science said it was. He could not be cured of his apostasy by a *willed* act of faith. Nor could he satisfy his human craving for transcendence through the mediation of art. Kierkegaard anticipated the advent of nihilism in the twentieth century when he emphasized the absurdity of faith as consisting of belief in that which is logically impossible.

> Nobody believes in the logically impossible. The logically impossible cannot be conceived, much less believed in. That was Kierkegaard's despair. He was a man who wanted to believe in the absurd, but who could not succeed. He was merely "the poet of Christianity."[47]

[44] John A. Lester, Jr., *Journey Through Despair 1880–1914* (Princeton, N.J.: Princeton University Press, 1968), p. 57.
[45] James M. Edie, "The Absence of God," in William Earle, James M. Edie, and John Wild, *Christianity and Existentialism* (Evanston, Ill.: Northwestern University Press, 1963), p. 117.
[46] The figure of Christ is "the crucial center of a moral drama and in literature this drama becomes more and more complex, as Christ is not only separated from the symbolic figure of the Trinity but—as is often the case—forced into the role of an exclusively human figure, the major key to secularization." Frederick J. Hoffman, *The Mortal No,* p. 395.
[47] Robert G. Olson, *An Introduction to Existentialism* (New York: Dover Publications, 1962), p. 99.

The decline of religious faith underlined the grotesque finality of death. The representative twentieth-century hero or anti-hero does not believe in the possibility of redemption in the Other World. He looks for fulfillment in a secular future, when mankind will establish the Kingdom of Heaven on earth. It is the brute fact of death as annihilation and oblivion that feeds the source of nihilistic anguish. It is the nihilist's desire to achieve a victory over death that motivates his renewed search for God.

2

Unamuno and the Quest for Faith

1. THE ARCHETYPAL FEAR OF DEATH

We wish to know how the conception of death will transform a man's entire life, when in order to think its uncertainty he has to think it in every moment, so as to prepare himself for it.[1]

Indeed analytic observation suggests that what we call the fear of death is the fear of something animistically conceived as an evil will hostile to our life, which is always as it were lurking in the shadows even when not manifest in a specific danger situation. Moreover, it is found to emanate from us.[2]

Ancient myths project the figure of the dying god and enact the cycle of death and rebirth. As men began wandering over the face of the earth and the stable society of a pastoral order broke up, the disruptive ideal of individual freedom emerged—the conception of the Promethean rebel challenging the gods to combat. He is finally overcome in battle but his perilous adventures exemplify the archetypal pattern of the death and rebirth of the dying god. Though these epic heroes are descendants of the gods, they are denied the gift of immortality. "They always live on the brink of death, while savouring beyond the rest the splendour of earthly existence, and their part in the after life is made unfruitful and meaningless to add poignancy to their courage and doom."[3] The later heroes of myth wander in solitude, cross fearful stormy seas,

[1] Søren Kierkegaard, *Concluding Unscientific Postscript,* trans. David F. Swenson (Princeton, N.J.: Princeton University Press, 1941), pp. 150–51.
[2] R. B. Money-Kyrle, *Man's Picture of His World* (New York: International Universities Press, 1961), p. 33.
[3] G. R. Levy, *The Sword from the Rock* (London: Faber and Faber, 1953), p. 94.

encounter dragons, explore strange shores, and thus learn the meaning of death.

Yet the death of the king, who must die because Nature dies, is not in vain, for it makes possible the miracle of rebirth. His death is a guarantee of life's renewal for his people.[4] That is the essential function and purpose of the mythic pattern: it provides the symbolic means for warding off the terror of death. Even in this realm of the symbol and the myth, there is never complete certainty; the participant believes, but his doubts fill him with anxiety.[5] The myth endeavors to throw off the painful oppression by affirming the ultimate triumph of life. It proclaims the glad tidings that there is no death.

But today the nonbeliever, deprived of the sacrificial figure of the Redeemer, is thrust back upon himself and must spell out for himself the dread meaning of death. It is not surprising that he often falls into moral despair. His confrontation of the ineluctable fate of death confirms the truth of his nihilistic vision. Time refuses to stand still. The biological ignominy of death must be accepted; no other alternative is open to the appointed victim. Yet the nihilist finds it impossible to accept this fate when death is utterly stripped of meaning. It is futile to resist this mortal ending; it is madness to submit to it. "It is absurd that we are born; it is absurd that we die."[6] Once the flame of life in the body is extinguished, everything is lost. As Paul-Louis Landsberg points out: "Every battle with death is lost before it begins."[7] Then he makes this paradoxical but perfectly true remark that "man never despairs entirely so long as he is alive. . . ."[8] Here we behold the working of the dialectic that governs the nihilistic conflict that is an unavoidable part of human destiny: man, while subject to

---

[4] James G. Frazer, *The Golden Bough* (New York: The Macmillan Company, 1958), pp. 448–49.
[5] See Herbert Weisinger, *Tragedy and the Paradox of the Fortunate Fall* (East Lansing, Mich.: Michigan State University Press, 1953), p. 66.
[6] Jean-Paul Sartre, *Being and Nothingness,* trans. Hazel E. Barnes (New York: Philosophical Library, 1956), p. 547.
[7] Paul-Louis Landsberg, *The Experience of Death: The Moral Problem of Suicide,* trans. Cynthia Rowland (New York: Philosophical Library, 1953), p. 49.
[8] *Ibid.,* p. 50.

death, must fight constantly against it. He cannot resign himself to a "law" of Nature that dooms him to die. He fears death because, like Nietzsche and Unamuno, he craves the boon of life everlasting. He yearns, such is his mad dream, to become immortal.[9]

It is this confrontation of death that enables the existentialist to achieve authenticity of being and gain the courage to break away from all those distractions that seek to bind him to the world of things. In his philosophy and psychology of death,[10] Sartre develops the idea that each man dies his own death. By being interiorized, death is individualized.

> Death is no longer the great unknowable which limits the human; it is the phenomenon of my personal life which makes of this life a unique life—that is, a life which does not begin again, a life in which one never recovers his stroke. Hence I become responsible for my death as for my life. Not for the empirical and contingent character of my decease but for this character of finitude which causes my life like my death to be my life.[11]

This is difficult to grasp at first. How can one become responsible for his death, when death is something contingent? How can life, in the Sartrean sense, be a preparation for death? For Sartre acknowledges that death is the supreme example of absurdity man encounters. Each one must die alone, but he can make his death

[9] The aim of *The Immortalist* by Alan Harrington is to rescue modern man from the atrocious tyranny of death. His fierce, relentless polemic against the Dark Angel of Death has been influenced by Camus, but his approach differs markedly from that Camus used in *The Myth of Sisyphus*. Harrington wishes to launch a crusade to defeat "the Enemy." He is confident that the fight can be waged with positive hope of success. Technology and the science of medicine can arrest the aging process and make man immortal. It is immortality that man demands. The very first paragraph of *The Immortalist* announces Harrington's "mad" thesis: "Death is an imposition on the human race, and no longer acceptable. Man has all but lost his ability to accomodate himself to personal extinction; he must now proceed physically to overcome it. In short, to kill death: to put an end to his own mortality as a certain consequence of being born." (Alan Harrington, *The Immortalist* [New York: Random House, 1969], p. 3.) He does not hesitate to say that man must settle for nothing less than that state of being which makes him divine. (*Ibid.*, p. 21.)

[10] See "The Philosophy and Psychology of Death," in Alfred Stern, *Sartre* (New York: Dell Publishing Co., 1967), pp. 161–77.

[11] Jean-Paul Sartre, *Being and Nothingness,* p. 532.

his own if he assimilates it subjectively. It is not a question of waiting patiently for time to take its course until the fruit falls from the tree, for death may come at any moment, without warning. "Thus death is never that which gives life its meaning; it is, on the contrary, that which on principle removes all meaning from life. If we must die, then our life has no meaning because its problems receive no solution and because the very meaning of the problem remains undetermined."[12]

Sartre derived many of his basic insights from Heidegger. Death, Heidegger points out, is not a disaster that strikes suddenly and cancels all obligations. "It is not only when he comes to die, but always and essentially that man is without issue in the face of death. Insofar as man *is,* he stands in the issuelessness of death."[13] For Heidegger, death is a mode of being and as such enters into the process of living, something toward which life inevitably tends. As the individual becomes aware of the fact not only that man is mortal but that he is himself destined to die, he is overcome by the experience of dread. It is this disclosure that darkens all of existence for him. "Everything that enters into life also begins to die, to go toward its death, and death is at the same time life."[14] Man must impose meaning on the chaos of meaninglessness if he is not to become a victim of the *nihil,*[15] but this is possible "only through the very recognition of meaninglessness—of the nothingness that underlies our lives."[16]

Emmanuel Mounier, an exponent of Christian existentialism, declares that it is not death that constitutes a philosophical problem, "but the fact *that I do die.*"[17] Life is characterized by this very fact of incompleteness, uncertainty, ambiguity, and dread. Man lives for the sake of dying.

I am constantly trying to forget about it, to escape from it, to misrepresent it to myself by means of such things as indifference, diversion

[12] *Ibid.,* pp. 539–40.
[13] Martin Heidegger, *An Introduction to Metaphysics,* trans. Ralph Manheim (New Haven: Yale University Press, 1959), p. 158.
[14] *Ibid.,* p. 131.
[15] Arland Usher, in *Journey Through Dread,* points out that Heidegger is a nihilist.
[16] Marjorie Grene, *Martin Heidegger* (London: Bowes and Bowes, 1957), p. 47.
[17] Emmanuel Mounier, *Existentialist Philosophies,* trans. Eric Blow (London: Rockliff, 1948), p. 9.

or religious myths. Living authentically, on the other hand, is living in conformity with this concept of life: to live in constant appreciation of death and its imminent possibility; to look squarely at this thing which is our fellow during every moment of our lives. Then we have attained "freedom in the face of death."[18]

Karl Jasper's concept of transcendence also issues out of the human sense of potential death. Each death, however, is an individual death. Jaspers maintains that the fact of death need not plunge man into the bottomless despair of nihilism. Once man becomes fully aware of the imminence and inevitability of death, he begins to seek out meanings that will account for his coming here on earth and his return to the original source of being. Potential death involves an act of knowing: the knowledge that death is certain and final. Potential death is the soil in which the idea of God grew; it is the mother of philosophy, the motive power behind the arts. Since man's freedom is rooted in death, such insights do not necessarily culminate in nihilism. Man can cherish his finiteness, the preciousness of his life in the fleeting present, and earn the right to his heritage of humaneness.

2. NIHILISM AND THE DEATH MOTIF

With your back to the wall, care-worn and weary, in the gray light of the void, read Job and Jeremiah and keep going. Formulate your principles without regard for anything else, because there will be nothing left of you but your words when this epoch comes to an end, making an end of all singing and chanting of poetry. What you don't say will not be there then. . . . But don't send out an SOS. First of all, there's no one to hear you, and secondly, after so many voyages your end will be a quiet one.[19]

To believe, in Unamuno's conception, is not a trivial matter; it is an emotional state in which are commingled hope, desire, and, simultaneously, feelings of lack and doubt.[20]

[18] *Ibid.,* p. 39.
[19] Gottfried Benn, *Primal Vision,* ed. E. B. Ashton (Norfolk, Conn.: New Directions, n.d.), p. 207.
[20] José Huertas-Jourda, *The Existentialism of Miguel de Unamuno.* University of Florida Monographs, Humanities no. 13 (Gainesville, Fla.: University of Florida Press, 1963), p. 14.

The above quotations help to explain why the fact of death is one of the archetypal motifs in the literature of the twentieth century. It is the realization on the part of those who are without the support of religious faith that there is no justification for the journey of man through time in a universe that recks not of his fate; it is this that generates a feeling of nihilistic futility. To shut out this terrifying vision of nothingness, man creates gods, builds churches, invents myths, and elaborates rituals. When Europe was dominated by the divine Absolute, this sense of the reality of the Beyond affected the character of earthly existence in every sphere. In the seventeenth century, however, the growth of the new science transformed man's conception of the cosmos and of his own nature and destiny. He now beheld a geometrical universe, with himself "an atom in a mathematically conceived whole," as Weber remarks in his *Farewell to European History* (p. 35). Whereas naturalism compels man to accept the knowledge that Nature is beyond good and evil and that death is the end of life, the Christian faith offers him the hope of life eternal, the fulfillment of his intense longing for immortality, the assurance that ultimately he will emerge the victor over pain, time, and dissolution. Despite the belief of Western man in the Incarnation, he cannot get rid of the insidious doubt that tells him that the Resurrection never took place. As a result, death is today regarded as the worst of evils.

The fight against nihilism is therefore essentially a fight against death and all that death represents. A doughty fighter like Unamuno quarrels with God and attempts to wrest the promise of immortality out of the very jaws of death. He resolutely confronts the accursed enemy of the human race: the Devil, who doubts and negates; the Emperor of Death who, utterly indifferent to man's fate, reduces the living human essence to a handful of dust; the Tempter, who on various occasions urges him to take his own life; the demon, who whispers in the night that all his striving is in vain. He refuses to heed the words of Ecclesiastes that the sons of men die even as the beasts perish.[21] Unamuno boldly demolishes the demoralizing premises of nihilism by proclaiming

[21] Ecclesiastes 3:19.

his belief in the higher truths of Christianity. His subjectivity, not to be balked in its desperate quest for salvation, rides roughshod over the objections raised by rationalism, affirms that it believes in God despite the absence of proof.

3. NADA AND GOD

If consciousness is ... nothing more than a flash of light between two eternities of darkness, then there is nothing more execrable than existence.[22]

I affirm, I believe, as a poet, as a creator, looking at the past, looking at memory. I deny, I disbelieve, as a rational being, as a citizen, looking at the present; and I doubt, I struggle, I am in agony, as a human being, as a Christian ... contemplating eternity.[23]

Unamuno presents the edifying spectacle of the religious seeker who must carry the dialectic of doubt to a nihilistic extreme and then soar above the damnable conclusions of logic by an anguished affirmation of faith. However overwhelming his vision of the power of blackness, even in his worst despairing moments of negation, he hopes for the theophany that will grant him the promise of life everlasting on his terms. He searches desperately for the answer to the riddle of the Sphinx, while inwardly aware that this is a quixotic, perhaps futile quest, since it is the mind of man that creates the Sphinx and propounds the question that cannot be answered. This is the nature of the spiritual conflict that rages in the heart of Unamuno's work. In his struggle against the absence of redemptive meaning, in his fight against the hell of nihilism, he composed soliloquies that rise to the level of "auto-dialogue" and achieve authentic existential communication.

The person who takes part in a dialogue, who converses with himself by dividing himself into two or three or more persons, or even into an entire people, does not soliloquize. Only dogmatists speak in mono-

[22] Miguel de Unamuno, *The Tragic Sense of Life,* trans. J. B. Crawford Flitch (London: Macmillan Co., 1926), p. 13.
[23] Miguel de Unamuno, *The Agony of Christianity,* trans. Kurt F. Reinhardt (New York: Frederick Ungar Publishing Co., 1960), p. 20.

logues, even when they seem to engage in dialogues, by means of questions and answers, as is being done in catechisms. But we skeptics, we who are in agony, we polemical spirits do not soliloquize. As for myself, I carry my agony, my religious and secular struggle, too deeply in my spiritual entrails to be able to live on soliloquies.[24]

Unamuno's conflict springs from the intolerable contradictions he encounters in his determined quest for ultimate meaning. He assumes that the meaning is there, *must* be there, but how can he be sure? If consciousness is but an epiphenomenon of the brain, a transient flash of light between two eternities of darkness, then Unamuno, the bearer of consciousness, pronounces his anathema upon existence. Even this curse is an expression of his insatiable hunger for the bread of meaning. In almost every period of history and in practically every literary movement since the beginning of the Renaissance, these archetypal motifs of the struggle against the fate of nihilism manifest themselves. In reality, the search for meaning goes on all the time. In Tillich's striking formulation of the problem, the writer who shoulders the burden of meaninglessness "shows that he experiences meaning within his desert of meaninglessness."[25] In short, nihilism must be experienced in depth before it can be transcended.

The Greeks, in their Dionysian excesses, had caught glimpses of the sheer irrationality of existence. It was not until the advent of Nietzsche, however, that nihilism became outspoken and, strangely enough, evangelical in tone, a kind of negative theology designed to confirm the conception of God as Nothing personified. In the twentieth century, the metaphysics of Nothingness gained increasing currency and entered literature in a variety of symbolic forms. Henceforth man, this interrogating animal, would be capable solely of asking questions, for he now knew there were no answers.[26] In his *Tractatus Logico-Philosophicus,* Ludwig

[24] *Ibid.,* p. 13.
[25] Paul Tillich, *Theology of Culture* (New York: Oxford University Press, 1959), p. 75.
[26] The impulse to question, the fact that man persists in asking questions of a universe that vouchsafes no answer, that remains impenetrably silent, unheeding of this impertinent jack-in-the-box who time and again pops his head out and shrilly cries "Why" of the interstellar spaces—is not this phenomenon in itself proof positive

Wittgenstein proclaimed with the assurance and ultimacy of a
logical positivist: "Of what cannot be said thereof one must be

that whatever else man may be he is first and last a questioning creature. Perhaps
this constitutes his original sin; perhaps the first act of man's disobedience con-
sisted of a sacrilegious question: why not taste of the forbidden fruit? Perhaps
man is guilty of hubris in raising questions that, by implication, criticize the
established order of things. The logical positivists, of course, reject the question
"Why" addressed to the cosmos as not meaningful in content since there are no
conceivable ways of framing an empirically warranted answer. Nevertheless, man
cannot live without persisting madly in this quest for ultimate meaning. He must
try to comprehend this mysterious, seemingly insoluble puzzle; he cannot find the
answer but this does not discourage him; it spurs him on to greater effort as his
perplexity increases. Ortega asks: "How can we live turning a' deaf ear to the last
dramatic questions? Where does the world come from, and whither is it going?
Which is the supreme power of the cosmos, what the essential meaning of life?
We cannot breathe confined to a realm of secondary and intermediate themes."
(José Ortega y Gasset, *History As a System,* trans. Helene Weyl [New York:
W. W. Norton & Company, 1961], pp. 15–16). The fact that man in the course
of the ages has found no finally satisfying answer is no reason why the search
should not go on. There is no escape from the need to face this issue that concerns first and last things. Such cosmological questions cannot be thrust aside,
they haunt the consciousness of modern man. The questions modern writers
in particular raise are not forced upon them from the outside; they are self-generated;
they comprise an internal dialogue in the form of metaphysical questions that breed
further questions. This obsession with questioning reveals the problematical
character of existence, the equivocal role of man's being in the world. Canetti
remarks: "Perhaps the most important question of all is about the future; certainly
it is one charged with tremendous urgency. But the gods to whom it is addressed
are not obliged to answer and hence, the more urgent the question, the more
despairing it is. The gods never commit themselves, never stand to be questioned;
no force can penetrate their intentions. Their utterances are ambiguous and defy
analysis." (Elias Canetti, *Crowds and Power,* trans. Carol Stewart [New York:
The Viking Press, 1962], p. 288).

This has been called, not without reason, an age of suspicion, an age of anxiety,
a neurotic age, but it might with better justice be called an age of interrogation.
The novelists and dramatists of our time of trouble (Kafka, Eugene O'Neill,
Lenormand, Gide, Sartre, Camus, Samuel Beckett, Paul Bowles) have created
the problematical hero, his consciousness perpetually resounding with questions,
questions, questions, for which he can find no answers. Or if he does provisionally
verbalize an answer, since he must perforce act out his decisions and these cannot
always be postponed, he soon enough proceeds to question the validity of his answer.
He introspects, he spies upon his own thought processes, watches himself act,
work, make love, and even analyzes his dreams. The twentieth-century philosophers
have also ventured to question the character of man, the nature of existence, the
meaning of death or Nothingness, but they are more thoroughgoing than the
literati in their art of interrogation. Why, they ask, is there a world at all and why
is there a charged consciousness that confronts the enigma, in Heidegger's terms,
of being-there? The questioning alters nothing; the world remains unaffected by
this metaphysical inquisition. The possibility, however, that there might be no

silent."[27] But the leading writers of the age could not keep silent even if in the eyes of the logical positivists they were guilty of uttering absolute "nonsense."[28] Though Nothing, like Nirvana or the nature of God, cannot be defined in meaningful conceptual terms, it is literally impossible not to rebel against the semantic tyranny of the Nothing. To talk about Nothing may be a contradiction in terms, for neither logic nor science can fathom its secret,[29] and yet the dialogue, the last extremity of existential man, must go on.[30]

Being at all discloses itself, and this is the horizon opened up by the questioning. The supreme question that is concerned with the problem of solving the mystery of being, arises in moments of severe inner crisis. "The question looms in moments of great despair, when things tend to lose all their weight and all meanings become obscured." (Martin Heidegger, *An Introduction to Metaphysics,* p. 1.) This is the most profound question we can ask, since it is concerned not with any particular thing but with the root-cause of being. But there is a further question: "Why the why?" (*Ibid.,* p. 4.) The function, the duty of metaphysics is to raise these fundamental questions. Wittgenstein, however, looked upon the anguish of being as a kind of disease, but how can it be cured except by ignoring the question of being. And that is precisely what he recommends. The question, "What is being?," is, according to him, illegitimate. It cannot possibly be answered. The sentence, as stated, is grammatically correct, but is not meaningful. There is the danger to be avoided: not to assume that objects correspond to the substantives we use. The characteristic of a metaphysical question is "that we express an unclarity about the grammar of words in the form of a scientific question." (Ludwig Wittgenstein, *The Blue and Brown Books* [Oxford: Basil Blackwell, 1960], p. 35.)
[27] Michael Polanyi, *Personal Knowledge* (Chicago: The University of Chicago Press, 1958), p. 87.
[28] On the problem of "nonsense," see George Pitcher, *The Philosophy of Wittgenstein* (Englewood Cliffs, N.J.: Prentice-Hall, 1968), pp. 154–57.
[29] In the *Tractatus Logico-Philosophicus,* Wittgenstein argues against the theory of the ineffable. What cannot be clearly stated belongs to the kingdom of silence. Wittgenstein insists that "The *riddle* does not exist. If a question can be put at all, it is possible to answer it." Quoted in Justus Hartnack, *Wittgenstein and Modern Philosophy,* trans. Maurice Cranston (New York: New York University Press, 1965), p. 17.
[30] It is astonishing and symptomatic, the degree to which a number of writers as well as literary critics and philosophers have focused their attention on the mystery of Nothing, as if the negative were an existing object or entity to be contemplated with a shudder of dread. Heidegger writes with oracular ambiguity on the subject. "Nothingness, even when we mean it only in the sense of the complete negative of what is present, in being absent, belongs to being present as one of its possibilities. If, therefore, nothingness prevails in nihilism and the essence of nothingness belongs to Being, although Being is the fate of transcendence, then the essence of metaphysics is shown to be the place of the essence of nihilism." (Martin Heidegger, *The Question of Being,* trans. William Kluback and Jean T. Wilde [New York: Twayne Publishers, 1958], p. 87.) To reduce such operations with the concept of

How then shall the writer name the unnameable, find concrete images to suggest the emptiness of being and, in the effort to express the numinous experience of Nothing, discover a way out of the desert of meaninglessness? Unamuno undertook this mission. Like Kierkegaard, whose work influenced his thinking,[31] he was a creature of paradox, an impassioned believer in "subjective truth."[32] He knew that his innermost thoughts were freighted with contradictions, and that contradictions and paradoxes lay at the heart of Christianity. Fighting against nada, the tormenting fear of extinction, he mobilized all his creative resources and, in defiance of reason, leaped by way of paradox into a faith that he believed because it could not be proved.

Living as he did in an age of science and methodological skepticism, Unamuno could not achieve perfect purity of faith; the poison of doubt weakened the will to believe. He could not

Nothing to their linguistic ground is to make it apparent that these are exercises in the jabberwocky of illogic, the deployment of grammatical fictions. According to Kenneth Burke, however, this may not be the result of irresponsible juggling of grammatical categories. "For if man is the symbol-using animal, and if the ultimate test of symbolicity is an intuitive feeling for the principle of the negative, then such 'transcendental' operations as the Heideggerian idea of 'Nothing' may reveal in their purity a kind of Weltanschauung that is imperfectly but inescapably operating in all of us." (Kenneth Burke, *The Rhetoric of Religion* [Boston: Beacon Press, 1961], p. 21.) Negative theology defines God in terms of what He is not. The experience of the Absolute through finite perceptions embodies a paradox. "The beginning and end of the paradox that is gnostic religion is the unknown God himself who, unknowable on principle, because the 'other' to everything known, is yet the object of a knowledge and even asks to be known. He as much invites as he thwarts the quest for knowing him; in the failure of reason and speech he becomes revealed; and the very account of the failure yields the language for naming him." (Hans Jonas, *The Gnostic Religion* [Boston: Beacon Press, 1958], p. 288.) Each religious symbol thus gives imaginative expression to that which human language only shadows forth in metaphors. (Edwyn Bevan, *Symbolism and Belief* [Boston: Beacon Press, 1957], p. 122.)

[31] Unamuno studied Danish-Norwegian or Norse-Danish in order to read Kierkegaard in the original. "In the works of this writer Unamuno recognized his own thirst for immortality and his own infinite God who was beyond man's understanding and hence must be accepted on faith alone." Margaret Thomas Rudd, *The Lone Heretic* (Austin, Tex.: University of Texas Press, 1963), p. 182.

[32] The only criterion of Unamunian truth is that truth which is lived. Unamuno trusts the wisdom of the heart, the revelation provided by the imagination, as opposed to the dictates of logic. "It is the distinctive property of subjective truth as Unamuno sees it, that it must be felt here and now, lived here and now." José Huertas-Jorda, *The Existentialism of Miguel de Unamuno*, p. 25.

establish peace between his head and heart, his religious faith and his reason, but he did not desire to do so. His mission, as he saw it, was "to destroy everyone's faith: faith in affirmation, faith in negation, and faith in indifferent abstention, and this is because I have faith in faith; and so it is my mission to wage war against all those who live resigned, be it to Catholicism, to rationalism, or to agnosticism."[33] Though his personal experience strengthened his conviction that reason was completely helpless in trying to grasp the reality of the supernatural, he could not silence the refractory voice of reason. This set the stage for his life-long crusade against nihilism. He realized that he could not be altogether successful in his jihad against the congregated powers of darkness, but this did not deter him from continuing the struggle. Though he insists that he seeks truth in life and life in truth, he is "conscious that I shall not find them while I live; my religion is to struggle tirelessly and incessantly with the unknown...."[34] He is determined not to be penned in by confining categories. Religion is not a doctrine that can be rationally set forth. Faith is a matter of the heart and not a question of empirical mathematical demonstration. He refuses to act on the premise that it is impossible to know. Perhaps this is so, but the desire to know the ultimate secret is not to be denied. He will persist in probing the mystery of the unknown, "even without any hope of penetrating it, because this struggle is my hope and my consolation."[35] The longing for eternity consumes him, despite the fact that he cannot stop himself from thinking that this longing is all in vain. "I can understand a man's not believing in another life, for I, myself, can find no proof of its existence; I cannot understand his being resigned to it and what is worse, not even desiring another life."[36]

Unamuno endears himself to the modern mind by the rigorous honesty of his search, the sincerity of his confession. He endeavored to salvage the integrity of the self in a mechanical universe that

[33] Miguel de Unamuno, *The Agony of Christianity,* p. xxvi.
[34] Miguel de Unamuno, *Perplexities and Paradoxes,* trans. Stuart Gross (New York: Philosophical Library, 1945), p. 2.
[35] *Ibid.,* p. 5.
[36] *Ibid.,* p. 13.

appeared to have no interest in the phenomenon of individual consciousness. The annihilation of the self, the *nihil* imposed by death—that outrage was not to be borne, but what assurance could he gain that the body survived after death? Throughout his life Unamuno wrestled with this obsessive but unanswerable question—what comes after death?—and it colored all his thinking.[37] He struggled desperately "to rescue God as well as himself from nothingness."[38]

4. UNAMUNO AND THE TRAGIC SENSE OF LIFE

If Unamuno grappled with the problem posed by nihilism, it was because nihilism sentenced him to death, and he was grimly determined not to be destroyed. The tragic conflict in Unamuno's thought is evident in his awareness of the war of opposites in his being: "the will to be, and the suspicion that one can cease to be...."[39] This interminable conflict between certainty and uncertainty, faith and doubt, makes itself felt in all his work: his philosophical meditations, his fiction, particularly in the novel *Abel Sanchez,* and even in his lyrics. As he declares in "On Credoes," his heart sweats in anguish "beneath the unending yoke of the infinite."[40] It is this never-ending conflict between the nihilism of doubt and the absolutism of faith that compels man to exist tragically. It is the coexistence of the rational and the irrational that underlies the "tragic sense of life."[41] Unamuno's quest for faith, like that of Kierkegaard, is essentially modern in temper; it avoids none of the pathos, none of the predicaments of the human condition. He is not satisfied with the gift of faith, if that were at all possible; he must test its degree of truth; he cannot trust his instincts and intuitions alone.

[37] See Marie J. Valdes, *Death in the Literature of Unamuno* (Urbana, Ill.: University of Illinois Press, 1964).
[38] Sherman H. Eoff, *The Modern Spanish Novel* (New York: New York University Press, 1961), p. 209.
[39] José Ferrater Mora, *Unamuno,* trans. Philip Silver (Berkeley and Los Angeles: University of California Press, 1962), p. 31.
[40] Miguel de Unamuno, *Poems,* trans. Eleanor L. Trumbull (Baltimore, Md.: The Johns Hopkins Press, 1952), p. 163.
[41] José Ferrater Mora, *Unamuno,* p. 31.

Unamuno succeded finally in casting off the paralyzing spell of ideas; he had to break the icy fetters of logic if he was ever to banish the terror of death. He possessed too critical an intellect, however, to rejoice for long in the pyrrhic victory of the absurd. Though his heart was perfectly willing to embrace Tertullian's *Credo quia absurdum,* his mind revolted against this surrender to intellectual folly. On the other hand, he knew that reason led to the dead end of skepticism, and skepticism stamped the seal of finality on the ignominious fact of death. Reason in itself is impotent, but faith that rests on irrational foundations belongs to the sphere of the absurd. Trapped in this irreconcilable contradiction, Unamuno redoubled his efforts to believe, as if the act of belief were of itself sufficient to insure the truth of a doctrine! Unamuno is at last forced to acknowledge the grievous contradiction present in his outlook.

> Since we only live in and by contradiction, since life is tragedy and the tragedy is perpetual struggle, without victory or the hope of victory, life is contradiction.[42]

Unamuno found no consolation in the award of fame or the vicarious immortality that the begetting of children conferred. Nor would he be stopped from undertaking this quest for ultimate meaning, which for him meant the same thing as the search for personal immortality, by the warning that the attempt to explore the unknowable was foredoomed to defeat. Man must cry out to God "even though God should hear us not. . . ."[43] Of what earthly use was the accumulation of knowledge and the conscientious pursuit of truth if in the end the philosopher winds up in the grave? Unamuno incisively defines the leading symptoms of the metaphysical and spiritual affliction known as nihilism. He wanted to know the meaning of man's brief, precarious existence. He was determined to solve, if he could, the mystery of death. He fought desperately against the fate of death that would overtake

---

[42] Miguel de Unamuno, *The Tragic Sense of Life,* p. 14.
[43] *Ibid.,* p. 17.

him. If death is to be his portion, "then nothing has any meaning for me."[44] If he finds that he is slated to die utterly, then he falls into a state of irremediable despair. If he receives the assurance that he will not die utterly, he is able to adopt a stance of resignation. If he cannot know what lies beyond the grave, then his despair generates a conflict that drains his spirit of the energy to affirm.

Unamuno cut the Gordian knot by assuming that everything vital is anti-rational. It is impossible for man to conceive of himself as not existing—certainly not for a vital personality like Unamuno, who could never get enough of life. Only one lifetime —and no more? And then the end, an eternity of oblivion? Unamuno will not have it so.[45] He desires more and more of life. Like Brand, his cry was: "Either all or nothing!"[46]

This is the mad cry of the metaphysical rebel, be he Manfred or Ahab, who would impose his unconditional demand on life: All or nothing! Unamuno, like Nietzsche, gives utterance to a type of hubris that violently rejects the limitations of the finite. No, he assails deaf Heaven with his bootless cries; he must live for ever and ever, beyond this brief mortal span. Nietzsche, in *Thus Spake Zarathustra,* declares that "Joys want the eternity of *all* things, they want *deep, profound eternity!*"[47] Uanmuno writes: "Eternity, eternity!—that is the supreme desire!"[48] Nothing less will do. There *must* be a life beyond death: that is the categorical demand Unamuno addresses to God.

Unamuno, like Pascal, is willing to gamble everything on his belief in the immortality of the soul. Unlike Nietzsche, he derives no shred of solace from the scientific doctrine of the conservation of matter.[49] He does not wish to be dissolved in the float of matter

---

[44] *Ibid.,* p. 33.
[45] Horace M. Kallen points out some of the flagrant contradictions in Unamuno's philosophy in *Freedom, Tragedy, and Comedy* (De Kalb, Ill.: Northern Illinois University, 1963), p. 15.
[46] Miguel de Unamuno, *The Tragic Sense of Life,* p. 39.
[47] Friedrich Nietzsche, *Thus Spake Zarathustra,* trans. Thomas Common (New York: Boni and Liveright, n.d.), p. 321.
[48] Miguel de Unamuno, *The Tragic Sense of Life,* p. 39.
[49] Unamuno was strongly influenced by Nietzsche, but he could not accept his atheism. As we have seen, Unamuno desperately needed to believe in the truth of immortality, the reality of an afterlife enjoyed for all eternity, but to discover

or energy. He insists on being what he is now. He fights desperately
against a destiny that would merge his identity in the infinite of
matter or energy. With equal desperation he resists the fate of
becoming one with God. He seeks to possess God, "to become
myself God, but without ceasing to be myself. . . ."[50] This comes
as close to downright blasphemy as the rebellious man of faith
dare go. Under no circumstances will Unamuno, in his rationalist
as well as anti-rationalist moments, consent to be sundered from
his flesh and bones, stripped of his unique personality. This is the
measure of his spiritual pride: he rebels in the name of Christianity,
and all because of his desire to live forever. If this be madness,
he will make the most of it. By the imperious thrust of his faith
he will create the God who will grant him the boon of immortality.
That is why God must exist—to make certain that his cry will be
heard, his prayer answered.

The specific character of truth is at stake in this tragic conflict.
The truth that reason finds acceptable is that which can be empirically
confirmed, but even the rationalists, much as they reject the belief
in immortality, seek to discover some motive for living, even
though they are aware that after the lapse of hundreds or millions
of centuries a time will come "when human consciousness shall
have ceased to exist" (p. 96). It is this made-to-order philosophy
of humanism that Unamuno contemplates with undisguised amaze-
ment. What possible justification is there for the cult of progress
or the striving for social perfection, if history culminates in the
grotesque anticlimax of death? He cites the example of Nietzsche,
the self-appointed Antichrist, who proved mathematically the

this truth and to believe in this reality he had to cast about for theological con-
firmation. Thus he both admired Nietzsche and attacked his views. "There you
have that thief of energy, as he clumsily called Christ, who tried to wed nihilism
with the struggle for existence, and who speaks to you of valor. His heart asked
him for the eternal All, while his head showed him Nothingness. Desperate and
mad to defend himself from himself, he cursed what he most loved. Not being able
to be Christ, he blasphemed against Christ. Blown up with himself, he wished to
be unending and he dreamed of the eternal return, a wretched solution for immortality." Quoted in Paul Ilie, *Unamuno: An Existentialist View of Self and
Society* (Madison, Milwaukee, and London: The University of Wisconsin Press,
1967), p. 178.
[50] Miguel de Unamuno, *The Tragic Sense of Life,* p. 47.

truth of the myth of eternal recurrence, "which is in fact the most stupendous tragi-comedy or comi-tragedy" (p. 100). If reason demonstrates that once the body dies consciousness is forever destroyed, then the only way to answer that rational demonstration is to affirm the truth of a faith that is absurd and that is based upon "the most absolute uncertainty" (p. 104). Rationalism, if carried far enough, opens the door to nihilism by disclosing that "there is no absolute truth, no absolute necessity" (p. 104).

Unamuno, the rebel as believer, is prepared to shake the world to its foundations in order to satisfy his craving for immortality. God is real because the believer is real. Like Kazantzakis in *The Saviors of God,* he held that God exists only because the believer exists. Subjectivity is truth, and subjectivity is the guarantee of immortality. For Unamuno, what he desired, if he desired it passionately enough, must be true. He readily concedes that this is not a rational argument, but why assume that only what is rational is true? We need God, he argued, in order "to give a meaning to the Universe" (p. 152). God, in other words, is not a God of reason but a heuristic fiction that invests the universe with the light of redemptive meaning.[51]

The work of each writer is dictated by his own special demon. Otto Rank composed *Art and Artist* to prove that the creative urge was governed fundamentally by the desire for immortality. This was certainly true of Unamuno, who created living images in order to achieve immortality in space as well as in time.[52] Unamuno knew, of course, how easily man can deceive himself, give himself

---

[51] Whereas Vaihinger looks upon a fiction as a legitimate error that is justified by the purpose it serves, Unamuno regards faith in God as "true." Vaihinger contends that the expression, "I believe in God," means "simply that 'I act as if a God really existed.'" (H. Vaihinger, *The Philosophy of "As If,"* trans. C. K. Ogden [New York and London: Harcourt, Brace & Co., 1925], p. 106.) For Unamuno this would have implied a surrender to the dark forces that make for death. Yet he is one with Vaihinger in maintaining that one does not believe in God because He exists; one gives birth to God out of a profound and despairing spiritual need, and therefore He exists. Man creates God. "To create Him, yes! This saying ought not to scandalize even the most devout theist. For to believe in God is, in a certain sense, to create Him, although He first creates us." (Miguel de Unamuno, *The Tragic Sense of Life,* p. 154.

[52] Margaret Thomas Rudd, *The Lone Heretic,* p. 188.

over to arbitrary but comforting illusions, but he felt that the craving for immortality is not born of illusion, for it is this craving that accounts for the origin of God. A depersonalized Divinity is only a personification of Nothingness. God exists because without Him life would be senseless, a nightmare of unrelieved nihilism. It is the miracle of faith that creates the object of worship. Faith must be affirmed, must be lived, despite the absence of proof.

Unamuno found no definitive solution for the problem of nihilism. To the last he remained a doubting Saint Thomas, and even God, as he envisaged Him, is stricken with the plague of doubt. Indeed, it is God who is the supreme heretic. In one of his sonnets Unamuno audaciously declares: "Perhaps God Himself/is an atheist."[53]

---

[53] José Ferrater Mora, *Unamuno,* p. 44.

PART II:

Revolt and Despair in the Russian Soul

3

Nihilism in the Russian Soul

If we strip the term "nihilism" of its contemporary existentialist en-
crustations, it should signify a doctrine advocating intellectual negation
and the sheer destruction of whatever may in fact exist, be it material
or spiritual. Such a theory would hold that it is of no interest whether
or not anything replaces that which is to be annihilated. A thoroughly
consistent nihilist would even consider it his duty to keep on ruining
anything that had been constructed or that would be constructed in
the future regardless of its utility. He should adhere to no positive
philosophical or religious beliefs at all.[1]

1. PRELUDE

Oh, if only one could accept one's own death. All our passionate hatreds
come from the fact that we're unwilling to die. We kill ourselves and one
another because we are unwilling to die.[2]

Men have the illusion that they are free. But when they are sentenced
to die they lose the illusion.[3]

I will keep faith with death in my heart, yet well remember that faith
with death and the dead is evil, is hostile to humankind, as soon as we
give it power over thought and action. *For the sake of goodness and
love, man shall let death have no sovereignty over his thoughts.*[4]

---

[1] Charles A. Moser, *Antinihilism in the Russian Novel of the 1860's* (The Hague:
Mouton & Co., 1964), pp. 18–19.
[2] Eugène Ionesco, *The Colonel's Photograph and Other Stories,* trans. Jean
Stewart (New York: Grove Press, 1969), p. 167.
[3] Albert Camus, *Notebooks, 1935–1942,* trans. Philip Thody (New York: Alfred
A. Knopf, 1963), p. 116.
[4] Thomas Mann, *The Magic Mountain,* trans. H. T. Lowe-Porter (New York: Alfred
A. Knopf, 1952), pp. 496–97.

The nihilist is a man in perpetual conflict with himself. One day, he knows not quite how it happened, he finds himself convinced of the fact that his life is utterly without meaning or purpose. For him this fact, however shattering its impact, constitutes an incontrovertible truth. This nadaistic epiphany did not come upon him suddenly; it was a slow, cumulative growth, like the insidious spread of cancer in the human body. Once the metaphysical infection set in, there was no arresting its malignant advance.

The curious thing about this process of inner conversion to a nihilist position is that the postulant who joins this order does not immediately question the truth of his belief. It is for him a universal, not a narrowly personal or neurotic truth. All men, he feels certain, are secretly of this persuasion, though they try to hide it from themselves. They are guilty of bad faith. They embrace consolatory faiths, they hail the promise of supernatural reward for all the suffering they have had to endure on earth, or they invent some myth that celebrates the glory and fullness of life and somehow manages to deny the reality of death.

But no man is a nihilist for long before a violent reaction sets in. He begins to fight against his recurrent moods of fatalistic despair. He has lost all incentives for living. The sky, as far as his eye can reach, is dark and overcast. Spiritually paralyzed like one of the living dead, he attempts to overcome this unbearable condition of life-in-death by resorting to a logical ploy. It is a contradiction in terms to argue that everything in the last resort is meaningless. If that is so, then his belief that everything is absurd is a questionable if not erroneous assumption. The grounds on which he based his nihilistic faith prove treacherous. But this is not enough to change his mind for good. He resists the mandate of logic by the simple Pascalian expedient of asserting that logic is not the ruler of life. He remains stricken, disconsolate, not to be comforted. Let others partake of whatever nostrums are offered them; he will refuse to blind himself to the truth of being: the truth of ultimate nothingness. To assume that existence is a fortuitous, purposeless explosion of biological energy is to commit intellectual suicide; it is to reduce man, the one creature who strives persistently toward the goal of transcendence, to the same order of importance as the amoeba, the worm, and the ant. It is to strip him completely of a sense of destiny.

The literary nihilists constitute an aberrant and self-defeating minority. Their situation is indeed a hopeless one. Despairing (though they profess to have gone beyond despair) and desperate, yet not knowing what to do if they are to save themselves, they have no alternative but to reject everything that makes up the body of values mankind cherishes in life. In doing so, they leave themselves exposed to the charge of sheer irrationality. This does not disturb them in the least, for the irrational reaches to the very heart of their complaint: the death of God, the total absence of purpose, the absurdity of a universe that manifests no concern for the fate of man. Despite the teleological pattern some philosophers are able to piece together, there is no good reason for the experiment of life on earth—none that the mind of the nihilist can grasp.

Nihilism goes beyond the most extreme form of pessimism, for the pessimist still adheres to some standard. He simply finds that life fails to measure up to the human ideal. Death is an outrage to which he cannot reconcile himself. Even if he recommends universal suicide, he does so for the sake of relieving men of senseless suffering. But the nihilist repudiates all standards— reason, ideals, purpose, meaning, truth. Hence he cannot take anything seriously. Love is a biological illusion, the quest for fame is an expression of vanity, the ambitious projects men undertake are designed to hide the emptiness of existence. Trapped in this state of utter disenchantment, he lacks the incentive to act. If he goes on living, it is because he cannot summon up the energy to take his own life. Besides, he realizes that individual suicide is an absurd and futile gesture: it solves no problem.

He is like Stavrogin, Dostoevski's nihilistic hero, devoid of will. He has no aim in life. He is tormented by his vision of the void, the *néant,* nada, the Nothing. The secret of his being is that he is bored by the spectacle life has to offer. He is alienated from his fellow men by his contempt for human nature's daily food. He suffers from the spleen, from acedia, the deadly sin of sloth. He abides by no moral law. He blows neither hot nor cold. Maurice Friedman, in *Problematic Rebel,* declares:

The secret of Stavrogin's boredom and his passionless indifference lies, more than anything, in the fact that he is not only cut off and detached but irreparably divided. He cannot do anything with his whole being and his whole heart. One part of him always looks on as the bored and listless observer, knowing that there is no extreme that can ever catch him up in such a way that he may really give himself to anyone or lose himself in anything.[5]

But Dostoevski's nihilists—the obsessed atheist Kirillov, "this maniac of a theophobe whose suicide is a protest against God's world"[6] and Ivan Karamazov, the rebel who believes that "everything is permissible"—do not conform to a single fixed pattern. Ivan, in many of his rebellious utterances, gives expression to "the essence of Russian nihilistic atheism."[7] The Russian nihilist in the second half of the nineteenth century was infected with a skepticism that poisoned his system and blighted his whole life. "The nihilistic superman recognizes no ethical truths, rejects all moral codes: nothing at all can be denied him."[8] He is the Man-God, satanic in his revolt, but his hubristic presumption in seeking to gain mastery over life and death results in a despair so extreme that it leads him to commit suicide. Dostoevski here confesses the split in his own being. He interprets nihilism not as a subversive philosophy imported from abroad but as a diabolical temptation that dwells in the breast of Russian intellectuals.

The nihilist is thus caught in the trap set and sprung by his own contradictions. In condemning life for its lack of purpose, he is betraying a religious hunger for ultimate meaning, but it is a metaphysical hunger which, on his terms, he can never hope to satisfy. He can deal with this problem in one of four ways. He can remain indifferent to it, deliberately ignoring, like the logical positivists, what cannot be solved. The scientist keeps silent about that which cannot be known. Or he can adopt a despairing hedonism,

[5] Maurice Friedman, *Problematic Rebel* (New York: Random House, 1963), p. 122.
[6] Julius Meier-Graefe, *Dostoevsky*, trans. Herbert H. Marks (London: George Routledge and Sons, 1928), p. 226.
[7] T. G. Masaryk, *The Spirit of Russia*, ed. George Gibian, trans. Robert Bass (New York: Barnes & Noble, 1967), 3:10.
[8] *Ibid.*, p. 11.

seeking to live feverishly in the present moment. Or, like Unamuno, he can affirm a transcendental faith in the face of all rational objections, creating the God he needs in order to triumph over death. Or, like Kafka, he can reject the Absolute and the world in an ironic gesture of impotence. Or he can revolt against the myth of the absurd by means of a humanistic affirmation of solidarity with mankind. In the last case, the nihilist realizes that if life is to have any positive meaning it must be one that man himself imposes on it. In this way he is able to fulfill his destiny, instead of being the architect of his own misfortunes. He does so without necessarily compromising his nihilist principles. Whatever may be the fate meted out to the race of man in the fullness of time, he will bear his existential burden in the problematical present and summon up the courage, like his forbears, to create art as well as shape the course of his own life. Perpetually confronted by the precariousness of existence, the nihilist who, in literature or life, seeks authenticity of being, never shuts the door completely on hope.

2. TURGENEV AND BAZAROV

Throughout the course of history, from the dawn of civilization, man has recurrently harbored the suspicion that life is a cruel and hideous joke, a meaningless episode in a meaningless dream. Resigned to this knowledge, the Oriental mind transforms nothingness into an absolute, making a veritable religion out of Nirvana, the blessed symbol of ultimate nonbeing. The texture of reality was woven of the stuff of illusion. The West countered the threat of nothingness by adopting the Christian mythos that promised the gift of immortality to mortal man. When the myth collapsed, when belief in God as a causal agent in the arena of history largely vanished, the Christian ideal was secularized, supplanted by the Promethean goal of striving for mastery of the world of Nature. The cult of progress was best exemplified in the Marxianized version of the Kingdom Come finally established in Soviet Russia.

Yet it was Russia that, paradoxically, was the generative ground of both nihilism and revolutionary messianism. It gave birth to the superfluous man and the positive hero, to Oblomov and Bazarov. Though Turgenev held that he coined the term *nihilism*, it was used as far back as 1790 in Germany.[9] Though the term *nihilism* existed long before Turgenev made it popular, it was not used in the sense ascribed to it in *Fathers and Sons* until the eighteen sixties. The new generation was radical in its demands, impatient of intellectuals who theorized but failed to act. The young critics Chernyshevski, Dobrolyubov, and Pisarev used literature as a springboard for trenchant sociological preachment. Art was meant to serve the cause of political emancipation and social betterment. The Russian nihilists were political extremists who fought to establish a better life for the masses. Not that they went to extreme lengths in carrying out their program. They believed, most of them, in a future socialist or anarchist society. Thus their negativism was, in fact, balanced by a positive, if vaguely formulated, hope. According to Moser, the basic tenet of the nihilistic outlook in the sixties was "a positivist, monistic philosophical materialism, in most cases fading into 'scientism' (a belief that all philosophical problems not already resolved through the researches of natural science would eventually be solved and that, necessarily, in a materialist sense)."[10] The nihilist movement in Russia was influenced by the work of Auguste Comte, Charles Darwin, and Ludwig Büchner. Büchner labored to demolish the pretensions of idealism and religion. Thus, to the regnant faith in materialism and utilitarianism, the nihilists added the evangelical motif of atheism. Chernyshevski boldly proclaimed his adherence to atheism. The Russian nihilists drew the logical conclusion that if God did not exist, a new basis for ethics, not grounded in supernatural revelation,

---

[9] August Closs, *Medusa's Mirror* (London: The Cresset Press, 1957), p. 147.
[10] Charles A. Moser, *Antinihilism in the Russian Novel of the 1860's*, p. 29. Moser deals with the Russian novelists of the period who were dissatisfied with the interpretation of life given by the literary nihilists. These novelists created a new genre, the tendentious novel, which attacked the radical movement. On the basis of newspaper accounts of the murder of Ivanov by the revolutionary Nechaev, Dostoevski became convinced that the nihilist group were motivated by criminal designs. Resolved to expose the true character of these nihilists, Dostoevski fashioned the figure of Stavrogin in *The Possessed*, the man who is incapable of distinguishing good from evil.

had to be found. Fourier's influence, which had been strong in the forties, still persisted. Chernyshevski's commune, described in his didactic novel *What Is to Be Done?*, was intended to start a movement of communal living that could spread throughout the world. The novel he composed drew the portrait of "the new man," the positive hero who would inherit the socialist world of the future. The nihilist as secular saint is embodied in the character of Rakhmetov, who lives abstemiously like the poor, though not abandoning his sole luxury—a cigar.[11]

Russian nihilism promulgated a methodological skepticism. It hailed scientific naturalism as the sovereign method of arriving at the truth—that is the chief identifying characteristic of the nihilistic concept among the Russian intelligentsia, which distinguished it from the philosophical nihilism of a Schopenhauer or Nietzsche. Though the doctrine embraced positivism and the ideal of scientific exactitude, in practice the writers who accepted the doctrine became accusers of the established order. Believing as they did that science offered the best available means of attaining salvation, the Bazarovs of Russia warred against the abstract, the metaphysical, the mystical; the truth they believed in was always concrete, factual, and practical. Inspired by the work of Comte, John Stuart Mill, Taine, Littré, Büchner, Moleschott, and Vogt, especially the last three, they exalted the figure of the natural scientist, the Prometheus of the modern age. They also derived ideological support for their outlook from Darwin's theory of evolution and from the writings of Feuerbach and Stirner.

The philosophy of materialism, which led to atheism, strengthened the critical spirit in the nihilists to such a degree that they questioned all things. As Masaryk remarks: "Atheism and materialism are at once preconditions and logical consequences of nihilist criticism and negation."[12] On the whole, however, nihilism in

---

[11] For a discussion of Chernyshevski's novel, see Charles I. Glicksberg, *Modern Literary Perspectivism* (Dallas, Tex.: Southern Methodist University Press, 1970), pp. 79–81.
[12] Thomas Garrigue Masaryk, *The Spirit of Russia*, trans. Eden and Cedar Paul (London: George Allen & Unwin, 1919), 2:72.

Russia was social and political in character; it aimed to overthrow
the absolutism of the Czar and the power of the theocracy. Not
until the appearance of Andreyev was nihilism couched in metaphysical terms. The Russian nihilists, whose portrait Turgenev
drew faithfully with a mixture of sympathy and distaste, never
gave way to despair; they submitted to a kind of revolutionary
discipline; in conformity with their ruling mystique of "the
people," they sought to identify themselves with the peasants.
"Since the sixties, nihilism had become the question of questions
for thoughtful Russians—and for thoughtful Europeans."[13]

Fathers and Sons introduces a tragic protagonist. It was Turgenev's
fundamental belief, which shaped his aesthetic of fiction, that there
existed a tragic element in every human being. As he declared: "we
are all condemned to die. Can there be anything more tragic than
that?"[14] The pessimism that informs his major novels grows
out of his constant awareness that the most precious achievement
of the history of culture, the development of the unique human
personality, is negated by the doom of death. Turgenev asked himself repeatedly what lay beyond the grave. Perhaps nothing but
the void. Like Bazarov, he realized that Nature was unaffected by
the aspirations and ideals of humanity. Bazarov, a man of strong
will, is unsparing in his search for knowledge, yet it avails him
naught: he must perish at the end. Turgenev, though himself not
a rebel, admired the heroic individual. Unlike Dostoevski, he
wanted the truth, not the assurance of salvation.[15] When the novel
was published, a storm of detraction broke out, the reactionaries
seizing on the invidious term *nihilism* as their target for a heavy
barrage of abuse.[16]

In focusing attention on the difficult problem the Russian intellectual then faced, his role in life and his relation to society,
Turgenev anticipated the modern dilemma. He had arrived at the

[13] *Ibid.*, 2:81.
[14] David Magarshack, *Turgenev* (New York: Grove Press, 1954), p. 216.
[15] Avraham Yarmolinsky, *Turgenev* (New York: The Orion Press, 1959), p. 95.
[16] For a more detailed analysis of *Fathers and Sons,* see Charles I. Glicksberg, *The Self
in Modern Literature* (University Park, Pa.: Pennsylvania State University Press,
1963), pp. 155–59.

conclusion that life was not made for happiness. Freedom of will
was but an illusion. His Schopenhauerian *Weltanschauung* is
evident in his interpretation of Nature as indifferent to human hopes
and needs. The individual counts for naught; he vanishes, leaving
no trace behind him, as if to confirm the lesson of his utter insignificance in the cosmic scheme of things. No matter how beautiful
Nature appears at times, it oppresses man with the sense of his
own mortality. Whatever fate befalls man, Nature remains imper-
turbable, unmoved by his quest for ultimate meaning. Turgenev
offers no hope of redemption through Christ. Death is incontestably
the victor in every encounter with the human adventurer; whatever fulfillment man is able to attain lasts but a moment and then
is rudely taken away. Death, the conqueror, wins every battle.
Bazarov, like the Communist protagonists in *Man's Fate,* attaches no importance to his own personality; he tries hard to be
self-sufficient. Since he believes in nothing, he must believe in himself as God. Freeborn points out: "Bazarov, the nihilist, has no
belief beyond himself, no will greater than his own, and in this
self-sufficiency he exhibits that 'bottomless abyss' of arrogance
and self-will which is characteristic of the man-God."[17] He recognizes no higher law. Once death overtakes him, then he ceases to
be; there is no resurrection.

This is a recurrent motif in Turgenev's work. In *On the Eve*
(1859), Turgenev introduced the character of a patriot, Insarov,
who is unlike Bazarov or Rudin, the dreamer and enthusiast.
Turgenev foreshadows the death of this Bulgarian hero. This is
how Yelena, the Russian woman whom Insarov has married,
broods while he is ill:

> why is there such a thing as death, why is there parting, sickness, and
> tears? Or otherwise why is there this beauty, this sweet feeling of hope,
> why the reassuring consciousness of a firm refuge, of constant defence,
> immortal protection? What is the meaning of this smiling, benedictory
> heaven, this happy, quietly resting earth? Or is it all really only within
> us, while outside us is eternal cold and silence? Are we really alone—

[17] Richard Freeborn, *Turgenev* (London: Oxford University Press, 1960), p. 124.

alone—and out there, everywhere, in all those inaccessible abysses and depths—everything, everything is alien to us?[18]

Here, as in other novels he wrote, Turgenev ends on the note that death comes to all. In *Smoke* (1886), the hero, Litvinov, realizes the evanescence of life; everything human and particularly everything Russian seemed as fugitive as smoke. It was while depicting the suffering of his characters that Turgenev voiced his perception of the perishability of all things beautiful, the impassivity of Nature, the defeat of man by powers he cannot cope with. Nevertheless, affirming his faith in man, Turgenev underlined the importance of the individual self. He insisted that he was not prejudiced against his hero, Bazarov.[19] In striving to capture the truth of the imagination, he had to include bad as well as good traits.[20]

3. GORKY AND ANDREYEV

Andreyev's nihilism goes far beyond the gentle melancholy of Turgenev; it involves a total, paroxysmal rejection of the accursed gift of life. Again I must mention the paradox that the same land that gave birth to Gorky's realism also produced the nihilistic despair of Andreyev. These two writers were initially drawn to each other but later, because of basic ideological as well as temperamental differences, their paths diverged. Gorky had written to the younger man expressing admiration for his realistic stories that unmasked the complacency and attacked the inertia of Russian life. Gorky then saw in Andreyev a kindred spirit. Gradually, however, Andreyev revealed a side of his nature that was bound to alienate Gorky and even arouse his antagonism. Fundamentally, it was Andreyev's nihlistic approach to life that Gorky found abhorrent. Andreyev had begun to explore abnormal states, to grapple with the dread mysteries of existence,

---

[18] Ivan Turgenev, *The Borzoi Turgenev,* trans. Harry Stevens (New York: Alfred A. Knopf, 1959), p. 549.
[19] Freeborn, *Turgenev,* p. 99.
[20] Ivan Turgenev, *Literary Reminiscences and Autobiographical Fragments,* trans. David Magarshack (New York: Farrar, Straus and Cudahy, 1958), p. 196.

the insoluble problems of life and death. There was a morbid streak in Andreyev as in Dostoevski, but whatever the reason for his obsession with the ultimate issues posed by the metaphysical vision, he drifted farther and farther away from the political radicalism of his day.

The two men were thus destined to clash, since they viewed the world from diametrically opposed perspectives. As Gorky's political outlook matured, he allied himself both as a man and as a writer with the revolutionary cause. He was troubled by Andreyev's anomalous development in the direction of symbolism. These two writers entertained opposing conceptions of the nature and function of art: one sought to capture the very heartbeat of the unintelligible mystery, while the other became more and more a zealous propagandist of the Revolution. A confirmed realist, Gorky, like Chernyshevski, rejected as quixotic the pursuit of unattainable ideals. Andreyev, however, remained the metaphysical rebel, impatient with those forms of literature that concerned themselves principally with the documentation of the ordinary. In a letter he wrote in 1911 Gorky complained that the basic tendency in Andreyev's work led to

> the de-socialization of man. Andreyev has absolutely no social instinct; he is deeply, sociologically egotistical. . . . [He considers that] life is meaningless, that thus all activity is purposeless. Man is the victim of life, not a constructor of life and not a master.[21]

Such a life-negating attitude was anathema to Gorky; Andreyev's nihilistic *Weltanschauung* constituted a form of betrayal that he could not forgive.

Gorky had decided for himself how the danger of nihilism was best to be avoided. Convinced that there was no God, he wished to deprive men of their illusions, especially the illusion of the supernatural—a theme that he deals with in *The Lower Depths.* He was determined to subdue his personal fear of death and face

---

[21] *Letters of Gorky and Andreev,* ed. Peter Yershov, trans. Lydia Weston (New York and London: Columbia University Press and Routledge and Kegan Paul, 1958), p. 9.

life with honesty and courage. Life is full of cruelty and horror, and to master it "a cold, rational cruelty is necessary."[22] The belief that man can conquer Nature by discovering its laws is held by both Chernyshevski and Gorky; it is the common ideological bond that unites the most diverse revolutionary thinkers. It informs their life with a sense of messianic purpose. Chernyshevski, like Turgenev, stressed the fact that Nature is indifferent to human concerns; "it knows nothing about man and his affairs, about his happiness or his death. . . . Nature is neutral towards man, it is neither his enemy nor his friend. . . ."[23] Unlike Andreyev, who was tormented by the thought of death, Gorky was undismayed by the realization that the earth would one day perish and that mankind, together with all its arts and artifacts, would turn into dust and ashes. The human spirit must accept the necessity of death, but before leaving the terrestrial scene it persists in carrying on its creative activities, it composes music and drama and fiction, it builds cathedrals, monuments, and cities, because it wants to do so. For Gorky the awareness of the inevitability of death is not inherently tragic; it need not rob the free man of his sense of worth. Man must proudly keep on working, keep on creating.[24]

As a dialectical humanist, Gorky believed there was only man to be considered. Man, the inventor of technology, was the sole measure of value. Hence there was no question of surrendering to the defeatist spirit of nihilism. As Gorky declares:

> I bow to man because beyond the incarnations of man's reason and imagination, I feel and see nothing in our world. God has been one of man's inventions, just like photography, with the difference that the

[22] *Ibid.,* p. 70.
[23] N. G. Chernyshevski, *Selected Philosophical Essays* (Moscow: Foreign Language Publishing House, 1953), p. 307.
[24] After the failure of the revolution of 1905, a number of Russian intellectuals turned their energies to religion. "After 1905 religious enthusiasm reached even the Social Democrats in foreign exile, and provoked among them Lenin's notorious quarrel with the heretical 'God-builders', Bogdanov, Lunacharsky, and others. The fundamental position of the God-builders was that the idea of God was neeeessary to mankind, but that God, as presented by all established religions, had failed them, and that it was therefore time to create a new God; this new God would not bear the character of a divine being who created men in His image, but

NIHILISM IN THE RUSSIAN SOUL

latter fixes that which really exists, whereas God is the photo of an
idea which man invents.[25]

The only thing proper to consider sacred is "the dissatisfaction
of man with himself and his striving to be better than he is. . . ."[26]
The questions raised by the nature of reality or the problem of truth
are to be answered, Gorky maintains, in pragmatic, not metaphysical terms.[27]

Andreyev's reading of life led him in an entirely different direction. Obsessed with his dark metaphysical speculations, he would
not give up his right to challenge the universe. A "realist" of the
imagination, he refused to become the dupe of dogma or the pawn
of the historical process. He had no faith in the promise held out
by the political utopias of his age. His brooding spirit of fatalism
could not embrace the revolutionary evangel. His nihilism, which
dismissed as a pathetic illusion the importance men attached to
the human enterprise, necessarily canceled out all social-minded
perspectives. Believing in nothing, he knew only the crushing
weight of despair. A precursor of the myth of the absurd, he
realized full well that suicide fails to solve the ontological mystery
and yet he attempted to take his own life.

Gorky, by contrast, was a committed writer who staunchly
believed that "one's attitude toward life and mankind should be
active."[28] He had no use for the nihilist who with supine irrationality
turns against the universe. If he had his way, he would not hesitate
to hang people of this stripe; they deserved death as the enemies
of mankind. It is not surprising, therefore, that the breach between
Andreyev and Gorky steadily widened and could not be healed.

would instead be created by men out of the noblest qualities of which throughout
the ages humanity had shown itself capable." F. M. Borras, *Maxim Gorky*
(Oxford: The Clarendon Press, 1967), p. 55.
[25] Nina Gourfinkel, *Gorky,* trans. Ann Feshbach (New York: Grove Press, 1960),
p. 184.
[26] *Ibid.*
[27] See the chapter on "Illusion Versus Reality," in Charles I. Glicksberg, *The
Ironic Vision in Modern Literature* (The Hague: Martinus Nijhoff, 1969), pp. 142–
51.
[28] *Letters of Gorky and Andreev,* pp. 120–21.

Gorky, the revolutionary novelist, would not care to preserve
the friendship of a writer like Andreyev who was convinced that
life is a wretched biological mistake and that reason is utterly impotent in its efforts to pierce the curtain of darkness that enshrouds
it. Unlike Gorky, who spoke to the Russian people as the voice
of militant class consciousness, Andreyev concerned himself
chiefly with the tragedy of the individual who sets out on his quest
for the redemptive light of meaning. The quest is a hopeless one;
the light, perhaps nonexistent, does not manifest itself. Andreyev
concludes that life is stale, absurd, profitless. Man is alone. Though
he acknowledged the power of reason in confronting the mystery
of existence, Andreyev was convinced, like Schopenhauer, that in
the last analysis even reason is under the blind governance of the
Will. However much he might pity man's fate, he never abandoned
his nihilistic outlook.

Though Andreyev was influenced by such writers as Pisarev
and Tolstoy, the dominant figures in his intellectual development
were Schopenhauer and Nietzsche, particularly the former. The
Nietzschean influence is discernible in Andreyev's distrust of the
masses and his deeply rooted faith in the individual, but his pre-
vailing tendency is to interpret the world in accordance with the
philosophy Schopenhauer advanced in *The World as Will and
Idea. The Life of Man* (1906), like Hardy's *The Dynasts,* pictures
life in Schopenhauerian terms as driven by inexorable biological
forces. In this dramatic parable, Andreyev attempts to show that
the life of man is controlled at every turn by the master puppeteer,
the Being in Grey, who symbolizes the Immanent Will.[29] Here
is the fatality, silent, invisible, and merciless, that presides over
human destiny, a destiny that culminates in the grotesque and
ignominious spasm of death. Like Tolstoy, Unamuno, and, today,
Ionesco, Andreyev was tormented all his life long by the thought
of death. As he declares in *Seven Who Were Hanged:* "It is not
death that is terrifying, but the knowledge of it: it would be utterly
impossible to live if a man knew exactly and definitely the day

---

[29] See Alexander Kaun, *Leonid Andreyev* (New York: B. W. Huebsch, 1924).

and hour of his death."[30] In *The Life of Man* Andreyev depicts how Man, the protagonist, rises up in furious but futile revolt against the tyranny of the Will. During his existence Man rushes feverishly hither and thither, engages in a multitude of diverse activities, and then makes the disconcerting discovery that throughout his headlong career the decisions he made were not his own; he was, from the very beginning of his pilgrimage, a predestined victim.

As a dramatist Andreyev was interested primarily not in the so-called objective world but in the conflicts and complexities of the inner self. The theater of the future, he contended, would be psychological in its orientation. Like Maeterlinck and Strindberg, he questioned whether "action" or "plot" constituted the heart of the drama. Though "public" events—wars, famines, revolutions, epidemics—still affect the life of the individual and that of society, the most revealing and important aspect of life, he held, is to be found in the dynamic play of thought: the dreams, fantasies, nostalgias, the myths and manias of the mind. For it is the mind of man that intolerably heightens the conflict between an alien reality and an alienated self, the specious present and the eternal—a conflict that finally ends and must end in his defeat. Man is the tragic victim of his own engendered illusions. The drama that is dedicated to the "truth" of being (how different is this truth from the social realism Gorky practiced!) must probe and illuminate these inner states.

Constructed like an allegory, *The Life of Man* is overlaid with symbolism. The characters, like those in Expressionist drama, are types, abstractions, personifications of philosophical ideas. The life of man is epitomized in the image of a candle that is gradually being consumed until it is reduced to a feeble, guttering end-piece—and then it goes out. The hero, Man, strives to fulfill himself, driven as he is by the force of his creative passion, but the result of his quest is not dependent on the purity of his commitment. Nature is the arbiter of destiny. It is not enough to

---

[30] Leonid Andreyev, *Seven Who Were Hanged,* in *Ten Modern Short Novels,* ed. Leo Hamalian and Edmond L. Volpe (New York: G. P. Putnam's Sons, 1958), p. 203.

struggle with single-minded devotion for the highest degree of perfection in art. Fame is a bauble, wealth a sorry illusion. Despite all the prizes and plaudits he receives in the course of his career, Man is still alone, frustrated in his existential needs, cruelly hoodwinked by the vanity of life. The Being in Grey is in charge of the weaving and the snapping of the thin threads of fate, and this Being is completely unmoved while the candle continues to burn itself out. Sustained by vain hopes and harried by dire forebodings, Man is unwitting of the everlasting darkness that waits to engulf him. That is the burden of the play: suffering makes up the life of man; beyond his mortal span there is only the vista of nothingness.

The Prologue sounds the central theme. The Being in Grey reads from the Book of Fate; he will unfold the pattern of man's life from birth to death. In this Book of Fate there is no mythic hope that can save man from extinction, not even the vaguely hinted promise of redemption in the hereafter. Andreyev's play is structured like the morality play *Everyman,* but it is thoroughly secularized in content, devoid of religious faith.

> Hitherto non-existent, mysteriously hidden in infinite time, without thought or feeling, utterly unknown, he will break through the barriers of non-existence and with a cry will announce the beginning of his brief life.[31]

Once thrust into life, Man will be made to suffer the same relentless blows of fate visited upon the others already inhabiting the earth. There are no happy exceptions.

> Irresistibly dragged on by time, he will tread inevitably all the steps of human life, upward to its climax and downward to its end. (p. 68)

The iron round of destiny pays no heed to prayers, it is deaf to the dolorous cries for pity. From the time the candle is first lit, the wax starts melting until the light flickers weakly and is then

---

[31] Leonid Andreyeff, *Plays,* trans. Clarence L. Meader and Fred Newton Scott (New York: Charles Scribner's Sons, 1925), p. 68.

extinguished. Man dies, returning to the night from which he came, "vanishing without trace into infinity" (p. 69).

This symbolic drama is composed in unrelieved colors of blackness. The old women in the first act (they reappear in an obscene dance at the end of the play) serve as a doleful, degraded substitute for the ancient Greek chorus as they comment shrilly on the folly of being born and the worse folly of dying. We hear the shrieks of the woman in labor and then the sudden wail of a child; the candle held by the Being in Grey lights up. The second act is focused upon the marriage that Man consummates in love and the misery of poverty the couple must endure. Hunger and poverty enable Man to perceive the senseless cruelty of life. Though he is steeped in misery, he remains defiant and challenges the Unknown: "No, you, whatever your name may be—Destiny, the Devil, Life— I throw down the gauntlet to you. I challenge you to battle" (p. 94). Urged on by his wife, he pits his strength against the invisible adversary. In the tradition inaugurated by the metaphysical rebels who appear in the work of Byron, Baudelaire, Swinburne, and Lautréamont, Man shouts his manifesto of defiance:

> You have a heart of stone that knows no pity. Stand aside! or I will pour into it the seething passion of rebellion (p. 94).

He is resolved never to give in, even though he falls under the brutal bludgeoning of fate. His body covered with wounds, he still possesses the courage and the strength to withstand this malignant foe of mankind. Then at last his genius as an architect is recognized; he wins fame and fortune. The Man and his wife give an elaborate ball in their mansion while the Being in Grey impassively witnesses this ostentatious display of vanity. He can afford to wait, and soon enough misfortune strikes: everything they have achieved is taken away from them; their son is dying. At this point Man kneels in prayer, hoping that eternal justice will heed his plea and save his son. The Being in Grey listens with stonelike indifference. When the son dies, Man curses the Unknown who laughs at both the tears and prayers of humankind. Like the modern Job, disillusioned, wrathful, and rebellious, he pronounces this curse:

> I curse the day when I was born! I curse the day on which I shall die! . . .
> I curse myself! . . . I hurl all back into your cruel face, senseless Fate
> (p. 127).

Then he dies. The Being in Grey, holding the burnt-out candle, watches the diverting spectacle. Absolute darkness falls as the old women dance their bacchanal about the corpse. Small wonder that Gorky could not appreciate the merits of this frenziedly nihilistic play. Since its hero has no roots in social reality, he is, according to Gorky, deprived of "tragedy, flesh, and blood."[32]

The Black Maskers (1908) is another allegory of the soul of man. Duke Lorenzo discovers that all is not well with him; his passions, his fantasies, his unacknowledged wishes, all these betray aspects of his being he had up to now successfully repressed. Now he beholds the hideous image of his other secret self and he kills him, but it is himself that he kills. Reason is dethroned. The citadel of the self is besieged and finally captured by the black maskers, the bringers of death, the mysterious, irrational forces man cannot hope to master. The masquerade mirrors the conflicts that rage in the heart and mind of Lorenzo. Around him he sees only masks. One masker, whom Lorenzo praises for his disguise since he looks exactly like a corpse, announces that Death was the artist who had altered his features. The maskers make known to Lorenzo the irreconcilable contradictions in his own being. The Masked Singer renders the song Lorenzo had composed, a hymn that pays tribute to the Lord of the World: Satan. Lorenzo asks himself whether he, the son of a crusader, could have composed such an infernally blasphemous song, but when he learns the shameful truth about his birth he cries out in anguish: "Oh, the horrible reality of human life!"[33] The Black Maskers arrive and darkness falls. Lorenzo kills his alter ego; madness overtakes him. Though Lorenzo is the ruler of the castle and therefore presumably in charge of his soul, these Black Masters, the demonic agents of the unconscious, fill him with the knowledge of the perversity of fate; they afford him a glimpse of the muddied depths of the soul of man whose mysterious nature can never be fathomed.

[32] *Letters of Gorky and Andreev,* p. 92.
[33] Andreyeff, *Plays,* p. 31.

Andreyev's spiritual agony was caused by his inability to believe in himself or in the meaningful destiny of the human race. The struggle and the suffering, the triumphs and the disasters of history, the achievements and the failures of the individual as well as society —all this seemed to him utterly pointless. As he saw it, life is a phantasmagoria of illusion, void of purpose. This pessimistic vision informs his more complex play, *Professor Storitsyn*. Unlike Kafka, who transmuted his metaphysical anxieties and terrors into art by viewing existence through the perspective of irony, Andreyev hysterically emphasizes the meaninglessness of the human condition. Kafka knew that he did not know and could not grasp the secret, if there was such a thing, of the universe, but Andreyev in his black rage passes harsh judgment on the ugly and intolerable truth of life. The truth for him is that man must die.

Professor Storitsyn is a sad study in frustration, betrayal, infidelity, and, of course, the curse of death. The wicked triumph; the professor, the innocent victim, suffers a heart attack and dies. Telemakhov, the doctor who had examined him and who is his close friend, tells him that he must be careful because he has a bad heart condition. The trouble is that the professor works too hard and smokes excessively. We discover soon enough what is wrong with this man, the impossible situation in which he is involved. His books are being stolen and sold in second-hand bookshops; it is his dissolute son who is the thief. The professor, the soul of honor, is sufficiently sensitive to identify himself with the evil-doer, but he is deeply depressed by all the corruption that surrounds him. He is convinced that this is not a local phenomenon. It infects all of Russia. If his heart is fatigued, though he is by no means an old man, this condition, too, is typical of Russia.

A poet at heart, a dreamer, a writer of books, he is unable to indulge his craving for beauty, poetry, and music. He has no time for such aesthetic pleasures, but he is certain that "one must live beautifully."[34] That marks the tragic irony of his life: he is trapped in a routine entirely devoid of beauty. The world he lives in is

[34] Leonid Andreyev, *Professor Storitsyn*, trans. Isaiah Minkoff, George Rapall Noyes, and Alexander Kaun, in *Masterpieces of the Russian Drama*, ed. George Rapall Noyes (New York: Dover Publications, 1960), 2:750.

drab, bleak, sordid: a tainted world. This infection has invaded his own home. His wife is guilty of adultery. He is loved by a student, Ludmilla, but he cannot possibly accept this love. He is not free; he is too old for her; besides, he feels he is being dragged down by "the coarseness, ugliness, and ignobleness of our life" (p. 765).

He cannot continue to live in this fashion; he must leave his home. His friend Telemakhov berates him for his naive idealism. The doctor, who professes to be a realist, points out that the two of them "are alone in this night, amid a pack of wolves" (p. 791). Ludmilla arrives to tell the professor that she, too, has left home. Now they are both homeless. The professor is tired, his will to live is broken; he is feverish from having been out in the rain. When he dies of a heart attack, Telemakhov, who has tried to wipe out in himself the last traces of pity, does not weep. Standing with his back to the corpse, he cries out: "It is a lie! A lie! A lie!" (p. 799). Shaking his fist toward heaven, he calls out furiously at the top of his voice: "Murderer!" (p. 799).

These were the existential paradoxes, the nihilistic passions, that tormented Andreyev throughout his life. He made no attempt to formulate a solution; though he found much in Schopenhauer that was congenial to his outlook on life, he could not get himself to believe in the validity of any philosophical system. Though he was a man of vision, he lacked the nourishing substance of faith.[35] Reality was too complex, too refractory, to be compressed within any Procrustean frame. Life remained inscrutable, beyond the power of reason to comprehend. A nihilist by conviction, he felt that life was purposeless, a brief passage from darkness to darkness. His literary work is shot through with the counterpointed motifs of dismay and defiance, despair and revolt. His is "the voice of the average intellectual of the twentieth century, restless, questioning, evaluating, sick at heart of disappointment and disparagement, yet ever seeking, always searching. . . ."[36] He is incapable of uttering the Everlasting Yea, no blessing ever crosses his lips; he aligns him-

---

[35] Stefan Schimanski, in his essay on Andreyev, declares that in the last analysis Andreyev failed "because he had no vision and no faith." *The New Spirit,* ed. E. W. Martin (London: Denis Dobson, 1946), p. 105.

[36] Kaun, *Leonid Andreyev,* p. 15.

self in despair with those victims who rebel futilely against their fate. Denied the possibility of adhering to a positive faith of any kind, he could create only nightmares of disillusionment, failure, and disaster.

For him there was but one universal and compelling theme: the mystery of existence. That is why he was impatient with the limited method of realistic narration; he would fain go beyond the confines of the actual world and express symbolically, as best he could, whatever scintilla of meaning the Absolute disclosed. Against those who severely criticized his work on the ground that it was too thickly allegorical and abstract, he defended himself by saying that he would never be understood by those who failed to grasp "that great riddle of existence—the appearance of darkness in response to the call of light, the emergence of black, cold beings knowing neither God nor Satan, shadows of shadows, beginnings of beginnings" (p. 110). Like Maeterlinck, he was certain that life was "a Mystery for all who think and live in earnest" (p. 121). A raging prophet of doom, nihilistic in his paroxysms of despair, he beheld no glimmer of hope on the horizon of the future. There was no balm of Gilead for the race of man. Whereas Gorky could shake off his awareness of the horror of life by his staunch faith in the masses and in the advent of Socialism, Andreyev specialized in the dialectics of meaninglessness. For him the struggle naught availeth.

Andreyev offers the singular and edifying case of a writer who not only failed to transcend his nihilism but gave in to it. Occasionally out of his anguished despair a cry of defiance is wrung, but the cry cannot be long sustained and subsides into silence. The imprecations the rebel hurls at the indifferent face of fate recoils upon his head as he goes down to defeat. Andreyev could not see life steadily nor see it whole. His obsessions stood in the way. His portrait of human existence is painted in a funereal monotone, unrelieved by the delicate art of chiaroscuro. He probes into the basic causes of human misery and suffering, but in the end what he holds up for our contemplation is the unmitigated horror of a life without meaning. He furnishes no categorical answers, not even provisional ones; what he communicates is the anguish of the questioner who is certain, even before he questions, that it is altogether impossible to make sense out of the appalling business of living. He wrote tragedies that contain no redeeming touch of comic relief. If he failed as an artist it was because the visionary truth he reported was morbidly one-sided.

Is nihilism, as the Communist critics loudly maintain, the bitter outcry of decadent intellectuals, rootless, alienated, illusionless, who are the product of a sick, exploitative society? Are such modern exemplars of futility as Andreyev, Kafka, Ionesco, and Samuel Beckett voicing the death-throes of a social order that is doomed to extinction? Would the triumph of Communism the world over cure the literary nihilist of his feeling of alienation? Does Gorky, the father-figure, establish the norm to be emulated by ideologically liberated writers, whereas Andreyev, like Alfred Jarry, Lautréamont, Artaud, and Céline, represents the psycho-pathological extreme? These are some of the questions we shall have to deal with as we turn to a critical discussion of another Russian novelist, Artzybashef.

4

Nihilism and Suicide

If human existence involves at its core an instinct toward nonexistence, an appetite in no way secondary to the craving for life itself, what crime does the work of art commit that recognizes the death wish, builds upon its deep-laid position in the human heart, and re-enacts within its own theater the brutal, inconclusive experience of life in irrepressible conflict with its own assumptions?[1]

It is not true that man always loves life unconditionally. Such is human suffering that any psychic life that is at all developed will necessarily be subject to this temptation or at least know moments when man wishes for death.[2]

Suicide is far from being contrary to human nature. The human animal's will to live is neither unlimited nor unconditional.[3]

What undermined the Christian faith was not the atheism of the eighteenth century or the materialism of the nineteenth . . .but rather the doubting concern with salvation of genuinely religious men like Pascal and Kierkegaard, in whose eyes the traditional Christian content and promise had become "absurd."[4]

---

[1] Robert M. Adams, *Strains of Discord* (Ithaca, N.Y.: Cornell University Press, 1958), p. 51.
[2] Paul-Louis Landsberg, *The Experience of Death: The Moral Problem of Suicide,* trans. Cynthia Rowland (New York: Philosophical Library, 1953), p. 67.
[3] *Ibid.,* p. 81.
[4] Hannah Arendt, *The Human Condition* (Chicago and London: The University of Chicago Press, 1959), p. 319. Quoted in A. Alvarez, *The Savage God: A Study of Suicide* (New York: Random House, 1972), p. 128n.

1. DOES NIHILISM LEAD TO SUICIDE?

Nihilism may be defined briefly as the philosophy that declares that life is not worth living. The definition is as incomplete as it is ambiguous and misleading. Under some circumstances life may prove so intolerable that death, self-inflicted, is chosen as the way out. But were the circumstances, whatever they happen to be, providentially changed, were the pain or the grief or the over-whelming sense of failure or guilt removed, then those who were ready to commit suicide would have found life perfectly desirable. Their self-sought death, then, is not a principled condemnation of life as a whole, whereas nihilism, which need not lead to suicide, rejects life under any and all conditions.

Even with this revised definition, a number of qualifications must be taken into account. Which species of nihilism are we considering? There are almost as many varieties of nihilism as there are sects within the body of Christianity. Or rather nihilism, once its root meaning is accepted, yields a host of different conclusions. Some nihilists simply go the whole hog and insist that life as a whole is a wretched mistake. There is no point in striving. The search for happiness is a pernicious illusion. The sooner death comes the better, though the nihilist as a rule will make no effort to hasten the end. Indeed, the best consummation of all, he feels, would be if the entire human race were to perish from the earth.

Once life is despaired of, once man realizes there is no hope of future life in the Other World, once he abandons as useless the quest for happiness on earth, he is, according to Eduard von Hartmann, ripe for the blessedness of salvation, though he has as yet taken only a few tentative steps toward his deliverance. The world as a whole, all of mankind, must be enlisted in this quest for salvation, which is to be fulfilled by making the ends of the Unconscious the ends of human consciousness. Instinct will be enlisted in this campaign to still the fever of volition. The energies of mankind will be mobilized to destroy the volitional impulse and shatter the cosmic scheme of things. The Unconscious Spirit (Hartmann's version of the Schopenhauerian Will), incarnate in humanity, will be given its death-blow. The assumption in all this is that the consciousness of mankind, having freed itself from the illusion of existence, will yearn for the painlessness of nonbeing. This will come to pass. Intellect will triumph over feeling, head over heart. This idea of annihilation of will and world will manifest itself as a profound craving for the ineffable peace of nonexistence. That is how to overcome the instinctive will to live. Once the blind will is brought under the light of understanding it will choose to die. This, Hartmann insists, is the way to redemption.[5]

This fixation on the beatitude of Nirvana is enough to convince many intellectuals that the nihilist must be a psychopath. He who summarily rejects the gift of life must be mad. If the nihilist categorically denies the value of life, then why does he bother to proclaim his views, why write, why live? The nihilist is not taken aback by these attacks. He does not question the sentence of "Guilty" that his judges have passed upon him. He has regarded himself as guilty long before the public pronounced its verdict. This Kafkaesque feeling of guilt on his part does not shake the fundamental character of his vision. Believing as he does in the ultimate meaninglessness of the human adventure, he has a number of options open to him, and the most logical option is that he can take his own life. If he refrains from doing so, it is not because he is afraid. He is no more cowardly or courageous than the general run of mankind. He draws back from committing *logical suicide,* for he is aware that logic is not the decisive force in life. He realizes, too, that his suicide would change nothing in the world. The carnival of absurdity would go on as of old.

Some nihilists, to be sure, do commit suicide. They are devoid of faith in themselves, they have no sense of purpose to keep them going; they suffer acutely all their life long from the curse of meaninglessness. They are not cynical but indifferent; like Stavrogin in *The Possessed,* they can blow neither hot nor cold. They can give themselves to no cause. Oftentimes they are without deep human attachments, even though outwardly they masquerade as husbands, fathers, friends. In short, they are spiritually lost, metaphys-

[5] Eduard von Hartmann, *Philosophy of the Unconscious,* trans. William Chatterton Coupland (New York: Harcourt, Brace and Company, 1931), 3:142.

ically bankrupt, overcome by despair. They struggle to bear up under the crushing weight of hopelessness. Before he commits the irreparable act, each nihilist must assure himself of the inescapable absurdity of all existence, past and future.[6]

Nevertheless, there is no necessary causal connection between nihilism and suicide, nor does commitment to the myth of the absurd trigger the decision to take one's life. There is no proof that if one is convinced life has no ultimate meaning, it therefore follows that life is not worth living. Yet people are frequently driven to a point beyond which they cannot go and then they kill themselves, but it is not the perception of the absurd that leads to suicide. Camus asks: "Does the absurd dictate Death?"[7] Do people obey the call of logic and arrive at the desperate conclusion that death is preferable to life? The reasoning here is itself absurd. The nihilist of the absurd faces a dilemma: is he to die voluntarily or go on living? The intelligence confirms the absurdity of the world while acknowledging the impotence of reason to grasp the irrational character of existence.

In the prologue to *The Savage God,* Alvarez narrates with quickened imaginative insight born of empathy (he, too, had tried to commit suicide) the self-willed death of Sylvia Plath, and the sad story of her death introduces and bears the burden of the central theme: the complex motives that enter into the suicide's decision to end his life. In this skeptical age the temptation to suicide cannot be set aside by dint of theological arguments or scriptural appeals. As Hannah Arendt says:

> For what matters today is not the immortality of life, but that life is the highest good. . . . Moreover, even if we disregard the details of Christian dogma and consider only the general mood of Christianity, which resides in the importance of faith, it is obvious that nothing could be more detrimental to this spirit than the spirit of distrust and suspicion of the modern age. Surely, Cartesian doubt has proved its efficiency

---

[6] "The absurdity and pathos of the life of suicide stems from the despairer's will to achieve—through suicide—his status as a moral human being. Leslie H. Farber, *The Ways of the Will* (New York and London: Basic Books, 1966), p. 93.

[7] Albert Camus, *The Myth of Sisyphus,* trans. Justin O'Brien (New York: Alfred A. Knopf, 1955), p. 9.

nowhere more disastrously and irretrievably than in the realm of religious belief, where it was introduced by Pascal and Kierkegaard, the two greatest religious thinkers of modernity.[8]

What precise means the suicide chooses to achieve his purpose—that does not matter. What counts supremely is his state of mind as he is about to cut the thread of life. Alvarez maintains that the motivation behind the act of suicide cannot be reduced to rational categories. What drives a person to take his own life is often obscure, irrational, inexplicable. Alvarez declares:

> The logic of suicide is like the unanswerable logic of a nightmare, or like the science-fiction fantasy of being projected suddenly into another dimension: everything makes sense and follows its own strict rules; yet, at the same time, everything is also different, perverted, upside down. Once a man decides to take his own life he enters a shut-off, impregnable but wholly convincing world where every decision fits and each incident reinforces his decision.[9]

The suicide-to-be goes ahead with his decision or abruptly reverses himself, without pausing to consider the reasons pro and con and weigh them in the balance. If he goes on living, it is because the option that suicide offers—the sudden termination of his life—leads nowhere. The beyond is a blank, and the would-be suicide knows this full well. Sometimes the planned act of suicide miscarries. Alvarez points out that unconsciously Sylvia Plath hoped to be saved in time, but in this instance luck was against her. Alvarez insists that "a serious suicide is an act of choice . . . a man dies by his own hand because he thinks the life he has is not worth living."[10]

Many writers have at some time in their career been overcome by the feeling that it is impossible for them any longer to bear the tedium or horror of life. Some react by planning to end their lives, some attempt it and fail, and some actually kill themselves. At random I cite such well-known cases as Heinrich von Kleist, Thomas Lovell Beddoes, Gorky, Andreyev, Otto Weininger, Eugene O'Neill, Ernst

[8] Arendt, *The Human Condition*, p. 319.
[9] Alvarez, *The Savage God*, p. 121.
[10] *Ibid.*, p. 56.

Toller, Pavese, and Stefan Zweig. It is extremely difficult to discover in each instance the motives that prompted the writer to take this step. Though many of them reveal the existential despair that brought them to this suicidal state, others leave us in the dark. Maya-kovsky and Essenin each died by his own hand in the prime of life, and we wonder why. All we can say is that the motives that lead to suicide are almost infinitely varied.[11]

Though literature contains many examples of suicides by charac-ters who are psychotic (Septimus Smith in *Mrs. Dalloway*) or who are broken in spirit by the competitive struggle (Willy Loman in *Death of a Salesman*), most literary suicides are caused chiefly by the total collapse of meaning and the conviction that existence is no longer supportable.[12] As he contemplates the ineradicable ab-surdity of the human condition and his own involvement in it, the nihilist hero or anti-hero falls into a state of incurable despair. If he commits or tries to commit suicide, that is because, a frustrated idealist at heart, he feels he cannot go on living. He serves as the sacrificial scapegoat offered up by the writer, his begetter, who thus pours out his metaphysical rage, symbolically acts out his fit of nihilistic madness, and is temporarily reconciled to the misery of existence. If, like Andreyev, he somehow manages to survive a number of attempts at suicide, he may, like the Russian novelist, transform art into anathema, but he cannot long persist in his battle of invective against a foe that remains silent, invisible—and invinci-ble.

The point is that the pursuit of literature affords no relief from the fatality of death. It offers neither escape nor solace nor solution. There is, as I have already indicated, the further irony that the literary nihilist, even as he pronounces his Everlasting Nay, has

[11] "The majority of persons who commit suicide are tormented and ambivalent; i.e., they are neurotic or have a character disorder but are not insane." (Norman L. Farberow and Edwin S. Shneidman, eds., *The Cry for Help* [New York and London: McGraw-Hill, 1961], p. 13.) In his classic study of the problem, Emile Durkheim concludes that "no psychopathic state bears a regular and indisputable relation to suicide." (Emile Durkheim, *Suicide,* trans. John A. Spaulding and George Simpson [Glencoe, Illinois: The Free Press, 1951], p. 81.)

[12] See "The Literature of Suicide," in Charles I. Glicksberg, *Modern Literature and the Death of God* (The Hague: Martinus Nijhoff, 1966), pp. 88–99.

really no intention of bidding the world good-bye. He may curse existence but he refuses to abandon it. Death he regards as the worst of evils, for it deprives him of the opportunity for condemning a world which he never made, a world in which he does not feel at home. If he dies, he loses everything. The whole problem of death is summed up in the question of suicide. Though there are limits of psychic or physical pain beyond which the will to live is destroyed, what holds many a man back from the brink is that he still retains some vestige of hope. However desperate his situation, he does not despair completely. It is only when he is convinced that nothing can save him that he gives up the struggle. In committing suicide, however, it is not Nirvana he seeks; it is not death he embraces as the way to salvation; he is protesting in the only manner open to him against the intolerable condition of life.

The metaphysical suicide is the man who passes judgment on life and finds it wanting. What it lacks is any rational principle of justification. It is this perception of the gratuitousness of the absurd that draws some literary nihilists to commit suicide. They achieve nothing heroic or exemplary by their act. They die and, unlike Kirillov, they expect to accomplish nothing by their voluntary deaths. There is this redeeming feature, however: the metaphysical suicide is neither pathetic nor psychopathological: he knows what he is doing and why. Cesare Pavese, long before he carried out his deliberate plan of action, was impelled by a suicidal urge:

> I know that I am forever condemned to think of suicide when faced with no matter what difficulty or grief. It terrifies me. My basic principle is suicide, never committed, never to be committed, but the thought of it caresses my sensibility.[13]

For a number of years he lacked the courage for the deed, but he could throw off his suicidal obsession for only short periods of time. Invariably the temptation returned, the mania for self-destruction. Then, at the age of twenty-nine, he penned this revealing confession:

[13] Cesare Pavese, *This Business of Living,* ed., and trans. A. E. Murch (London: Peter Owen, 1961), p. 29.

> Consider this point carefully: nowadays, suicide is just a way of disappearing. It is carried out timidly, quietly, and falls flat. It is no longer an action, only a submission.
>
> Who knows whether an optimistic suicide will come back to the world again? (p. 53)

This philosophy of optimistic suicide is the brain-child of a despairing nihilist. Pavese cannot let go of the idea of suicide. He knows that death cannot be avoided, it will come to one and all in due time, but he is unable or unwilling to wait for its fated arrival. Like a twentieth-century Kirillov but without his negative religiosity, he asks: "Why not seek death of one's own free will, asserting one's right to choose, giving it some significance? Instead of letting it happen? Why not?" (p. 47). He has no answer for his insistent question: the logic of his reasoning is at this point badly confused. He realizes all too well that once death is embraced the freedom to act is lost, but he wants to protest against the ignominy of dying "naturally." In 1950 he committed suicide.[14]

The logical upshot of nihilism is silence or suicide, but then nihilism is not logical in structure or substance. The nihilist does not reason his way into this cul-de-sac nor is he able to reason his way out. The motivation behind every *Weltanschauung* is emotional and intuitive; very often it is conceived and supported by impulses of which the thinker may himself be unaware. Contradiction governs the inner life of man. In any event, it is clear that the writer who takes the pains to voice his nihilism is in effect protesting against it. Were he convinced that the human condition was absolutely hopeless, he could not summon forth the energy to go ahead with his creative work. The artist is, by definition, a living refutation of the nihilistic ethos. Literature presents a curious paradox. The creative nihilist is never resigned to things as they are; it is because he cannot be silent or indifferent that he speaks out so bitterly. The specter of

---

[14] Through death, self-inflicted, he hoped to find the road to the absolute. "Since even the word is part of the world, Pavese finally commits the act that will negate the word and destroy the relationship between literature and life . . . the ultimate maturity for him, will not be a book but silence." Gian-Paolo Biasin, *The Smile of the Gods: A Thematic study of Cesare Pavese's Works,* trans. Yvonne Freccero (Ithaca, N.Y.: Cornell University Press, 1968), p. 257.

the absurd haunts him. The myth of Sisyphus symbolically reveals the nature of the trap in which mankind is caught. The formulation of the myth, however, is in itself an act of revolt; it protests against the monstrous injustice of the human condition. In accepting this myth as true, the nihilist, even when he opts for suicide, is casting about for ways and means of overcoming it.

2. ARTZYBASHEF AND UNIVERSAL SUICIDE

We are fortunate enough if there still remains something to wish for and to strive after, that the game may be kept up of constant transition from desire to satisfaction, and from satisfaction to a new desire, the rapid course of which is called happiness, and the slow course sorrow, and does not sink into that stagnation that shows itself in fearful ennui that paralyses life, vain yearning without a definite object, deadening languor.[15]

The man who is a nihilist at heart is thus faced with a number of options. Having ceased to believe that life has an ultimate meaning, he must stop raising questions about the possible purpose of human existence. If he decides to go on living despite his total disillusionment with self and the world (and that is the choice he usually makes), he must live meaninglessly. If he is tempted to commit suicide, he must wonder what he hopes to accomplish by eliminating himself, before his time is up, from the ranks of those privileged—or condemned—to be alive. Michael Artzybashef (1878–1927), the Russian novelist, works in the pessimistic tradition exemplified by Andreyev; he depicts the various strategies, all of them useless, that men adopt when their faith in life is shattered. Artzybashef articulates a nihilism more uncompromising than that of Andreyev. Whereas in *Sanine* he glorified the life of instinct and seemed to support the Nietzschean conception of love and sex, in his more representative, though less popular novel *Breaking-Point* (1911–1912), he takes for his theme the omnipotence of death and seems to preach the desirability of universal suicide. What saves this work from sheer melodrama is the use

[15] Arthur Schopenhauer, *The World as Will and Idea,* trans. R. B. Haldane and J. Kemp (London: Kegan Paul, Trench, Trübner & Co., 1906), 1:215.

of ironic counterpoint in highlighting the absurdity of rushing to meet the fate of death that everyone fears.

Artzybashef's suicidal pessimism is altogether different in tone and content from the tragic pessimism of Dostoevski. Artzybashef rejects the Christian doctrine in its entirety. The blend of Schopenhauer and Nietzsche yields a nihilism that finds suicide the only "logical" way out, even though this solution is full of absurd contradictions. But *Breaking-Point* is, like *The Possessed,* the classic novel of the absurd. Cornet Krause, methodical in his reasoning, a fanatic in his reliance on logic, his intellect ever active while his heart remains underdeveloped, is a twentieth-century version of Kirillov, but he differs from Kirillov in that he possesses none of his ecstatic mysticism and is not motivated by his sacrificial craving to liberate mankind from the bugaboo of death. Cornet Krause suffers from acedia: the curse of indifference. Cherishing no illusions, drained of hope, infernally bored, he broods constantly on the idea of taking his own life. He is determined to carry out this project without fuss or fanfare. Artzybashef describes how this character is held back by an incomprehensible impulse, a blind, irrational clinging to life; he cannot shoot himself in the dark, when he is alone in his room, and he decides to do it in the company of others at the club, where nothing will distract him from acting out his fixed purpose.

He is confirmed in his decision by the rabid spouting of the engineer, Naumoff, who proclaims the salvationary doctrine of universal suicide. The latter argues that life is a cruel farce, full of misery and suffering; freedom from all this can be achieved by the extinction of the race of man. A minor epidemic of suicides breaks out in this provincial town. Naumoff is not the direct instigating cause; he is merely the catalytic agent. The opposition to Naumoffism is represented by Tchish, a student who supports himself by giving lessons. He had been arrested and imprisoned for his revolutionary activities, but he still believes ardently in a glorious future for mankind to be ushered in by Communism. In the meantime, however, he, too, is a victim of boredom; he is poor and lives as a lodger in a widow's boarding house. Finally, after his "fall," he comes to realize that his dazzling vision of a utopian future is a pipe dream.

After succumbing, while drunk, to "the charms" of the fat, sensual widow, he hangs himself.

There is no touch of comic relief, no glimmer of hope or humor, in this depressing picture of life in Russia before the October Revolution. Love is presented as a biological trap. The local Don Juan, Dchenieff, an artist, after ruining a number of women, perceives at last the emptiness and futility of his life, and shoots himself. Lisa, one of his conquests, drowns herself. Ryskoff, a poor clerk without talent who nourishes pathetic dreams of becoming a professional writer, hangs himself. Nelly, another of Dchenieff's victims, tries to take her own life. Trenieff, after being drawn again into one of his chronic quarrels with his wife, cuts his throat.

This bald summary omits the number of cases Artzybashef piles up of various characters stricken with some incurable disease. We witness the death of a child and the inconsolable grief of the parents. Professor Ivan Rasumovski is dying and knows the end is near; in his state of terror he turns to prayer but immediately before his death he lapses into silence and then laughs aloud with satanic strangeness. Eugenia Samoilovna, formerly an actress, is dying of tuberculosis. Dr. Arnoldi, who inwardly despairs of life, is moved by deep compassion for all those who suffer, but there is nothing he can do.

It is difficult to determine Artzybashef's intention in all this. He is responsible, of course, for the composition as a whole: the selection of naturalistic details, the grim scenes delineated of disease and death, the wave of suicides, the brooding atmosphere of boredom and wretched despair. He evidently considers life an incomprehensible and futile affair, but he is able to distance his material sufficiently to make us realize the ridiculousness of such a conclusion. He shows that Naumoff, for all his impassioned evangelism, is loath to take his own life; he is buoyed up by an inflated sense of his own importance as a prophet of doom. What drives him to choose this path, to preach this grotesque message of redemption by means of universal suicide, is his overweening egotism. Yet there can be little doubt that Artzybashef sympathizes with a character like Krause and the miserably disillusioned Tchish. He exposes the folly of all ideals directed toward the achievement of a paradisal future. Life is the fatal sickness from which these cruelly afflicted creatures will

never recover. Death is the trap sooner or later sprung, from which
there is no possibility of escape.

It is perhaps Dr. Arnoldi who sums up most closely the author's
position. He is surprised at nothing; he seeks to ease the pain of life
in others, whereas he himself has died within. He goes through the
monotonous ritual of living: he drinks, visits his patients, spends
time at the club, but he sees no meaning in any of his actions. He
has died spiritually long ago. He feels there is no point in his committing suicide. He has no answer for the questions the principal characters in the novel ask him in their anguish. His reply is that he does
not know. As far as he is concerned, there are no solutions. Dr.
Arnoldi's humanity, his unfailing compassion, his readiness to do
whatever he can to help others—all this offsets his nihilistic conviction and makes him the most lovable character in the story.

The action of the novel, however, is so constructed as to confirm
and reinforce the pervasive philosophy of nihilism. Death represents
the nadir of futility; the sooner it is made welcome the better. That
is how some of these Russian characters plan to revenge themselves
upon life: they will commit suicide when they finally realize that
there is no reason for going on living and every reason for bringing
this hideous mummery to an end. The instinctive clinging to life, the
superstitious dread of what might lie beyond, these obstacles must
be overcome. We observe how a few of the suicides *reason* their way
to death; before they take the irretrievable setp they must make
certain that their logic is foolproof.

Situated in the Steppes, this God-forsaken town, which forms
the fitting background of the plot, accentuates the atmosphere of
oppressive tedium. Everything about the place is "as formless and
insignificant as a heap of ashes before the wind scatters them."[16]
The dismal images used to describe the hamlet stress the point that
here, in this desolate region of Russia, terrible thoughts are being
born, thoughts that will later shake the town to its depths, compelling the inhabitants to confront the idiotic specter of death.

Artzybashef foreshadows the nature of the catastrophe that is
to occur, a catastrophe precipitated by the new engineer Naumoff,

[16] Michael Artzybashef, *Breaking-Point* (New York: B. W. Huebsch, 1917), p. 7.

but the author insists that the trouble could not rightly be attributed to a human agency; his declared belief is "that the human will is incapable of changing in any minute detail what Life has ordained. Sooner or later it must lead to one inevitable end" (pp. 7–8). Artzybashef uncovers the determinism that shapes the course of events, humdrum and trivial as they may seem, and brings them to a disastrous end. The dreary round of existence, however, gives no indication that there is anything brewing that will cause a violent break in the unvarying routine, just as a healthy man suspects naught of the germ of a fatal disease that has insidiously lodged itself inside his body and is beginning to undermine it. Tchish, for example, is enraged by the apathy induced by his environment, but his rage is pointless. "He understood as well as anyone the complicated web of fatality that enmeshes people even in such remote places" (p. 9). And yet he clings all the more fervently to his revolutionary, utopian expectations. He prides himself in particular on not being one of those who believe that the game of life is not worth playing. Artzybashef analyzes the specious content of the romantic faith he embraces.

> He believed that only the life of yesterday and to-day, and perhaps of to-morrow also, presented such a chaotic, aimless outlook. After that a mighty wave would come, sweeping away all that was old and dirty and bringing with it a harmonious, mathematically regulated happiness, in which he, the young exiled student, that paltry mortal creature, should have his share, his value and his duty. (p. 12)

The phrase *a mathematically regulated happiness* registers the controlling mood of deflationary mockery. Bitter irony is present, too, when Tchish, in his discussion with such fanatical pessimists as Cornet Krause and Naumoff, defends his philosophy of strenuous social optimism.

Tchish and Dr. Arnoldi form an excellent study in contrasts: one enthusiastic and idealistic, and the other sunk in indifference, aware that the struggle for existence is basically the same everywhere. He knows that everyone is fated to die, and that no one is happy. A change of government, technological innovations, the conquest of the air by the wings of man—all this will make no difference in the human condition. Tchish, for his part, believes in the greatness of humanity. He looks upon the vicissitudes of history, the creative efforts made by artists, the works of philosophers, the battles fought in the arena of politics, as integral parts of a Promethean epic to conquer Nature and arrive at the Truth. Nevertheless, Tchish, despite his bravely affirmed utopian hopes, suffers from painful seizures of depression, when everything around him seems drab and uninteresting. The old doctor, on the other hand, doggedly pursues "an aimless path, without reason and without joy" (p. 25). He has seen too many people die to be stirred by desire or moved by regret. When the dying ask him what is the use of all this human suffering, his invariable reply is: "I don't know" (p. 30). Death at least grants the victim release from the bed of pain, a way out of the biological trap, but he cannot say why human beings must be tortured before the blessed peace of death descends upon them. Gazing upon his patient, the battered wreck of this once brilliant professor, who is fighting against the terrible realization that his life is over, Dr. Arnoldi saw

> how unmeaning were the dreams of man's immortality, as humanity, death's prey, vainly tried to picture them. It was as though he saw some absurd, crude picture, painted upon a curtain by a dilettante, hiding the black emptiness beyond. . . . What were they, God, heaven, the cosmos? . . . a little heap of decaying bones, a light flickering out, and nothing more. One might argue about religion and believe in immortality as long as the intellect could work and the body enjoy life to the full, but now, when all might see how man turned to a dying animal, an idiot, a mass of crumbling bones and failing organs, these ideas seemed as ludicrous as old-wives' tales of demons and fairies. (p. 32)

For these characters in *Breaking-Point,* whether they seek relief in wine and sex and pleasure or fall into indifference and take their own life, there is no Dostoevskian crisis of conversion, no theophany, no promise, however ambiguous, of redemption. Death is the common sordid end, that is all. Nothing more remains to be said. Words are of no avail, faith is illusion, pity a vain indulgence. Yet life goes on steadily and renews itself as if in fulfillment of some great purpose. Though *Breaking-Point* contains some lively scenes of love-making and merry-making, these are but pathetic, ineffectual distractions; the primary theme drives home the lesson that death reduces all human pride and ambition to nothingness. Children are born in pain, and all for what? That in time, as Dr. Arnoldi sees it, the next generation "too should be crushed by the wheels of fate" (p. 35). Death is inescapable; one may fend it off today, only to be forced to face its terrors on the morrow. Though Dr. Arnoldi is, like Dr. Rieux in *The Plague,* a man who has lost his faith in God, he is no secular saint fighting to the last ditch against the tyrannical power of death. He would gladly have sacrificed his own life if by so doing he could have helped to cure the sick.

> And had he known who was guilty of this mass of useless agony, the old doctor would have gone up to him with fearless, open countenance, and cursed him—nor feared pain, death, or the last judgment. . . . So full of pity and bitterness was this man's weary soul.
> But he knew that help was impossible and that neither entreaty nor arguments would ever make reply. (p. 38)

In a sense it is merciful that the sick child he is attempting to save will perish before learning the fear of death or experiencing a strong attachment "to this beloved or accursed existence" (p. 38).

The most gripping parts of the novel confront the problem of suicide. Cornet Krause, the Mephistophelean persona, seeks to find a valid justification for suicide, whereas Naumoff, the egregious believer in salvation through universal death, keeps harping on his mythomania. The latter insists there is no necessity that binds the individual to life. Tchish continues to uphold the ethic of striving. He tells Krause: "You can propound any theories you like about the futility of life, and I shall always say that they are the outcome of your own slackness and nothing else. Damn it all, life never promised you anything. It was left you to make what you pleased of it (p. 129). Man can choose his own weapons in his battle with Nature and thus be able to conquer it. The main thing is not to lose heart and cry aloud but to keep up the struggle. The world is not a lazar-house; there are man-made evils to be eradicated, freedom to be won, art to be created, scientific advances to be made. Krause, the skeptic, is not in the least impressed by these humanistic arguments. Suppose, he asks, he cares naught for progress but prefers to cast away the privilege of life? Is he to be accounted a criminal? He is not at all interested in promoting the happiness of mankind. Such an attitude brings Tchish up short.

> To a certain extent he was convinced that it was everyone's duty to believe in something, that phrases like: "A person who believes in nothing, who only thinks of himself," were insults. . . . He could not imagine how anybody could help trying to clear himself from this imputation. (p. 131)

He cannot understand how Krause is capable of advancing, with apparent conviction, precisely such irresponsible and "insane" views. Enraged, Tchish accuses him of being dead, a living corpse, and cries out that such people ought to be killed. "If you believe in nothing, and have no use for humanity, if your soul is a blank and your life is uninteresting, then be good enough to put a bullet through your head . . . (p. 132). Krause replies by asking calmly how Tchish can tell whether that is not what he intends to do.

Tchish must contend with another formidable adversary, Naumoff, who attacks his condemnation of suicide as an act of moral cowardice. Fanatically the engineer argues that

> every death is monstrous, though it were a thousand times a law of nature. Death is an act of violence against the race, and only suicide is free. You can't say it's natural if I want to live and have to die, but still less can you say it's unnatural if I die of my own free will as soon as there is nothing left for me to live for, simply because I don't want to live any longer. (p. 146)

Tchish concedes that suicide is understandable if one has no desire to go on living, but what seems to him positively morbid is that death should be painted in glowing colors. "I am convinced that it would never occur to anyone who was not ill, mad, or had gone off the tracks in some way, to send a bullet through his head, or crawl into the noose, the devil only knowing why" (p. 146). But Naumoff sticks grimly to his Schopenhauerian thesis that life is incurably unhappy: it is irrational and unnatural for humanity not to realize that death is their best remedy. He can comprehend the fear of death but not the will to live.

Naumoff is bent on exploding the pernicious myth of happiness. Life consists of suffering, sorrow, conflict, pain. Why must this demented martyrdom be allowed to go on forever? He does not deny the titanic strength of the incomprehensible will to live, but it is this very instinct that must be suppressed. He will point the way. When Tchish retorts that human nature will frustrate his mad plan of universal suicide, Naumoff maintains that since everything in Nature dies, a time will come when people will grow tired of living and regard death as a blessed deliverance. The men who had in the past been hailed as benefactors of the race were really its enemies, for they perpetuated a lie, a harmful illusion, thus exposing men to more and more senseless suffering.

The debate over the justification of suicide is continued at the picnic. Naumoff holds the floor, asserting that it is sheer folly to die for a cause. Nothing on earth can bring man the gift of happiness. Since death always waits in the offing, no revolution can do any good. Even if men were allowed to live forever, they would be horribly bored and beg for the boon of death. The best thing, he concludes, is to die. That brings life at last to an end. But first people must be shown "that they have no right to protract the senseless comedy" (p. 120).

That is the theme reiterated with gloomy, unsparing emphasis: there is no possibility of happiness, but death, fortunately, terminates the misery of man. All things come to that at last. When Dr. Arnoldi is at the cemetery where the professor and the actress lie buried, he thinks to himself that Naumoff is right. "Every human thought and action can have only one end . . . death (p. 229). Even Tchish suffers recurrently from doubts about the future. He tries to whip his ebbing enthusiasm for the social ideal, but he knows that by the time it is achieved, if it is ever achieved, he will be dead and utterly forgotten, and what will it avail him then?

Krause is the absurd hero who plans to commit suicide, but he must first make sure of his ground; he tests the logic of the engineer's argument. If Naumoff lives on while preaching that life is meaningless and that death is to be deliberately chosen, then why should others not follow his example? Naumoff retorts that his theory is stronger than himself. He refuses to make his exit from the earthly scene until he has done everything possible to spread his gospel. He does not hate his own life, he hates life in general. He is even prepared to kill in support of his theory. It is his unshakable faith in death as salvation that gives him the right to kill. He has abandoned all ideas of progress, sacrifice, revolution, the emancipation of the proletariat from bondage. It is under the banner of death that he fights against life. Though he is but an infinitesimal speck of energy in the universe, he has to affirm his individuality "so that I could oppose it to the whole universe, to the universal will, God. . . or whatever else there may be" (p. 261). Krause, who is a more complex if less articulate person than Naumoff, makes the point that Naumoff does not actually believe in his theory but clings to it out of an overweening ambition. He challenges Naumoff to prove his sincerity by immediately approving of Krause's suicide. Krause raises his revolver but he does not shoot himself—not this time.

Though Krause has not pulled the trigger, Naumoff is convinced that he will surely kill himself later on, perhaps this very night. He hates the man because he had disclosed the truth about his own conflicting motives. There were two beings in Naumoff: "one believed in his theory with a fanatic's obstinacy, desiring annihilation and death; the other feared them, choked with detestation and vented his own cowardice and despair on everyone else" (p. 266). He is consumed by a maniacal self-love. Artzybashef unmasks his devouring egotism. Krause, on the other hand, struggles with himself as he tries to summon up the strength to act on his fixed beliefs. Joy and sorrow, love and hate, everything, he feels, "is useless. It is futile to begin a new day, to dress, to eat and drink, to speak, to think. Not that he was tired of it all . . . no, it is merely that it is so pointless" (p. 270). He holds the pistol in the darkness of his room; one impulse from his finger and it will be all over, he will know Death, but he cannot act; he is filled with an indefinable dread.

Instinct is stronger than the force of logic; the living draw back in horror from the final step. The conscious will gives way before this nameless fear, and this, Krause perceived, betrayed some serious flaw in his chain of reasoning. "It must mean that his life

was precious to him . . this empty, unessential life was, in spite of
its proved absurdity, dearer to him than his inmost self, which
clung grovelling to the life that had cursed it" (p. 272). He would
have to consider the case for suicide all over again, he would have to
marshall his forces anew. Life and death, he muses, are intertwined.
"Nothing can sever life from death. Death conquers and vanishes
in the victory, and the dread of death exists only as long as life
lasts!" (p. 273). Resolved to overcome this indwelling terror, he
makes up his mind to commit suicide not in darkness, which rein-
forces his terror, but in public.

Then comes the riotous scene at the club. Trenieff, the officer
who will later slash his own throat, twits Krause on his suicidal
obsession. Krause, in full dress, wearing a resplendent uniform,
announces that he intends to shoot himself, at once. The others
imagine he is joking, but Krause never jests. Rising to his full height,
he declares that his action is of no special importance; he wants
to take his own life at the most ridiculous moment so as to rob
the deed of any special significance. There is, he assures his audience,
nothing heroic or tragic about his gesture. The truth is he cannot go
on living.

> To me life is not a tragedy, nor a horror, nor a senseless episode, but
> merely uninteresting. Nature and beauty are so trivial, one gets so tired
> of them. . . .love is so petty . . . humanity—simply foolish. The mysteries
> of the universe are impenetrable, and even should one fathom them it
> would be just as dull as before. Everything is as uninteresting as what we
> know already. In eternity there is nothing either small or large, and there-
> fore even a match is a mystery and a miracle . . . but we know the match
> and it is uninteresting. And it's the same with everything. In the same way
> God would be tedious if we could see Him. Why have a God at all? It's
> superfluous. (p. 306)   .

Then he says goodbye and before anyone can prevent him he puts
the barrel of his pistol into his mouth and pulls the trigger.

His suicide is indirectly responsible for a wave of suicides in the
town. The officers who knew him well recall his oddities of behavior,
especially his remark that life and everything connected with it is
loathsome. The revolver shot that Krause fired shatters the accustomed and reassuring routine of life. Now the presence of death

overshadows everyone's consciousness. Those who frequent the club cannot believe in the reality of what has taken place. Naumoff denies that he is responsible for Krause's death on the ground that "nobody can force a man to believe that he must die if he wants to live . . . no persuasion and no theories can accomplish that" (p. 312). He regrets nothing that he has said or done. Once more he announces that happiness is impossible and nonexistent. He repeats the old familiar arguments. What is the good of life? Why live if all that life brings is sorrow? What good are the gods man invented or the lofty ideals he professes to believe in or the opiate dream of everlasting bliss in heaven? What is the value of this mythical post-humous reward if existence on earth is so full of misery? God, if He exists, cannot be forgiven for imposing this terrible burden of suffering on mankind. If he [Naumoff] drove Krause to his self-inflicted death, then that is entirely to his credit. "And I'd drive the whole world to it, if I could . . . with the greatest pleasure" (p. 314).

Even Tchish is affected by this suicide. Ryskoff, the clerk, has been converted to Naumoff's view of things; he is sick of life. Tchish attempts to argue him out of his suicidal mood. Why should Ryskoff allow himself to become infected by the present morbid intellectual atmosphere? Society will soon recover from this craze of Naumoffism. The future belongs to the people, the golden age will soon dawn. Ryskoff, thrilled by the thought that in taking his own life he will become, like Krause, a tragic figure, one who nobly despises life, goes home and hangs himself.

The sudden wave of suicides stirs the town to its depths, especially the death of this nonentity of a clerk. Many feared "that this one impetus would shatter the majestic fabric of centuries and cause them to fling away their lives in masses" (p. 351). Only Dr. Arnoldi is unsurprised and unmoved. It was as if he had expected nothing else. If he does not kill himself it is because, as he says, he has been dead for a long time. And Tchish, despite his brave affirmation of faith in the future of humanity, comes to a point where he can no longer endure his wretched existence. He believes that he "believes in something, suffers for something, and is full of zeal for the cause. . . .He does not himself know in what, but he believes! Full of grief, full of tormenting agonies he believes without hope!"

(p. 413). He tries hard to persuade himself that life is noble and beautiful, but he realizes that all this means absolutely nothing to him; he has been an utter failure; he can no longer fool himself with vainglorious dreams, and so he hangs himself.

Like Dostoevski, Artzybashef reveals that the Nemesis of the nihilist is that he can give himself to no project, at least not for long. Whatever work he sets his hand to, whatever cause he supports, sooner or later seems foolish and futile. He is the man devoid of faith, but life without some kind of faith is insupportable, and therefore he acts on his own negative faith—he takes his own life. Nothing, not even life, is sacred. The nihilist as suicide achieves nothing. His death leaves the universe of the absurd intact, unchanged, and unchallenged.

PART III:

The Nihilism of the Absurd

5

The Universe of the Absurd

1. STRATEGIES AND STRUGGLES AGAINST THE ABSURD

The nihilism of the absurd is based on the belief, provisionally held but nevertheless regarded as essentially true, that the life of man is not only incomprehensible but pointless. The belief is held provisionally because the nihilist is not sure of his ground; secretly he hopes that he will be proved wrong in his incredible life-negating judgment. That is why he sternly examines his conscience and conducts an elaborate trial in which he, taking on the roles of both culprit and prosecuting attorney, proceeds to question his degree of guilt in condemning the gift of life; but the questioning, too, turns out to be a senseless ritual, for, as in Kafka's fictional cosmos, there are no answers his skeptical mind can accept as valid. The answers men formulated in the past, which identified the ultimate meaning as God, the Kingdom Come in Heaven or on earth, the future perfection of society, the Marxist millennium—these abstractions are all human and therefore fallible constructs. The anthropomorphic projection of value, of telos, is, when viewed from the perspective of nihilism, born of illusion. Man interprets the universe in accordance with his own needs and desires. There is no truth, no causal necessity the mind can grasp.[1]

The literary nihilist is, of course, not a trained philosopher; he does not, in his novels or plays, work out a systematic and logically

---

[1] As Wittgenstein, following in the footsteps of Hume, says: "Belief in the causal nexus is *superstition*." Quoted in George Pitcher, *The Philosophy of Wittgenstein* (Englewood Cliffs, N.J.: Prentice-Hall, 1964), p. 73.

coherent body of thought. Indeed, it is questionable if fiction can be effectively utilized as a medium for the expression of philosophical ideas. Can generalized concepts be fitted into an art-form that is concerned primarily with the particular, the concrete, the individual? But the metaphysical novel, when it truly fulfills its purpose, does not present a series of abstract ideological systems engaged in bitter conflict. It attempts to reveal the impact of ideas on the protagonist or on a group of character—how they react. The metaphysics embodied in *Man's Fate* or *The Trial* or *The Plague* is lived, felt, experienced in the flesh.[2]

> The importance of metaphysical fiction lies not so much in the conclusions arrived at as in the questions asked; not so much in the goal reached as in the journey taken....The metaphysical novelist goes beyond the methodological restraints imposed by scientific determinism, beyond the limits of the rational. He questions the sphinx, he seeks a thread of meaning through the labyrinth of chaos that is without beginning or end.[3]

In coping with this unheard-of situation of meaninglessness, the literary nihilist adopts a variety of strategic methods, either to remove the danger that threatens him or at least to render it powerless. Like Kafka he may exploit the resources of ambiguity and paradox. Like Ionesco, he may confront the absurd fatality of death by refracting it through the prism of irony and the mask of comedy. Beckett, in handling the theme of human impotence, emphasizes its grotesque and farcical aspects. The literary nihilist describes the desperate efforts of his persona to make the quest on which he is launched meaningful—his sisyphean tasks, the straws at which he clutches while drowning, the fantastic illusions he embraces, the pipe dreams to which he clings.

How did all this come about? Why do some writers cultivate the nihilistic strain? The Age of Enlightenment undermined the foundations of faith and left a spiritual void that none of the pro-

---

[2] See John Cruickshand, ed., *The Novelist as Philosopher* (London: Oxford University Press, 1962).
[3] Charles I. Glicksberg, "The Metaphysical Novel," *Meanjin* 8 (Winter 1949):103.

posed secular remedies could hope to fill. Mankind was liberated from the prison-house of ignorance and superstition; men were free at last, but they did not know for what. They were told that they could now master their environment, that they were now in full control of their destiny. Medical science could make it possible for man to live to the age of Methusaleh. But science, as I pointed out in the Introduction, had no answer for the insistent metaphysical questions the people raised; it ruled out as illegitimate such questions bearing on the ultimate meaning of life.

Metaphysical questions of this kind could not be outlawed. Those intellectuals who were at home in both cultures, the scientific and the literary, became convinced that the indwelling mystery of existence could not be solved. That the world *is,* that the world exists—this, as Wittgenstein declared, is the mystical fact. If being was a kind of disease, and Wittgenstein looked upon it as such, it could not be cured except by entirely ignoring the question of being. That is exactly what Wittgenstein recommended. He asserted that the question "What is being?" makes no sense, since there is no empirical way of answering it.[4] As it stands, the interrogative sentence, though grammatically correct, is not meaningful.

If logic concludes that it is useless to pose the "nonsensical" question of life's meaning[5] then this strengthens man in his suspicion that he is the victim of the wanton sport indulged in by the gods of chance. "To say that the *being of man* is radically con-

---

[4] Morse Peckham argues that the statement "God created the world" is not meaningless. "The fact is, of course, that infinite numbers of people have had their behavior stringently controlled by that statement, such as being bound to a stake and burned to death." (Morse Peckham, *Art and Pornography* [New York and London: Basic Books, 1969], p. 140). Insisting that all sentences are metaphysical, Peckham disposes of the criteria of empirical validity set up by the logical positivists.

[5] Freud categorically declares: "The moment one inquires about the sense or value of life one is sick, since objectively neither of them has any existence. In doing so one is only admitting a surplus of unsatisfied libido, and then something else must happen, a sort of fermenting, for it to lead to grief and depression." (Ernest Jones, *The Life and Work of Sigmund Freud* [New York: Basic Books, 1957], 3:465). Is that really the case? In every age thinking man is driven by the irrepressible need to solve the riddle of the Sphinx. The existentialist quester starts his journey with a question, but his hope of finding an answer is frustrated. Fallico remarks: "We arrive instead, not at any answer, but at the questioner himself. For questions are asked only by existing men. Except for a living man of flesh and blood, not a ques-

tingent and ultimately meaningless is to say that man knows not why he exists and cannot rise to a knowledge of his destiny."[6]

The modern writer seems to be waging a losing battle against the myth of the absurd, for the outcome is never in doubt. He has ceased to believe in the vicarious immortality that literary fame is supposed to confer. He knows at last that he, like the art he practices, is mortal; his only means of defense is to protest against the evil powers leagued against him, to rebel, like Camus, against the cruel and incomprehensible mandate of death. He rejects the values handed down by previous generations and starts off anew on the quest for ultimate meaning, despite the intimidating thought that he is on a wild-goose chase, that this "metaphysical" enterprise is bound to lead nowhere.

He tries to describe the features of the absurd universe he beholds. The myth of the absurd is an archetypal reality, a universal experience. Though in some periods of history it is unacknowledged, the awareness of its presence is not to be denied. In times of trouble it comes out of hiding. It is today a haunting presence, a nightmarish obsession, a shadow that blots out the light of the sun. It is absurd that life should be absurd: that was the paradox the nihilistic writers could not resolve. If they proclaim the absolute reign of the absurd, then the creative passion that possesses them constitutes a repudiation of the myth of the absurd. Art, even tragic art, represents a celebration of life. They cannot have it both ways, of course. They cannot silence the voice of reason, though they are aware of its limitations. Unlike Kierkegaard, they will not compromise the life of reason by speciously identifying the needs of their subjectivity with the dictates of a "higher" truth or confusing the thrust of desire with the authentic substance of faith.

In his encounter with the reality of the absurd, Kierkegaard, a

---

tion would be heard in the boundless ocean of being in which we are cast. Galaxies could thunder through the heavens, Sputniks unwind their pre-arranged beeps, but otherwise all would be silence. Except for an existing man, everything remains unnamed, unaccounted for. . . . In the universe only human voices are heard even though they report the hearing of superhuman voices." (Arturo B. Fallico, *Art & Existentialism* [Englewood Cliffs, N.J.: Prentice-Hall, 1962], p. 12).
[6] Robert G. Olson, *An Introduction to Existentialism* (New York: Dover Publications, 1962), p. 37.

religious prophet, foreshadowed the advent of nihilism in the twentieth century. He demonstrated that the Christian faith, if it is to be
achieved in depth and in full sincerity, is beset with thorny contradictions. What is the concept of the absurd but a paradox shot
through with existential contradictions that formal logic cannot
dispose of? Christ, the God who takes on human form, the scapegoat
sacrificed for the sins of mankind, is an example of the paradox of
the fortunate Fall. Why must the mystery of redemption be mediated
by a crucifixion? Kierkegaard, to be sure, insisted that for the man
of faith Christianity is not infected by the taint of the absurd. The
absurd comes to life when doubt attacks the heart of belief, but then
doubt is a potent adversary in the struggle for faith. No faith is irre-
proachably pure.

Kierkegaard's idea of the absurd is a perception that goes beyond
the confines of reason. He does not minimize the force of the
objections that have been raised against man's irrational venture
into faith. He knows how indefensible it is, when judged by the
canons of logic, to believe in the emergence of the God-Man, the
existence of Christ as a definite individual in the past, the supernatural assuming the lineaments of the human. Yet, as an entry in
his *Journal* indicates, he did not regard the absurd as a gratuitous
leap into folly:

> it is superficial to suppose that the absurd is not a concept, that by it can
> be meant all kinds of absurdities. . . . The absurd, the paradox, is so com-
> posed that reason by itself can in no way turn it into nonsense and show it
> to be nonsense; no, it is a sign, an enigma, a composite enigma, about
> which reason is forced to say: I cannot solve this, it cannot be understood,
> but this does not mean at all that it is nonsense. But of course if faith is
> discarded and the whole sphere ignored, reason will become presumptuous
> and will perhaps conclude: ergo, the paradox is nonsense.[7]

With but few exceptions, the modern intelligentsia were not impressed
by Kierkegaard's religious mysticism; they delight only in those
passages which deal with alienation and existential despair.

[7] Quoted in N. H. Søe, "Kierkegaard's Doctrine of the Paradox," in Howard A.
Johnson and Niels Thulstrup, eds., *A Kierkegaard Critique* (New York: Harper
& Brothers, 1968), p. 220.

6

Franz Kafka:
The Prophet of the Absurd[1]

1. THE DIALECTICS OF NIHILISM IN KAFKA

Kafka, whether he says so openly or not, is an atheist. An atheist, though, of that modern species who regard God's removal from the scene not as a liberation . . . but as a token of the "God-forsakenness" of the world, its utter desolation and futility.[2]

For Kafka . . . the meaning of this world lies with God, which is beyond this world. Therefore, the meaning of this world is incomprehensible to Kafka. All that God does, therefore, seems to be senseless. God is the absurd.[3]

The most gifted and influential exemplar of nihilism in modern literature is Franz Kafka. It is fascinating to watch the way in which he experiments with his refractory material and deploys the resources of his imagination to suggest the dim outlines of a reality beyond the reality mediated by the senses. He utilizes expressive symbols to communicate his tantalizing glimpse of the numinous, which is ineffable, beyond the reach of language, but shorn of its traditional association with the idea of the sacred. The tormented prophet of the absurd, he, like Kierkegaard, finds it impossible to speak out directly. In order to sketch the character of that which transcends

[1] In order to show that there were forerunners of literary nihilism in the nineteenth century before the advent of Nietzsche, I have included a study of Georg Büchner. See Appendix B.
[2] Georg Lukács, *Realism in Our Time*, trans. Necke Mander (New York and Evanston, Ill.: Harper & Row, 1964), p. 44.
[3] Friedrich Dürrenmatt, "Kafka and the News," *The New York Times*, July 11, 1971.

finite reality, he relies on the use of parable, but his parables, like the novels and plays of Samuel Beckett, give no hint, however faint, of the existence of a divine order. Instead, they seem to imply the absence of any rational order or controlling purpose the human mind can discern. If his work offers any intimations of the supernatural, it is "super" only in the special sense that it defies "natural" understanding. The parable, as Kafka handles it, is designed to discuss the presence of something behind or beyond phenomena while at the same time denying that it has any "reality." Whereas Christian paradox stresses the incommensurability of the divine and the human, and reasons that since man cannot know he must therefore believe, Kafka refuses to believe and resigns himself to a permanent state of not knowing. Delivering no message of hope or redemption, he projects with wry touches of irony the tragic dilemma of being human.

In his unwillingness to perpetuate the vital fictions that men have invented to dispel the fear of the dark unknown, Kafka is neither cruel nor anti-human. He is no misanthrope. Though he suffers because of his utter lack of faith, he is not ashamed of his nihilism. Johannes Urzidil recalls what Franz Werfel once said to him: "I would love Kafka much more, if he were not so nihilistic."[4] Urzidil proceeds to defend Kafka against this groundless aspersion on his character.

> All of us loved the genius of Werfel's affirmation of the world and his approval of life, for after all we all wanted the world and life. Kafka also wanted them. Indeed, no one fought as hard and despairingly as he did in their behalf, no one took a position such as he did against the incessant disappointments and frustrations which life, the world, and its inhabitants evidenced to all who embraced them wholeheartedly. Kafka was that kind of devotee, not a nihilist.[5]

Kafka, however, requires no defense because of his attachment to the nihilistic vision.

Kafka belongs to our age, and to the future as well, because

---

[4] Johannes Urzidil, *There Goes Kafka*, trans. Harold A. Basilius (Detroit, Mich.: Wayne University Press, 1968), p. 188.
[5] *Ibid.*

he dares to seek the meaning of the human condition, though he knows that his creative work fails to pierce the heart of the mystery incarnate in the universe. He cannot justify his own existence. His struggle to find a meaning when he is convinced that it does not exist or that it remains impenetrably ambiguous, becomes emblematic of the quest of all metaphysical seekers in our naturalistic age. He wrestled alone with these issues of ultimate concern, despairing of the outcome, yet he never ceased to "trouble deaf heaven with his bootless cries." Despite repeated disappointments and defeats, he did not give up his search for the Absolute that always eluded him. Kafka "defines the value and logic of life in terms of what they *are not,* knowing that what they *are* is undiscoverable, indefinable, forever in question."[6] Or, as Roland Barthes says in his essay, "Kafka's Answer": "For the writer, literature is that utterance which says until death: I shall not begin to live before I know the meaning of life."[7]

A number of critics (Max Brod, Edwin Muir, Ronald Gray, and Rebecca West) have engaged in the esoteric game of symbolic interpretation in order to present Kafka as a mystic manqué, a profound, if thoroughly ambiguous, religious writer.[8] Their interpretation is open to serious objections. It can be demonstrated with an impressive display of internal evidence that Kafka is a visionary who never beheld the face or heard the voice of God. Kafka is an atheist, but one who keeps on questioning the ways of a God he does not believe exists. In the words of Dürrenmatt, he does not believe in the possibility of recognizing God. God is

---

[6] R. M. Albérès and Pierre de Boisdeffre, *Kafka: The Torment of Man,* trans. Wade Baskin (New York: Philosophical Library, 1968), p. 88.
[7] Roland Barthes, *Critical Essays,* trans. Richard Howard (Evanston, Ill.: Northwestern University Press, 1972), p. 135.
[8] Georg Lukács, the prolific Marxist critic from Hungary, is a notable exception. He attacks Kafka on different grounds. He cites Kafka as "the classic example of the modern writer at the mercy of a blind and panic-stricken *angst.*" (Georg Lukács, *Realism in Our Time,* p. 77). But it is not an autonomous, unconditioned state of anxiety or dread that Kafka calls forth. "The diabolical character of the world of modern capitalism, and man's impotence in the face of it, is the real subject-matter of Kafka's writings." Kafka is denounced as the neurotic prophet of unreality, the writer who tries to shape an image of the transcendental world that lies outside the realm of history.

unknowable because he is only the phantom creation of the mind of man.

This poses a difficult problem. Gunther Anders states it by raising a series of challenging questions:

> How does it come about that a writer, who did not practice any form of belief and saw himself living in a completely godless world, should consider himself a religious man; that he should describe writing as a form of prayer, and that he should be hailed as a religious prophet by a cultured class normally indifferent to religion?[9]

Anders provides the answer to his own questions. If Kafka sought some means of salvation, it was not because he was religious in outlook

> but because he felt compelled to find some form of affirmation, to affirm something, be it the bare fact of existence alone, life simply because and as it is. If Nietzsche was not Kafka's teacher he was certainly his proto-type in the desperate attempt to overcome nihilism and discover the secret of a new strength of soul, the strength perhaps merely to *be,* without the need of religious meaning. (p. 74)

Hence Anders concludes that "the meaning of Kafka's entire work is governed by his awareness of the 'death of God' (p. 82).

Kafka is at his best as an artist in picturing the irrational and inexplicable character of the finite world as viewed against the backdrop of the infinite. The conjunction produces a grotesque as well as uncanny effect, for the two worlds cannot be reconciled. In Kafka's world of the imagination the reality of the earth is decep-tive, and people wander on its surface like sleepwalkers. His tech-nique reveals much of his meaning. His characters sense that something lies beyond, but they cannot make out what it is. Kafka's fiction, like his diaries, explores the dimensions of a self that is nihilistically alienated. With consummate skill he evokes a set of images that reflect the hopelessness of man's fate. His anti-heroes engage in anguished but futile introspection, they grope their way

[9] Gunther Anders, *Franz Kafka,* trans. A. Steer and A. K. Thorlby (London: Bowes & Bowes, 1960), p. 72.

confusedly in the dark; lost and forsaken, they struggle to find the road, if such there be, that leads to the Castle. Kafka is himself the lonely and forlorn pilgrim seeking a faith that he can never attain. He frankly confesses his own neurotic weaknesses, which are, paradoxically, the source of his creative strength. He is not endowed with a spontaneous and exuberant love of life. He accuses himself of lacking the power of will to make decisions and abide by them and bear the full responsibility for his actions. And his protagonists cannot rise above their insectlike existence. They protest bitterly against the fate that overtakes them, but their protest in each case is without effect.

2. MANIFESTATIONS OF NIHILISM IN KAFKA'S EARLY WRITINGS

> Now literature is only a means, devoid of cause and purpose; in fact, that is what defines it. You can of course attempt a sociology of the literary institution; but you can limit the act of writing by neither a *why* nor a *wherefore*. . . . To ask oneself why one writes is already an advance over the blissful unconsciousness of "inspiration," but it is a despairing advance—there is no answer. Apart from demand and apart from success . . . the literary act is without cause and without goal precisely because it is devoid of sanction.[10]

Kafka's early writings reveal that his technique, his method of composing fiction that captures the Expressionist "logic" of the dream, is not something he learned from any of his predecessors or contemporaries but an integral and essential part of his creative vision. His nihilism is a temperamental trait that owes nothing or very little to historical or social conditions. A Marxist critic, Howard Fast, assailed Kafka in *Literature and Reality*[11] because of his "reactionary" contempt for the ideology of social commitment. Georg Lukács finds the real subject matter of Kafka's work in the demonic character of capitalism. Kafka's metaphysical vision cannot be fitted neatly within the confines of any *ism*. Steeped in subjectivity, locked

---

[10] Roland Barthes, *Critical Essays,* p. 135.
[11] Published in 1950, before Fast left the Communist Party.

within the belly of the whale, he introduces characters and situations that mirror his inner state of conflict and confusion, but do so in a manner that lifts them above the narrowly personal confession and seeks to invest them with the aura of the universal. "Description of a Struggle," a story Kafka wrote at the age of twenty, contains in germ some of the ambiguities and paradoxes that appear in his later, more mature work, reading at times like a rough excerpt from an early version of *The Castle* or *The Trial*. The second part of this story is called, significantly, "Diversions or Proof That It's Impossible to Live." Everything in this piece of fiction is strange; reality is dematerialized; houses suddenly collapse without reason, people fall dead in the street, and yet no one seems to be afraid.

It is the parables, however, that strongly support the impression that Kafka's technique, his method of composition, is a function of his nihilistic obsession. "The Departure" is the story of a man who saddles his horse and starts off on his journey. When he is asked what his destination is he replies that it is to get out of here. This cryptic tale hints at the disorientation of Kafka's characters; they are, many of them, outsiders who do not feel at home in the world of common sense. "Give It Up" is another metaphysically charged parable. A man on his way to the station early in the morning, not being well acquainted with the town he is in, asks a policeman for directions: which is the way? The latter replies: "Give it up! Give it up!"[12] Then the policeman turns away suddenly, "like someone who wants to be alone with his laughter."[13] This affords some measure of insight into Kafka's state of alienation, into his intuitive awareness, which his personae share, that there are no answers to the questions man keeps on asking about the meaning and purpose of his brief stay on earth.

In "Wedding Preparations in the Country," which also belongs to his earliest writings, Raban, a clerk, is amazed at the sight of the street, the strangeness of moving traffic, the anomaly of the familiar background and habitual routine in a world that remains incomprehensible. He works hard at the office, but why, he muses, should

[12] Franz Kafka, *Description of a Struggle*, trans. Tania and James Stern (New York: Schocken Books, 1958), p. 201.
[13] *Ibid.*

he expect to be treated lovingly by others? On the contrary, "one is alone, a total stranger and only an object of curiosity."[14] Thus, even in his youth, Kafka the story-teller sounded the motif of alienation and wrestled with the terrifying problem of depersonalization: the transformation of the existential "I" into the anonymous "one" or the reified "it."

Kafka used a variety of symbols to picture his spiritually uprooted and homeless condition: prisons, animals, cruel rulers who are figures of arbitrary authority, gates that suddenly close, doors that are too narrow to permit anyone to enter or to leave. He presents a gallery of characters who suffer from the torment of subtly refined indecisions, unable to make up their minds on the perplexing problems that confront them, unable to choose as they face a multiplicity of alternatives, all of them perhaps valid, perhaps not. They scent danger at every turn of the road; every step forward or backward is fraught with peril. Every pulsation of consciousness heightens the contrast between the outer and inner world, one bustling with frantic but senseless activity and the other shadowy and insubstantial like the scenario of a dream. How is Raban ever to feel at home in either world or establish a bridge between the two? As he lies in bed, he assumes "the shape of a big beetle, a stag beetle, or a cockchafer . . . (p. 6). This imagined "transformation," which foreshadows the theme of "The Metamorphosis," would serve as an effective alibi, as a way of avoiding the painful need for making decisions. No Kafka protagonist ever undertakes a journey that is not attended with vexatious obstructions, unaccountable delays, detours, internal struggles, enigmatic mishaps.

In "Reflections on Sin, Suffering, Hope, and the True Way," Kafka probes the baffling mystery of existence, the nature of sin, and the paradoxical craving for death. The wish to die—that marks the first sign of the beginning of true understanding of the human condition. These "reflections" embody Kafka's nihilistic outlook. "This life appears unbearable, another unattainable" (p. 35). Perhaps life is nothing more than a bad dream. There are, Kafka

---

[14] Franz Kafka, *Dearest Father,* trans. Ernst Kaiser and Eithne Wilkins (New York: Schocken Books, 1954), p. 3.

reiterates, no answers to the persistent questions man raises. Kafka writes that in the past he could not comprehend why he received no answer to his questions; now he fails to understand how he could ever have believed that he had the capacity to ask these questions. "But I didn't really believe, I only asked" (p. 37). That is how Kafka confronted the contradictions inherent in the process of living. One voice in his dialectically counterpointed exercise declares that, after all, one cannot "not-live," and the alter ego replies: "It is precisely in this 'Cannot, after all,' that the mad strength of faith lies . . . (p. 48). There is no end to this despairing spiritual conflict. Kafka cuts himself off from all the sources of illusion. If he dreads the night, he also dreads the "not-night" (p. 63).

The Kafka anti-hero fights this spectral battle alone. He engages in hand-to-hand combat with his own distorted shadow, which seems to mimic his unavailing gestures of rebellion. More terrible than the song of the sirens, Kafka notes cryptically, is their silence. One of the most characteristic *faits accomplis,* he remarks, is the act of suicide; he compares the suicide to the prisoner who observes that a gallows is being built in the prison yard. He assumes, erroneously, that it is meant for him. He forces his way out of his cell in the night "and goes down and hangs himself" (p. 87). A man utterly deprived of the sustenance of hope or faith, Kafka cannot make out why he feels this longing for eternity when the very thought of it depresses him. What he finds oppressive about the idea of the eternal "is the justification, incomprehensible to us, that time must undergo in eternity and the logical conclusion of that, the justification of our-selves as we are" (p. 94). Such a brooding, benighted spirit could never achieve the miracle of assured faith. He saw life as governed by the unpredictable god of chance. He cannot get himself to adopt any of the expedients men have devised—love, marriage, family life, professional activity, not even the literary calling—as a screen that temporarily shuts out the vision of the void. He has, he declares, absorbed chiefly the negative influences of his age. Unlike Kierke-gaard, he was not guided through life by the redemptive light of the Christian faith nor could he, like the Zionists, attach himself to an attenuated version of the Jewish religion. "I am an end or a beginning (pp. 99–100).

Though Kafka was an incorrigible skeptic, as lacerating confessions of this type attest, he never gave up the quest for ultimate meaning, impossible as the task proved to be. And it is this steadfast refusal to give in to the nihilism of the absurd that makes him an exemplary figure of our time. According to him, every man "must be able to justify his life (or his death, which amounts to the same); he cannot escape this task" (p. 100). Every human being, he pointed out, is under the necessity of living his life or dying his death; "no human being can live an unjustified life" (p. 100). Throughout his life he was haunted, like Unamuno, by the thought of death. He descried no glorious consummation in the distant future climaxing the evolution of the human race; he beheld only "a growth of death-force" (p. 101). And death, he asserted gloomily, is salvation. What made death so fearful and so oppressive, he declared, was not that it meant the abrupt termination of life but that it brought life into question, so that each person was forced in some way to justify his existence. Most people, to be sure, feel confident that they can pass this test with ease, but they are the ones most deluded; their faith in themselves and in life rests on no secure foundation. Kafka would not deceive himself. He could not feel at home in this world nor could he be like the others and adjust his life to "objective" standards. His nature is such that he can only obey a commandment that was not meant for him. Like Unamuno, he can live only in a contradiction. "But this doubtless applies to everyone; for living, one dies, dying, one lives" (p. 270). Though Kafka says he spent all his life "resisting the desire to end it,"[15] his nihilistic insights do not represent an impotent surrender to despair, an abject ethic of defeat. Like the voices to be heard later in the Theater of the Absurd, he believes that "the dignity of man lies in his ability to face reality in all its senselessness; to accept it freely, without fear, without illusions...."[16]

---

[15] *Ibid.,* p. 303. Kafka was frequently tempted by the thought of suicide, though there were no circumstances in his life that would account for this death-wish. See ·A. P. Foulkes, *The Reluctant Pessimist* (The Hague and Paris: Mouton, 1967), p. 55.
[16] Martin Esslin, *The Theatre of the Absurd* (Garden City, N.Y.: Doubleday & Company, 1961), p. 316.

3. THE VERDICT OF THE TRIAL

All his life long Kafka felt that he had been put on trial. He concurred in the sentence of guilty that the court invariably pronounced; he not only accepted the prescribed punishment but proceeded to inflict it on himself. Deeply distrustful of himself, he was convinced that he was incapable of coping with the realities of life; it was not for him to struggle, to overcome difficulties, to love, to marry and beget children. As a writer who was born a Jew, he manifested all the recognizable symptoms of *Angst*. He knew that the specific syndrome of Jewishness is anxiety. Insecure, surrounded by danger on all sides, the Jews develop paranoiac patterns; they are, as Kafka says, "threatened with threats."[17] He was himself the sufferer from chronic attacks of anxiety and was driven to withdraw from contact with people and the world, but this withdrawal, instead of restoring his peace of mind, only intensified his sense of alienation. He is consumed by a nameless fear. What is he afraid of? He is afraid of "only this inner conspiracy against myself" (p. 73). This existential fear, this persecutory *Angst,* cannot be cured by mental therapy, for it is not the result of a crippling neurosis.

The metaphysical terror that Kafka experienced furnishes the nuclear themes of his fiction. His creative imagination, by achieving the order and universality of art, triumphs over the irrational fears that threaten to disrupt the integrity of the self. These fears, Kafka acknowledged, are a part of him, perhaps the best part of him. When someone remarked that Kafka must have made extensive studies in a lunatic asylum, his reply was: "Only in my own . . . "(p. 149). Though various critics have stigmatized Kafka as a morbid or psychopathological writer, his anxiety stems from metaphysical rather than neurotic sources. He was not, as a matter of fact, favorably impressed by the psychoanalytic method of treating mental illness:

I don't call it illness and I consider the therapeutic part of psychoanalysis to be a hopeless error. All these so-called illnesses, sad as they

[17] Franz Kafka, *Letters to Milena,* trans. Tania and James Stern (New York: Schocken Books, 1953), p. 51.

may appear, are matters of faith, efforts of souls in distress to find moorings in some maternal soil; thus psychoanalysis also considers the origins of religions to be nothing but what (in its opinion) causes the "illnesses" of the individual. (p. 217)

But this alleged "illness," Kafka contends, this oppressive anxiety, is rooted in the human condition and is therefore incurable.

It is in *The Trial* that Kafka unveils his nihilistic vision. Joseph K. is summoned to stand trial by powers that have no interest in his personal destiny. He had lived "the normal" life as a head clerk, and then, on his thirtieth birthday, suddenly, without warning, the blow falls and his worst fears are realized. Gradually the slow, protracted, tortuous, and incomprehensible procedure of the trial overwhelms him and robs him of the will to resist. He cannot discover the meaning of his life. A self-condemned victim, he is guilty, regardless of the outcome of the trial. "He sinks into absolute nihilism, because he cannot find a remedy for this anguish either in religion or in the inoffensive world of day-to-day existence."[18]

The pattern of the plot unfolds. The Kafkaesque anti-hero is at odds with himself, a stranger in a world that is mysterious, irrational. The "real" world exists but it is a commonplace and yet also threatening reality. *The Trial* opens with the ambiguous statement: "Someone must have traduced Joseph K., for without having done anything wrong he was arrested one fine morning."[19] From that moment, Joseph K., though he has not done anything wrong, is thrust into a situation that moves forward with the sinister illogic but irresistible momentum of a nightmare. He is no longer a free agent. He attempts to assert himself, to find out why he is under arrest, but all he can gather from his warders is that proceedings have been instituted against him and that there is no telling how long his case will last. All this strikes an ominous note of foreboding, of menace. Who could these warders be? On what authority did they act? After all, he was a citizen in a country that protected him with a legal

[18] René Dauvin, "*The Trial:* Its Meaning," in Angel Flores and Homer Swander, eds., *Franz Kafka Today* (Madison, Wis.: The University of Wisconsin Press, 1958), p. 159.
[19] Franz Kafka, *The Trial,* trans. Willa and Edwin Muir (New York: The Modern Library, 1956), p. 3.

constitution. At a time of universal peace, when the laws were in effect, who would dare to arrest him without cause in his own domicile?

> He had always been inclined to take things easily, to believe in the worst only when the worst happened, to take no care for the morrow even when the outlook was threatening. (p. 7)

Kafka is skillfully setting the stage for the extraordinary series of events about to take place. At first, the cheerful, ambitious clerk, "the normal man," tends to dismiss the entire incident as a practical joke and plays his role as if this were the improvised script of a *commedia dell'arte.* The first thing he does on getting back to his room is to search for his birth certificate, his identification papers. Displaying his documents, he demands to see the warrant for his arrest. The warders tell him that his papers mean nothing to them, that they were but obeying orders; the authorities, however, knew all about his case before ordering his arrest. Even the lowest-grade officials, though they do not go in search of those who commit crimes, are drawn unerringly to the guilty person. They carry out the Law, which makes no mistakes. When K. remarks that he does not know this Law, one of the warders replies that it is all the worse for him.

K. receives the summons for the interrogation by the Inspector, which is held, strangely enough, in Fräulein Bürstner's room. When the Inspector declares that K. must be surprised at the events that occurred in the morning, K. replies that he is surprised but not very surprised. He does not now regard the whole thing as a joke but then, surely, it cannot be of much account either. He has been accused whereas he cannot "recall the slightest offense that might be charged against him" (p. 16). Who is preferring charges against him? The Inspector informs him that he does not know whether K. is charged with an offense and advises him not to worry about what is going to happen to him but to think more about himself. K. can make no sense of this outrageous affair. He attempts to bribe the Inspector but the latter disabuses him of the notion that he can get out of his difficulties so easily, but he does not suggest that he give up the struggle. He is only under arrest, nothing has as yet been decided. Though he is under arrest, he will not be hindered from going about his business.

There is nothing particularly outstanding about K. As chief clerk he is diligent, conscientious, and reliable, but that is all. Once a week he satisfies his sexual needs by visiting a girl named Elsa. What he wants is that everything should go on as usual, that there should be no disruption of his routine. He still persists in his belief that the strange events of the morning were all a mistake. When he receives the summons for a short inquiry into his case, he vows to put an end to this senseless persecution of an innocent man. He starts out for the court inquiry on Sunday, but encounters unexpected difficulties in locating the place. The hearing is to be held in the poorest section of the town. When he finally reaches the house and starts climbing the stairs, he recalls the saying of the warder "that an attraction existed between the Law and guilt" (p. 45).

When K. at last enters the room where the investigation is to be held, he is rebuked for being late. Kafka paints a Goyasque scene of a mad, lurid, yet psychologically revealing court of conscience. The examination starts and K. protests the character of the trial to which he is being subjected under compulsion. He addresses the Examining Magistrate: "You may object that it is not a trial at all; you are quite right, for it is only a trial if I recognize it as such" (p. 51). K. conducts his own defense, and he cites his reasons for doing so; his case, he points out, is typical of a misguided policy that affects many other people as well, and he is championing the cause of these people. He recounts the incredible circumstances of his arrest, all part of a dastardly conspiracy to undermine his reputation and damage his position at the Bank. He behaves like a paranoiac, as if the scene were the surrealistic rehearsal of a drama acted out on the stage of his mind.[20] He pretends to be calm, detached, though he has raised his voice and banged the table. He is convinced that

[20] One critic interprets Kafka's work in the light of the spiritual conflicts that beset the moral nature of man. Kafka's narrative form, he argues, is modeled on the dream. "Kafka became a major writer when he discovered his dream narrative." (Martin Greenberg, *The Terror of Art: Kafka and Modern Literature* [New York and London: Basic Books, 1968], p. 8). By means of this technique, which was finally perfected in *The Trial* and *The Castle,* he was able to explore aspects of the self, which would otherwise pass unnoticed.

there is a great organization responsible for his arrest and interrogation, a hierarchical order that has its corrupt underlings, but also its
police, its judges of the highest rank, and perhaps even hangmen.
K. works himself into a frenzy of indignation, emphasizing the
senselessness of the whole case.

After this first interrogation, he waits in considerable anxiety for
another summons. Though he has received no call, he returns next
Sunday at the same time, but finds the room empty. He sees several
books lying on the table, those belonging to the Examining Magistrate; he thinks they are probably law books, but when he opens
one he beholds an obscene picture. The title of the second volume
he picks up is that of a pornographic volume, *How Grete Was
Plagued by Her Husband.*

The information the washerwoman on the premises gives him only
adds to his confusion and his growing disillusionment. She tells him
that the Examining Magistrate makes out written reports, which
are sent to the higher officials. Last Sunday he was kept up late
preparing reports about K., and these certainly cannot be without
importance. She tells him, too, that the Examining Magistrate was
trying to win her favor by giving her a pair of silk stockings, and she
shows him, provocatively, how they look on her. The intrusion of the
erotic motif at this juncture accentuates the grotesque and distracted
character of his quest for vindication. K. decides there is no good
reason why he should not yield to this woman who attracts him
physically. Besides, by possessing this woman, he would revenge
himself upon the Examining Magistrate. At this moment the law
student Bertold appears and carries her off. She offers no resistance
as she is being taken, so she says, to the Examining Magistrate. K.
watches helplessly as she is being abducted. The woman's husband
arrives and confesses that he can do nothing in this matter, especially
since his wife, the hussy, is to blame. He can take no action against
such a powerful official. Such are the disconcerting ways of justice,
but K. is destined to make discoveries of a more painful nature.

He accompanies the husband to the offices, where he sees people,
the accused, the defendants, crowded in the lobby. No one has any
knowledge how the Court operates—only hints, rumors, guesses,
conjectures. There is no certainty as to the right procedure that

must be followed. K., lost in the maze of lobbies, asks himself what
he is doing here. What can be his motive in exploring these labyrinths?
To find out the exact date of his next interrogation? Or is he prompted
by a desire, which he does not acknowledge, to confirm his suspicion
that the inner working of this intricate legal system is as repellent
as its external appearance? He is thoroughly depressed by what he has
seen thus far. His quest has borne no fruit. The atmosphere of the
place is suffocating and he faints, but the fresh air, when he gets
outside, restores his energy.

Further surprises are in store for him. His "case" pursues him even
within the sacred precincts of the Bank. When he opens a door in the
Bank, he sees three men in the lumber room; he recognizes the two
warders who had placed him under arrest; the third man is wearing
a leather garment. K. hears the warders cry out that they are to be
flogged because of his complaints to the Examining Magistrate, but
the man in charge bids him not to be deceived by their pleas: "the
punishment is as just as it is inevitable."[21] They must strip and
be beaten. K. seeks to bribe the Whipper, arguing that the warders
are not guilty. "The guilt lies with the organization. It is the high
officials who are guilty" (p. 107). The Whipper, the incarnation of
the mindless, sadistic bureaucrat, refuses to be bribed: "I am
here to whip people, and whip them I shall" (p. 107). K. broods
miserably on this traumatic incident. It is clearly his duty to intervene,
since he had vowed to fight the corrupt machinery of the Court.
Even the next day he cannot get the warders out of his mind. When
he opens the door of the lumber room, he sees the Whipper with his
rod and the warders with all their clothes off. He hears their cries
but he quickly slams the door shut and then beats on it with his fists
in impotent fury.

K.'s affairs are now in a sorry state. K.'s uncle arrives and urges
him to hire the services of a lawyer. Together with his uncle, he visits
the house of the lawyer, Herr Huld, where he meets Leni, who urges
him not to be obdurate and unyielding in the future. She tells him
that it is useless to "fight against this Court, you must confess to
guilt. Make your confession at the first chance you get. Until

[21] Franz Kafka, *The Trial*, p. 105.

you do that, there's no possibility of getting out of their clutches, none at all" (p. 135). She cannot help him unless he follows her advice. She gives herself to him; he can come to her whenever he likes. Again, the erotic principle serves to draw him away, temporarily, from his single-minded quest for justice. By this time, however, he is so obsessed with his case that he can think of nothing else.

The lawyer attempts to explain the complexities of the law. It is difficult to fathom the established system of justice. There is no point in trying to reform this or that detail. One must learn to accept conditions as they are. There is no way of ascertaining how the machinery of the law works; there are no fixed rules of jurisprudence; the higher up a case goes, the more incomprehensible it becomes. K. seeks to regain his balance, to banish all thoughts of guilt from his mind, but that is sooner said than done. He cannot decide what action to take.

He next visits the painter Titorelli, who works for the Court. The painter asks him point blank whether he is innocent. K. once more asserts his innocence and complains of the web of subtleties, woven by the Court, in which he is enmeshed. Titorelli informs him that once the Court brings charges against a man it is already fully convinced of his guilt and pays no attention to any proof of innocence he may offer. Of all the cases Titorelli had known no one was ever definitively acquitted; perhaps none was really innocent. But the Court, K. insists, is really a pointless institution, since it could just as well hire an executioner.

Is K. formally guilty or is he guilty only in the all-seeing eyes of God? It is possible to consider him entirely innocent and the action of the Court as arbitrary and persecutory, or to assume, on the contrary, that he is somehow guilty and the Court justified in its judgment, even though its actions cannot be rationally comprehended. Neither interpretation stands up under critical scrutiny. Bathed in ambiguity, this fantastic narrative, full of startling paradoxes, limns the dark and inexplicable aspect of reality. It depicts a kingdom of the absurd in which incompatibilities and contradictions coexist. The life that Kafka portrays in this novel violates the categories of reason. He presents no solution, for there is none to be had. Indefensible as the process of the Law is, it works inexorably. Accused, arrested, the security of his career disrupted, K. is forced to confront the unmitigated absurdity of existence. He wants to be acquitted, he wishes to justify his life, he demands nothing less than justice, but at the end he realizes it is useless to resist. The Higher Court finds him guilty, though he has committed no crime against society. *The Trial* dramatizes the failure of K.'s quest: the story of his progressive disillusionment, his final acknowledgement of impotence, and his ignoble execution. Kafka, like his anti-hero, cannot reconcile himself to the human condition, man's precarious place in the cosmic scheme, and the absence of justice in a world that inflicts on man the ignominious punishment of death.

In *The Castle* as in *The Trial,* the Kafka protagonist is pitted against a universe that vouchsafes no meaningful reply to the questions he hurls at it. He moves in a sphere where improbability reigns and unreason is the rule; the unpredictable overwhelms him; there is no guide he can follow, no firm ground under his feet. The impact of contingency and the eruption of the irrational generate in him a feeling of dread. He cannot interpret the meaning of the actions of those around him; the real takes on the lineaments of the absurd. All this is a painful source of guilt. Obviously the established laws must be right and it is clearly man's duty to obey them, but how, Kafka asks, shall they be interpreted? Where is the court or the judge who speaks with unequivocal authority? What if the powers that be are not only irrational but unconscionable? In debating these issues of ultimate concern, the Kafka protagonist is a rebel in spite of himself; whether or not he obeys the mandate of the law, he is always in conflict with himself. Though he knows that it is the better part of wisdom to submit, his consciousness, a perpetual question mark, drives him to rebel. As a rebel and an outsider, one who is not at home in this world, he continues to feel guilty. Like the millions of innocent inmates of German concentration camps who were slated for extermination, he is trapped in a situation from which there is no possibility of escape. From the start he is destined to suffer, without reason, the fate of victimization. He is guilty before he has committed any crime. Kafka's aim is to show that man is gratuitously and therefore unjustly punished, because he is not actually guilty. His only crime is that of having been born.

Kafka's fiction brings into focus the dichotomies of existence in a concretely detailed, seemingly "realistic" way, yet everything in the world of the imagination he creates appears equivocal and mysterious: time, space, reality, the self. The strangeness is not frightening because it is problematical; the reality that is so mystifying, so appallingly out of tune with the expectations of Kafka's questing anti-hero, gives off intimations of something wholly other, something not to be apprehended in terms of the familiar world of experience, something numinous but never divine; it is the unaccountable, the emergence of the absurd. In breaking out of the trap of explicit analysis, the closed formal world of concepts, Kafka transcends both logic and reason. Like Kierkegaard, he demonstrates the limits of reason by holding it up to the ubiquitous light of the irrational, and he undermines the irrational by viewing it through the perspective of the rational. In either case he fills the mind of the reader with a sense of the inexplicable, of the absurd, and it is this sense that is so terrifying. He is "religious" in his awareness of the distance of God from human cognizance, the incommensurability of the human and the divine, but he is nihilistic in his perception of the total absence of God and the futility of the quest for ultimate meaning. Man torments himself with questions for which there are no answers, and yet Kafka goes on asking questions and his personae earnestly wait for an answer. But all they hear is the derision of silence.[22]

---

[22] The interpretation set forth in this chapter of Kafka as a nihilist is not one that writers on Kafka are willing to accept. Professor Theodore Ziolkowski, for example, agrees with those critics who contend "that there are no sufficient grounds for calling Kafka a nihilist. Kafka limits the horizons of his characters, but never implies that there is no meaning beyond that horizon." Theodore Ziolkowski, *Dimensions of the Novel*. Princeton: Princeton University Press, 1969, p. 62n). The Surrealists, when they discovered Kafka, canonized him as one of their patron saints. His fiction, they felt, was born of a nihilistic vision of life in the universe. The existentialists hailed him as the inspired prophet of the absurd. See Albert Camus, "Hope and the Absurd in the Work of Franz Kafka," in *The Myth of Sisyphus and Other Essays,* trans. Justin O'Brien (New York: Vintage Books, 1955), pp. 92–102. Nevertheless, there are scholars who deny that Kafka can legitimately be called a nihilist. Paul Conrad Kurz writes: "Today most interpreters agree that Kafka is neither a nihilistic prophet nor an existentialist saint as the French understood the terms." (Paul Konrad Kurz, *On Modern German Literature,* trans. Sister Mary Frances McCarthy [University, Ala.: University of Alabama Press, 1967], 1:39.)

7

The Battle against the
Absurd in France

From the day when consciousness awakened in man, he began to feel
himself separated from the whole, isolated, exiled, in a universe to which
he clings with all the fibers of his body and his soul, but which remains
alien to him. It is impossible to escape from this dualism which consciousness had introduced into life, to abandon oneself to the world without
reservations, but also to abstract oneself from it. To veer and tack,
to accept intermediate paths between mind and things, sometimes closer
to the mind and sometimes to things, such is the fate of man.[1]

When God and the creation become objects of consciousness, man
becomes a nihilist. Nihilism is the nothingness of consciousness when
consciousness becomes the foundation of everything. Man the murderer
of God and drinker of the sea of creation wanders through the infinite
nothingness of his own ego.[2]

1. NIHILISM AND FREEDOM OF THOUGHT AND
EXPRESSION

Just as the literary interpretation of the Absurd is diverse, no
two writers investing the term with the same connotative range
of meaning (compare, for example, the conception of the Absurd

[1] Marcel Raymond, *From Baudelaire to Surrealism*, trans. G. M. (New York:
Wittenborn, Schultz, 1950), p. 161.
[2] J. Hillis Miller, *Poets of Reality* (Cambridge, Mass. Harvard University Press,
1965), p. 3. Miller examines Joseph Conrad's nihilism and perspectivism. Conrad
sees the world as a deliberately created illusion. The ideals to which men swear
allegiance are mental projections; the universe fails utterly to confirm their validity,
their value, or even their existence. There are no universal ethical laws, no immutable standards of conduct. Man himself invents these laws and formulates
these standards.

described by Kierkegaard or Unamuno with that to be found in the work of Camus, Beckett, or Ionesco), so is the literary response to the challenge of nihilism highly differentiated. Those who are haunted by the vision of the Absurd agree on no first principles, form no doctrinaire school, and attract no disciples. They are very much on their own as they explore the wasteland of nightmare through which their life's journey takes them.

Literary absurdists are not fitted for the role of preachers or missionaries. This is not at all surprising when we consider some of the alternatives open to the writer who has caught a blinding glimpse of the irremediable absurdity of existence. He may, first of all, simply decide to ignore the reality of the Absurd and devote his creative energy to the enterprise of art. Second, he may resolve not to surrender to its debilitating influence and in the name of reason fight against it with his last ounce of strength. Third, he may wish, like the dadaists, to celebrate the triumph of the irrational and seek to exemplify his extreme spirit of negation by shaping his life in the image of the Absurd. The first option represents a flagrant evasion of reality, a case of "bad faith" in the Sartrean sense, a cowardly evasion of responsibility. The second option is the one to which many writers are drawn; they combat the power of the Absurd and the nihilism to which it often leads. The third option is definitely a suicidal gesture, as is illustrated by the life and work of Alfred Jarry.

The writer who is without religious faith of any kind, who has given up his belief in the transcendental goals that the mass of humanity hope to reach, need not conclude that the struggle naught availeth. On the contrary, by the force of his intellect and by relying on the use of reason rather than faith or intuition, he confronts the ontological mystery with courage and lucidity.[3] As he beholds

---

[3] Somerset Maugham's hero in *Of Human Bondage,* who is the mouthpiece of the author, arrives finally at the liberating nihilistic insight that the history of man can be summed up in a single line: "he was born, he suffered, and he died. There was no meaning in life, and man by living served no end. It was immaterial whether he lived or ceased to live. Life was insignificant and death without consequence." (W. Somerset Maugham, *Of Human Bondage* [New York: George H. Doran Company, 1915], p. 559). Philip Carey is not crushed by this revelation; he was free to shape the pattern of his life.

these negative epiphanies of the cosmic enigma, he is aware of the limitations of the intellect. The more tenaciously the intellectual clings to consciousness, the more he comes to realize the tricky and deceptive character of his perceptions; the disorderly world intrudes upon his solitude and upsets the tenuous sense of harmony his mind has created. By remaining hermetically sealed within the privacy of his inner self, he shuts himself off from vital sources of being and renders himself incapable of experiencing anything that he might consider genuinely "real." This is the price he must pay for rooting himself in the pride of consciousness. He intellectualizes everything he touches; his feeling of nihilistic alienation grows upon him.

It is France, which traditionally granted writers, no matter where they came from or what they believed in, the right to freedom of thought—it is in this land that nihilism frequently manifested itself. Anarchists, avant-garde rebels, revolutionaries, political exiles, Surrealists, and nihilists found here, particularly in Paris, a congenial home. Mallarmé, whose poetic theory defended the ideal of purity against the Philistine preachers of morality, later discovered that his restrictive concept of Beauty failed to satisfy him. It cut him off from life. The aesthetic resolution led nowhere: it was not a viable surrogate for philosophy or religion. His pessimism grew worse. He had ceased to believe in the immortality of the soul. In his state of spiritual desperation he beheld "a cosmic *Néant*."[4] Mallarmé had gazed into the bottomless depths of "le néant." Hamburger says apropos Mallarmé: "there is no denying that a profound nihilism underlies the extreme aestheticism of the late nineteenth and early twentieth centuries."[5]

2. HOW VALÉRY COMBATED THE ABSURDITY OF EXISTENCE

Early in life Valéry discarded the illusions that helped to sustain man in his brief and lonely pilgrimage on earth, but he did not attack

---

[4] D. J. Mossop, *Pure Poetry: Studies in French Poetic Theory 1746–1945* (Oxford: At the Clarendon Press, 1971), p. 130.
[5] Michael Hamburger, *The Truth of Poetry: Tensions in Modern Poetry from Baudelaire to the Sixties* (New York: Harcourt, Brace & World, 1969), p. 29.

Christianity or proclaim the death of God in the manner of Nietzsche. He was neither an iconoclast nor an evangelist; he made no effort to convert others to his point of view. He was chiefly interested in analyzing the internalized drama of thought, but at the same time he fully realized how treacherous and largely ineffectual language proved to be when one made the attempt to "translate" the adventures of the mind. Like his memorable character creation, Monsieur Teste, he struggled hard not to become the victim of the skeptical method he had himself devised. The mind, he insisted, must not be allowed to deceive itself. Even though he thus sought to safeguard himself against the ever-present danger of the mind's betraying the complex and susceptible self, he nevertheless relied on the intellect as the sole touchstone of whatever truths it might discover. If he returned to poetry after a long period of renunciation, the poetry he produced did not neglect the demands of the intellect. He was engaged in a lifelong task of demystification. He warred against the romantic myth of spontaneous, effortless inspiration. Influenced by Poe in this respect, he maintained that consciousness in the creative process must be alert and active, deliberately shaping the body of the form. In his poetry as in his prose, his aim is to capture, if he can, the elusive meaning of selfhood in relation to the world. Carefully avoiding all metaphysical abstractions, he confronts the mysterious relationship of the self to an alien and unknowable universe.

Despite the keenness of his intellect and the prodigious range of his knowledge, Valéry could not arrive at a truth, much less a faith, that would satisfy the fastidious requirements of his mind. That is often the "original sin" as well as typical misfortune of the dedicated intellectual: he is held back in his search for viable values by a skepticism that is virile but unfruitful. His persistent quest for truth turns out to be a singularly unrewarding occupation. Committed to this quest, the best a writer like Valéry can achieve is the scrupulous record of his own fluctuating states of consciousness.

Valéry uses his high-powered rational intellect as an efficient instrument to exorcise the demons of the irrational, to banish the troublesome and inexplicable specter of the absurd. But skepticism, if carried far enough, brings about its own defeat. Though Valéry distrusted the overdeveloped intellect and critically examined the

motives behind its passion for understanding the self and the world-
stage on which it acted out its mortal destiny, he was nonetheless a
slave of the intellect, dependent on it for all that he could provisionally affirm. Not only as essayist but also as literary critic, poet, and
playwright, he interpreted the enigma of existence without the mediation of faith, remaining, as it were, in a state of negative capability,
accepting nothing as true on the evidence that others provided. He
tried to live intensely and completely the life of the mind, following
the spoor of thought to its ultimate lair. Like Teste, he is the skeptic
who, if he speaks, does so by indirection, in terms of paradox. Everything he writes is, he knows, a confession. As he remarks: "In fact,
there is no theory that is not a fragment, carefully prepared, of some
autobiography."[6]

Though Valéry explored the recesses of the hidden, mutable self,
he also endeavored to discover the nature of the world he lived in.
Instead of indulging in the luxury of introspection and dwelling in
the realm of subjectivity, he set himself the task of mastering the exact
sciences. He wanted to understand the structure and function of the
physical universe, but to gain some degree of understanding in this
highly specialized field of knowledge, he found that he had, first,
to train and discipline his mind. If he was to succeed in this supremely
difficult task, he would have to reconnoiter the frontiers of consciousness, for it was consciousness that constituted a mystery. The
undertaking proved more formidable than he had anticipated; he
could not solve the mystery of consciousness, since it is consciousness that knows it knows; it is the observer who watches the observer
making his observations. Valéry here anticipates the infinite regres-
sion of introspection that characterizes the existentialist protagonist.

Valéry's persona, Teste, gives himself wholly to the life of
thought. *Monsieur Teste,* though nominally a novel, is actually an
intellectual autobiography, a series of monologues distributed among
a small number of *dramatis personae,* all of them revealing some
facet of the protean self of the author. It is concerned with ideas,
analysis, reflection, which mirror the internal conflicts of a single

[6] Paul Valéry, *The Art of Poetry,* trans. Denise Folliot (New York: Pantheon
Books, 1959), p. 58.

character, Monsieur Teste. Valéry found that the Narcissus myth was best suited to his purpose of describing the character of the man who watches himself in the fountain or the mirror. The myth symbolizes the divided consciousness of modern man, his split self. Narcissus is no longer the creature enmeshed in the net of self-love; he becomes, in Valéry's treatment of the theme, the figure who illustrates the conflict between the self as individual and the self as universe. What Valéry wishes to disclose, as in the Teste cycle, is the precise relationship between consciousness and the self.[7]

We learn little about Monsieur Teste as an individualized person, but we do get a portrait in depth of his inquiring intellect, a picture of his mind in action. The portrait is a subtle and ironic study of the attempt made by a disciplined consciousness to know itself, of the struggle it puts up not to be frozen into a single role or attitude. Valéry spells out the danger the intellectual runs in cultivating the intellect at the expense of his sensibility: the man who becomes all intellect is not taken in by the devious shifts and stratagems of his own thought, but gradually he is transformed into a monster, a logical machine, and ceases to be human.

What was reprehensible in this rigorous method of inquiry? Why was the charge of nihilism brought against Valéry as if he had committed a crime against humanity, as if he were the carrier of the plague? In seeking to elicit those basic values which the mind can affirm, Valéry hoped to work his way out of the nihilistic impasse. In his preface to *Monsieur Teste,* he tells us that he created Teste at a time when his will felt capable of coping with all things. In this patient and protracted effort to understand himself and the world and to develop his critical powers to the utmost, he selected only that which was difficult, avoiding the pitfalls of the sentimental, the romantically vague. He was not propounding a misanthropic, anti-human, life-negating doctrine. If he was suspicious of literature, it was because "the act of writing always requires a kind of 'sacrifice of the intellect.'"[8]

---

[7] See Christine M. Crow, *Paul Valéry: Consciousness & Nature* (Cambridge: At the University Press, 1972).
[8] Paul Valéry, *Monsieur Teste,* trans. Jackson Mathews (Princeton, N.J.: Princeton University Press, 1973), p. 3–4.

M. Teste is the civilized man who believes he knows himself. He insists that the mind must strive to reach ever-higher levels of consciousness. Teste does not take the trouble to write or read books. An athlete of the mind, his memory superbly trained, he was filled with the ambition to identify his own "nature." "He was a being absorbed in his own variations, one who becomes his own system, who gives himself up wholly to the frightening discipline of the free mind . . ." (p. 12). Unfortunately, his intellectual activities do not culminate in a series of affirmations. Teste is aware of his own ineradicable limitations. If Montaigne repeatedly asked himself, What do I know?, Teste keeps asking, "What is a man's potential?" (p. 20). All his efforts have been in vain. He has reached the end of his resources. He knows at last "that he doesn't know what he is saying!" (p. 18).

Teste's ambitious project to extend the frontiers of consciousness gets stuck in the quicksands of Pyrrhonism. The intrepid seeker encounters nothing except the mobile, ever-changing masks of the self. A mystic without God, as his wife describes him, Teste has abandoned hope. In the excerpts included from his logbook, Teste confesses that he has made an idol of his mind, "but I have found no other."[9] His restless intellect, as it sounded the depths of being, gleaned no certain knowledge. He climbs the loftiest mountain peaks of thought and he is master of all he surveys, but he descries nothing of what he is looking for—no God, no Absolute, no final truth. "It is impossible to receive the 'truth' from oneself" (p. 37). He cannot capture the innermost secret of consciousness.

If Teste rejects the concept of the infinite, he is also suspicious of the claims of science. For Teste, Valéry's alter ego, the first indispensable hypothesis of science is this: "the world is not known" (p. 73). Valéry does not share the arrogant but premature faith of some nineteenth-century thinkers that science could solve all problems. "What is really peculiar to the modern world," according to René Dubos, "is the belief that scientific knowledge can be used at will by man to master and exploit nature for his own ends."[10]

[9] *Ibid.,* p. 35.
[10] René Dubos, *The Dreams of Reason* (New York and London: Columbia University Press, 1961), p. 16.

Valéry was not guilty of this type of hubris. He looked upon the scientist not as a narrow specialist but as one whose research is designed to unlock the secret of nature. He would probably have agreed with the confident assertion Dubos makes: "Whatever questions are asked concerning the universe and human destiny, the answers of theologians and philosophers must be consistent with the demands of informed intelligence—that is, with scientific facts."[11] Valéry might have raised some troublesome questions about what constitutes a scientific fact.

Adept in the art of rational analysis, Teste is the type of intellectual hero who incessantly spies upon himself. He questions all things but reaches no conclusion. Finally he realizes that his self is an unknown. But if that is so, then it follows that life, too, is completely baffling, "a matter of going from zero to zero. . . . From unconsciousness and insensibility to unconsciousness and insensibility."[12] What saves Teste from succumbing to the nihilistic malaise is that, like the author who created him, he will not give in to his dark moods. The inveterate foe of the mystical and the mystique of the Absurd, he is resolved, like Valéry, to work only with those elements which are pure and distinct, with forms that have definite outlines. In the light of all this, it comes as no surprise to learn that Teste distrusts the art of literature and its preoccupation with words, just as he distrusts the sterile sport of metaphysical speculation. "I rejected not only literature but almost the whole of philosophy as belonging amongst those Vague and Impure Things which I denied myself with all my heart."[13] This ethic of renunciation is characteristic of the secular saint who must find out for himself the meaning of life, whatever it be, track down the truth regardless of consequences, casting aside everything else, even literature, philosophy, and religion, that might stand in his way. In setting his house of intellect in order, Teste must first of all reject all established beliefs and values. Valéry realizes that his persona, who is the personification of intellect, is impossible to accept as a man; there is nothing recognizably human about him.[14] "He

[11] *Ibid.*, p. 167.
[12] Paul Valéry, *Monsieur Teste*, p. 79.
[13] *Ibid.*, p. 4.
[14] William H. Gass, who is a professional philosopher as well as novelist and

knows only two values, two categories—those of consciousness reduced to its acts: the *possible* and the *impossible*."[15]

All his life long Valéry fought against the dark oppression of mystery, the romantic exaltation of the unknown. Things are what they are; the uncanniness of their appearance is overwhelming, but man must not allow himself to be overcome by the forces of the irrational. The sun, naturally, is the image Valéry delights in; darkness is the enemy to be routed. This conflict, Cartesian rather than Manichaean in nature, is fought out on the inner stage of the mind by the two adversaries, the agents of light and those of darkness, both of whom are aspects of the one self. This explains why Valéry is drawn irresistibly to the form of the monologue, though some of these monologues transform themselves into quasi-dialogues.

Valéry, who possessed a sensibility and trained intelligence that sought above all things to achieve luminous clarity of insight into the working of his mind, presents a test case of the writer who is damned as a nihilist because of the negative implications of his leading ideas. This represents a simplistic rendering or misinterpretation of his literary work as a whole, for he never wrote with dogmatic finality—it was foreign to his method. Nor did he spend all his creative energies in brooding skeptically on the ontological mystery. His problem, as Philip Wheelwright points out, was "to conquer the Absurd," and this could be done "only by accepting, assimilating, and dominating it. . . ."[16] He did not conquer the Absurd but at least he kept it at bay. A poet as well as amateur philosopher, he emphasized that the

literary critic, draws a perceptive portrait of Monsieur Teste. He shows that Valéry, as befits a poet who believes, like Poe, in keeping full control of the creative process, views Monsieur Teste with a measure of skeptical detachment. This fictitious being nevertheless embodies the supreme example of a "hero" devoted, like his begetter, to the free working of the mind. In a sense he represents, perhaps to an extreme degree, the ideal person Valéry aspired to become: "a Narcissus of the best kind, a scientific observer of consciousness. . . ." (William H. Gass, "Paul Valéry," Crisis and Resolution," *The New York Times Book Review*, August 20, 1972, p. 7). Gass notes that Monsieur Teste also resembles Valéry in his persistent preoccupation with the shifting and treacherous meaning of words.

[15] Paul Valéry, *Monsieur Teste*, p. 6.
[16] Paul Valéry, *Idée Fixe*, trans. David Paul (New York: Pantheon Books, 1965), p. xvii.

mind of man cannot grasp the essence of nature. Subjectivity interposes a screen on which images of the external world are projected, but he does not, like Kierkegaard, "leap" to the conclusion that subjectivity is God.[17] The universe is like a sphinx that propounds puzzling existential questions but fails utterly to vouchsafe an answer. Valéry discloses that the quest for knowledge ends in failure; the mind cannot comprehend the *why* and *wherefore* of the human condition. Valéry is reformulating the dilemmas posed by the Cartesian *Cogito*. He maintains that art, too, is an illusion. He entertains no hope of life beyond the grave; when the body dies, what we call the soul perishes with it.

Valéry has been consistent in shaping his nihilistic outlook. In *Mon Faust* he shows that God, like the Devil, exists only as an idea in the mind of man. The modern Faust, as Valéry portrays him, is deprived of God and professes to have cast off all illusions. He is not deceived by talk about the world beyond; the world he lives in is without ultimate meaning or purpose. He is the hero who is haunted by the specter of meaninglessness. He is repelled by the thought of clinging to life fearfully and without reason. *Mon Faust* incorporates Valéry's relativistic vision, his innate skepticism, his rejection of the deified Absurd.

Both parts of Valéry's *My Faust* are left incomplete, and for good reasons. Art, in its confrontation of the ontological mystery, is defeated; it cannot discern the shape or utter the name of that which lies beyond the reach of the senses; it can go so far, only a short way, and no farther. If there is no ascertainable meaning or purpose in life, and that is

---

[17] Kierkegaard knew the temptation of doubt. That is why he fought against the virus of doubt with unrelenting irony. Skepticism, he believed, is not a methodological exercise in logic; it is a perverse display of will, a refusal to believe in God. The doubter holds back; he will not commit himself but remains rooted in uncertainty. He resists the faith that can overcome his doubts. But faith, Kierkegaard reminds us, is not a logical process. It represents a decision by means of which the serpent of doubt is slain. Ortega holds that skepticism is not enough. "What is essential is that the skeptic be fully convinced of his skepticism. . . . The evil thing is for the skeptic to doubt that he doubts. . . ." José Ortega y Gasset, *Man and Crisis,* trans. Mildred Adams (New York: W. W. Norton & Company, 1958), p. 109.

the incredible conclusion to which nihilism leads, then what justifiable function can art serve?[18]

Faust is the skeptical quester who has freed himself from the enticing clutches of the Absolute. Believing in neither heaven nor hell, he has ceased to look upon life as either tragic or comic in character.

This, in brief, sums up the type of nihilism Valéry elaborated, but this lucid espousal of a nihilistic metaphysic did not prevent him from keeping faith with his fellow men, devoting himself to his literary career, and defending those values which assure the continuity of culture. Like Malraux and Camus, he transcended the nihilism of the Absurd. If we judge Valéry by his life and work, and not by the invidious labels some critics have affixed to him, then it is clear that he is a humanist at heart. Scarfe, for example, contends that there is no justification for calling Valéry, or his Faust, a nihilist.

> If Faust seeks complete detachment, even that cannot be described as nihilism. The essential thing is that he continues to think and to write, he creates in his unbelief, and therefore he obviously has at least two important "values," thinking and writing.[19]

This would imply, quite correctly, that nihilism as it achieves triumphant expression in a work of art, is a contradiction in terms. To create is to affirm. The writer's existential choice and commitment demonstrate his implicit belief in the intrinsic importance of literature, even though he may insist with ironic counterpointing that it is a vain and useless passion. But to apply this principle too rigorously would, in effect, blot out all semantic distinctions and overlook the dialectic of opposition inherent in the nihilistic obsession. It is clear that Valéry's Faust, in contradistinction to Marlowe's Doctor Faustus and Goethe's Faust, has gone beyond the categories of good and evil and knows that nothing can save him.

Valéry was humanistic in his conviction that the mind must stand in opposition to Nature and the pull of instinct. Humanistic,

---

[18] Charles I. Glicksberg, *The Ironic Vision in Modern Literature* (The Hague: Martinus Nijhoff, 1969), p. 192.
[19] Francis Scarfe, *The Art of Paul Valéry* (London and Toronto: William Heinemann, 1954), p. 305.

too, is his faith in the uses of intelligence. A relativist in his outlook, Valéry is prepared to discard his most cherished ideas if they are not in accord with the truth. He would keep his mind open, free to explore all points of view. If he railed persistently at Pascal it was because the latter despised the intellect and became the prophet of the irrational. Valéry for his part is not frightened by the infinite spaces. While acknowledging the mysteriousness of the universe, he seeks to know that which can be known. Descartes, who respected the canons of logic, is a better guide than Pascal. The world must be mastered by knowledge so that it conforms to human thought. Otherwise our life has no meaning whatsoever; the sense of purpose that motivates our efforts and aspirations is, after all, a human creation. As Suckling remarks in his book on Valéry, "there are no grounds for supposing the processes of life and the world, apart from human reactions upon them, to have any spiritual significance worthy of 'affirmation.'"[20] Valéry's views go beyond the nihilism they postulate by upholding the unique role of intelligence in human affairs.

Valéry cheerfully admits his nihilistic leanings. He has been called many harsh names by some of his critics, perhaps the worst being that he is an absolute nihilist. He was vilified because he argued that the course of evolution betrayed no shred of evidence that it was controlled by an immanent purpose. Life was not geared to the fulfillment of a cosmic design—a theme to which we shall return in the final chapter. All values are hypothetical, born of the rational mind. Once man begins to question what traditionally has been taken for granted as the truth, the foundations of his life begin to crumble. He finds himself dwelling in a world in which the essential values of the human spirit are being steadily undermined. Sooner or later, however, he comes to perceive that he alone is responsible for organizing the forms of life. He passes beyond the needs that make for survival and engages in an adventure "whose objective and end it does not know and even whose limits it thinks it does not

[20] Norman Suckling, *Paul Valéry and the Civilized Mind* (London and New York: Oxford University Press, 1954), p. 175.

know."[21] As one of the characters in *Colloquy* declares: "There is no 'why' when life is involved."[22] It is by the sovereign force of his intellect, by his inveterate hostility to all types of mysticism and mystification, that Valéry was able to combat his haunting awareness of the absurdity of existence.[23]

[21] Paul Valéry, *Reflections on the World Today,* trans. Francis Scarfe (New York: Pantheon, 1948), p. 158.
[22] Paul Valéry, *Dialogues,* trans. William McCausland Stewart (New York: Pantheon Books, 1956), p. 21.
[23] Valéry writes: "What do we teach other people by continually telling them that they are nothing, that life is vain, nature hostile, knowledge an illusion? What is the point of belaboring their nothingness, or telling them over and over what they already know?" Paul Valéry, *Masters and Friends,* trans. Martin Turnell (Princeton, N.J.: Princeton University Press, 1968), p. 93.

8

Henry de Montherlant:
Hedonism and the Absurd

1. COURAGE WITHOUT HOPE AND PASSION
WITHOUT FAITH

Kafka is the prototype of the prophet of the absurd. Montherlant is utterly unlike him in style and sensibility, in character and outlook. His life, like his work, further illustrates the theme that it is perfectly possible, and by no means illogical, to be a nihilist (as I have defined the species) without renouncing life. Montherlant suffers from no morbid compulsion. He knows how to deal with the miasma of despair generated by the vision of the absurd. His fiction offers added proof that nihilism, like romanticism or classicism, cannot be reduced to a single category; its productions run the whole gamut of differentiated responses called forth by the realization that there is no reason to life, no available principle of justification for the destiny that man seems to choose. Montherlant declares that a world without God, a world without the final triumph of justice, is the only world worthy of the man of courage.[1]

The nihilism of the absurd does not commit the writer to a belief in universal suicide. The literary nihlist has no intention of taking his own life. That would be a foolish and futile act of rebellion, an abject confession of defeat. If he is to voice his protest against

---

[1] Henry de Montherlant, *Selected Essays,* trans. John Weightman (New York: The Macmillan Company, 1961), p. 110.

the indignity of death he must live his life, but how is he to live in the light of his nihilistic convictions? Each writer answers the question in his own way. Schopenhauer invokes the idea as the best safeguard against the tyranny of the Will, hailing art, especially the art of music, as capable of opening the gates of nirvanic salvation in a godless world. Nietzsche hoped to conquer the furies of nihilism by releasing the full scope of what he called the will to power. Unamuno overcame nada by an affirmation of faith that creates the God who will assure him of personal immortality. Georg Büchner engaged in revolutionary activity while composing *Danton's Death,* which voiced his tragic realization of the futility of revolution. Kafka exploited an ambiguous form of irony that is resigned to the human condition and yet remains rebellious in its art of interrogation. Montherlant, while haunted by the thought of death, adopted a hedonistic ethic, devoting himself to a life of unabashed sensuality and to, second in importance, his writing.

A skeptic, a lapsed Catholic, Montherlant could not break away completely from the moorings of his faith. He jeered at it, his mind refused to accept the doctrine of immortality, and yet he continued to dwell on the possibility that life may go on beyond the grave. His experience in the First World War, the wound he received, his stay in the hospital, his remembrance of the dying and the dead, all this intensified his inner need to find some meaning in life. He fought to survive, to overcome the diseases that attacked his body. Professing himself to be a pagan in the mechanized twentieth century, he made a cult of the art of sensuality. Consequently he gave himself wholly to Eros and the pursuit of literature, in that order.

As a novelist he was determined not to play a partisan role; the ephemeral passions of politics could not command his allegiance or awaken his interest. Both sides were right as far as he was concerned, and both were wrong. In any event, he would not commit himself to the left or the right, and he had no desire to identify himself with the epicene ideas of liberalism. In one of his notebooks he made an entry, dated December 23, 1938, that voices his determination to steer clear of the Spanish Civil War, since he feared he would become too deeply involved in that fratricidal struggle. The natural consequence of his withdrawal from the political arena was that, during the Second World War and after it was ended, he was condemned as socially and morally irresponsible. Not to be committed, and "commitment" meant only one thing to the Marxist critics and their militant camp followers—that, it was charged against him, was worse than a sin; it was a crime against humanity. The condemnation left him unmoved; it did not affect his way of life. That was the way he chose to live, like it or not, for good or evil. He would remain unattached as well as detached. He would hide himself, in his novels and dramas, behind his persona.

As a confirmed skeptic, an observer of life without preconceptions or prejudices, he valued intelligence highly. In order to protect himself against being duped, he was resolved to consider all points of view, all ideas and perspectives, even those that seemed at first uncongenial and abhorrent. It is a notion held by professors, he remarked in 1923, that yes and no must stand in polar opposition to each other.[2] He prefers to reconcile these antinomies. Not that in his personal life he displayed no preference of any kind. On the contrary, as is shown in his first novel, *The Dream,* which is partly autobiographical in content, he believed in the virtues of comradeship, honor, sympathy, and compassion.

He was not taken in by the masks of distinction people wore or the moral shibboleths they mouthed. The intellect, he knew, is not the lord and ruler of life. The body does not lie. The sexual instinct represented the purpose for which life was made, its crown and consummation. Next to it he ranked the joy of creativity. But it is sensuality, not romantic love, that he exalts. He does not fall down in worship before that which he enjoys in the sexual experience. Physical desire coupled with tenderness—that is all there is to the art of loving. Talk about romantic love and its beatific folly, he will not countenance such nonsense. All these contradictions in his being—his determination to live dangerously, his love of a life of action, his celebration of sex, his attraction to

---

[2] *Ibid.,* p. 14. In the Introduction Peter Quennell quotes Montherlant's views on the subject of affirmation and negation.

Catholicism even though he has abandoned it—all these contradictions are the result of his persistent quest for authenticity. His
heroes are impelled, no matter what the cost, to search out the
truth, not the abstract, rational truth, but the more difficult and
elusive truth about themselves—who they are, what they feel and
desire.

But the sensual man, the quondam Catholic who has rejected
his religious heritage, is haunted by the thought of death. Here
is the mystery that overshadows existence and reduces everything
men do to nullity: their sexual exploits, their heroism in battle,
their ambition, their creative achievement, their pride. Montherlant
early in life freed himself of the vanity of authorship, the craving
for fame, the last infirmity of noble minds. He would not allow
himself to be intimidated by the fickle judgment of the public. He
would go his own way. He would write as if he were already dead.
Not that he foolishly believed that justice would be accorded his
work posthumously. No, the expedient was simply a means of being
honest with himself, indifferent to the opinions of his contemporaries. In "Explicit Mysterium," he sets down what are supposed to be the confessions of a writer who knew that he was
going to die before the end of the year. The device is no more than
that; Montherlant is using this stratagem in order to conceal himself
behind this conveniently distanced alter ego, but the pattern of
preoccupation in the essay betrays the presence of the authentic
Montherlant self. How, he asks, shall men die if they have given
up all faith in a life after death? It is not death, however, but life
that is the great mystery. And it is incomprehensible that men
should pursue their hunt for pleasure while the seed of death is
planted in their flesh and growing rapidly like a carcinoma.
Nevertheless, there is some justification for this outpouring of
passion, this indulgence in sensuality. Though Montherlant places
a high value on intelligence and heroism and art, they are, he feels,
subordinate to what he considers the supreme Good, "which is
loving someone" (p. 94). He could do without intelligence, if
that were taken away from him, though the quality of life he led
would be impaired, but if he were deprived of someone to love,
his life, he felt, would be ruined.

It is death that unveils the appalling specter of the absurd. When the end approaches and the dying man attempts to sum up all he knows, he is utterly at a loss. He has gained no essential wisdom through the years, no understanding of why he was placed on earth. The world on whose stage he appeared one day, and the role to which he was assigned or that he thinks he freely chose—both remain unknown. The dark curtain falls, the light of consciousness is extinguished, and there is nothing more to be said. All that happened during a lifetime was the outcome of chance: the work produced, the friendships formed, the love affairs one enjoyed, the illness that proved fatal; and this summing up applies to all people the world over. Like Thomas Hardy, Montherlant argues that it is the element of chance that governs the course of our life, but we are unwilling or unable to accept this unpalatable truth. Only as the end draws near does one lose his illusions and realize his insignificance in the cosmic scheme.

But if death is an impenetrable mystery, it is ridiculous to spend precious time thinking or worrying about it. "There is," Montherlant contends, "only one way to prepare for death"—and that is to live life to the fullest possible extent. The only kind of immortality worth having, according to Montherlant, is "the immortality of life" (p. 98). If only the screen that hides from us the knowledge of what lies beyond could be torn aside and we could see the ultima Thule of nothingness that greets us at journey's end and come back to report that there is absolutely no ground for hope. There is only the fugitive present; the past is gone forever; the future is a mirage. The one thing that can fire the blood and raise us higher than art or music is capable of doing, is physical sensation. It is the *summum bonum*. Montherlant confesses that he has never exerted himself except in the pursuit of sensual pleasure.

Montherlant defeats the power of nihilism by glorifying the life of the senses. Death, as far as he can make out, does not demonstrate the vanity of life on earth. Nonsense! It makes life here and now all the more precious. The anticipation of death can furnish a surprising source of vitality. Death, as the behavior of brave men in battle demonstrates, can be treated with the contempt it deserves. Even if there were a possibility of life after death,

Montherlant does not believe in clinging desperately to this illusion of hope; one should embrace that philosophy which enables him to live his life with dignity and courage, though such manifestations of courage must, of course, be judged by relative standards. One man, Montherlant points out, may be afraid to visit the dentist and yet manage to come to terms with a universe "where there is neither God, punishment nor immortality" (p. 108). Montherlant will engage in no Pascalian wager. He is not afraid to face an eternity of nothingness. Hope—that is the insidious drug which turns us all into cowards and slaves. And so Montherlant concludes this essay, "Explicit Mysterium," written in 1931, on the following note of nihilistic affirmation: "A world without God, a world without final justice"—that, he is convinced, is the only world worthy of man (p. 110).

Just as in a dramatic work the dialogue reveals what the characters say while their actual feelings and the actions prompted by these feelings may be strikingly different, so we must differentiate between the portrait of himself a writer paints and the secret self that emerges from the totality of his life and work. If the writer dwells on his feelings, his variable moods, the values he honors, the crucial experiences that shaped the chief lines of his character, he is bound to fall into contradictions, especially if he cherishes the quality of honesty, Montherlant pictures himself as alone, beyond pity, self-sufficient on the whole, surprised by nothing, and yet the most striking note in his writing is that of compassion. No one reading his account of the misfortunes and miseries of war, or the decay of France and the dry rot of prudential morality that has eaten into the soul of its citizens so that they treasure, above all other things, security, a job, regardless of the shameful conditions to which they must submit—no one reading this can possibly miss the anguish Montherlant feels and communicates. Even though he pretends to remain aloof and uncommitted, he is personally involved in the fate of his countrymen. How overwhelming is his sense of shame when France capitulates to Germany! It is as if he had suffered the loss of a leg or arm. The country he loved dearly and for which he had again and again risked his life, had betrayed its trust, and this he could not forgive. No, Montherlant is not withdrawn and unconcerned, indifferent to the vicissitudes of history. On the contrary, because life is so precarious and so brief, and because the dead are given no second chance—for those very reasons he insists that life must be lived joyfully but not without honor in the present.

Though Montherlant contradicts himself at times in the sphere of feeling, this is part of his complex nature, but he is on the whole remarkably consistent in his *Weltanschauung*. In 1923, in "Hold Fast to All Things, While Keeping Each in Its Proper Place," he formulates a line of conduct that he had followed through the years. For him the question of renunciation does not arise; he has displayed an admirable capacity for throwing off the claims of possession, even of beautiful, costly objects, and he had denied himself the alleged pleasures of matrimony, fatherhood, and family life. For him, as for Gide, the chief difficulty is to decide which principle he should choose above all others and then support it loyally, while keeping each thing "in its proper place" (p. 24). This seems to resemble the Greek ideal of the golden mean, but it is much more than that. Indeed, it goes so far beyond the Greek ideal that it turns out to be something qualitatively different. It embraces all the contradictions of existence and glories in them. It acknowledges that no single point of view is sufficient to encompass the full truth of being. The mystery remains, and it is not to be dissipated by rational modes of inquiry. Nothing, in fact, is to be renounced.

Montherlant declares that he would renounce nothing because he believes in the basic truth of the ancient Greek doctrine of the union of opposites. To keep contrary forces in balance—that is his definition of the good life. Nature is the source and ground of all these polarized contrasts: night and day, rain and drought, winter and summer, work and rest, sleep and waking, creation and destruction, life and death. Nature, a prodigal principle of contradiction, is impartial in her operation, and he would like to emulate her example by not limiting his pattern of fate. Like Gide, he wishes to develop all his potentialities, to be effective in all directions. That is the distinctive mark of a healthy soul: its capacity to achieve a higher synthesis, a unity that will reconcile most of the apparent contradictions in life that oppress the fearful. Montherlant wants to experience all that life has to offer: suffering and happiness, good and evil, wisdom and madness, life in all its splendid and sometimes frightening plenitude. He seeks to experience everything in order to understand everything, thereby to be able to give it expression. In thus living his life joyously, to the full, the human adventurer will be greatly rewarded when he sees God "as made in the image of man" (p. 26).

This sums up Montherlant's ethic of revolt, his defiance charged with the Luciferian pride of blasphemy. He would exhaust the entire universe of experience within the brief compass of a lifetime, excluding nothing; he elevates man to the pinnacle of Godhood, but this God made in the image of man is no more than the personification of an operative principle, infinitely resourceful but aimless, of contradiction; in fact, Montherlant abolishes God by making him a product of the fecund human imagination. He sets forth a modernized and essentially anomalous version of the Renaissance ideal of striving to achieve a kind of orchestrated perfection of human possibilities—an ideal that is impossible of realization. It comes closer to the Paterian conception of hedonism: that in the brief interval of life that remains to us, after which the world knows us no more, we are justified

> in getting as many pulsations as possible into the given time. Great passions may give us this quickened sense of life, ecstasy and sorrow of love, the various forms of enthusiastic activity, disinterested or otherwise, which come naturally to many of us. Only be sure it is passion—that it does yield you this fruit of a quickened, multiplied consciousness.[3]

This dream of a heightened consciousness that would result from the attempt to savor all of life's varied experiences, cannot, alas, be fulfilled on earth. One must choose among rival possibilities. As Montherlant's own life discloses, one cannot walk down all roads at once. One choice negates for the moment all the others the human adventurer might have made, and there is no turning back. Montherlant has never regretted the decision he made; he

[3] Walter Pater, *The Renaissance* (London: Macmillan and Co., 1924), p. 252.

gave himself to a life of sensuality that was not held in check by the factitious idealization of love.

Montherlant was a heretic by temperament, determined to obey the law of his own being, regardless of what the world might think. He would leave nothing out of his account, omit no truth he cherished that might perhaps be censured as unpalatable to human susceptibilities, leave unrecorded no vision or experience he once had for fear that society would condemn him as immoral. He will celebrate the excellence of madness, glorify the creative power born of obsession and aberration, trust the sense of mystery wherever it leads him, and give free rein to the rebellious skepticism that will question all things sacred and certain. He will relish the abusive title of "enemy of the people" because of his uncompromising opposition to the idolatry of his age, especially the craze of conformity. He remains the unbending aristocrat, intent on preserving his honor and integrity at all costs. If he disposed of his possessions and left his native land, he did so in order to intensify his sense of life and, secondly, "to be uncommitted."[4] His books had won him the guerdon of fame; he had achieved what he set out to do; why repeat himself?

Montherlant lives dangerously. He was wounded by a young bull in Spain and was hospitalized. After contracting typhoid fever and pneumonia, he had to spend some time in nursing his weakened body. One of the wounds he had received in the war acted up again. He strove to bear up under the weight of all this physical suffering, and struggled to save himself from falling into despair. He kept on writing. The crisis ended; he had come through. He had passed through a period of intemperate sensuality, but he managed to regain his balance and his spirit of serenity returned. He could not, however, find a solution for the metaphysical problem, which continued to trouble him. Unlike Unamuno, who could not reconcile himself to a life that ends in the anonymity of dust, Montherlant was able to integrate into his being the metaphysical crisis posed by the question: why are we alive?—and thus learned to live with it (p. 115). In the past, the question as to the meaning and

---

[4] Henry de Montherlant, *Selected Essays,* p. 112.

purpose of it all drove him to despair; now it had the power to soothe him.

The new man emerged, born of his renunciation of all worldly interests and ambitions. He had, after all, made a choice. His spiritual nature was coming to the fore. By indulging his senses fully, he quieted the demons of sexual desire and was free to live spiritually; the exhaustion of his sexual energies made it possible for his spirit to come into its own. He turned against violence, cruelty, and oppression. Before 1925, which marked the turning point in his life, he had followed the bidding of his powerful will; he had carried everything before him, but this aggressive will, he now realized, was satanic in origin. Now he forsook this source of evil temptation; his will became identified with that of the universe. Willing was a species of illusion, action a form of vanity. When his will subsided, hope died with it, but it inaugurated the beginning of inner calm. He was now in full possession of himself and therefore able to trust mankind. But the purpose which had originally prompted him to leave France—that persisted unchanged. He knew what he was doing. He refused to burden himself with onerous responsibilities; he was resolved to welcome all the possibilities of experience.

Despite his professed inner calm, he could not rid himself of the religious question. Before 1925 he had preached "a Catholicism totally devoid of Christianity" (p. 118). Then for a time he indulged in the sport of blasphemy, but these outbursts against God led him nowhere. He could no longer accept the Christian faith, but he had been brought up as a Christian and his feelings were deeply rooted in the Christian mythos. He kept aloof from the Church, but he "respected religion" (p. 119n). In 1929 he stated that he was not a believer, but since he had been baptized as a Catholic he remained a Catholic. This was only a nominal attachment, for he was clearly "outside Catholicism" (p. 119n). He took from Catholicism what happened to suit his spiritual and creative needs, even including the practice of religion up to a certain point. He frankly acknowledges that he makes use of it, "in a human way" (p. 119). This is, of course an equivocation, a transparent bit of casuistry. One cannot play with the elements of religion as if it were a game of make-believe and make use of it in a human or poetic way. That is to trifle with God, to transform faith into a purely "aesthetic" category, as Kierkegaard defined "the aesthetic" stage in *Either/Or*. The religious discipline, the act of faith, demands all of the believer. One cannot be a half-baked or part-time Catholic.

In the meantime, Montherlant lived under an assumed name in North Africa. He read, wrote, thought, satisfied his sexual hunger, doing very much as he pleased. His chief object in life was not to produce literature nor to revel in uninhibited sexuality; his aim was to understand himself, to come into full possession of himself, for herein lay "the origin of creative work" (p. 121). That is why he had divested himself of useless duties and distractions. He strove to get down to essentials, to perform only those actions that mattered supremely. Unmoved by the thirst for fame, he could give himself, when he wished to do so, wholly to his work. Indifferent to the world and the values it held up for emulation, he felt free, self-sufficient.

He was severely criticized for adopting this austere regimen; even his friends admonished him to respond to the call of duty, to play his part in the affairs of the world instead of running away, but he would not listen to their advice. He was not running a race in order to win a prize. What he hoped to achieve was inner happiness, and he had to achieve it on his own terms. He was now able to rejoice in the miracle of life as it is. He worshipped the glory of the earth, the beauty of the body; he was happy. He had gained pleasure for himself and given pleasure to those he loved. In doing all this, he had been true to himself. As he put it, "I had seen things as they really are" (p. 130). That, he declares, is his impelling passion, his controlling purpose: to fulfill himself. He had found the means whereby to overcome the nihilistic crisis of despair engendered by his loss of religious faith.

The course of sensual or creative fulfillment, however, does not run smooth; the world breaks in rudely upon the privacy of the self and drags it by *force majeure* into the vortex of public events. The literary nihilist obviously plays a diversity of roles; he suffers from internal conflicts as well as embarrassing contradictions. Montherlant is a case in point. Despite his profession of egotism, he is the least self-obsessed of writers. It is not a cult of personality to which he is addicted, like that inspired narcissist Salvador Dali, who publicly advertises his genius. What Montherlant strives to achieve is the highest degree of sincerity.[5] Hence he deliberately confesses those urges and impulses which most men (and many writers) hide beneath a veil of decent obscurity or genteel circumlocution. What keeps Montherlant's vision straight and true is his profound disillusionment. He sees through the humanitarian pretensions of his age, its blague of patriotism, its rhetoric of idealism, its cowardly craving for peace at any price. In September 1938 he accurately foresaw the shape of things to come; he knew that war was inevitable. He had no love for the Nazis and was even then ready to oppose them. The conciliatory attitude of Chamberlain and the French leaders, their strategy of appeasement, sickened him. He was prepared to fight but he was

[5] What is meant by sincerity in literature? In his book, *Literature and Sincerity* (New Haven and London: Yale University Press, 1963), Henri Peyre shows us that the question is bafflingly complex. Is it principally an aesthetic issue or is it fundamentally a matter of keeping faith with the private self? How is sincerity achieved? Some artists sought to cultivate their creative power as members of an esoteric cult devoted solely to the worship of beauty. Thus they could negate the indifference of the universe and dwell in their own created world of the imagination, unmindful of such disturbing metaphysical enigmas as the existence of God or the ultimate meaning of life. But the twentieth century blew up all ivory towers and revealed to the writer the absurdity of the ideal of self-sufficiency or exclusive dedication to art for its own sake. Wars, revolutions, concentration camps, crematoria utilized efficiently for genocidal purposes the atomic bombs dropped over Hiroshima and Nagasaki, the collapse of the Marxist dream of brotherhood, all this made him aware of the horror of the modern world, a world from which no one could hope to escape by retiring inside the belly of the whale, and there enjoy the unique privilege of aesthetic contemplation. Henceforth writers would be wary of the pitfalls of language and resist the insidious enchantment of rhetoric. In their quest for sincerity, they would get rid of eloquence and shut their ears to the siren song of style. That is how they would capture the pure state of experience, the flow of sensibility undistorted by the habit-frozen forms of language. Or they tried to explore unknown and forbidden territory, to break down taboos, to reveal what most men fearfully conceal even from themselves. There is much to be said for this literary crusade in behalf of sincerity, but as Professor Peyre points out, it can be carried too far. Complete sincerity implies the acceptance of the coexistence of good and evil, of contradictory states of feeling, in the same person. This principle of polarity emerges fully panoplied in the work of writers like Gide, Julian Green, Montherlant, and Ionesco. For a cogent critical analysis of the function, uses, and abuses of what we call sincerity, see Lionel Trilling, *Sincerity and Authenticity* (Cambridge, Mass.: Harvard University Press, 1973), pp. 1–25.

under no illusions about the catastrophic character of the war that would soon break out. War, he knew, meant death for millions of men on both sides, and he wanted above all things to go on living. When he left for the front he was not, he maintained, actuated by a sense of duty; the impending outbreak of war was, for him, a test of strength and he therefore welcomed it.

His dominant purpose during this period of crisis remained the same: he would not glorify this or any war; he would simply assimilate those experiences, and only those, which would further his own development. At this juncture he faces a glaring contradiction: he is prepared to risk his life, but for what? Not, he assures us, for the sake of France, and yet his concern for his country is not to be mistaken. With what anxiety he broods about its demoralized state, the fecklessness and bumbling ineptitude of its leaders, the blindness of the deluded populace. But if one were asked to select a single personal motive that dictated his actions immediately before and during the Second World War, it would be his unswerving loyalty to a code of honor. He will be himself at all times, in the worst hour of adversity, even in the face of death. Throughout his life he was resolved to keep faith with his sense of destiny. All this, of course, comports ill with the picture we generally form of the outstanding character of the nihilist.

With Montherlant it was not a question of supporting the right cause against the evil one. He was not much concerned about the side he had chosen to defend. What mattered to him greatly was the knowledge that, in fighting under a particular flag, he could "achieve fulfillment."[6] War, he asserted, is valuable solely as a wager with death, though he has no intention of dying. He is intelligent: why should he perish in this holocaust? But he is also heroic and therefore voluntarily runs the risk of being killed in battle. His code of honor overrides all considerations that are prompted by the instinct for survival.

The truth is that Montherlant thrives in an atmosphere of crisis. The presence of danger deepens his awareness of the precariousness of life and the relativity of all things under the sun.

[6] Henry de Montherlant, *Selected Essays*, p. 203.

Let others cry aloud and mourn for their children foredoomed to annihilation. Not Montherlant. His withers are unwrung. Let the world perish, let mankind die, if that must be. There is no reason for falling into despair. The cycle of death initiates the countermovement of rebirth. If civilization should be destroyed, this would mark but a passing episode in the geological history of the earth. A new race, a new civilization, would take over. Even if Armageddon were being waged, Montherlant would keep his poise. In the hour of catastrophe, particularly then, he would rely on himself alone. Death, he contended, is best defeated by facing it bravely. Beneath a godless sky, man stands alone. "Absolutely alone . . ." (p. 159). At this point Montherlant dwells on the Mystery in which all contradictions coexist without being reconciled, though in eternity they will fuse and become one.

But when the 1940 Armistice was signed, he could not console himself with the law of equivalence that would fulfill itself in eternity. The humilation of his nation was worse than any personal affliction of disgrace. His mother country had fallen into dishonor. This was more than he could bear. Under the Occupation life was degrading, utterly intolerable, without meaning. He derived some comfort from the thought that time effaces all distinctions, just as it wipes out the monuments of victory, so that the categories of time and space are only relative containers. His all-inclusive vision abolished the law of contradiction; he beheld the world as a constant process of transformation, a world in which "everything comes to the same thing" (p. 228).

In "Extracts from the Notebooks of Henry de Montherlant— 1930–1944," Montherlant gives us a close picture of the working of his mind. He interprets the world by viewing it through the dialectical perspective of contradiction. Action begets reaction. Each day of life is a battle, a rhythm of creation and destruction, but he labors under no illusion as to the outcome of this conflict. Always, in the end, nihilism triumphs, the void is the winner. Though he tries to keep the balance even between life and death, he knows that this precarious balance can not be maintained forever. As he contemplated the starry spaces that frightened Pascal, as he gazed into what he called "the void," he realized that the only thing that could support him in this experience of nothingness was the conception he had formed of himself. "The void," he concluded, "is acceptable" (p. 290).

This, in a nutshell, poses the tragic dilemma of the nihilist: his confrontation of the void is countered by the imperative need for action. For he continues to live in the ephemeral world that is destined to be swallowed up in the nothingness of eternity, and therefore he feels obliged to taste its pleasures and bear some of its responsibilities, "the rules of the game and the game without rules . . ." (p. 290). There is also the countervailing play of intelligence, the power of lucid contemplation that obliterates all differences in the crucible of time. That is the nature of the conflict the nihilist must undergo: intelligence pitted against instinct, detachment opposed by the irresistible craving for action. Montherlant is constantly aware of this tension of opposites. He faces this conflict honestly, but the battle is fought essentially within himself. Even if this conflict saps his energy and interferes with his literary output, he is not perturbed. He confesses that he is interested only in his private life, which is devoted to the satisfaction of his sexual hunger and to his "creative work in literature" (p. 293). The rest does not move him.

His interest is focused on himself. He will endeavor to tell the truth, even though he realizes it will not be the whole truth, only that fraction of it which he can encompass. He is no evangelist, no fanatic of the persuasion that he is in possession of *the* Truth. His sense of irony is too highly developed for him to indulge in such folly. He tells us that he has never written anything without feeling the impulse "to write the opposite" (p. 300). Though he perceives how the relativity of values affects all areas of life, he nevertheless holds on to his own convictions, regardless of the orthodoxies that prevail in the marketplace. As a writer he is sufficiently imaginative to perceive the psychological basis of the value-system we adopt as our own; we embrace a given set of ideas and beliefs because they are pleasurable, consolotary, or strength-giving—an insight he may have gleaned from Nietzsche. That is why he identifies himself with the most diverse passions and perspectives. He considers all sides of an issue, even to the point of acknowledging the cogency of his opponent's position. Like Valéry, he writes his books but attaches little importance to their publication. For him the creative act is not something mysterious or sacred, a quasi-divide seizure of inspiration; it is "a physiological relief of the same nature as copulation" (p. 301). Montherlant may also have derived this psychologically illuminating idea from Nietzsche, who anticipated Freud by disclosing the sexual genesis of art. Nietzsche asserts that artists are sexual by nature, endowed with a powerful energizing sex instinct.

Though Montherlant is too complex, both as a writer and a man, to be summed up in a formula, he is nihilistic in his reading of life. He sees existence as basically a comedy that must be interpreted tragically. He describes his restlessness, his ennui, his feeling of metaphysical "nausea," his sense of uselessness. How is he to achieve peace, how is he to escape from the pressure of other human beings and above all from himself? Even if he were assuredly in possession of God, he would soon tire of Him. Whatever is attained is immediately deprived of value. Satisfaction does not bring happiness. There is no point in struggling or aspiring. One is faced, always, with the problem of how to kill time. Montherlant has gained everything he sought in life and should therefore consider himself relatively happy, but what, he asks, is happiness? It is happiness that somehow eludes him. Time destroys him. All he has achieved, all he has been, will dissolve into nothingness, "without memory and without dreams, where at last I shall finally be through with myself."[7] This is the testament of a man for whom death represents the acme of absurdity. Death, as he shows in his novel *Chaos and Night,* renders null and void all dreams, all hopes, all political aspirations and ideals.

2. CHAOS AND NIGHT

Chaos and Night is a curious novel when judged in relation to Montherlant's previous work. It departs from the themes that

---

[7] Henry de Montherlant, "The Hounded Travelers," in *From the N.R.F.,* ed. Justin O'Brien (New York: Farrar, Straus and Cudahy, 1958), p. 297.

appear in his earlier fiction. It seizes upon a political theme, only to reveal its utter insignificance. The protagonist, now an old man, formerly an anarchist who fought in the Spanish Civil War, has been an exile in Paris for a period of twenty years. What had he done during that time? Brooded bitterly on the reasons for the defeat of the Republican forces in that fratricidal conflict, written articles on his political views that the newspapers declined to print. He dreams nostalgically of returning to his native land. When that dream is at last realized, he discovers, in Spain, the blinding truth about himself.

It is strange that Montherlant should be interested in dealing with a quasi-political theme and in minutely analyzing a character who is an anarchist, though the author makes Celestine "a bogus leftist," an absurd eccentric, a descendant of Don Quixote. Montherlant had no personal knowledge of the Spanish Civil War and therefore had to imagine what his central character must have experienced and felt. In his preface he warns the reader against the fallacy of imputing to the author sentiments he has placed in the mouths of his various characters. This is a particularly dangerous practice when the novelist ventures into the mine-laden territory of modern politics. The writer of fiction, Montherlant declares, is bound to incorporate some aspects of himself into all the varied characters he creates in a given work, even when he feels a personal antipathy for their temperament and their behavior. Montherlant is right in his insistence that the novelist identified himself closely with his protagonist (as he does in *Young Girls* and *Pity for Women* and *Costals and the Hippogriff*),[8] though in the foreword to *Young Girls* he also warns the reader not to commit the error of identifying the author with his hero, Costa. If the novelist reveals a great deal of himself in portraying his principal character, he reveals just as much of himself in drawing the portrait of characters whom he does not like. True enough, but there is no mistaking the fact that Montherlant despises the quixotic protagonist

---

[8] Despite Montherlant's denial that Costa is a picture of himself, it is evident that Costa resembles his begetter in some particulars. He is writer, a novelist; he sees things as they are and he is a realist in matters of love. He is proud of the fact that he has never contracted the romantic disease known as love.

in *Chaos and Night;* he uses him as a medium for venting his hatred of political fanaticism and voicing his philosophy of death.

Celestino is now living in Paris with his daughter Pascualita, a girl of twenty. He spends his time reading the newspapers, the evening as well as morning editions, looking for signs of progress in the world. He is particularly hungry for news about Spain. He is supposed to be gathering material for a book, but he has not written it as yet because, as he says, his mind teems with too many ideas. He breaks off all relations with his friend M. Ruiz, who accuses him, not without reason, of living in the vanished past. It is the friend who remarks with Sancho Panza pessimism that the modern world bears witness to the fusion of the tragic and the grotesque. Whereas everybody recognizes the tragic element, "few people see the grotesque. . . ."[9]

Celestino ardently defends his political faith, for without it he is lost, his life a waste of foolish endeavor. An eloquent and impassioned ideologist, he judges politics by the degree to which it contributes to the destruction of Christianity. He will brook no half-way measures; total destruction must be the aim. If the Spanish Republicans had won the war, he would have asked for the post of Minister for the Destruction of Religion. His friend good-naturedly remarks that Celestino is perhaps the only man in France who is a devout free-thinker, and considers his secularism to be as anachronistic as his anarchism. The Church is now in a dominant position. As Ruiz declares scornfully, practically all people today have lost their faith, but they continue to play the role of believers. And that is because of the widespread myth that "to go through the motions of believing is supposed to exorcise Communism" (p. 16). Ruiz exposes what he regards as the ridiculous illusions his friend cherishes. He tells him bluntly that he is not going anywhere and that he understands nothing about the world. The mental confusion he suffers from is "the characteristic sickness of our age" (p. 16). He condemns Celestino's quixotic folly, his failure to think clearly and to practice the virtue of discrimination.

[9] Henry de Montherlant, *Chaos and Night,* trans. Terence Kilmartin (New York: The Macmillan Company, 1964), p. 10.

He compares him to Don Quixote, whom he calls the first anarchist. His contempt for Celestino's obsession is evident in his derisive summing up of the man as "a caricature of a man of the Left" (p. 17). He is a useless creature, living on the stale political crumbs of his dreams of a past that can never be recovered.

This is too much for Celestino. His pride wounded to the quick, he resolves never to see Ruiz again. The latter maintained that if the Revolution had been successful it would have been attacked by the cancer of corruption, whereas in defeat it still beckoned the believer as a pure and shining ideal. This interpretation of the matter disgusts and enrages Celestino. It is the skeptics and cynics of this type that he would, if he had the power, place before a firing squad. Then the suspicion enters his mind that perhaps his friend is a spy, an *agent provocateur*. As a young man Celestino had devoted all his time to political discussions and as a result failed his final law examinations. Unable to establish himself in a professional career, he turned as a compensation to socialism, but he did not take the decisive step of joining a party. He admired the Encyclopaedists and read with fervor the work of Proudhon and Leo Tolstoy. If he studied closely the writing of Bakunin it was because he was "so intelligent and such a good atheist" (p. 26). Gradually he came to hate not only the State in itself but "authority in any shape or form" (p. 27). Montherlant ironically underlines the contradictions inherent in the philosophy of anarchism. Celestino, though he was fearless in the fighting that took place during the Spanish Civil War, was not amenable to discipline of any kind.

Now he lived the life of a bachelor in exile. He was, as Montherlant portrays him, the victim of a singular obsession, feeding on the opiate of hope, cut off from the world, completely alone. An honest, guileless man, an "innocent," he believed that politics was more important than money. He did not work for a livelihood, since this would consume the precious time which he urgently needed for his study of politics. He was extremely just in his judgments, when political issues were not at stake. His private maxim read: "Justice through injustice" (p. 31). In France, he kept to himself, with the exception of two friends and his lawyer; he did not even associate with the exiles from his country. In order not to endanger the right of asylum France had granted him, he studiously avoided left-wing groups. He detested the Communists just as he was too undisciplined to accept any collectivist or party control, but in Paris, where anarchism had taken no hold and socialism was too compromised by its leanings towards democracy, Communism seemed the only doctrine that could be made to work. The logic of events convinced the unhappy and restive Celestino that Communism, regardless of his personal dislikes in the matter, "represented the future of the proletariat . . ." (p. 36). His cautious efforts to effect a rapprochement with the Communists were fruitless and he retired within his shell. An outcast from his mother country, spurned by the Communists, he feels thoroughly sorry for himself. Montherlant pictures him as a confused man, the political Don Quixote who would never "see reality for what it is" (p. 37). Loyal, brave, self-sacrificing, he was densely ignorant of military matters. An intransigent individualist (Celestino and the author have at least this much in common), he had participated in the war out of hatred rather than love. In the future development of mankind that Bakunin prophesied, he eagerly welcomed the day of judgment, not the millennium of peace and brotherhood: "Scorched earth, rather than the Promised Land" (p. 38). By portraying Celestino in this heartless manner, it is as if Montherlant were exorcising the spirit of Don Quixote that dwelt in his own breast.

Montherlant underlines the flagrant shortcomings of this man, this thinker who never thought things through. Though he was deeply interested in social, economic, and political issues, he was indifferent to art and beauty and the sensuous manifestations of life. He is the perennial dreamer who cannot distinguish between the imaginary and the real. He develops gloomy ideas. Like Don Quixote whose remarks he quotes, he is beginning to realize that he is dying, bit by bit, every day. He looks upon his exile as a punishment that is at times too painful to bear. He suffers from it, and he suffers even more because he believes he does not suffer enough. His inner guilt at not being killed or wounded or imprisoned troubles him. His cause has been defeated, he has been a total failure. Montherlant, pitiless in his analysis, makes the comment that "muddle and eccentricity were his natural state of mind" (p. 75).

Montherlant debunks the political abstractions of the Left and uncovers the real motives of the political activists, those who achieved their goal and are installed in the seats of power as well as those revolutionaries who are still on the outside looking in. He holds up Celestino as an exemplary case of the self-deluded and ineffectual radical. Celestino in his old age is depressed by the thought of wasted time. Since he had of late looked with indifference upon all things under the sun, why was he troubled about how he spent his time, "or even if he did nothing?" (p. 91). He knows, however, that time is his enemy. He has passed the peak of his career, and the rest of the way leads precipitously downward. There is nothing now to arrest his falling into oblivion. Death becomes his obsession. (That is the secondary theme which emerges and gradually becomes the dominant concern of the novel). He realizes that he will soon cease to be, and this will constitute his worst and final defeat, for it will rob him of autonomy and put him at the mercy of others. Now he walks in the valley of the shadow of death. Who can say with perfect assurance that he will be alive on the morrow? Celestino wonders how and when his end will come and how he will meet it. In such a crisis-situation, one cannot fall back for support on either philosophy or religion. One is left alone with himself, and sheer courage is called for. But why display courage? And why, Celestino asks, has the fear of death suddenly become so pronounced? Were people terribly oppressed by the fear of death ever since "they had ceased to believe in God?" (p. 94). He finds himself trapped between "a horror of living and a horror of dying" (p. 95).

Then he receives the news that his sister in Spain has died. He must go there to claim his inheritance. He is afraid that the police will apprehend him, and yet he ardently desires to revisit his native land. Pascualita tries to reassure him that he need have no fear, but he cannot get rid of his paranoiac suspicions. He decides finally to accept his destiny, come what may. Perhaps the danger he suspects exists only in his own mind, though one of his favorite axioms is: "Everything one dreads eventually happens . . ." (p. 127).

That is how Montherlant foreshadows the meaningless fate that overtakes his protagonist.

Once Celestino enters Spain, the land of the enemy, he feels himself surrounded on all sides by hostile forces. He had pictured Spain under the rule of Franco as a vast concentration camp, but he perceives that the widespread suffering and oppression he had imagined do not exist. As he reviews his past, his lifelong devotion to the revolutionary movement, he begins to suspect that he has betrayed *the cause;* old age has unmanned him, the specter of death has stripped him of his idealistic fervor. What, he asks in despair, is the point of living? The ideal for which he had lived and sacrificed everything had ceased to exist for him. He is but waiting to die. He must leave Spain at once, without his daughter, but not before seeing a bullfight.

The bullfight, which is described in vivid detail, leads him to identify himself with the bull, the victim sentenced to die. He is the bull who is being drawn and deceived into death. He is now in a demoralized condition, disillusioned, fearful. Revolution, war, anarchism, the proletariat, the bulls—all have failed him. At this moment he gains the nihilistic insight that death is more important than the triumph of socialism, and yet, in the past, he had not regarded human life as sacred. As he faces the dismaying, ineluctable fact of death, all his former beliefs are brought into question. What does the overthrow of Franco or the victory of socialism throughout the world matter to him? Why should he be aroused by the prospect of another world war breaking out or the annihilation of the human race in an atomic holocaust? These dreadful contingencies are overshadowed by his perception of the fact "that he was going to die. . . ." He was utterly without hope, and knew that his end was near. This was happening to him, now. He would "cease to be: the most banal, the most improbable, the most unbelievable thing" (p. 229).

Anguish grips him, though why should he be made to endure this unrelieved mental suffering? Had he not expected this to happen? Death, after all, this disaster without precedent that overtakes every son and daughter of Eve, would mark the end of everything: his fear of being arrested, his frustrations and failures, his fears themselves. What, then, is the use of struggle and sacrifice if, after death, one ceases to exist? During the Civil War, the Left on the battlefront used loudspeakers in an effort to induce soldiers on the opposing side to desert. These loudspeakers called out: Why should you bear all this suffering? Why suffer "for the sake of chaos, which will dissolve into night"? (p. 232). Celestino no longer cares what becomes of his beloved country or who rules it. Why should he worry about the destiny of Spain when "his *own death*" was a meaningless fiasco? His vision expands as his political faith loses its hold over him—a vision in which everything is murkily confused. He is startled to find that there is "no 'yes' and 'no.'" (pp. 233–34). The "yes" and "no," the positive and the negative, constitute a mixture that can not be reduced to its separate and seemingly opposed elements. In the cold light of death, everything stands confounded. But he has been condemned to die from the very beginning; the only question confronting him now is when the blow will fall. He feels that he should have viewed the world as an aesthetic spectacle, enjoyed its beauty, "but never taken part in it" (pp. 234–35).

Montherlant is at his best—his imagination catches fire—in describing this epiphany of the negative, this scene of "recognition," in which the death-haunted Celestino repents of his fanaticism. The only certitude was life, "which was confused, incoherent, and unstable" (p. 236), and death represented the absolute of darkness, the triumph of the void. In short, life was an expression of Chaos, and Night represented the state of nonbeing that existed before life emerged and after life disappears. Perhaps there was only nonbeing, Celestino reflects, and life was only an illusion. *"Nothing exists, since everything ceases to exist when I cease to exist"* (p. 236). This is the numinous truth—namely, that nothing exists—he should have discovered sooner. Death has called forth this destructive vision. He can now see into the heart of things. In his mind Celestino clutches the light to him, hailing indifference as the supreme power in this world.

Chaos and Night, written between July 1961 and May 1962, is an astonishing fictional performance. Despite his disclaimers, Montherlant is Celestino, especially in the second half of the novel, even though he presents him in a poor light. He is at one with his persona in the same sense that Flaubert is Madame Bovary. Montherlant possesses many of the traits of the philosophical anarchist, though, unlike poor Celestino, he eschews politics and has only contempt for the ideologist. That is why he treats this aspect of Celestino's character—his obsession with the abstractions of politics, his ideas of messianic redemption, his hatred of the State and the Church—with deflationary irony. It is in his hour of death that Celestino is converted to Montherlant's conception of life. He realizes at last that he is a bogus intellectual, that politics is a futile passion, that Franco and Stalin are one and the same. Death alone matters. He cares about nothing now; the truths for which he had fought now seemed foolish illusions. Indifference is the only remedy. Though he leaves instructions that his body is to be cremated and his ashes strewn to the winds, he is—and this is the crowning irony—buried by the Church in hallowed ground.

Montherlant rejects both the eschatological promise of Christianity and the utopian mystique of politics, but he has nothing to put in their place except a romantic Titanism that is incongruously combined with an attitude of soical indifference and a belief he never gave up in the intrinsic goodness and rightness of a life of sensuality. Chaos remains chaos. His nihilism is generated by his fixation on the absurd fatality of death.[10]

---

[10] Montherlant committed suicide on September 21, 1972, by shooting himself in the mouth. He was seventy-six years old. In the obituary that appeared in The *New York Times,* Andreas Freund noted that in Montherlant's novels and plays a number of characters had taken their own lives. Montherlant had consistently defended the individual's right to commit suicide. "This was a typical, Montherlant attitude, that of a nihilist preoccupied with ethics." The *New York Times,* September 23, 1972.

9

Malraux: The Riposte of Conscience

In an article of 1959, set out in the form of answers to questions put to him [Gottfried Benn] in an interview, he wrote: "When you announced your visit, you promised not to ask me whether I'm a nihilist. And indeed the question is just as meaningless as to ask me whether I'm a skater or a stamp collector. For the important thing is what one makes of one's nihilism.[1]

Negative passions play a very great part among the intellectuals. . . . Nietzsche wrote that since 1860 nihilism (which for him was what I have called the absurd) had little by little overtaken all artists. Since then, consider! Eighty per cent of genius from Baudelaire to our present writers, has been nihilists![2]

1. PRELUDE

Nihilism, as it functions in the body of twentieth-century literature, gives birth to its own dialectic of irony. Could anything be more superbly ironic than the spectacle of a *creative* nihilist, a writer who professes that he believes in nothing, and then proclaims, through the mouths of the various masks he assumes, that he believes in nothing? For whatever he is prepared to abandon in keeping with his negative vision, he will not give up the enterprise of art. If all is illusion, this is the last illusion to which he will perversely cling until the end. Hence his singular devotion to art gives rise to what might be called existential irony: a conflict

[1] Michael Hamburger, *Contraries* (New York: E. P. Dutton & Co., 1970), pp. 325–26.
[2] André Malraux, *Felled Oaks: Conversation with de Gaulle,* trans. Irene Clephane, rev. Linda Asher (New York: Holt, Rinehart and Winston, 1971), p. 96.

between mind and heart, reason and intuition. This is the kind of irony that we find in Pascal and Kierkegaard: the awareness in the former of the grandeur and misery of man, and the awareness in the latter of the despair that springs from the epiphany of the Absurd.

What the *creative* nihilist produces (and it is indeed difficult to understand, on his terms, how he can continue to be productive, for what purpose, on what justifiable grounds) is instinct with overtones of irony. His imagination brings into play all the dichotomies of the human condition: the dynamic flux of energy in the universe and the inability of human intelligence to comprehend what it is all about; the enduring faith of the masses in God, a personified First Cause, to whom they address their petitionary prayers, and the total absence of any warranted evidence for the existence of the supernatural.

The twentieth century has witnessed the collapse of all absolutes. When that happens, not only the place of man in the universe but his intrinsic nature becomes equivocal; he can no longer define himself or relate himself to some objective, continuing purpose. The concept of man is discarded; there are only individuals, isolated monads. The character of human nature undergoes a radical transformation so that universals as well as absolutes are abolished. The lines of communication between men break down if only because the dialogue between man and God is ended. If God is dead, if the absurd reigns in the kingdom of nothingness, then modern man is doomed to be alone and incommunicable, imprisoned in a solitude from which there is no hope of escape. "Indeed, the only really satisfactory cure for solitude is not intercourse with others, but the belief that there is a reason for our existence, that our presence on earth fulfills, in some way, a Purpose."[3] That is perfectly true. Unfortunately, the human condition in our time is such (or is interpreted as such) that the intellectual hero feels alienated, dwelling in a solipsistic universe, unable to achieve the beatitude of faith. His longing for spiritual union

[3] Everett W. Knight, *Literature Considered as Philosophy* (London: Routledge & Kegan Paul, 1957), p. 152.

with a power other and greater than himself is frustrated at every turn.

In every writer who reveals some aspect of the secret of the absurd, there is the countervailing impulse to transcend the absurd, to rise above the fate of victimization, to make the choice of freedom meaningful; modern literature frequently portrays its awareness of the fact that man is besieged by the forces of chaos that threaten to destroy the cosmos he and his forbears have fashioned. The best way to overcome that threat is not in surrendering to the absurd as if it were a primal curse or aboriginal Fall that is the heritage of the children of Adam, but in boldly making use of it. Man has the choice of taking on himself the burden of existence and thus negating the fatality of the absurd. He comes to realize that there is no justification to be sought outside the sphere of history for the brief upsurge of consciousness that constitutes a life, but life is all a man has to work with.

The nihilist faces a world in which God or the Absolute is absent; he must therefore formulate his own body of values, his own conception of what is desirable in a life that has lost the support of the divine. He must take God's place and become the demiurge and architect of his own mortal destiny. He must create his own viable myths and treat his vital fictions as if they were the mandate of Heaven. He is the one responsible for preserving the fabric of civilization.

Not that all nihilists belong to this abstract typology. As I showed in the discussion of Valéry, it is extremely difficult in all conscience to pin down the definition of a nihilist, either as applied to the writer himself or to his persona. Obviously no writer is all nihilist and nothing but a nihilist, nor is he a nihilist at every stage of his career. The fact that he pursues the profession of letters, even if he publicly accounts it of little value or creates what he calls "anti-literature," constitutes a positive value, even though it does not necessarily entail the relinquishment of the absurdist outlook. A writer may not even acknowledge being a nihilist, and yet the world view implicit in his work will inevitably betray him. Or, as is more often the case, he may resist the deadly spiritual infection and strive like Dostoevski to combat the rampant atheism of his age in *The Brothers Karamazov* and in *The Possessed* to expose the suicidal folly of Russian nihilism. The writer may, like Unamuno, counter the terrors of the void by affirming his faith in God, whom he creates and sustains by the sheer force of his will to believe. Those writers who cannot take the irrational leap from nada to the blessedness of religious faith generally adopt some form of secular humanism. Driven out of the Kingdom of Heaven and deprived of the assurance of eternity by the ideologies born in the Age of Enlightenment, the modern intellectual frequently comes to terms with his metaphysical dilemma, his alienation from God, by resigning himself to work as best he can within the finite and ephemeral domain of history. Are writers like Valéry, Camus, and Malraux, then, to be regarded as nihilists or humanists? The exact label does not matter, of course, if the two seemingly opposed positions can be reconciled. What counts supremely is, as Gottfried Benn points out, what one makes of one's nihilism. That is the decisive test.

The nihilistic protagonist is as a rule not a tragic figure. The exception occurs when he displays, as in Malraux's novels, unfaltering courage as he rebels against the order of the universe. Malraux depicts his hero as refusing to be fooled or to fool himself. He is resolved to face life honestly. He will not in his extremity resort to spiritual opiates. Nor will he silence the refractory voice of reason in an effort to transform the Absurd into the Absolute, the vision of nothingness into the ineffable image of God. He is willing to risk his life for the sake of helping the victims of oppression, but he does not expect that his sacrifice will vindicate a cosmic law of justice. He sees no cogency in the argument often advanced "that every tragedy is a demonstration of the unalterable conditions of human experience."[4] Malraux early in his career as a writer suspected

> that life, death and the universe are impenetrable mysteries, unillumined by the presence of God. Yet he ... has refused passive submission to

---

[4] Henry Alonzo Myers, *Tragedy: A View of Life* (Ithaca, N.Y.: Cornell University Press, 1953), p. 53.

despair, and has sought deliverance in the powers that set men apart from the physical existence of insects and the stars.[5]

The heavens are empty, Nature is indifferent to human aspirations and ideals. The gods of the past are dead, yet Malraux is convinced that man can rise above his own insignificance in the cosmic scheme of things. "The miracles of human existence, to Malraux, are man's willingness to consecrate himself to transcendent values, unsupported and undirected by belief in any religious code. . . ."[6]

Whereas Albert Schweitzer preached the sacredness of life and called for an attitude of reverence toward *all* living things, Malraux, irreligious in his outlook, denies that there is anything intrinsically sacred in the uses of life. There is no ultimate goal of felicity or salvation to be reached. Since the present is all in all, Malraux rooted himself in particular things and accepted the toll of suffering that action entails. Malraux, as one critic points out, "was one of the first to see that the 'death of God' involves that of man. God understood not only as the Deity, but as any principle purporting to render the universe intelligible. . . ."[7] Malraux firmly rejected not only the Absolute that is equated with the divine but also the postulated absolutism of reason. As the pre-existentialist poet of freedom, he recognizes the ineradicable ambiguity of life. Man must fashion his own sense of purpose, since it is through the application of his will that he shapes the world. Men make history by the force of their commitment to a life of action. That is how they banish the crushing knowledge of the absurd. Each one must choose his own way of life, even as he realizes that his efforts may utterly fail or prove in the end to be altogether useless.

Accepting the challenge of death, the Malraux hero decides to live dangerously. He plays a given role on the world's stage, finding in action a means of heightening his sense of life. His defiance of death is, as it were, an act of revenge against an alien universe. Garine, the "conqueror," is a Nietzschean nihilist who knows that his revolutionary work in behalf of the Chinese masses

---

[5] Avriel Goldberger, *Visions of a New Hero* (Paris: M. J. Minard, 1965), p. 147.
[6] *Ibid.,* pp. 148–49.
[7] Knight, *Literature Considered as Philosophy,* p. 134.

is bound to come to naught.[8] In 1925 Malraux went to China, where he did propaganda work and helped to edit a revolutionary newspaper, but he was not a Communist, not even philosophically, for "Marxism had no answer to individual death."[9] There is no avenue of escape from the human condition. In this brief interlude of consciousness before everlasting darkness falls, the only values worth cherishing are those of human courage and the sense of solidarity with mankind. Man must act in order to invest his life with vital meaning, but it is a meaning he has imposed. It is not the achievement that counts. What matters supremely is the spirit of dedication the project calls forth in the protagonist, even if it culminates in failure and results in his death.

2. THE WALNUT TREES OF ALTENBURG

Thus Malraux looks only for the human greatness that man "wrests" from his imperfect self in defiance of the indifference of the universe and the cruelty of death. . . . In a letter to Armand Hoog, he commented: *"I do think that Altenburg, rewritten, would only pose more clearly the problem that underlies everything I write: how to make man aware that he can build his greatness, without religion, on the nothingness that crushes him."*[10]

In *The Walnut Trees of Altenburg,* Malraux attempts to resolve his inner conflicts. He allows the Devil's advocate to speak and recapitulate all that can be said in favor of the destructive element —the death of God, the evanescence of time, the eventual disappearance of all things human, even humanity itself. He then affirms the redemptive function of art in imposing the order of meaningful form on the universe. It is art that demonstrates the continuity of culture and vindicates the importance of man.

Malraux's art of fiction interrogates the world. Through all the vicissitudes of his extraordinary career, Malraux never ceased to question the meaning of the ontological mystery. In fact, he

[8] Geoffrey Hartman, *André Malraux* (London: Bowes & Bowes, 1960), pp. 23–24.
[9] Cecil Jenkins, "André Malraux," in John Cruickshank, ed., *The Novelist as Philosopher* (London: Oxford University Press, 1962), p. 62.
[10] Goldberger, *Visions of a New Hero,* p. 236.

insisted that the character of man is revealed by the kind of questions he asks of the Sphinx. He was convinced that "man can never plumb the depths of his own being; his image is not to be discovered in the extent of the knowledge he acquires but in the questions he asks. The man who will be found here [in *Anti-Memoirs*] is one who is attuned to the questions which death raises about the meaning of the world."[11]

Whereas religious faith in the past gave man the assurance that his prayers would be heard, the hero in Malraux's world of fiction is denied that solace. The latter must confront a universe over which no God presides. Exiled from Nature as well as bereft of God, he ponders the meaning of death. He realizes that, for all his rebellious questioning, the universe remains unmoved by his craving for certitude. Only through action can he affirm his uniqueness. Like Nietzsche, Malraux is constantly struggling to defeat the deadly logic of nihilism.

First published in 1943, *The Walnut Trees of Altenburg* is the surviving part of *La Lutte avec L'Ange,* a larger work the manuscript of which was destroyed by the Nazis. The novel opens with a symbolically fitting scene placed in Chartres Cathedral, which has been turned into a prison camp. God is dead, but the children of God are held in captivity. Vincent Berger, the protagonist, remembers the past; he is the narrator who recounts the life of his father and grandfather. We thus witness the fate of three generations. The grandfather commits suicide; the father fought in the First World War and is involved in an attack by poison gas launched against the Russian trenches. Years later, the Second World War breaks out and Vincent Berger, fighting for France, is taken prisoner. In a number of vivid, intensely moving scenes, Malraux shows how man, transformed into a raging demon, dehumanizes the world he lives in. In this novel that consists largely of metaphysical colloquies, the narrator is essentially an observer who broods on the nature of humanity. Through this persona, Malraux projects an apocalyptic image, deeply

[11] André Malraux, *Anti-Memoirs,* trans. Terence Kilmartin (New York and Chicago: Holt, Rinehart and Winston, 1968), p. 6.

colored by Nietzschean influence, of the conflicts that are acted out in his own mind. Möllberg, one of his alter egos, voices an uncompromising nihilism. He gives utterance to the fearful suspicion that man is only a freakish accident in the course of evolution. Civilization is but a façade that is doomed to perish. The fate of man is overshadowed by the specter of meaninglessness. Malraux, however, seems to suggest that the grandeur of man lies in his ability to question the apparent order—or lack of order—of the universe. Art provides a means of escape from the absurd fatality of the human condition. Instead of submitting to the arbitrary requirements of a world he did not create, the artist transforms it and thus humanizes it.

Though thematically rewarding in content, *The Walnut Trees of Altenburg* is structurally the weakest of Malraux's novels. It begins with a description of the French prisoners in the camp at Chartres; we see the faces of the wounded and the windows of the cathedral, and hear the rumors that spread like wildfire and the roar of the German tanks. The French Army has suffered a humiliating defeat in the early years of the Second World War. Malraux pictures the exhaustion of these captured soldiers, their pathetic eagerness to send letters to the world outside, a world that is scarcely human. In the face of misfortune and disaster they manifest a remarkable capacity for endurance, a secret faith in their power to survive the ordeal of war, perhaps the same faith "as the cave-man used to have in the face of famine."[12] Vincent Berger dwells on the undying instinct in these haggard men, their ability to endure: they are symbols of mankind locked in a nightmare, fantastic yet palpably real. Vincent Berger reflects:

> Every morning I watch thousands of shadows in the restless light of dawn, and I think: "It's mankind." (pp. 22–23).

This scene, as it develops, achieves the effect of timeless continuity, the vision of mankind on the march through countless cycles of suffering. In the gaunt faces of these bearded men, Malraux

---

[12] André Malraux, *The Walnut Trees of Altenburg*, trans. A. W. Fielding (London: John Lehmann, 1952), p. 21.

beholds the Gothic visage, the Middle Ages reborn. The life led by these weary and defeated soldiers is like that of a bad dream. Vincent Berger writes—and the passage clearly sounds as if Malraux is speaking through him—of this experience. For the past ten years he has as a writer been obsessed solely by the thought of mankind. Here in the camp at Chartres, a captive like the other men, he beholds the essence of the human race. His experience of captivity and his awareness of death as a constant presence, lead him to recall the words of his father:

"It is not by any amount of scratching at the individual that one finally comes to mankind." (pp. 23–24).

The link is here provided between his life and that of his father, whose fate was decided twenty-five years ago. He seeks to discover a common thread, to search out the meaning of the cruel destiny that had overtaken these men and the world as a whole.

The novel proper begins with the story of his father's life: his arrival at the time of the suicide of Vincent's grandfather. The father declares that he respects the courage of the man who kills himself. Whether or not suicide represents an act of courage, a question of this kind "concerns only those who have not killed themselves" (p. 28). The only one who is not present at the funeral of Diedrich Berger, the grandfather, is Walter, who is appointed, together with Vincent's father, as the legal executor. It is Walter who is made the heir of the estate. All the other members of the family, businessmen and merchants, look up to Walter as a great professor, a brilliant intellectual. He had founded the "Altenburg Discussion Groups," which were held at the priory of Altenburg. To this colloquium, held annually, he invited fifteen of his distinguished colleagues from all parts of the world and the most talented of his old students. These discussion groups produced contributions by such eminent figures as Max Weber, Freud, Emile Durkheim, and Sorel. We learn that Walter had once been a friend of Nietzsche. Since Walter had a lively appreciation of fame in all its forms, he invited his brother, Vincent's father, to the colloquium. The latter had earned a degree in Oriental languages and been appointed to the faculty of the University of Constantinople. His first course of lectures there was entitled "The Philosophy of Action." A romantic adventurer who effectively utilized his intellectual resources, he performed a number of important services in Turkey, playing the role of a kind of T. E. Lawrence. He loved power but cared nothing for money. Devoted to the cause of Ottomanism, he undertook a mission designed to unite the Ottoman Empire, but he soon came to realize that Ottomanism did not exist and could not be brought into being. He had been blinded by the dazzling light of a myth. Now that he has cast off this myth, he returns to Europe. Five days after his arrival at Reichbach his father kills himself.

The next section of the novel takes us to the library at Altenburg, where the two brothers discuss the motives that led Diedrich to take his own life. Vincent's father relates that two days before his death Diedrich had said: "Well . . . *whatever happens,* if I had to live another life again, I should want none other than Diedrich Berger's" (p. 65). The premeditated suicide is implied in the expression: *"whatever happens."* Walter remarks that as a child he was terribly afraid of death but now that each year brings him closer to it he is indifferent to it. They wonder, too, what induced Diedrich to express a wish that he be given a church burial. It may have been fear or the impulse to abandon the useless struggle. It is then Walter voices his conception of man. He declares that fundamentally man is what he hides. Vincent's father, on the other hand, maintains that man is what he is able to achieve—a point of view that Malraux himself supports.

Walter, now seventy-five years old, discusses Nietzsche with his brother. He describes how Nietzsche went mad and had to be taken to an asylum—the trip by train from Turin to Basel, the critical period of thirty-five minutes it took to pass through the St. Gothard tunnel in the dark, the fear that Nietzsche might become violent. Then Nietzsche sings a poem, a late composition of his, a sublime song. Walter has never forgotten the strangeness of that experience. He remarks that, while in that train in the dark with the mad Nietzsche, he felt convinced that the timeless radiance of the star-strewn sky was completely eclipsed by the genius of man. Though Walter has never known a love that lasts until death, he does know that man, through the works of art he creates, triumphs over the world. Walter then utters the faith that is in him, a faith that Malraux later set forth in *The Psychology of Art*. The supreme mystery is not that by a stroke of chance we have been thrust between earth and sky, but that we are endowed with the power to project images of ourselves that are sufficient "to deny our nothingness" (p. 74).

Malraux makes the whole scene come alive—the smell of the walnut trees filtering in from the outside, the darkness of the room, Walter's spoken words, his remembered vision of Nietzsche singing his song above the metallic clattering of the wheels as the train sped through the dark tunnel, the discussion of the suicide, the sight of the coffin being carried out. But this human and unique gift of transcendence achieved through art, this endowment that Walter Berger, like Malraux, valued so highly, had its limitations. While it could shut out the immensity of the star-studded sky, it provided no armor against the piercing sword of grief. It should be added at this point that Walter and Vincent's father represent two contrasting attitudes toward life. Walter believed that man was summed up by the miserable bundle of secrets that motivated and impelled his creative urge, but his father felt that the star-illuminated immensity of the sky was already present in the mental outlook that induced a man, one desirous of death and at the end of a life that had had its full share of pain and no redeeming touch of glamor, to remark that if he were given the opportunity to choose another life, he would choose his own.

We learn that Möllberg, who had returned to Europe, has arrived for the colloquium. Walter had originally planned the discussion to focus on the theme "The Eternal Element in Art," but now, after the death and burial of Diedrich, he has changed the subject to read: "The Permanence and Metamorphosis of Man." Möllberg, a scholar of international repute, is to play an important part in the colloquium. He has delayed the publication of his monumental work, for which he had gathered a vast and fascinating mass of material. It was believed that from the data he had collected he would create a masterpiece, a unified science that would be Hegelian in its scope. While other scholars at the time stressed the diversity of civilizations, Möllberg strove to impose unity on the difficult study of ethnology, which would support the conception of man "as a strict continuity" (p. 82). His opus, when completed, would supply a badly needed system of thought and furnish a clue to the meaning of man's destiny. When he is asked if the manuscript of this work, *Civilization, Conquest and Fate,* is finished at last, he replies that it has been destroyed. He left the scattered leaves hanging on the lower branches of trees stretching from the Sahara to Zanzibar. Later, during the colloquium, we learn why he had tossed his masterpiece to the winds, why he had become converted to a nihilistic philosophy.

The various eminent intellectuals participating in the discussion are introduced—Walter Berger, Vincent's father, Möllberg, Edme Thirard, and Count Rabaud, but it is Möllberg who is accorded the position of honor. Count Rabaud comes to the end of his talk, in which he has eloquently propounded the theme that the great artist is able to achieve the universal and to demonstrate how the continuity of culture springs out of himself. Certain men, the great artists, are endowed with that rare gift of discovering within themselves, and transmitting to others, the secret means of transcending the limits set by time and space and of triumphing over the fatality of death. As Edme Thirard points out, the Count seems to accept the conception of man eternal, and the Count agrees that this is so. He believes in eternal man, he says, because he believes "in the everlastingness of masterpieces" (p. 85). Thirard proceeds to question the validity of the underlying assumption. What, he asks disconcertingly, have the masterpieces ever taught us?[13] And silence fills the room for a few minutes.

The discussion then continues. The illustrious names of the dead are invoked and brought into the argument. Each one defends

---

[13] Ever since the fiendish crimes committed by the Nazi regime against millions of innocent men, women, and children were brought to the attention of an appalled but still incredulous world, some critics, men like George Steiner, began to question the prevalent belief that culture acts as a humanizing influence. See George Steiner, *In Bluebeard's Castle* (New Haven, Conn.: Yale University Press, 1971), pp. 77–79.

his own brand of faith in culture. Thirard persists in the denial that culture has the power to teach us the truth about the nature of man. Compassion, he contends, is a greater teacher than all the books in the world. "Culture, regarded as the be-all and end-all, inevitably results in the production of Chinese mandarins. . . ."[14] Thirard examines the meaning of the endless quest for knowledge, its different connotations and unexpected consequences. What, he asks, is meant by "knowing about" man? The great novelists like Tolstoy, Stendhal, and Dostoevski would have replied: "Not being surprised by him."[15] This is a form of negative knowledge that is gaining ground of late. The consequences are that we cannot anticipate the important actions of those nearest to us. The self of others is a dark, unfamiliar country that must be explored.

The discussion takes up the uses of psychology, the art of self-analysis, and the relation of great art to psychology. Vincent's father remarks that the need for psychology makes itself felt only in the West. And that is because the West refuses to conform to the world as it is or to accept the outer sense of fatality, whereas in psychology it seeks what it considers an inner fatality. Vincent's father goes on to show why psychology exists, the particular function it performs. The Christian, he argues, seeks his salvation first of all, but is held back from achieving it by the weaknesses implanted in his nature, by his belief in original sin, and by the activity of the Devil. Here Vincent's father, himself a man of action, penetrates to the heart of the problem. The knowledge of man is not to be confused with the knowledge of his secrets. Only in the West is it taken for granted that man is what he conceals.

When the subject of art comes up, Vincent's father proceeds to relate it to the awareness men have of their destiny. But what is destiny? He explains that we had no choice in the matter of being born, and that it is not within our power to prevent the coming of death. Time defeats us in the end and all of us know that the world

---

[14] Malraux, *The Walnut Trees of Altenburg,* p. 86.
[15] Dostoevski writes: "What cannot a man live through! Man is a creature that can get accustomed to anything, and I think that is the best definition of him." Fyodor Dostoevski, *The House of the Dead,* trans. Constance Garnett (New York: The Macmillan Company, 1917), p. 7.

exists independently of our will and that it will continue to exist long after we are gone. It is the father who at this point unfolds the themes that Malraux developed in his previous novels and, later, presented in his critical writing on art: namely, the effect on man of his alienation in the universe and the conception of art as a rectification of the absence of order in the world. Man is aware that the world dwarfs him in size and reduces him to insignificance, and he wishes it could be made to fit within the human frame of reference. When he tries to rebuild the world, he does it invariably in terms of the human scale. Then Vincent's father formulates what is virtually the aesthetic philosophy Malraux holds. Art, he says, seems to be a means of rectifying the alien and often inimical world that man confronts, a way of rising above the human condition. It is basically a method for the humanization of the world around us. This is the unique contribution art makes to human culture and its supreme virtue is that it enables men to rise above the world of fatality, and thus break out of the trap of nihilism.

If the father stands for one pole of thought, the humanist ethic that affirms its belief in transcendence achieved through great works of art, Möllberg represents the nihilist extreme. He considers the idea of destiny Vincent's father had broached and declares that it leads to the question whether we can attach any definite meaning to the nature of man. Is it possible, he asks, from the bewildering variety of faiths men embraced in the past, the myths they have fashioned and then abandoned, the philosophical perspectives they believed would reveal the ultimate truth of being, to single out a factor that will be accepted as valid throughout the vicissitudes of history, on which one can then erect one's conception of man? The mental structure changes in the course of time and man has to find some way of not being defeated in his encounter with death. Conceiving of himself as mortal, man was driven by necessity to struggle against the oblivion that death imposes, and the idea of dualism emerged. The notion of the soul was devised to insure the validity of the belief in immortality. After thousands of years of spiritual travail, mankind finally invented the immortal soul. This was the consoling faith man required in order to make it possible for him to survive. According to Möllberg, it is the task of history to lend a pattern of meaning to the human pilgrimage. He dwells on the singular paradox of man in relation to the sphinx of history. Thought is the source of man's grandeur but it is also the Pandora's box which, when opened, reveals the doom of nihilism, the vision of ultimate nothingness. Möllberg concludes by saying that if civilizations rise and fall in order at the end to hurl men into the gulf of nonbeing, then the culture that flourishes richly for a few centuries matters not at all, for man is at the mercy of chance and "the world consists of oblivion."[16]

This marks the climax of the colloquium: the startling announcement that man is no more than a chance element in Nature and that the world is headed for oblivion. Möllberg has brought into the open the suicidal logic that if life is a part of death, a haphazard throw of the genetic dice in the biological gamble of the universe, then absurdity, which is fittingly symbolized by an eternity of oblivion, triumphs. History is not even a nightmare: it is but a whirl of shadows in the void. As Möllberg points out, though it is possible to conceive the idea of the everlastingness of the race of man, "it's an everlastingness in nothingness" (p. 110). Everyone at the colloquium feels that his existence has been put on trial by this spoken manifesto of nihilism. Möllberg completely strips man of his illusions. He argues, in opposition to the theme eloquently upheld by Vincent's father, that fundamental man is a myth. Oblivion consumes the intellectual just as it does the peasant and the clown. Man is essentially an animal, however much he may try to gloss over his zoological origins. The only thing all men have in common is "sleeping, when they sleep without dreaming —and being dead" (p. 111). Man's essence, despite all his heroic striving to achieve lasting fame in a lifetime, is, alas, perishable.

Count Rabaud maintains that something eternal lives in thinking man, a godlike quality that lies in his "ability to call the world in question" (p. 112). Möllberg is not impressed by this rejoinder. He asserts that Sisyphus, too, was eternal. It was Africa that had

---

[16] Malraux, *The Walnut Trees of Altenburg,* p. 107.

unveiled for Möllberg the blank nihilating face of nada. He learned the truth about man by studying ant hills. That is the upshot of the discussion of the mysteries of man's fate, a discussion that took place at a time when Europe had not been ravaged by war for a period of forty years.

The section that dealt with the colloquium is followed, approximately a year later, by a memorable account of the father's experience in the First World War. On June 11, 1915, he is stationed with the German army on the Vistula front, assigned to a section of the Secret Service. He is later shifted to work with Professor Hoffman, who has perfected the use of gas as a lethal instrument of chemical warfare. The extraordinary virtue of the latest gas he has invented is that it is capable of poisoning the enemy without their being aware of the danger. The Professor warmly defends his invention on the ground that Germany has no other choice. Besides, victory won in this manner will prevent the loss of hundreds of thousands of soldiers. This part of the novel continues, as it were, the colloquium on the nature of man, though it is conducted in a different environment and under radically different circumstances. The Professor argues that if the subject is logically examined, the use of gas is unquestionably "the most humane method of warfare" (p. 135). Here is an intellectual of a peculiar kind, infected with his own species of madness. All this leads up to the description of the preparations for the gas attack. The scene builds up a mood of dramatic suspense: men waiting for death to strike unexpectedly and in wholesale fashion. The father keeps nervously glancing at his watch as he views the Russian lines from the observation post; he sees the high clouds overhead, a flight of birds sweeping down toward the Vistula, and hears the voices of men, "the only species that has learnt—and learnt so badly—that it can die" (p. 152).

The gas moves on steadily toward the Russian trenches, which are silent. The Russian guns start firing furiously at the advancing mass of deadly gas, but then the artillery suddenly stops. The first-line infantry troops march forward into action, but the valley is strangely silent. The father sees some German soldiers coming back through the barbed wire, bearing white spots on their shoulders. They are running through a lunar landscape, past black and slimy trees, through dead grass and withered leaves. As they come closer, the father realizes what has happened. Each German soldier is carrying the stricken body of a Russian. The sight of the Russians lying gassed in the trenches was too much for the German infantrymen to bear. Military discipline broke down and the feeling of compassion, of brotherhood, asserted itself. The father knows that it was not pity that moved the German troops to react in this way but something deeper—an archetypal urge, a sense of empathy, that enabled them to identify themselves with the pain and suffering of the victims. Suddenly the father recaptured the memory of Altenburg, for opposite him there were some clusters of walnut trees. Out of this encounter with the horror of gas-inflicted death is born the sense of fraternal solidarity that provides an answer to the nihilism of Möllberg.

The final section completes the cycle by returning us to Chartres Camp and to the son who is writing about his father's adventures. Vincent Berger continues to wonder "what holds out against the spell of nothingness" (p. 189). What sustains these French captives so that they can raise their voices in song? This is the mystery that absorbs him: how account for the nobility in man that they do not know exists within themselves. The interior dialogue then comes to an end.

3. CODA

The theme of nihilism sounded in *The Walnut Trees of Altenburg* is not negated; it is transcended.[17] The continuity of life is affirmed; even in the inferno of the gas attack the men instinctively

---

[17] See the chapter "Malraux and the Myth of Violence," in Charles I. Glicksberg, *The Tragic Vision in Twentieth-Century Literature* (Carbondale, Ill.: Southern Illinois University Press, 1963), pp. 137–47; and the chapter "The Discovery of Transcendence in *Les Noyers de l'Altenburg*," in Thomas Jefferson Kline, *André Malraux and the Metamorphosis of Death* (New York and London: Columbia University Press, 1973), pp. 121–56. "The walnut trees give the work its title because they constitute the only symbol which incorporates the three major discoveries of the novel: the discovery of Art as a humanization of the world, the possibility of harmony between man and the world, and the discovery of a notion on which one can found a concept of man." *Idem.*, pp. 145–46.

feel that the senselessness of death must be defeated. Malraux does not allow total meaninglessness to triumph. The history of the race, its culture, its works of art—all testify to the creative power of man and his ability to question the character of existence. In thus framing questions and formulating his own speculative, never definitive, answers, man revolts against the absurdity of the human condition. It is through the energies and endeavors of art that he asserts his own conception of destiny. He knows, of course, that these energies, incarnate in the forms of art that have lasted through the ages have no coercive power over fate, time, and death; these remain untouched, but his attitude toward them undergoes a progressive qualitative change. Malraux, the novelist, offers no solution. The burden of the unintelligible mystery is not lifted even when, as in *Man's Fate,* Malraux succeeds in giving the tragic vision effective dramatic embodiment.[18] For how viable and enduring are the existential values to which man gives birth and to which he swears allegiance? What does he achieve, finally, by confronting his fate with undaunted courage? "By asserting his humanity against the void what does he assert? These questions remain to trouble Malraux.... But perhaps the most specific and immediate contribution of existentialist humanism, and of Malraux's in particular, is to give us a more profound and dramatic sense of human reality in the face of the void."[19]

In *The Walnut Trees of Altenburg,* as in *Man's Fate,* the genius of darkness makes its presence felt, but it is not encountered with a feeling of nihilistic fatalism; it is challenged. The individual human soul pits its will against the adamantine indifference of

[18] William Righter, *The Rhetorical Hero* (London: Routledge & Kegan Paul, 1964), p. 74. Righter makes the point that "the exaltation of man does not lessen the tragedy of man, it deepens it—the greater the creature the more monstrous the fact of his fall." *Ibid.,* p. 78.

[19] Wayne C. Booth, *The Rhetoric of Fiction* (Chicago: The University of Chicago Press, 1961), p. 299. C. L. Sulzberger, an American journalist writing from Paris, pens a portrait of Malraux that bears no trace of the darkly brooding nihilist, the writer whose work is instinct with "negative" passions. He is cited as an inspiring example of "the committed" writer. The intellectuals among the younger generation in France are convinced that it is their duty to become "engaged" in world affairs. Though there are a few young revolutionists who are willing to fight for their ideas, the young generation cannot boast of many who "really put their

the world. It is in the experience of reaching out toward com-munion—in the apocalyptic scene during the gas attack, when the German soldiers disobey military orders and rush to the aid of the stricken victims—that Malraux's protagonist achieves tran-scendence of self. He does not throw off his finiteness or shut out the grievous knowledge of his mortal lot, but since he shares his fate with other men, he is no longer alone and no longer tormented by a derisive awareness of the futility of all effort. By his readiness to sacrifice his life for that which is more precious than life itself, he conquers his fear of death. That is how the dialectic of nihilism is resolved. Malraux's fiction confirms the correctness of one critic's contention that "most so-called nihilistic works are . . . really works of active protest or even of affirmation."[20]

money where their mouth is and none can equal Malraux's splendid record." (C. L. Sulzberger, "Europe: The Long View," The *New York Times,* January 21, 1972). David Wilkinson, however, declares that Malraux "was always a spiritual fascist, or at least a nihilist: he has never surpassed his initial perception of the world's absurdity, for all his principal characters are nihilists and all their lives are empty cycles of struggle and death. . . ." David Wilkinson, *Malraux: An Essay in Political Criticism* (Cambridge, Mass.: Harvard University Press, 1967), p. 120n.
[20] Wayne C. Booth, *The Rhetoric of Fiction,* p. 299.

10

Albert Camus:
From Nihilism to Revolt

Camus simply lived through and documented what Nietzsche saw looming up in the twentieth century: namely, the nihilism which would result while the technological world adapted to its horrifying discovery that God was very, very dead, and that there was no ultimate and absolute meaning to either human life or the universe: they simply *were*.[1]

There is nothing more incontestable than the fact that Meursault, in certain of his aspects, embodies that temptation toward an active nihilism and impersonality which constitutes, among others, one of the permanent characteristics of Camus's work.[2]

Camus had never expressed any nihilistic point of view as being his own. On the contrary, from the outset his explicit intention had been to counteract in his works what he felt were dangerous nihilistic tendencies of the twentieth century.[3]

An equally impressive example of the dialectic that transforms a philosophy of the absurd into a call for rebellion against the nihilist imperative is to be found in the career of Albert Camus. Like Malraux but in a spirit of inquiry characteristically his own, a spirit that sought to define with lucidity the complex process

---

[1] Thomas Hanna, *Bodies in Revolt* (New York and Chicago: Holt, Rinehart and Winston, 1970), p. 193.
[2] Roger Quilliot, *The Sea and Prisons,* trans. Emmet Parker (University, Ala.: The University of Alabama Press, 1970), p. 79.
[3] Emmet Parker, *Albert Camus* (Madison and Milwaukee: The University of Wisconsin Press, 1965), p. 109.

whereby nihilism could be transcended without necessitating the abandonment of the myth of the absurd, Camus set out on a quest for meaning that would justify the pilgrimage of man on earth. Though his explorations at the beginning of his quest led him to adopt nihilistic conclusions, he was never happy in or reconciled to his role as prophet of the absurd. His so-called nihilistic works— *The Stranger, The Myth of Sisyphus, Caligula,* and *The Misunderstanding*—are protests against the fate of meaninglessness. Camus's development as a writer strikingly illustrates the paradox that nihilism carries within it the seeds of its own dissolution. If the writer carries despair to its utmost limit, he is, in effect, trying to go beyond it. As Camus declared in an essay published in 1950: "A literature of despair is a contradiction in terms."[4] And he went on to say: "In the darkest depths of our nihilism I have sought only for the means to transcend nihilism."[5]

This furnishes the most rewarding clue to his life and work. He would be the resolute spokesman of the truth, but the truth he beheld entailed the elmination of the absolutes of the past. Mankind would have to give up the old, comforting illusions. There was no ideal of perfection to pursue, no divinely ordained destiny to fulfill. Not that rationalism could supplant the repudiated religious faith. The blood-soaked history of the twentieth century demolished the quaint fiction that man was preeminently a rational creature. The rise of Fascism and the horrors of Belsen and Auschwitz demonstrated the inhumanity of man to man. The outbreak of the Second World War deepened Camus's sense of the irremediable absurdity of life. The logic of the situation was such that no sensitive mind could bear it. If life is inescapably absurd, then literature is certainly an indefensible preoccupation. Camus did not yield to a mood of despair. He made this revealing entry in his notebook: "we can despair of the meaning of life in general, but not of the particular forms it takes; we can

[4] John Cruickshank, *Albert Camus and the Literature of Revolt* (London and New York: Oxford University Press, 1950), p. 3.
[5] *Ibid.,* p. 3.

despair of existence, for we have no power over it, but not of history, where the individual can do everything."[6]

Death renders life absurd and forces many people to decide that life is not worth living. What justification, however, is there for suicide? There is, to be sure, a close connection between the feeling of the absurd and the decision to commit suicide. But what conceivable advantage can the suicide derive from his desperate act? For whatever decision his mind arrives at, the body prefers to go on living. Camus states: "The body's judgment is as good as the mind's, and the body shrinks from annihilation."[7] In his youth in Algiers, Camus had learned to love the earth, the light and heat of the sun, the flesh. If he fears death, it is because of the overwhelming strength of his will to live.

The perception of the absurd effects a revolution in the ordered continuity of time. Once hope lies shattered, the future ceases to entice man. There is only the fugitive, problematical present. The mind, having broken out of its biological bondage, beholds Nature bare, without the mediation of culture and art. Always man confronts the absolute certainty of death, and it is out of this confrontation that he becomes aware of the ubiquitous absurd.

The Absurd must be accepted even when one rebels against it. Man must not surrender his dignity and pride before these unknown and irrational powers. His only trustworthy frame of reference is the earth, the world of sensory experience; there is nothing beyond. What lies outside the range of awareness cannot become the legitimate object of faith. Man can understand and believe only in what is open to his senses. The world does not lend itself to his craving for unity. The more clearly he perceives

---

[6] Albert Camus, *Notebooks, 1935–1943,* trans. Philip Thody (New York: Alfred A. Knopf, 1963), pp. 151–52. Rayner Heppenstall places Camus in the tradition of romantic pessimism represented by Baudelaire, Rimbaud, and others. He points out that Camus's heroes denounce bitterly the fact of death. "They have swallowed their disappointment about Father Christmas and are reconciled to the way babies are born, but the fact of death sticks in their throats." *The Fourfold Tradition* (London: Barie and Rockliff, 1961), pp. 197–98.

[7] Albert Camus, *The Myth of Sisyphus,* trans. Justin O'Brien (New York: Vintage Books, 1955), p. 6.

the truth of the Absurd, the more thoroughly is he committed to an ethic of revolt.

The Stranger is the dramatic embodiment of the myth of the absurd. Its absurdist hero faces a reality that his reason cannot comprehend. Time is an illusion. Death marks the end of the human story. The protagonist is unable to derive any meaning from the universe. He has come to the realization that success, courage, sacrifice, devotion to duty are meaningless terms. All men are sentenced to die: therefore life is unutterably absurd. Passive, taciturn, indifferent toward all things, Meursault endures the tedium of existence. He is without the spur of ambition and he is incapable of love. The fate that awaits him, as it waits for all of us—this constitutes his chief obsession, though he does not take the trouble to philosophize about it. A creature of settled routine, he is upset by nothing except the heat of the sun. He lives alone. The death of his mother draws no tears from him. He is too honest with himself to pretend to feelings of grief that he does not have. As far as he is concerned, nothing really matters much, if at all. After all, he and his mother had nothing in common. Why should he grieve? Meursault is a loner; he keeps for the most part to himself. For him, the only realities that count are visceral sensations: the smoking of a cigarette, sleep, sex.

He sleeps with Márie and is willing to marry her (it is she who raises the issue), but he does not love her and frankly admits that he does not. It is his dogged devotion to the truth that others— the judge, the lawyer who defends him, the prosecuting attorney— find so disconcerting and this trait of character brings about his undoing at the trial. He is not impressed by the sound of moral rhetoric or religious appeals. It is his settled conviction that nothing is of any importance. He does not care one way or the other if he is put in charge of the Paris branch that the owner of the firm he is working for plans to establish. He would prefer to remain where he is. There is no such thing, he is convinced, as a change of life; "one life was as good as another, and my present one suited me quite well."[8]

[8] Albert Camus, *The Stranger*, trans. Stuart Gilbert (New York: Vintage Books, 1954), p. 52.

Meursault's encounter with the Arab on the beach illustrates the intrusion of the absurd element of contingency; the sun beats down on the sand with blinding heat, and Meursault feels befuddled. He could have turned back and nothing would have happened, but he steps forward, the Arab draws his knife, the blade of which glints in the sunlight. At this moment Meursault pulls the trigger of the gun he happens to be carrying (it is not his) and then, unaccountably, fires more shots into the inert body of the Arab. His behavior at the funeral of his mother has, of course, no bearing on his case in court, but it is the one thing that leads to his being sentenced to death. The efforts of the magistrate to convert him to religion produce no results. Meursault cannot follow the magistrate's evangelical discourse; he is tired of all this talk. When the question is put to him, he replies that he does not believe in God. The magistrate indignantly asks him if he wants his life to have no meaning, and Meursault reflects ironically: "Really I couldn't see how my wishes came into it . . ." (p. 86).

We see him in his cell, this absurdist anti-hero, and observe how he grows used to the routine of life in jail. He loses his craving for smoking. His chief problem is how to kill time, how to prevent the onset of boredom. At the trial he behaves with his usual directness, hiding nothing. He would have liked to explain that he had never been able to regret anything in his life. "I've always been far too much absorbed in the present moment, or the immediate future, to think back" (p. 127). He is resigned to death (he is to be beheaded for his crime) and the oblivion to which it will consign him. After death there is only an eternity of nothingness. The only life he craves is life here on earth. Only the living could be ranked among the privileged. Once he has vented his rage on the priest who wishes to minister to his spiritual needs he is emptied of hope. Gazing up at the sky, he "laid his heart open to the benign indifference of the universe" (p. 154). Thus, in dying bereft of illusion, he enacts the fate of mankind, all of whom are condemned to die.

Just as *The Stranger* underlines the futility of all striving, so *The Myth of Sisyphus* constitutes the manifesto of the absurd. It declares that religious faith is powerless to save the race of man. Salvation to be achieved through the instrumentality of reason or fullness of knowledge—that, too, is compounded of illusion. The human quest for ultimate meaning is foredoomed to defeat. The questions man raises are unanswerable. No explanation furnished by the limited intellect can penetrate the heart of the cosmic mystery. The feeling of the absurd originates and grows in the mind of man, but it emerges as the result of his interrogation of the universe. His steady awareness of the absurd does not lead him to embrace an ethic of renunciation. He cannot behold this vision of the void without changing his whole attitude toward life. It conditions everything he does and drives him at the same time to break out of this intolerable bondage. Unreconciled to this fate of the absurd, he adopts the only attitude compatible with his human pride, an attitude of "defiance."[9]

It was with the tragedy rather then the comedy of the absurd that Camus was concerned. Whereas later dramatists of the absurd like Samuel Beckett, Adamov, and Ionesco freely utilized comic devices that would generate black humor—inane dialogue, pratfalls, vaudevillian stunts, burlesque, caricature, farce—Camus remained strictly within the orbit of tragedy. In *Caligula* and *The Misunderstanding,* he presents protagonists who look the Medusa squarely in the face; they will not turn aside from their calamitous fate. Caligula is no hater of mankind, but he is bent on depriving his people of their opiate illusions. He abhors their weak-kneed spirit of resignation, their acceptance of the outrageous conditions life imposes on them. In trying to teach them the meaning of nothingness, he uses a "nihilist logic in which the classic demonstration of the Absurd is rigorously triumphant."[10] He has discovered a truth, namely, that death exists, which renders all of human existence meaningless. He will teach the world that mankind is unimportant. "And the play on one level is a demonstration of Caligula's capricious madness in denying both the value of human life and the world."[11] *Caligula* carries the nihilist theme to an extreme.

[9] Camus, *The Myth of Sisyphus,* p. 41.
[10] Quilliot, *The Sea and Prisons,* p. 51.
[11] Robert Emmet Jones, *The Alienated Heroes in Modern French Drama* (Athens, Ga.: University of Georgia Press, 1962), p. 112.

Camus was not satisfied to reiterate that life is a thing of sound and fury, signifying nothing. Even if one feels deeply the pervasive and ultimate absurdity of existence, he still finds that some things are infinitely precious—the experience of love, the privilege of being alive, the power man possesses of protesting against the ignominy of death. Life is its own unarguable and supreme value. It is Camus's signal merit that he has raised these metaphysical questions anew and sought his answers within a rational rather than supernatural context.

Camus, of course, recognizes that if life is absurd, then the creative quest is also absurd. The artist working in a universe of the absurd realizes that he knows naught and is tempted to fall into silence. He decides nevertheless to speak out, to embody his tragic vision which, by affirming the unique value of life, repudiates the nihilism on which it is based. The artist goes beyond the plane of the personal and the constriction of the absurd. His imposition of order on the chaotic flux and superfetation of the universe constitutes a revolt: the upsurge of creativity.

Camus in his notebooks recorded "the fact that we are suffering from nihilism,"[12] but he never surrendered to the spirit of nihilism. For him, an attitude of negation did not presuppose an abdication of the moral sense. Negation represented the deliberate choice of the man who is without God. In his preliminary reflections on the ideas that were eventually incorporated in *The Plague*, Camus conceived of "a sort of arduous progress toward a sanctity of negation—a heroism without God—man alone, in short" (p. 20). In October 1945 he penned this thought on the aesthetics of revolt:

> Impossibility for man to despair utterly. Conclusion: any literature of despair represents but an extreme case and not the most significant. The remarkable thing in man is not that he despairs, but that he overcomes or forgets despair. A literature of despair will never be universal. (p. 112)

Camus did not remain a prisoner in the closed universe of the absurd; it was a stage he had to pass through and rise above. A

[12] Albert Camus, *Notebooks, 1942-1951*, trans. Justin O'Brien (New York: Alfred A. Knopf, 1965), p. 15.

humanist by conviction, he did not choose the role of negation; it was thrust upon him. In *The Rebel* as in *The Plague*, Camus promulgates a distinctively humanist philosophy of revolt. Man must create his own values and make them prevail. By affirming his faith in a humanist ethic, Camus managed to halt the advance of the absurd. Thody declares: "From being a description of man's fate in a world deprived of value and significance, Camus's work becomes after 1945 a study and exploration, no longer of the nihilism of the absurd, but of the problems of action and of the service of humanity."[13] Camus is convinced that radical nihilism can never be put into action. Camus writes that "I have sought only reasons to transcend our darkest nihilism."[14] Basic to his humanist outlook is the belief that man is the measure of all things. He warns against the danger of transforming history into an absolute.

There was no abrupt break between Camus, the contemplative nihilist, and Camus, the "committed" writer. Even when he was elaborating the myth of the absurd in *The Stranger*, he did not withdraw from participation in the social and political struggles of his time. He spoke out boldly in his journalistic work, which deals with the Algerian revolt, the Spanish Civil War, the question of Communism. From the beginning of his career he took his responsibility seriously, but "commitment" did not mean for him what it meant for Sartre. He left the Communist Party when he found that it followed a Machiavellian policy of expediency in formulating its ideological principles. He could not remain a supporter of nihilism. One critic, who has made a study of Camus's journalistic contributions, warmly defends Camus against the blanket charge of nihilism.

> The labels "pessimistic" and "nihilistic" were incorrectly applied to these writings [namely *The Myth of Sisyphus, Caligula,* and *The Stranger*] and to their author when the works first appeared, and they have persisted in the criticism of nearly all of Camus's writing to the present day.[15]

[13] Philip Thody, *Albert Camus* (London: Hamish Hamilton, 1957), p. 27.
[14] Albert Camus, *Lyrical and Critical Essays,* ed. Philip Thody, trans. Ellen Conroy Kennedy (New York: Alfred A. Knopf, 1969), p. 160.
[15] Parker, *Albert Camus,* p. xiv.

After his comparatively short period of involvement with the nihilism of the absurd, Camus composed *The Plague,* which belongs to the literature of revolt. It rejects the abstract ethical commandments of the past. Dr. Bernard Rieux devotes himself selflessly to the treatment of the patients stricken by the plague in the town of Oran. He does all he can to alleviate the suffering of the victims. He does not know why the plague has broken out. He cannot accept the priest's explanation that it serves some mysterious purpose of God. But why, if he does not believe in God, does the doctor labor so self-sacrificingly to combat the ravages of the plague? Dr. Rieux replies "that if he believed in an all-powerful God he would cease curing the sick and leave that to Him. But no one in the world believed in a God of that sort. . . ."[16] Instead of throwing himself on the mercy of Providence, he fights against creation. He cannot resign himself to seeing people die. His reasoning is cogent and challenging:

> since the order of the world is shaped by death, mightn't it be better for God if we refuse to believe in Him and struggle with all our might against death, without raising our eyes toward Heaven where He sits in silence. (pp. 117–18)

Tarrou, too, is opposed to any movement which for any reason justifies the act of putting people to death. He is content to let others have the honor of directing the course of history. He will not become a legalized murderer. But since the plague exists and is spreading, he will resist the power of the pestilence. Like Dr. Rieux, he does not believe in God, and yet he desires strongly to become a saint. Camus asks: "Can one be a saint without God?" (p. 230). It is Rieux, the narrator, who is allowed to have the last word. He exemplifies the secular saint in that he has always taken the side of the victims, without presuming to judge them; he has endeavored "to share with his fellow citizens the only certitudes they had in common—love, exile, and suffering" (p. 272). He is transcending not only nihilism but the narrow boundaries of the

---

[16] Albert Camus, *The Plague,* trans. Stuart Gilbert (New York: The Modern Library, 1948), p. 116.

self. He is acting in the name of humanity. Through his rebellion, the individual overcomes his alienation; he is no longer alone. He rebels, however obscurely, in behalf of higher values, he wants to remake the world in the image of justice. In refusing to submit to the power that sentences him to death, he engineers a metaphysical revolution.

> When the throne of God is overthrown, the rebel realizes that it is now his own responsibility to create the justice, order and unity that he sought in vain within his own condition and, in this way, to justify the fall of God.[17]

In *The Rebel* Camus traces the inception and insidious growth of nihilism. He reveals its limitations and its dangers. "Nihilism is not only despair and negation, but above all the desire to despair and to negate" (pp. 52-53). Its final product is an inhuman logic. Once man assumes that he can become God he is at liberty, if he has the power, to act irresponsibly; there is nothing to stop him from engaging in crime. If the universe is absurd, then everything is permitted. Nothing is sacred or forbidden. The murderer is as justified in his behavior as the saint. Good and evil are but relative terms. If mass murders have taken place with impunity in our time, "this is because of the indifference to life which is the. mark of nihilism" (p. 14). Camus is speaking in this connection of the moral nihilism which, applied recklessly to the realm of politics, is transformed into an unconscionable and deadly will to power. The Nazis were thoroughgoing nihilists who gave vent to their passion for an amoral life of action. Success was its own justification. The history of contemporary nihilism is thus "nothing but a prolonged endeavour to give order, by human forces alone and simply by force, to a history no longer endowed with order" (pp. 190-91).

Camus resolutely opposed the type of nihilism, regardless of the political banner it flaunted, that struggled to achieve absolute power, for this is the type of nihilism dedicated to Caesarism,

---

[17] Albert Camus, *The Rebel,* trans. Anthony Bower (New York: Alfred A. Knopf, 1954), p. 31.

which ushers in a reign of inhumanity. If he denies the existence of God, he also denies the validity of the argument that there is no appeal beyond history. It is this pragmatic reliance on the verdict of history that is essentially nihilistic in character. Dedicated to life, the rebel sets himself a limited goal. "All of us, among the ruins, are preparing a renaissance beyond the limits of nihilism" (p. 272).

Even during the painful years of the Occupation, Camus never lost his faith in justice, the life of the spirit, the power of the truth. Though the truth is at times difficult to ascertain, the lie can easily be detected. In *Letters to a German Friend,* published in 1943 and 1944, he defends the ideal of justice above the claims of patriotism. He tells his German friend: "Man is that force which ultimately cancels all tyrants and gods. He is the force of evidence. . . . If nothing has any meaning, you would be right. But there is something that still has a meaning."[18] Camus here takes his stand against nihilism, upholding the principle of the unity of mankind and the viability of the European cultural tradition. He admits that, like his German friend, he had once believed that the world was devoid of ultimate meaning, and he still thinks so. But what conclusions is one warranted in drawing from this premise? Does it imply that nothing matters and that good and evil are without distinction? According to the logic of nihilism, the will to power becomes the sole touchstone of morality. Camus cherished a radically different body of values. It seems to him "that man must exalt justice in order to fight against injustice, create happiness in order to protest against the universe of unhappiness" (p. 28).

Camus is clearly no nihilist, even though he has not given up his belief that the universe is devoid of ultimate meaning.

> I continue to believe that this world has no ultimate meaning. But I know that something in it has meaning and that is man, because he is the only creature to insist on having one. This world has at least the truth of man, and our task is to provide its justification against fate itself. And it has no justification but man; hence he must be saved if we want to save the idea we have of life. (p. 28)

[18] Albert Camus, *Resistance, Rebellion, and Death,* trans. Justin O'Brien (New York: Alfred A. Knopf, 1961), p. 14.

Camus knew that though man is nothing vis-à-vis the universe, he is a nothing endowed with conscience and the indomitable courage, which is the mark of his greatness, to rise above the human condition. As for the charge that he was a nihilist, a charge preferred by both Christian and Marxist critics, Camus maintained that there was no incompatibility between a negative philosophy and a positive morality grounded in justice.

> If the epoch has suffered from nihilism, we cannot remain ignorant of nihilism and still achieve the moral code we need. No, everything is not summed up in negation and absurdity. We know this. But we must first posit negation and absurdity because they are what our generation had encountered and what we must take into account. (p. 59)

11

Sartre: From Nausea to Communism

There are two fundamental reactions to *Angst:* we can say that the realization of man's insignificance in the universe can be met by a kind of despairful defiance. I may be insignificant, and my life a useless passion, but at least I can cock a snook at the whole show and prove the independence of my mind, my consciousness. Life obviously has no meaning, but let us pretend that it has. This pretence will at any rate give the individual a sense of responsibility: he can prove that he is a law unto himself, and he can even enter into agreement with his fellow-men about certain lines of conduct which, in this situation, they should all adopt. He is free to do this, and his freedom thus grows into a sense of responsibility. This is Sartre's doctrine.[1]

In reply to the question, "What are we saved by?", Sartre answered: "By nothing. There is no salvation anywhere. The idea of salvation implies the idea of an absolute. For forty years I was conscripted by the absolute, the neurosis. The absolute is gone."[2]

Existentialism is not atheist in the sense that it would exhaust itself in demonstrations of the non-existence of God. It declares, rather, that even if God existed, that would make no difference from its point of view. Not that we believe God does exist, but we think that the real problem is not that of His existence; what man needs is to find himself again and to understand that nothing can save him from himself, not even a valid proof of the existence of God.[3]

Nihilism, "the philosophical disease of our time," is a condition of despair "that overcomes man whenever he looks into the

[1] Herbert Read, *Anarchy and Order* (London: Faber and Faber, 1954), p. 142.
[2] Quoted from an interview in *Encounter,* June 1964, in Anthony Manser, *Sartre* (London: The Athlone Press, 1966), p. 166.
[3] Jean-Paul Sartre, *Existentialism and Humanism,* trans. Philip Mairet (London: Methuen & Co., 1949), p. 56.

abyss of nothingness and realizes his own insignificance."[4] One who believes in the fundamental truth of this doctrine is a nihilist. Sartre, however, has denied that existentialism can be categorized as nihilist in character. His early work did betray some nihilist sentiments. Salvation, damnation, God, immortality—Sartre rejected such transcendental abstractions. There is neither heaven nor hell. The universe that man inhabits is alien to his purpose and indifferent to his needs. Once God created him, as Orestes defiantly tells Zeus in *The Flies,* He ceased to have power over him. The one thing that neither God nor Nature can take away from him is his freedom of choice.

But nihilism is not, as we have shown, a fixed category; it is a dialectical process that seeks to go beyond itself. The continuing conflict between nothingness and the Absolute, between nihilism and faith in redemptive action in the realm of history, is to be found in the fiction of Malraux as well as the writing of an atheist like Sartre. If the world is denuded of meaning, if man as he confronts an incomprehensible and therefore absurd universe is reduced to a single cry, frenetic or forlorn, of negation, then Nothingness is elevated to the height of the Absolute. For Sartre God is dead. Sartre asserts that he no longer suffers because of God's absence. As a youth he needed God and found Him "without realizing that I was seeking Him. Failing to take root in my heart, He vegetated in me for a while, then He died."[5]

God died in him, but his need for the Absolute persisted. This is the dilemma he faced: if there are no a priori essences, if existence is the primary datum, then the reasons for human existence, if there are any such, lie beyond the reach of cognition. There is no Providence that directs the pilgrimage of man, no rational principles that can explain or justify it. Man is the sole author of history. He must choose both his goal and the means of realizing it; the responsibility for choosing his life-project rests upon himself alone. He can consult no oracle who will tell him whether what he proposes to do is fundamentally right and will turn out well. He must act

[4] Read, *Anarchy and Order,* p. 150.
[5] Jean-Paul Sartre, *The Words,* trans. Bernard Frechtman (New York: George Braziller, 1964), p. 120.

in full knowledge of the possibility of falling into grievous error, of failing to reach his intended goal, or of selecting the wrong goal. He can invoke no cosmic teleological law to sustain him in his brief march—whither bound?—through time. He is here on earth, at this cross-road of history, filled with a sense of astonishment that he should be here at all. All this provides the philosophical underpinning for the experience of "nausea."

The absurdity of the world triggers the reaction Sartre describes as nausea. The individual is thrust at birth into a world in which he feels estranged. Both the religious and nonreligious existentialists look upon human existence as "absurd." As Kathleen Nott phrases it: "We are contingent or accidental beings and there is no reason why we should be—or for that matter why anything else should be or come into existence."[6] It is man, the time-binding animal, who imposes value on a world that is alien to his desires and void of purpose. This is the character of the human condition, which gives rise to the nihilistic myth of the absurd, but the existentialist does not abjectly succumb to this myth; he defeats it by devoting himself to his freely chosen project. Thus both Camus and Sartre transform the myth of the absurd into a humanist ethic that emphasizes the central importance of individual moral responsibility. Each individual must commit himself to a life of action in cooperation with his fellow man even though the world remains unintelligible. It is this freedom to choose that constitutes his dignity as a man.

In Sartre's existentialist novels and plays, however, it is the absurdity of existence that is stressed, the ineffectuality of both thought and action. That is what Roquentin, the Sartrean hero in *Nausea,* feels: the tastelessness of existence, the inchoate and incomprehensible quality of experience in relation to things. The objects he encounters seem strange, superfluous, and yet obtrusive. There is no reason why they should exist at all; they do not form part of a necessary pattern. In this phantasmagoria of the absurd, not even consciousness can make the encounter with

---

[6] Kathleen Nott, *Philosophy and Human Nature* (New York: New York University Press, 1971), p. 106.

"nausea" endurable. The metaphysical vertigo that attacks Roquentin is caused by his awareness that man is a useless passion. He suffers because he has no destiny to fulfill, he is bound by no sense of social commitment, and he is unable to establish personal relationships. He is convinced that there are no universal truths and no categorical imperatives.

Existentialism may represent, as Sartre argues, a type of humanism, but nihilism and humanism, though they differ in many essentials, have a number of traits in common. Certainly *Nausea* (1938), Sartre's first novel, offers a good example of the existentialist version of nihilism. In telling the story of Roquentin, Sartre brings to light the spiritual conflicts of an age of unfaith. A novel based on a diary, it describes the severe inner crisis through which the protagonist is passing. He has undertaken the thankless task of preparing a historical study of the Marquis de Rollebon. While engaged in this exacting labor of scholarship, he comes to realize that he is living only vicariously, and decides to abandon it. The theme of nausea pervades the book.

The existentialist hero is determined not to delude himself; he avoids the guilt that is born of "bad faith." When he strives to be true to himself, however, he discovers that he has no self he can call his own. As his attenuated or nonexistent self confronts the world, it is stricken with an overwhelming sense of the absurdity of being in the world at all. In these moments of heightened awareness and relentless introspection, the Sartrean protagonist has to assure himself that he is not going insane. He sees himself changing as he perceives the mysterious and frightening otherness of objects. His state of mind grows progressively worse. Something is definitely wrong with him. He feels disoriented and depersonalized: for example, he is overcome by the uncanny strangeness of his hands. An unaccountable horror of existence assails him. He cannot make out what is wrong with him. He feels empty inside, and yet all around him in the town of Bouville, where he is doing research and writing his book, he meets solid, well-adjusted citizens with happy faces, who do not question the established order of things. Though he fights against this spiritual affliction, he finds himself becoming more and more alienated. His will has ceased to function. He is no longer in command of his actions. He is defenseless against the objects that invade his consciousness and take possession of him.

The novel analyzes the nature of this malady. "Nausea" attacks the protagonist at the oddest times, seizes upon him in the most unexpected places. It lies in wait for him, like a hidden foe. Before this condition overtook him he could escape from himself by going to a well-lighted café full of people,[7] but now "nausea" grips him even there. Unlike the epileptic seizures Dostoevski describes in *The Idiot,* this experience produces no ecstatic vision, no sublime epiphany, only a sensation of nonbeing so that he no longer knows where he is. He feels disembodied. The objects he beholds are disconnected from their familiar and reassuring *Gestalt*: a pair of suspenders stands out with disconcerting distinctness, apart from their wearer, and this is enough to bring on an attack of Nausea. He knows the Nausea is not inside of him. It is, he feels, somewhere outside of him. It is present everywhere around him. It merges with the wall and the café. The rest of the novel attempts to trace the root cause and define in dramatic terms the existential meaning of this numinous experience. Nausea is but another name for the myth of the absurd. Roquentin watches the men in the café playing cards, passing the time, whereas he knows that time cannot thus be disposed of. As the Nausea spreads and grows, he realizes that it is "at the bottom of *our* time,"[8] that, far from being new, it has been weighing him down for the past twenty years, only he stubbornly refused to acknowledge it.

Cut off from all in his environment that is reassuring, deprived by the experience of Nausea of the illusions that others regard as both necessary and true, Roquentin gazes with disgust at the portraits of the dignitaries of Bouville: their self-important bearing, their restricted horizon, their fussy devotion to the ideal of public service. They are sure of the present, sure of the recorded past,

[7] See the story, "A Clean, Well-Lighted Room," by Ernest Hemingway, for a pre-existentialist description of Nausea. Ernest Hemingway, *The Short Stories of Ernest Hemingway* (New York: The Modern Library, 1938), pp. 480–81.

[8] Jean-Paul Sartre, *Nausea,* trans. Lloyd Alexander (New York: New Directions, 1964), p. 33.

and confident of the direction in which the future is bound to move, whereas for him time is a trap. The past has faded like an old photograph; it is memory that is shadowy, phantasmal, perhaps fictional. His present self tries to revive and take possession of the memories of the past, but it cannot root itself in the fugitive present, and he is unable to return to the past. For him there is no avenue of escape. His past is a dream, a tissue of self-deception. He perceives that he has never been free. Things have simply happened to him. Each instant passes irrevocably and one can do nothing to arrest the inexorable flow of time. He seeks to extract the essence of each moment, trying to implant it alive permanently within himself, but always he is driven forward. Time is irreversible.

Roquentin represents the detached and rootless intellectual. He despises those who sink themselves in their occupational roles, those who bequeath their burden of tradition to the next generation, those who cling jealously to the past, those who believe, or profess to believe, that the passing years bring the ripened fruit of wisdom. It is all a downright lie. He is even more contemptuous of those who take refuge in general ideas. The only important truth to be grasped is that each person is headed toward death. This is the bitter, ineluctable truth the good citizen would vehemently deny: that he is utterly alone in the world, forever alienated from the past. Such a man flees from the knowledge that his intelligence is limited, imperfect, and that he inhabits a body that carries within it the seeds of corruption. It is Roquentin's constant awareness of this truth that accounts for his recurrent attacks of Nausea.

Nothing seems real in the world around him; anything can happen. He looks closely at his surroundings in order to make sure that the objects he beholds are what their names represent. Then he is overcome by the "sudden revelation that *things can be almost everything*—that they are not essentially stable, permanent, and immutable as we had believed."[9] Under his gaze, objects become strangely transformed, lose their identity, escape from the

[9] Claude-Edmonde Magny, "The Duplicity of Being," in *Sartre,* ed. Edith Kern (Englewood Cliffs, N.J.: Prentice-Hall, 1962), p. 24.

concept that tied them to a given name. Now Roquentin knows that "things" cannot be confined within their conceptual habitation; they are protean, ineffable, part of existence: "something absolutely gratuitous, totally contingent, which is there . . . because of a fundamental absurdity. . . ."[10] Roquentin experiences a feeling of revulsion, of sheer disgust, as he perceives that the world of things is not subject to necessity. He sees that "things are what they appear to be—and behind them . . . there is nothing."[11] His disgust turns into horror when he discovers "the capacity for indefinite, lawless proliferation which things carry within them. . . ."[12] Roquentin cannot halt the feverish flow of his thoughts. What does it mean to exist? He tries to keep from thinking, from the futile, interminable process of introspection. He seems to succeed in stopping the chain of associations called forth by the feeling that he exists, but then the mind resumes its useless inquisition: ". . . not to think—don't want to think . . . I think I don't want to think."[13]

Out of this compulsive game (is it only that?) of thought giving birth to thought, nothing positive emerges. This is the curse of consciousness: it can never stop. The self is thought in perpetual flight, a consciousness that is forever recoiling upon itself. Roquentin cannot arrest this unceasing St. Vitus dance of thought because the thought is himself. He is under the governance of the Cartesian *Cogito*. "I exist because I think . . . and I can't stop myself from thinking" (p. 135).

And it is consciousness that leads him to the realization that he is cut off from existence. That is the nature of the horror that takes possession of him: the thoughts that negate existence, the consciousness that reduces him to the volatile play of thought, the persistent need to feel that he exists. He continues to wrestle with the tormenting problem of what it means to exist. He cannot be, but must always inquire what it means to be; he must analyze his moods and state of mind, dissect the contents of consciousness,

[10] *Ibid.*, p. 25.
[11] Sartre, *Nausea,* p. 131.
[12] Magny, "The Duplicity of Being," p. 26.
[13] Sartre, *Nausea,* p. 135.

engage in solipsistic soliloquies. ". . . I exist, I think, therefore I am; I am because I think, why do I think?" (p. 137).

Such a process of inquisitional self-analysis can go on ad infinitum. It illustrates the basic difference between Sartre, the existentialist, and Kierkegaard, the knight of faith. The latter transcends the abstract; his thoughts and introspections flower into existential decisions; he transmutes the Absurd into a categorical affirmation of faith that leaps beyond the finite limits of reason. Roquentin, the Sartrean hero, can do nothing but question himself, with the result that he never lives. He hangs suspended over the gulf of nothingness; he cannot partake of the mystique of the irrational nor can he resign himself to the nihilism of the Absurd. He is the rationalist *par excellence* whose reasoning power, which he distrusts but, *faute de mieux,* nevertheless relies upon, paralyzes his capacity for action. Like a Narcissus who gazes fixedly at his own image in the water, scrutinizing every feature minutely, he watches every pulsation of thought, every flicker of consciousness. He is a peeping Tom of the intellect, a spectator who critically observes himself feeling, thinking, and reacting.

All things conspire to alienate Roquentin: making love, the ritual of sex, dancing, eating, and drinking. He cannot hide from himself the absurdity of existence. He believes that he is different from other people—the serious-minded folk, the Philistines—in that he knows that he exists; he knows what existence means; he knows that "really there is nothing, nothing, absolutely no reason for existing" (p. 151). He refuses to embrace the quasi-religion of humanism, but he has nothing to put in its place. There is no niche where he can fit in. He is aware that he is "de trop" (p. 164). He knows that he exists and that the world exists apart from him, but that is all. This knowledge makes no difference. The insight he has gained affords him no relief. At last he comprehends that the Nausea will not leave him; he will have to put up with it. Whereas before he had viewed existence conceptually, now it revealed itself nakedly; it ceased to be an abstract category: "it was the very paste of things . . ." (p. 171). He now beheld existence unveiled, denuded. He could never become one with it; he had no reason to be where he was or anywhere at all.

Sartre thus builds up the cumulative vision of the Absurd. The key to existence, he concluded, lay in this vision of the Absurd. Here was the source of his Nausea, the clue to the meaning or lack of meaning in his own life. This is the oppressive revelation that Nausea made possible. Existence is everywhere, but reason cannot explain this proliferation of forms of life that stubbornly wage their struggle to survive in the face of death. "Every existing thing is born without reason, prolongs itself out of weakness and dies by chance" (p. 180).

Roquentin finally leaves Bouville, but before leaving he questions this freedom with which he is burdened: "I am free: there is absolutely no more reason for living, all the ones I have tried have given way and I can't imagine any more of them" (p. 209). He is without energy, ambition, or hope. He knows that the Nausea will come back since it constitutes his normal condition. He knows, too, that man is completely alone in the universe. One day even the humanists will experience this terrible solitude of the self, this incurable malaise of alienation. Roquentin at the end finds that he has lost his selfhood. His "I" is stripped of reality. "The only real thing left in me is existence which feels it exists" (p. 227). He possesses nothing but consciousness, a consciousness of the world of things, a consciousness of consciousness, a consciousness that tells him that he is superfluous. He simply wants to be. Perhaps by writing a novel, by creating a work of art, he will be restored to being and cured of Nausea.

This novel indicates that Sartre was not satisfied with the nihilist principles on which his existentialism is based. He endeavored to work out an ethic, rooted in sincerity, that would compel each individual to face the truth of the situation he finds himself in, without seeking support from an established system of moral values. Since man is free, he is required at each instant to choose those values that will commit him to a given course of action. What happens as the result of his choice cannot be justified in terms of determinism, materialism, God, or the pressure of economic forces. No voice from on high, no external authority, can grant him a guarantee that he has chosen wisely. The approval of society offers no touchstone of value. Nor can he appeal to a set of moral

absolutes. Each choice is unique and unpredictable in its consequences. The individual makes his own free choice, and he has
no prior assurance that his choice will ultimately be justified. He
must live dangerously if he is not to fall into inauthenticity. He is
responsible to himself alone.

This challenging ethic is coupled with the belief, which is the
source of Nausea, that life is contingent, that no one at birth is
invested with the right to exist. Life is as much a matter of genetic
hazard as the direction in which dust particles are borne by the wind
through the atmosphere. The only thing that binds men together
is the human condition, their finitude. It was not long before Sartre,
without repudiating his existentialist philosophy, defined his
position as being that of an independent Marxist. The fate of
France during the Second World War led him to commit himself
politically. His play *The Flies* and his postwar articles conform
to his conception of commitment. He argued that the writer had
to be responsible for what he writes. Sartre declared in an article:

> Man's response to the absurdity of his condition does not lie in a great
> romantic rebellion, but in daily effort. Our *true* revolt lies in seeing
> things clearly, keeping our word and doing our job. For there is no
> reason for me to be faithful, sincere and courageous. And *that is precisely
> why* I must show myself to be such.[14]

That is how Sartre endeavored to extricate himself from the
dilemma posed by nihilism. He realized, of course, that this espousal
of the politics of the Left, this earnest alliance with the cause of
Communism, involved him in a series of contradictions. He was
no die-hard materialist, he did not accept the Marxist interpretation of man as a mere economic unit of energy. Marxism formulates a revolutionary imperative that is instinct with overtones of
eschatological faith in a future that will give birth to the classless
society; it projects a myth designed to fortify the will of the masses
to change the world. But a materialist universe logically entails
the supersession of the human will and prevents the individual

---

[14] Quoted in Benjamin Suhl, *Jean-Paul Sartre* (New York: Columbia University
Press, 1970), p. 82.

from assuming responsibility for himself and his relation to the world. For Sartre the human condition, not economics, is the prime motor of history. He accepts those aspects of Marxism which he believes can be reconciled with existentialism and which will enable him to transcend the iron logic of nihilism.[15]

In a lecture delivered in Paris in 1945, Sartre vigorously denied that existentialism leads to a philosophy of nihilism. The Communists had criticized him on the ground that his outlook ignored the organic ties that bind the individual to the collectivity. In rebutting the charge, Sartre maintained that though all truth and action presupposed a human subjectivity, it did not follow that he was guilty of antisocial and irresponsible pessimism. The existentialist, he insisted, shoulders responsibility not only for his own individuality but for all men.

When we say that man chooses his own self, we mean that every one of us does likewise; but we also mean by that that in making this choice he also chooses all men. In fact, in creating the man we want to be, there is not a single one of our acts which does not at the same time create an image of man as we think he ought to be. To choose to be this or that is to affirm at the same time the value of what we choose,

---

[15] Critics differ in their attitude toward the alleged nihilism of Sartre. For example, Greene declares: "Whatever may be said in criticism of Sartre's ethics, it does not seem fair to call him a nihilist even by implication." (Norman N. Greene, *Jean-Paul Sartre* [Ann Arbor, Mich.: The University of Michigan Press, 1960], p. 161.) Guido de Ruggiero, on the other hand, remarks, apropos of existentialism, that "the dark, pessimistic, anxious mood of existentialism reflects a state of human disintegration." (Guido de Ruggiero, *Existentialism.* New York: Social Science Publishers, 1948, p. 14). For a sweeping attack on existentialism as a philosophy of unregenerate despair, see Norberto Bobbio, *The Philosophy of Decadentism,* trans. David Moore (Oxford: B. Blackwell, 1948). As far back as 1943 Hans Mayer, a Marxist critic, wrote an article that analyzed Sartre's existentialism and appraised its nihilistic content. Sartre, he says, is convinced that "existence in and by itself is meaningless; there is neither the beautiful nor the good, neither the heroic nor the treacherous, neither the Christian nor the humanistic life." (Hans Mayer, *Steppenwolf and Everyman,* trans. Jack D. Zipes [New York: Thomas Y. Growell Company, 1971], pp. 214–15. One German scholar argues that it is a misunderstanding of what Sartre meant by "nothingness" that led some critics to accuse Sartre of being a nihilist. But this word, Leo Pollman observes, "has nothing to do with what is commonly meant by nihilism." Like Greene, he is convinced "that Sartre's ethics is not nihilisic." (Leo Pollman, *Sartre and Camus,* trans. Helen and Gregor Sebba (New York: Frederick Ungar Publishing Co., 1970), p. 7.

because we can never choose evil. We always choose the good, and nothing can be good for us without being good for all.[16]

Man is the architect of his own being. Each individual is accountable for everything that happens to him, even for those events that seemingly take place through no fault of his. Indeed, Sartre contends that everyone is responsible for the condition of the world. "I am abandoned to the world . . . engaged in a world for which I bear the whole responsibility without being able, whatever I do, to tear myself away from this responsibility for an instant."[17]

Despite this spirited defense, the contradictions between existentialism and Marxism were too glaring to be ignored by the Communist critics. One Polish philosopher condemns existentialism as defeatist because it is grounded in "the a-social concept of the individual who, being isolated and lonely, must determine his behaviour entirely for himself and, with nothing but his own judgment to guide him, grapple with hostile living and non-living forces."[18] It is the subjectivist foundation of existentialism, a subjectivism that culminates in nihilist despair, that is fundamentally wrong. Existentialism and Marxism cannot be wedded, but Sartre has made up his mind in which direction he wishes to go. He has aligned himself more closely with the Communist cause.[19]

---

[16] Jean-Paul Sartre, *Existentialism,* trans. Bernard Frechtman (New York: Philosophical Library, 1947), p. 20.

[17] Jean-Paul Sartre, *Being and Nothingness,* trans. Hazel E. Barnes (New York: Philosophical Library, 1956), pp. 555–56. See Hazel E. Barnes, *An Existential Ethics* (New York: Alfred A. Knopf, 1968), pp. 113–14.

[18] Adam Schaff, *A Philosophy of Man.* New York: Monthly Review Press, 1963, p. 25.

[19] Hazel E. Barnes loyally defends Sartre's decision to become an independent Marxist and do all he can to relieve suffering, fight against man-made evils, and denounce injustice wherever it manifests itself—in Algiers, Vietnam, the United States. "Sartre has on occasion worked with the Communists; he has sharply criticized them at other times, both theoretically and apropos of specific events. He has never allowed the Party line to become his own conscience." Barnes, *An Existentialist Ethics,* p. 417.

12

Ionesco and the Comedy of the Absurd

"And what do you understand about nihilism? For myself, I do not know very well what that means."[1]

The "absurd" is a very vague notion. Maybe it's the failure to understand something, some universal laws. It is born of the conflict between my will and a universal will; it is also born of the conflict within me between me and myself, between my different wills, my contradictory impulses: I want simultaneously to live and to die, or rather I have within me a movement both towards death and towards life. Eros and thanatos, love and hatred, love and destructiveness, it's a sufficiently violent antithesis, isn't it, to give me a feeling of "absurdity."[2]

1. THE COMIC VERSUS THE TRAGIC

In a face-to-face encounter, Ionesco presents a genial and engaging personality. Witty, humorous on occasion, highly articulate without taking time off for thought in immediate response to questions, he belies the false impression that some of his work, especially

[1] The *New York Times*, March 21, 1960. Ionesco's remarks were provoked by the "loaded" question of the reporter, who had asked how Ionesco accounted for the nihilistic trend in his work. In "Problems of the Theatre," Dürrenmatt deals with the charge leveled against many writers of our time that they are guilty of producing nihilistic art. "Today, of course, there exists a nihilistic art, but not every art that seems nihilistic is so. True nihilistic art does not appear nihilistic at all; usually it is considered to be especially humane and supremely worthy of being read by our more mature young people. A man must be a pretty bungling sort of nihilist to be recognized as such by the world at large. People call nihilistic what is merely uncomfortable." Friedrich Dürrenmatt, "Problems of the Theatre," in *The Modern Theatre,* ed. Robert W. Corrigan (New York: The Macmillan Company, 1965), p. 294.
[2] Claude Bonnefoy, *Conversations with Ionesco,* trans. Jan Dawson (New York and Chicago: Holt, Rinehart and Winston, 1971), p. 120.

The Bald Soprano, his first play, has created that communication is rendered impossible in an age of technological coordination. He by no means fits the stereotype of the saturnine nihilist of the Absurd, contemplating a death's-head. Like Beckett, he does not take literature seriously, though he keeps on writing plays.[3] He acknowledges his indebtedness to Kafka, who shared his obsessions. His plays, like the fiction of Kafka, are not intended to convey a message, a rationally defined meaning. He composed *The Bald Soprano* in order "to prove that nothing had any real importance" (p. 55). He finds existence "sometimes unbearable, painful, heavy and stultifying, and sometimes it seems to be the manifestation of God himself, all light" (p. 63).

It must take a great deal of courage for a dramatist of the absurd to write at all. He must fight his own battle of the mind against the enervating feeling of futility. He is caught in the meshes of the destructive logic that supports his aesthetic of the absurd. If life, insofar as he can make out, is without meaning or purpose, then why take the trouble to repeat the lugubrious theme that life is without meaning or purpose? If, however, he is not bothered by the need to justify his creative venture, he is brought up short by the difficulty of embodying his vision of a reality that cannot be framed in words. How, as he practices the art of the absurd, can he name the unnameable? How give flesh and form to the ineffable experience of nada?

Small wonder that the dramatist of the Absurd often fails in his undertaking, though he is not discouraged by the experience of failure. He anticipates the failure of his creative quest. He has no solution to offer, no magic key that will open the gates of deliverance. Utopian schemes, Marxist ideologies, technological panaceas, the flourishing mystique of progress, the cult of self-

---

[3] "I think that literature is neurosis. If there's no neurosis, there's no literature. . . . The real question is whether this 'neurosis' is significant or representative of a human tragedy, or whether it's just an individual case. If it's an individual case, then it's certainly less interesting. To the extent that this neurosis is representative of the human condition (isn't man 'the sick animal'?), or of a metaphysical anguish, or else is the echo of psycho-social conditions which are the fault not of the writer but of objective realities, then it can be interesting, vastly significant. . . ." *Ibid.,* p. 36.

fulfillment, the messianic faith in the classless Kingdom of Heaven to be established on earth by the embattled proletariat—he rejects these illusions as firmly as he spurns the otherworldly absolutes of religion.

In order to capture the elusive features of the Absurd, Ionesco focuses on the elements of the comic, the grotesque, and the contingent in the life of man. Death for Ionesco represents the upsurge of the uncanny, the threat of nothingness, the quintessence of the Absurd. He protests against the fate of death, though he realizes that his protest is but an ineffectual gesture, an empty outburst of rhetoric. The finality of death reveals the distinctive character of the Absurd. The tragic and the comic interpenetrate. The drama of the Absurd is born of the dismaying insight that modern man, despite all his technological conquests, cannot escape his mortal lot. A victim of contingency, he may, in his last extremity, mouth fervent prayers or curse whatever gods there be, shake his fists at the heedless skies, appeal to his fellow men to apprehend the wanton Killer who sends the young and the old to the grave, but these desperate measures produce no results. The absurdist hero struggles fiercely against annihilation, but in the end, as in Ionesco's *The Killer,* he is overcome.

The type of drama called forth by this numinous encounter with the Absurd eliminates the possibility of tragic affirmation in the manner of the ancient Greeks. The Absurd is simply there, a *tremendum mysterium* that is neither to be worshiped as divine nor assailed as diabolical; it is a haunting consciousness of the nothingness that waits for man. The tragedy of the absurd, like the nihilistic tragedy, seems to be a contradiction in terms. There is nothing the dramatist of the Absurd can affirm. Born of paradox and culminating in paradox, his plays abandon all illusion, though he is aware that these illusions constitute the essential humanity of man, his never-ceasing search for transcendence. The intimations of the Absurd emerge from this conflict between these all-too-human illusions and the adamantine indifference of the universe. The absurdist hero is defeated and dragged under, but he never pretends that the outcome will be other than it turns out to be. A dauntless truth-seeker, he prefers, like Bérenger, the protagonist of

The Killer, to know the worst that will befall him rather than to remain deluded. He is able to endure the wounds that existence can inflict upon him and laugh at his mortal predicament.[4]

The drama of the absurd relies heavily on the resources of irony, counterpoint, incongruity, parody, paradox, and farce in order to demonstrate the unavoidable unity of tragedy and comedy. It prefers comedy to tragedy because it probes deeper and reveals the utter pointlessness of life.[5] The comedy of the absurd portrays man as alone in a mysterious and alien, if not hostile, world. The protagonist of this genre, having gone beyond illusion, can find no cure for his metaphysical anguish. The only relief open to him is the catharsis of laughter.[6] The humor Ionesco employs is at bottom a method for ordering the inchoate mass of material that the world places at the disposal of his imagination. "Comedy,

---

[4] "Ionesco is not committed to a point of view because he realizes that all points of view are useless. His plays are demonstrations of the incongruity between the human condition and the human being's desires. As such, they are true tragedies, for tragedy, as Ionesco himself points out, lies in the unbearable." George E. Wellwarth, *The Theater of Protest and Paradox* (New York: New York University Press, 1964), p. 51.

[5] The belief is gaining ground that the comic is a more complex, more demanding and expressive form, than the tragic. Dürrenmatt declares: "Comedy alone is suitable for us. Our world has led us to the grotesque as well as to the atom bomb. . . ." ("Problems of the Theatre," p. 291.) He goes on to say that "we can achieve the tragic out of comedy." (*Ibid.*, p. 292.) Ionesco contends that "the tragic feeling of a play can be underlined by farce. . . . For my part, I have never understood the difference people make between the comic and the tragic. As the 'comic' is an intuitive perception of the absurd, it seems to me more hopeless than the 'tragic'. The 'comic' offers no escape." (Eugène Ionesco, *Notes and Counter Notes*, trans. Donald Watson (New York: Grove Press, 1964), p. 27.

[6] "In a universe without absolutes tragedy is impossible. In such a universe pure comedy is no longer possible either, for man seems to belong nowhere, is the constituent of no hierarchy, either divine or social. Man examines himself as a peculiar, suffering animal in the zoological garden of the world, and the result is often amusing. But when he turns to the infinities that surround him, the result is disquieting. Precisely because the dramatists of the avant-garde usually see man not only in a horizontal context, but in a vertical one as well, they blend the amusing with the disquieting. Those who are the most hopelessly pessimistic and the most clearly 'meta-physical' are often the most laughable, perhaps because their pessimism leaves no recourse but laughter." Leonard Cabell Pronko, *Avant-Garde* (Berkeley and Los Angeles: University of California Press, 1962), p. 205.

therefore, is an essential factor, not merely in Ionesco's outlook, but in his actual creative method. . . ."[7]

2. THE ABSURDITY OF DEATH

The truth of life could be seen only in the shadow of death; living and dying were simultaneous and inseparable.[8]

When you read Western writers, you are suddenly confronted with the following fact: the thought with which these writers are chiefly concerned is that of death. It is beginning to appear that mankind never feared death as much as it does today. Perhaps in the middle ages—but in the middle ages people believed in God, in the after-life, and then the thought of death took on more impressive, more musical forms. Nowadays, the artist of the West does not believe in God, and the thought of death, of all living things being doomed, leads him to deny that life has any meaning at all.[9]

It's to Death, above all, that I say "Why?" with such terror. Death alone can, and will, close my mouth.[10]

I have always been aware of the impossibility of communication, of isolation and encirclement; I write in order to fight encirclement; I also write in order to cry out my fear of death and my humiliation at the thought of dying. To live in order to die is not *absurd*, it is just the way things are.[11]

Death is an imposition on the human race, and no longer acceptable. Man has all but lost his ability to accommodate himself to personal extinction; he must now proceed physically to overcome it. In short, to kill death: to put an end to his own mortality as a certain consequence of being born.[12]

[7] Richard N. Coe, *Ionesco* (Edinburgh and London: Oliver and Boyd, 1961), p. 18.
[8] George Santayana, *My Host the World* (New York: Charles Scribner's Sons, 1953), p. 13.
[9] Yuri Olesha, "About Formalism," *International Literature*, no. 6 (June 1936), p. 91.
[10] Eugène Ionesco, *Fragments of a Journal*, trans. Jean Stewart (New York: Grove Press, 1968), p. 27.
[11] *Ibid.*, p. 27.
[12] Alan Harrington, *The Immortalist* (New York: Random House, 1969), p. 3.

Ionesco's personal confessions reveal the mystical streak in his make-up; he is the visionary poet who can never get used to the strangeness of existence. He can make no sense of this phantasmagoric universe, these phantom presences that represent people, these moving lights and shadows and the all-enveloping curtain of darkness. He looks on the world as a rare spectacle, an incomprehensible and yet amusing show and he reacts to it with a sense of wonder, but it also induces anxiety and dread. He is caught in a series of irreconcilable contradictions. "Nothing is atrocious, everything is atrocious. Nothing is comic. Everything is tragic. Nothing is tragic, everything is comic, everything is real, unreal, possible, impossible, conceivable, inconceivable."[13] His work, despite its exploitation of the comic vein, gives expression to an obsessive pessimism. Death is the epitome of the Absurd. As Richard N. Coe says: "And where death is, there can be no optimism. What act or thought is *not* meaningless, when the end of all is annihilation?"[14] Death overtakes all men, regardless of their merit, and if that is so, then what is the purpose of living? Ionesco remarks: "We are made to be immortal, and yet we die. It's horrible, it can't be taken seriously."[15] He cannot forget himself because he cannot forget that he must die, those he loves will die, and the world will ultimately come to an end.

Death is the supreme humiliation man is made to suffer, the outrage he is powerless to prevent. Death is meted out to all, and it is this knowledge that leads Ionesco to stress the vanity of life. All his reading, all the works of art he has studied, emphasize the implacable truth he perceived early in life: the inevitability of death. Why should he concern himself with the social, economic, and political problems of the hour when he knows that we are slated to die and that no revolution can save us from death. Ionesco writes:

> We are in life in order to die. Death is the aim of existence, that seems to be a commonplace truth. Sometimes, in a trite expression,

[13] Ionesco, *Notes and Counter Notes,* p. 216.
[14] *Ionesco,* p. 7.
[15] *Ibid.,* p. 73.

the banality may vanish and truth appear, reappear, newborn. I am living through one of those moments when it seems to be that I am discovering for the first time that the only aim of existence is death. There's nothing we can do.[16]

Though Ionesco's obsession is fixed on death, it is not, like the work of Edward Young and Thomas L. Beddoes, morbid in content. It voices a universal theme. It is a source of anguish, and it is this metaphysical anguish, which never lets up, that incites him to creativity. By writing he keeps the issue of mortality alive even though this intensifies the anguish he feels, anguish born of the "fear of nothingness" (p. 26). It is this accursed knowledge that we are doomed to die that turns us into killers. Death is the tormenting question mark for which we can find no answer. Though this perpetual "Why" that we ask gets us nowhere in the end, we continue to interrogate the world of being. Why for millennia should the sons of Adam resign themselves to the intolerable imposition of death? If they begin to love life, they are soon overcome by the certainty that it will shortly be taken away from them. "This is the incredible thing: to love a life that has been thrust upon me and that is snatched away from me just when I have accepted it" (p. 32). He is afraid that in dwelling repeatedly on this archetypal theme he may yield to the vice of self-pity or indulge in sentimentality. He writes: "I have been, I still am tormented at once by the dread of death, the horror of the void, and by an eager, impatient desire to live. Why does one long to live, what does living mean?" (p. 40). He does not know the answer. It is the thought of death that makes living an impossible burden to bear. Like Camus, Ionesco rejects suicide as "unforgivable failure; and we must not fail" (p. 83).

Ionesco comes to grips with the theme of death in *The Killer* and, later, in *Exit the King*. He kept some of the notes he jotted down when he was struggling with the composition of the latter play: fragments of dialogue not used in the printed text, personal comments, philosophical reflections, the difficulty of reconciling the King to his imminent death, the meaning of nothingness.

---

[16] *Fragments of a Journal*, p. 25.

3. EXIT THE KING

Offhand no theme seems less promising than the one Ionesco has chosen to deal with in this play. What dramatically fruitful results can be derived from the thanatopsian motif? The agonizing struggle to cling to life of a king who is dying and knows he is dying—what, after all, can the most gifted and original playwright do with such refractory material? The words of the Preacher in *Ecclesiastes,* the poignant cry of *memento mori,* the Dance of Death, the sermons and sonnets of John Donne, the lucubrations of the Graveyard School of poets—the potentialities of such an essentially static and sterile theme have already been exhausted. Nothing new can be added; no genuine conflict can possibly arise. The battle the condemned person wages is cruelly unjust. As in Andreyev's play *The Life of Man,* Death is always the winner. There is never a moment of doubt as to the final outcome. However desperate his resistance, the chosen victim must give in. It is only a matter of time.[17] Here is the grim drama each man acts out at the end of his life: a drama that lacks the element of suspense. The plot must, of necessity, follow a preestablished pattern. Why did Ionesco revert to this theme that he had already sounded in *The Killer?*[18]

Because it sums up the distinctive aesthetic of the Absurd. Because, as I have shown, death is Ionesco's constant obsession, the primary source of his inspiration. In *Exit the King* he is writing a twentieth-century version of *Everyman,* in which the theological and moral gloss is left out. There is no God to pass judgment on life or to intercede for the dying man. Heaven and hell no longer exist. After death, there is—nothing.

Ionesco invests the theme with universal overtones. Each man is the virtual ruler of a kingdom, his body, which he is forced to surrender after a comparatively brief reign. The outlying prov-

[17] See "The Literature of Death" in Charles I. Glicksberg, *Literature and Religion* (Dallas, Tex.: Southern Methodist University Press, 1960), pp. 39–48.
[18] Ionesco reports that his play, *The Epidemic in the City,* based on Defoe's *Journal of the Plague Year,* sets out to denounce "the scandal of death." The *New York Times,* January 23, 1970.

inces renounce their allegiance; the parts of the internal kingdom
refuse to obey their sovereign. Or they break down, one by one,
and are no longer capable of responding to his commands. He
ceases to be in control of his subjects; he lacks the strength to
support his crown and scepter.

Behold the King, Bérenger the First (he appears in other plays
by Ionesco), whose second wife, Marie, has mercifully kept from
him the knowledge that he is dying. The first wife, Queen Marguerite, a stern realist, does not believe in pretending that things
are not what they are. Why preserve the pernicious illusion of
hope? The King, she insists, should be told the truth and thus be
prepared for his exit. She sees no good reason why he should be
taken by surprise. One must not be allowed to forget the truth of
death. Too many people know what awaits them but then they
proceed to forget what they know. This must not happen to the
King. The kingdom is falling apart, the palace is crumbling, the
population of the land is shrinking. All signs and portents point
to the coming calamity.

When the King appears on the stage, he is a physical wreck. He
feels that everyone is staring at him in a peculiar fashion and wonders why. Queen Marguerite informs him that he is dying, but he
reacts with unconcern. He knows the syllogism—all men must
die sometime, but his hour has not yet come. Though the Doctor
confirms the diagnosis that he is going to die, he cannot believe it.
That dread event will take place in the remote future, not now. The
Doctor and Marguerite advise him to abdicate, politically, physically, and morally. He is a broken man. His commands are ignored.
He tries to walk and falls. He then gets up by himself but not without
a tremendous effort. He falls down again and once more manages
to rise with painful difficulty. His crown slips to the ground, the
scepter drops from his nerveless hands. The Doctor tries to make
him understand the nature of his fatal illness. Marguerite announces that he will die in one hour and twenty-five minutes.

The King is powerless to arrest the march of time. When the
Doctor declares that the King is more dead than alive, the latter
cries out that he does not want to die and begs for help. Marie

bids him to hold out bravely, not to give up hope, but the rapid deterioration of his body is not to be stopped. His hair suddenly turns white. He feels that he has been trapped, taken unawares. Kings ought to be immortal. He should have conditioned himself every day of his life for this confrontation. Unfortunately, he never really believed that this could happen to him. As the Doctor says: "He never looked ahead, he's always lived from day to day, like most people."[19] And now, as the last minutes of his life are being ticked off, he is not ready to face this ordeal. Nothing can be done for him. No miracle can avert this stroke of fate.

In his distress, the King wants everyone to know that he is dying. He cannot comprehend the meaning of the Doctor's words asking him to die with dignity. He continues to call out to his people for help. He is thoroughly frightened. He cannot reconcile himself to the thought that *he* is dying. It cannot be. As Marguerite callously declares: "He imagines no one's ever died before" (p. 41). He breaks into tears, still calling for help at the window. The others watch his panicky reactions with cold curiosity; only Marie, who loves him, is filled with compassion as she observes his physical break-down. He is staggering as he stands. In his terror he screams aloud and then collapses. He is still not altogether convinced that this is happening to him. Perhaps he is suffering from a nightmare. He does not wish to hear the truth and he has no use for pity. As he struggles against the inevitable, he moans piteously: "Why was I born if it wasn't forever? Damn my parents! What a joke, what a farce!" (p. 45). He says he will never resign himself to this miserable ending, but the inner fortress of his will has already been breached. When reminded that he had faced death many times on the battlefield, he maintains that at the time he knew that death was not meant for him. He had on a number of occasions ordered the execution of his enemies, but now he is himself the victim. He is not exempt from the universal law of mortality. When he is gone, the others will soon forget him and remain preoccupied

---

[19] Eugène Ionesco, *Exit the King,* trans. Donald Watson (New York: Grove Press, 1963), p. 37.

with their own affairs. He longs to be remembered by posterity, his name perpetuated in school textbooks, his body preserved, but the thought of being embalmed fills him with horror. "I don't want to be embalmed. I want nothing to do with that corpse. I don't want to be burnt. I don't want to be buried . . ." (p. 49).

The indifference of Marguerite, the Doctor, and Juliette, who plays the part of both the maid and registered nurse, heightens the note of doom. They are amused by the King's desire to be remembered until the end of time, for they are aware that all things human sink into oblivion. It is Marie who implores him not to torture himself, but he is by this time deaf to all appeals. He now realizes that no one can help him. In his extreme anguish he is willing to let the rest of humanity perish provided he can live on, even under the worst of conditions. The others are not moved by his agonized outcries. There is nothing new in his outburst of hysteria. Perhaps he can derive some comfort from turning his pain into "literature." He is fast reaching a point where nothing can console him. He addresses the countless hosts who died before him. How did they manage to accept death? Perhaps they can help him. "Assist me, you who were frightened and did not want to go! What was it like? Who held you up? Who dragged you there, who pushed you? Were you afraid to the very end?" (p. 54). Now that the end is rapidly approaching, he fights more desperately against death. As he says, even an insect struggles against the fate of extinction. "It's not natural to die, because no one ever wants to. I want to exist" (p. 57). He is steadily growing weaker. He is at this moment enchanted by the miracle of the seemingly commonplace—the changing color of light in the sky, the growth of vegetables in the garden, the ritual of getting dressed, the routine—how fascinating!—of shopping for food, the cooking of meals. He envies the maid the inestimable privilege of being bored.

Marguerite reminds him that there is no escape from the common lot, even for the King. Death does not come suddenly; it is present in the embryo, in the body of the child at birth. Marie seeks to reassure the King by telling him that love can save him, but all his mind can grasp now is the fact that he is dying. Nothing can alter that fact. Now that he is brought face to face with death, he cares not a whit about religion or the future of mankind. At last he is left alone—and dies.[20]

[20] Julian H. Wulbern's *Brecht and Ionesco: Commitment in Context* is a sustained polemic disguised as a work of balanced scholarship. The title is misleading. It should have been changed to read: *Brecht Versus Ionesco,* which suggests the contentious spirit that informs the body of the text. Ionesco, the representative of the Absurd, the opponent of the mystique of commitment, is given short shrift. He is brought in for the most part to demonstrate the fallaciousness of his dramaturgic views, the invalidity of his repeated attacks on Brecht, the minor quality of his achievement in the drama as compared with the major contribution made by a world-renowned dramatist like Brecht, who was actively engaged in the production of plays in the theater. This is how Wulbern disposes of Ionesco's opposition to Brechtian socialist drama:

"In essence . . . Ionesco's severe criticism of Brecht does not draw upon direct experience of representative plays, but is rather based entirely upon his rejection of Brecht's avowed commitment to Marxism and his use of the theater to serve political ends." (*Brecht and Ionesco: Commitment in Context* [Urbana, Ill. and London: University of Illinois Press, 1971], p. 5). Wulbern's attempt to prove that Ionesco, in *Rhinoceros,* is a politically committed playwright, fails to come off. There is a world of difference between a didactic set piece like *The Measures Taken,* an equivocal defense of Communist Party ethics in action, and *Rhinoceros.* Wulbern concludes that Ionesco "remains socially and politically nihilistic. . . ." (*Ibid.,* p. 26).

13

Samuel Beckett: The Cosmic Nihilist

Even as we define the Absurd condition, we undermine its validity, and, even as we speak of the anguish which is our common fate, Sisyphus begins to assume Promethean qualities indicative of our response. Absurdity and Revolt are very closely linked in the ideal pattern.[1]

For more than a century the rebel has insisted that existence is absurd, that man does not live authentically until he accepts the inexplicable.[2]

The vacancy left by God's dethronement, which in itself is a gesture of revolt ... inspired a drama of negation, desolation, and defeat.[3]

If God is dead, then nothing is permitted, and man is superfluous. A universe drained entirely of life or consciousness, drifting ever slower into empty spaces—such may be his [Beckett's] vision of apocalypse.[4]

Human beings who do not doubt that life has a direction and a goal are not prone to despair. The despair of modern man is born of his belief in the absurdity of the world.[5]

[1] Arnold F. Hinchliffe, *The Absurd* (London: Methuen & Co., 1969), p. 45. William I. Oliver, in "Between Absurdity and the Playwright," defines the genre of absurd drama by its subject matter, not its technique. Its subject is absurdity; the absurdity of being born, the absurdity of being sentenced to die, and the absurdity of nothingness. He calls the absurdists of our time ironists. "The realization of absurdity makes ironists of all of us who undergo it and continue to live in action. . . ." Travis Bogard and William I. Oliver, eds., *Modern Drama* (New York: Oxford University Press, 1965), pp. 12–13.
[2] Wylie Sypher, *Loss of the Self in Modern Literature and Art* (New York: Random House, 1962), p. 65.
[3] Eric Sellin, *The Dramatic Concepts of Antonin Artaud* (Chicago and London: The University of Chicago Press, 1968), p. 54.
[4] Ihab Hassan, *The Literature of Silence* (New York: Alfred A. Knopf, 1967), p. 131.
[5] François Mauriac, *Words of Faith,* trans. Edward H. Flannery (New York: Philosophical Library, 1955), p. 73.

Both Beckett and Ionesco represent the anguish caused by the disappearance of one side of the cosmic equation:

the majesty of God + the nothingness of man = the Universe.

For many agnostic and aestheistic [*sic*] writers the disappearance of God is compensated for by faith in social progress and so on. But for Beckett and Ionesco all that is left is the nothingness of man.[6]

Beckett is the literary nihilist *par excellence,* though he does not call himself by that name; he does not compromise his position by indulging in the inflated rhetoric of hope. Dedicated to the elaboration of the single theme of failure, he reveals the pointlessness of life, the insignificance of man vis-à-vis the universe, and the impotence of art.[7] A metaphysical novelist, he writes fiction that differs markedly from such philosophical novels as Broch's *The Sleepwalkers,* Mann's *The Magic Mountain,* and Sartre's *Nausea.* Though the dynamic thrust of ideas is to be found in *Murphy, Watt, Molloy, Malone Dies,* and *The Unnamable,* his fiction is for the most part rooted in specific actions that call forth the response of an agitated, insecure Cartesian consciousness. He is a profoundly committed writer in that for him the problem of art for art's sake never arises. Through the mediation of literature he seeks to capture the truth about the elusive, indefinable self, to discover, if possible, the meaning of and reason for existence, to be delivered at last from the vanity of his creative calling and the misery of being. He turns to art, in short, as a means of achieving "salvation," but he fails in his mission, as he knew he would. His effort, through the alchemy of the word, through the therapy of "fiction" and "plays," to understand the human condition, is foredoomed to defeat. He can make no sense of the world he inhabits. There is no God to whom he can address his appeal. Though

---

[6] Colin Duckworth, *Angels of Darkness* (New York: Barnes & Noble, 1972), p. 104.
[7] "Beckett's aesthetic concerns itself with failure. To write is to fail, a self-imposed necessary doom, for man is unknown and unknowable, his existence a logical impossibility encircled by Nothing." Michael Robinson, *The Long Sonata of the Dead* (New York: Grove Press, 1969), p. 229.

he accepts this state of affairs as the donnée of his art, the defeat of his quest for ultimate meaning fills him with anguish.

Beckett strives to achieve the impossible: to create an objective correlative that will suggest the dread experience of Nothingness. In his attempt to communicate this negative epiphany, to embody his conception of a mysterious, unintelligible universe from which the light of the divine has been drained, he resorts to extremes of paradox, flashes of irony, parodies, puns, ambiguity, passages of black humor. He knows full well the madness of his undertaking, his struggle to convey the meaning of nothing. "For the only way one can speak of nothing is to speak of it as though it were something. . . ."[8] The strategic function of language is to provide this "something." Language is therefore to be distrusted. Using this treacherous medium, Beckett holds up for our contemplation the irreducible absurdity of existence.

Beckett rebels against the cruel, incredible fate that subjects each man to the infirmities of old age and the humiliating knowledge that he is sentenced to die. He dwells with compassion on the unavoidable frustrations his absurd anti-heroes suffer and the despair that overcomes them when they realize the utter meaninglessness of their plight. Their confused wandering, their futile search, demonstrates the limitations of the faculty of reason. Cognition is an exercise in uncertainty; the exploration of the unknowable yields no assured knowledge. Throughout life man is tormented by implacable powers, but his mind cannot make out who or what they are or why they punish him for the aboriginal crime of being born, if that is what constitutes his guilt. Beckett's protagonists are the victims of doubt, rebelling in vain against the grotesque death that is bound to overtake them sooner or later. Through their agonized consciousness—their consciousness that creates God in order to dispel the nihilism that they find unbearable[9]— Beckett portrays their alienated state in a universe that cares not a whit about their spiritual suffering.

[8] Samuel Beckett, *Watt* (New York: Grove Press, 1959), p. 77.
[9] "Godot's existence is the result of man's inability to be a nihilist: he is the creation of man's profound need for meaning." Robinson, *The Long Sonata of the Dead*, p. 259.

The absolute of despair that Beckett voices in his work is counter-pointed by the sound of ironic, deflationary laughter. The characters, who are his spokesmen, safeguard themselves against an outburst of sentimental tears or the weakness of self-pity by debunking the idea of God, an idea chockful of irreconcilable contradictions, and demolishing the philosophical concepts that occur to them as a possible explanation for the fate that has befallen them. These crippled anti-heroes are in quest of the peace that will arrest the fever of consciousness and lead them to the blessed kingdom of silence, but the journey they undertake ends, always, in failure. The trilogy, *Molloy, Malone Dies,* and *The Unnamable,* records the saga of their failure, but they never give up their quest for meaning. It is their destiny to pursue this unattainable goal. They lose their certainty as to their identity, their location in space, the original purpose of their journey. They are the victims of illusion.[10] When they realize that their ordeal, their interminable monologue, their struggle, are all purposeless, they long for death. If these failures do not generate an intolerable feeling of gloom, that is because they are balanced by Beckett's effective use of comic devices. The injection of black humor reduces the tragic tension without dissipating it.

Watt sets out to search for the solution to the enigma of existence, but the result is zero. He arrives at the blinding knowledge that there is no solution. The Mr. Knott he encounters is not God.[11] The world remains inexplicable, threatening, the ultimate of absurdity, the quintessence of the negative.[12] Beckett imaginatively depicts the inevitable failure of literature in its effort to reveal the

---

[10] "Basically there are three types of illusion that beset the characters of the trilogy—the illusion of the possibility of objective knowledge, the illusion of freedom or motivated behavior, and the illusion that the principal causes of their anxiety are external rather than within themselves." Eugene Webb, *Samuel Beckett* (Seattle, Wash.: University of Washington Press, n.d.), p. 88.

[11] "To those driven mad by the need for a meaning, Knot is the meaninglessness, the nothingness, at the heart of the universe." *Ibid.,* p. 61.

[12] "The fundamental idea behind Beckett's fiction may be termed an affirmation of the negative." Raymond Federman, *Journey to Chaos* (Berkeley and Los Angeles: University of California Press, 1969), p. 6.

truth of the human condition; he discloses the utter absence of God.[13]

The novels and plays of Beckett offer an unsparing revelation of the ubiquitous Absurd.[14] His protagonists, deprived of God, cannot dedicate themselves to some ideal end. In Watt, Beckett introduces a grotesque quester. He cannot make sense of the world. He discovers that life is without a discernible pattern of meaning, but he keeps looking for signs of the Absolute. His failure is the cause of his mental breakdown.[15]

Watt is a strange character. It is hard to make out at first where he is bound for; it is difficult to distinguish the features or form of this solitary, shambling figure. Mr. Hackett, old and infirm, who sees him on the far side of the street, is intrigued by this scarecrow, even though he has reached the age when "even the extraordinary, even the supernatural, intrigues so seldom, and so little."[16] All we know of Watt is that he is starting out on a journey, though it is not until later that we learn where he is going. Those who observe his movements as he gets off the tram, wonder what he is up to. They know that he has no fixed address and they speculate on what his destination might be. Watt is devoid of energy; he half desires to keep moving and half desires to remain stationary; he seems incapable of forming a decision as to which direction to take in the infinitude of time-space. And yet he is an experienced traveler. The Irish group of observers have no personal knowledge of this singular clown. They know nothing of his family, birthplace, nationality, occupation, or means of subsistence. All they can gather is that he is gentle, inoffensive, and strange, and

---

[13] For a bibliographical survey dealing with the religious motif as it appears in Beckett's work, see Melvin J. Friedman's introduction in Melvin J. Friedman, ed., *Samuel Beckett Now* (Chicago and London: The University of Chicago Press, 1970), pp. 18–29.

[14] "Beckett's theatre partakes of the cruelty, and the ridiculousness, of a life devoid of meaning. It reflects the world: *theatrum mundi* in our time. Man is an actor in the cosmic farce." John Fletcher, *Samuel Beckett's Art* (New York: Barnes & Noble, 1967), p. 74.

[15] For an analysis of Watt as a psychotic, see G. C. Barnard, *Samuel Beckett* (New York: Dodd, Mead & Company, 1970), pp. 16–27.

[16] Samuel Beckett, *Watt*, p. 17.

that he has a huge red nose. He may be a university man, but even that is pure conjecture.

Watt does not remember how he entered Mr. Knott's house, whether he got in by the back door or by climbing through a window. There is a light burning in the kitchen. Then the gentleman who had seen Watt but said nothing reappears, ready to depart. Before he leaves he remarks:

> All the old ways led to this. . . . All led to this, to this gloaming where a middleaged man sits masturbating his snout, waiting for the first dawn to break. (p. 40)

In this extraordinary passage, a statement addressed to Watt, is summed up the foiled quest of man for the light of meaning— a theme that is also developed in *Waiting for Godot, Endgame,* and the trilogy of novels. Watt is still unable to account for the fact that he ever found the way to this neighborhood and the entrance to the interior of this house. He must be in the right place, however, for this is where he obviously belongs. He will sense the harmony of the world, feel that he belongs by right to this establishment, not exiled to the perimeter as an unwelcome intruder. He takes off his hat, unbuttons his coat, and is ready to perform his appointed duties. For the first time since he was nursed at his mother's breast, "definite tasks of unquestionable utility are assigned to him" (p. 41). The discovery of Watt that he is in a definite place where he belongs and that he is assigned tasks that are unquestionably useful he regards as vastly reassuring, but this mood does not last long.

After remaining in Knott's house for some time, he leaves, his mission fulfilled. He has failed to find out what actually goes on in Knott's house, and the failure brings about his mental breakdown. He cannot cope with the irruption of the irrational. He is confused as to his identity. He is diligent in his search for meaning, he questions the nature of the objects around him, and he examines the equivocal relationship between things and the words that are supposed to represent them. He can make no progress in his efforts to find words that will do justice to the world of appearances;

the phenomenal universe is too densely irrational to be comprehended by rational means.[17] The human mind is poorly equipped to gain access to authentic knowledge of reality. Reason is powerless to grasp the truth of life. Language, like reason, is defeated in its struggle to solve the mystery of being. Watt hears voices, a babel of sound, and sometimes he understands and sometimes he does not understand what these voices are saying. The reality outside the mind cannot be known, the report of the senses proves deceptive, the obtrusive doubt—what Whitman in *Leaves of Grass* calls "the terrible doubt of appearances"—is never overcome. Man is barred from learning the secret of the ultimate. The Beckett pilgrim in the time-space continuum is brought up short before the solipsistic impasse. "Watt's rationalism leads to insanity. . . ."[18]

Beckett, the novelist, attempts to convey the sense of the phantasmagoric absurdity of existence. Watt considers the possibilities open to him of interpreting the meaning of all that takes place in Knott's house. What conclusion can he draw from his observations and experiences? Arsene, the servant who had preceded him, speaks to Watt, but the latter pays no attention and does not understand what he is told. Erskine, now in attendance on Knott, divulges no information at all. This is how Beckett pictures the befuddlement of Watt in his frantic but ineffectual endeavor to gain knowledge about himself in relation to a reality that remains forever unknowable.

> Looking at a pot, for example, or thinking of a pot, at one of Mr Knott's pots, it was in vain that Watt said, Pot, pot. . . . For it was not a pot, the more he looked, the more he reflected, the more he felt sure of that, that is [*sic*] was not a pot at all.[19]

---

[17] Watt rediscovers one of Wittgenstein's basic principles: "that a word hasn't got a meaning given to it, as it were, by a power independent of us, so that there could be a kind of scientific investigation into what the word *really* means. A word has the meaning someone has given to it." Ludwig Wittgenstein, *The Blue and Brown Books* (Oxford: Basil Blackwell, 1960), p. 31.

[18] Ruby Cohn, *Samuel Beckett* (New Brunswick, N.J.: Rutgers University Press, 1962), p. 94.

[19] Beckett, *Watt*, p. 81.

This state of alienation from reality—the disjunction of words from things, the bewildered feeling that our perceptions betray us—is an experience not far removed from the "nausea" that assailed Roquentin. These metaphysical queries, these delirious monologues, these inconclusive debates of a consciousness cut off from the world, these intellectual perturbations and semantic doubts, are characteristic, more or less, of all of Beckett's fictional progeny. The language they use retains its surface of logical meaning, but the reality to which it is applied eludes the drawn net of words. Watt is obsessed by the epistemological question: how does one know what he knows? Through the medium of Watt's consciousness Beckett reveals the astounding lack of correspondence between language and reality, the name and the object to which it refers. That is how Beckett probes the ontological enigma: the emergence of life out of nonbeing, the plunge into the maelstrom of being, the temporary interlude of service in Knott's house, and in the end the inevitable return to nonbeing—the completion of the cycle. Watt seeks to be reassured that everything is as it should be, but he can find no reassurance in his present condition. The problem that plagued him without remission was his inability to declare with conviction that the object before him, which seemed like a pot, was a pot, and that the creature invested with a number of definitely human characteristics was a man.

Is all this feverish mind-searching, this inquisition of the disintegrated self, to be taken seriously? How long can one retain interest in these divagations of a schizophrenically tormented consciousness that is surrounded by things that are never the same, things that are unnameable? Beckett manages to sustain our interest to the very end in the misfortunes and aberrations of this woebegone descendant of Don Quixote. If Watt could only talk with Erskine and gain some inkling of *his* reality, *his* naming of things. Then perhaps, for nothing is ever certain, Watts would have felt that his dilemma, his dissociated self, was caused by poor health, caused by the effort of his body to adjust itself to this strange milieu, and that when his health was restored everything would fall into place and names reassume their rightness of signification. Not that he really craved such reassurance, for if he entered the ultimate dark of being he would at last know the peace of silence and the anguished cries within him would be stilled.

Watt tries hard to puzzle things out for himself; he observes what goes on, listens intently to every sound, but gains little by way of understanding. He obeys the regulation that requires that whatever food Mr. Knott leaves over after his meal is to be fed to a dog and entirely consumed. Watt then considers the various possibilities of providing a regular series of dogs for carrying out precisely such an assignment. He is supposed to watch the dog consume the food to the last drop, but when he fails to do so nothing happens, no punishment follows this sin of omission, though punishment might come later, who knows. And this business of the dog whose sole purpose is to eat Mr. Knott's food on those days when the master did not dispose of his entire meal, fascinates the ever-curious mind of Watt. What a complex mechanism is made to function in this house! The house is full of conundrums, but Watt knows nothing of Mr. Knott.

Since Watt is telling the story of his past disjointedly, we get only a fragmentary, confused, and conjectural narrative. Watt himself can report only what he has observed or knows. There is no other source that can confirm or correct his tale, and Watt in his present disoriented condition is an unreliable and often incoherent witness. Beckett thus underscores the point that it is impossible to arrive at the truth of what actually took place in Knott's house.

Though Beckett in this novel works with only the bare bones of a plot, he succeeds in raising a number of universal issues that he treats in his characteristic manner. He succeeds in satirizing the extremes to which men go in order to pass the time. Their rituals, their games, their relationships, their contests and prizes, these are shown to be ridiculously unimportant. All of life's joys and pains, ordeals and triumphs, all the adventures and mishaps on this "poor old lousy old earth" (p. 46), this earth that housed our forefathers and their forefathers back to the beginning of time, the memories that men sigh over nostalgically, the beauty of growing things, the turning green of leaves, the smell of new-mown hay, the song of birds—they all amount to nothing. This descant on the vanity of earthly existence is told by the inmate of Mr. Knott's house who is now leaving. If he were granted a chance to repeat the performance, knowing what he knows now, the result, he insists, would be the same, no matter how often "the play" was repeated. He is telling Watt what's what.

This disillusioned former servant, about to depart from Mr. Knott's premises, both regrets and doesn't regret the past. He is weary of the time he spent in this house, the happy hours and the unhappy hours and those that were neither. Since Watt is about to take his place, he decides to reveal something about himself, and tells Watt about Mr. Knott in his bed. Servants keep entering the household while others leave, but for each the hour will strike when the light drains out of the sky and the summons for him to depart is sounded. The only one who neither comes nor goes is the employer; he remains in his place. Yet he must have appeared once, otherwise how account for his presence here? This former inmate of the house dwells on the mystery of the beginning of things, the mystery that attends the arrival and departure of the servants, the mystery of birth and death. He can make no sense of the furious proliferation of life; it seems purposeless. Watt learns some of the sly conjectures current about Knott, namely, that he needs to have someone to look after him, though little enough that is trustworthy is known about him. It is impossible to speak positively about Mr. Knott; one is forced to fall back on hearsay, rumor, superstition.

Watt does not gain much inside knowledge while serving his master, for he has no direct dealings with Mr. Knott, who sees no one and hears from no one, as far as Watt can make out. Mr. Knott never leaves the grounds, though Watt is not sure of this detail or of anything else he observes. When the Galls, blind father and son, come to tune the piano, Watt broods on the meaning of this incident. Did it really take place? Did it perhaps contain a hidden, esoteric significance? Watt hears voices and sees visions. Strange things occur in this house, and Watt in his perplexity tries to interpret what they mean. He cannot get himself to believe that nothing has happened. Were the lights he saw, the sounds he heard, but the products of his imagination? He cannot rest until he untangles these knotty problems in his own mind. He seeks to identify the sounds, the light, the objects he perceives, so that he will at least know where he is, but if nothing has happened then he can deduce nothing from that. Then comes this philosophically illuminating passage:

> For the only way one can speak of nothing is to speak of it as though it were something . . . and the only way one can speak of man . . . is to speak of him as though he were a termite. (p. 77)

Watt is nonplussed; he is beset by phantoms, and his mind spins hypotheses that would somehow account for their presence. If he could furnish a truly convincing explanation, one that his mind would be willing to accept as reasonable, then the mystery would be dispelled. Unfortunately, the hypotheses he cooks up do not carry conviction. Nor did these hypotheses stand their ground. No, they changed their content, gave way to different hypotheses. The events he seeks to understand resist all his efforts to interpret their meaning. Watt and Knott never conversed; the latter from time to time indulged in song, in a rush of meaningless words. God is unapproachable, unknowable, ineffable.

Beckett is bearing witness to the collapse of the religious absolute, the breakdown of communication at a time when the electronic media are reaching mass audiences by the millions. He records the failure of the metaphysical quest, the loss of faith in life. His novels and plays give utterance to the spirit of nihilism rampant in our time. *Waiting for Godot* exhibits none of the characteristics associated with the Christian God.[20] One critic considers "utterly misguided the efforts of certain critics to find in the actual content of his work some sort of crypto-religiousness."[21] Beckett makes

---

[20] Wallace Fowlie, *Dionysus in Paris* (New York: Meridian Books, 1960), p. 214.
[21] Nathan A. Scott, *Samuel Beckett* (London: Bowes and Bowes, 1965), p. 130. Kenneth Allsop declares that "Beckett is unconcerned with writing requiems for humanity, for he sees life as polluted and pointless: he merely scrawls its obituary, without bitterness or compassion because he cannot really believe it is worth the words he is wasting." Kenneth Allsop, *The Angry Decade* (New York: British Book Centre, 1958), p. 39.

no concession to the all-too-human craving for the bread and wine of meaning. His plays and novels spell out the death of the Absolute. The impressive contribution Beckett has made to modern literature, the books that have been written about his work, all this is an exercise in futility, a frivolous pursuit. David H. Helsa provides this perceptive summing up of Beckett's nihilism:

> By means of the dialectic, Beckett achieves in his art what he observed to be true of Joyce's art and his own confused world—the absolute absence of any Absolute at all. Nothing is left standing which could be thought to be independent, autonomous, or immune to negation. Author cancels character, circle cancels line, ending cancels beginning, question cancels answer, no cancels yes, tragedy cancels comedy, pessimism cancels optimism, pain cancels courage, suffering cancels wit, isolation cancels love, fatigue cancels action, and despair cancels hope, the dark cancels the light.[22]

---

[22] David H. Helsa, *The Shape of Chaos* (Minneapolis, Minn.: The University of Minnesota Press, 1971), pp. 226–27.

14

Various Aspects of Modern Nihilism

Sensible people accept the contingency of the world and get on with the business of living in it, while existentialists cry out in anguish that they are gratuitous in an impossible world![1]

1. PROLOGUE

In every generation, exceptional men of vision appear who take it upon themselves to challenge the funded wisdom of the race. They are the metaphysical rebels who reject the world as meaningless and man's fate as absurd and yet cling to life because there is nothing to be gained and everything to be lost by spurning it. They raise again the age-old, troublesome questions: What am I living for? What is life worth, in the last analysis? Since death is bound to overtake all those who are now alive, what is the ultimate purpose, if any, of life here on earth? To what can I give myself that will save me from the despair born of my vision of the Absurd? On their lips these questions sound like a bitter indictment. These are the very questions, however, that thinking men from the beginning of recorded time have attempted to answer. What is the function of the ancient myths if not to affirm the unbroken continuity of life, the rebirth of the dying god, the triumphant renewal of the failing energies of the earth each season of spring. What is the underlying purpose of the myth and ritual pattern if not to persuade men to accept the inexorable decrees imposed by the order of nature? The religious mythos encourages its com-

---

[1] Arnold P. Hinchliffe, *The Absurd* (London: Methuen & Co., 1969), p. 24.

municants to root themselves in the mystery of faith so that they can live their lives with a measure of courage and dignity and a sense of justice in a world that cares nothing for these values. Through the mediation of myth and sacred rituals, the believer is able to transfigure the character of existence so that he feels he is in tune with God and the universe. That is how he wards off the evil forces that conspire to destroy him and his kind. Hence the anomalous persistence of the religious impulse despite the steady advance of science and the rise of secular surrogates for the lost Absolute.

It is this frustrated yet continuing quest for ultimate meaning that accounts for the emergence of a literature of nihilism. The literary nihilist never completely abandons the hope that he may finally hit upon a solution. That is why he obsessively reviews the evidence for and against the Absurd. Perhaps there is a cure for his metaphysical madness. Though he suspects that there is no answer to the riddle of the Sphinx, he keeps on searching for "Something" or "Someone," perhaps a new incarnation of God, that will rescue him from his terrifying predicament.[2] Imaginative literature repeatedly uses the archetypal image that life is a play of shadows, a dream devoid of substance, a thing of sound and fury signifying nothing, a game without consequences. The game is

[2] It is only modern man who is exposed to the terror of history but is deprived of any of the myths and archetypes that could safeguard him against terror. His only defense against that terror is "through the idea of God. In fact, it is only by presupposing the existence of God that he conquers, on the one hand, freedom (which grants him autonomy in a universe governed by laws or, in other words, the 'inauguration' of a mode of being that is new and unique in the universe) and, on the other hand, the certainty that historical tragedies have a transhistorical meaning, even if that meaning is not always visible for humanity in its present condition. Any other situation of modern man leads, in the end, to despair." (Mircea Eliade, *The Myth of the Eternal Return,* trans. Willard R. Trask [New York: Pantheon Books, 1954], p. 162.) But historicism commits man to a belief in relativity. There is no one overarching and abiding truth, no one true faith. Culture itself is an achievement based on illusion. Religion, God, justice, mythology, are all products of consciousness. "The drama has all been moved within the minds of the characters, and the world as it is in itself is by implication unattainable or of no significance. Love, honor, God himself exist, but only because someone believes in them. Historicism transforms God into a human creature. . . . Historicism . . . brings us back to the absence of God." (J. Hillis Miller, *The Disappearance of God* [Cambridge, Mass.: Harvard University Press, 1963], p. 12.)

so rigged that whatever the outcome, man is bound to lose. The metaphor of the game, which can be applied to gambling, sports, play-acting, chess, cards, is eminently suited to the literary mind, which views life from some Olympian height. Many writers have relied on this metaphor to shadow forth their vision of contingency, whether it be the fall of a card, the capricious turn of the wheel of fortune, or the throw of a pair of dice. Borges, for example, beholds the world as a prodigious but inscrutable dream, for it is a dream in which the dreamer himself may be dreamed. Consequently his love of paradox, his perception of the pervasive role contingency plays in life. André Maurois says of Borges: "Attracted by metaphysics, but accepting no system as true, Borges makes out of all of them a game for the mind."[3] Surrealism made objective hazard the basic feature of the creative process. So long as the mystery remains, so long as there is no way of answering the question why things are as they are, so long will existence be pictured in the figure of a dream or a game.[4] Georg Lukács, in *The Metaphysics of Tragedy* (1908), defines tragedy as a game "which is watched by God. He is nothing more than a spectator, and he never intervenes, either by word or deed, in what the actors are doing."[5]

The Black Humorist plays the game of art for all it is worth, but he knows full well that it is a game he is playing. Hence he is prepared to let his imagination go the whole hog. The realization on his part of the gratuitousness of art leads him to experiment with extreme forms of comedy and satire. Nothing, not even art, is to be taken seriously; everything can be reduced to laughter.

> The Black Humorist is not concerned with what to do about life but with how to take it. In this respect Black Humor has certain affinities with some existentialist attitudes, roughly distinguishable in terms of

[3] José Luis Borges, *Labyrinths,* trans. Donald A. Yates & James E. Irby (Norfolk, Conn.: New Directions, 1962), p. xii.
[4] See "The Rules of the Game," in Charles I. Glicksberg, *Modern Literary Perspectivism* (Dallas, Tex.: Southern Methodist University Press, 1970), pp. 51–61.
[5] Quoted in Lucien Goldmann, *The Hidden God,* trans. Philip Thody (New York: The Humanities Press, 1964), p. xxi.

the difference between seeing the universe as absurd and seeing it as ridiculous—a joke.[6]

The saving idea is to accept the cosmic joke and appreciate it to the full. "To present life as a joke is a way of both acknowledging its absurdity and showing how that very absurdity can be encompassed by the human desire for form."[7]

Closely connected with the above metaphor is the image provided by *theatrum mundi,* the picture of life as a stage[8] on which is enacted a drama that is either comic or tragic or both, though the actors, unwitting of the fate that is in store for them, enter wholeheartedly into the roles assigned to them, strutting their brief hour before the footlights of history, mouthing their lines with passionate intensity, declaiming bitterly against God or fate when things go wrong, playing the part of circus clowns when they have to, until the time comes when the lights suddenly go out, the curtain drops, and they are thrown into a common grave. Then the curtain rises again and the dramatic cycle repeats virtually the same scenario but with a new cast. The protagonists do not know who is directing their actions and prompting their utterances. Perhaps the script has been prepared for them in advance. Perhaps they are only rehearsing a plot the outcome of which has been predetermined from the very start.

Aware of this fatality, the literary nihilist may react like Camus by protesting against the doom of death visited upon mankind or he may, like Beckett and Ionesco, soften the tragic strain by combining it with the comic element. He is convinced, to begin with, that the nature of reality, whatever it may be, is beyond his comprehension, a mystery not to be fathomed. Since he has decided to live and not to die, he believes that he can make existence more bearable by viewing it through the comic perspective. He has given up the hope that he can be saved through the practice of literature. He does not labor under the illusion that his negative outlook is the one that conforms to "the truth." He realizes that

[6] Robert Scholes, *The Fabulators* (New York: Oxford University Press, 1967), p. 43.
[7] *Ibid.,* p. 46.
[8] See "Life Is a Stage," in Glicksberg, *Modern Literary Perspectivism,* pp. 62–74.

others may think him deranged. Why kick against the pricks? Why assume that the Absurd is a universal condition? Why not accept the universe as given, without hysterically fretting because it does not satisfy *all* human needs? Why not make the best possible adjustment to the miraculous or chance emergence of human life on this minor planet? Others in the past have passed through this dark night of the soul and succeeded in coming to terms with life. Such arguments utterly fail to impress the literary nihilist. In an age that proclaimed the death of God, witnessed the genocidal campaign of the Nazis that sent millions of victims to their death in crematoria specially manufactured for that purpose, and unleashed the atom bomb against Japan—in such a catastrophic age the Absurd, whether in a tragic or comic version, asserts itself as the uniquely expressive myth of modern man.

2. MAN THE PUPPET

Isak Dinesen portrays the life of man in the image of a marionette comedy. One must play his part in this game of life, accepting the evil and the tragic as intrinsic ingredients in the overall design. One must join affirmatively in the dance of creation. "To be in a marionette play is to know that your purpose is part of a grand design."[9] The characters Dinesen brings to life are moved by the invisible hand of fate; they struggle and suffer until they find out who they are and the end toward which they are journeying. They may or may not be aware of it, but throughout the performance they are subject to the will—or the whim—of the manipulator of the puppet show. It is he who makes them laugh, cry, twitch, fall, rise up again, gesticulate, dance like a dervish, pray, call upon the gods for mercy. To themselves they seem to be in full control of their destiny, but for their creator they are but wooden figures whose strings he pulls. He is their begetter and director, who decides that the "show" is to be a tragedy, a comedy, a roistering farce, a melodrama, a morality play, an allegory. Indeed, some of Dinesen's characters look upon themselves as marionettes

---

[9] Robert Langbaum, *The Gayety of Vision* (New York: Random House, 1964), p. 12.

in uniform, drawn into mysterious plots that are beyond their comprehension or control, though a few perceive at the climactic moment, just as the curtain is brought down and darkness falls, the meaning of all they have gone through. They gain a luminous instant of insight, even if it is only the realization that they are mechanically controlled figures in a puppet show.

In utilizing the figures of puppets, Dinesen reveals that their role is assigned; they are automatons without consciousness; they do not brood about the future and pine for what is not; they have no prevision of the destiny that they will fulfill. The human actor in the drama of life, however, is endowed with consciousness and is in a position to contest the prearranged working out of his destiny. "Consequently man has the doubtful, even dangerous privilege of being able to live according to his own will and ideas, rather than simply carrying out God's purpose like the puppet obeying the puppet-master."[10]

This metaphor of the puppet show provides the writer with a distanced point of view and enables him to present the life of his characters against the backdrop of eternity. The creator of fiction is an illusionist who spellbinds his audience by telling them a story that represents a technique of deception, "disguising the essential nothingness of life. As such, it does, however, become a heroic defiance of nothingness, for it requires courage to meet the deception of life with a still greater form of deception."[11]

Dinesen is a master of the art of spinning a tale. There is nothing "experimental" or "avant-gardeish" in her method of narration. The stories in *Seven Gothic Tales* follow a leisurely pace and even include digressions. The time is set in the nineteenth century so that the author can treat her varied group of characters and the events in which they participate with fine objectivity and detach-

---

[10] Donald Hannah, *"Isak Dinesen" and Karen Blixen* (New York: Random House, 1971), p. 117. Wolfgang Kayser writes: "Among the most persistent motifs of the grotesque we find human bodies reduced to puppets, marionettes, and automata." (Wolfgang Kayser, *The Grotesque in Art and Literature,* trans. Ulrich Weisstein [Bloomfield, Ind.: Indiana University Press, 1963], p. 183).
[11] Eric O. Johannesson, *The World of Isak Dinesen* (Seattle, Wash.: University of Washington Press, 1961), p. 52.

ment. In reality Dinesen is concerned with neither time nor place as determinant naturalistic factors in the resolution of the conflict; her aim is not to build up verisimilitude of detail, though the background is depicted in vivid, authentic colors, but to paint a picture of life as she sees it. And it is her vision of the universe that makes her fiction so memorable.

Her stories are steeped in an atmosphere that is predominantly skeptical, ironic, and resigned. Death is a constant threat, a frightening presence. God is absent from the scene of action or is reduced to a metaphor that betrays his blind and blundering importance. In portraying the mechanical operation of fate, Dinesen highlights the extraordinary power of illusion in directing the erratic course of human affairs. Men and women are marionettes, animated dolls, though they each assume a self that is an artificial cover-up, a socially approved mask worn for the occasion. Dinesen calmly delineates all these elaborate strategies of accommodation. In "The Deluge at Norderney," she comments sagely on the difference between youth and age in their attitude toward death:

> When we are young, the idea of death or failure is intolerable to us; even the possibility of ridicule we cannot bear. But we have also an unconquerable faith in our own stars. ... As we grow older we slowly come to believe that everything will turn out badly.[12]

This expression of pessimism is neither bitter nor rebellious; it is a sober and mature acceptance of the way things are. Dinesen's metaphysical realism perceives that life is a game in which "the hand of the Lord moves us where he wants us to be" (p. 15). As for the truth, who can honestly argue that the Lord demands it of us? Miss Malin, in "The Deluge at Norderney," is convinced that the good Lord must find existence a bit dull. She has always maintained "that the Lord has a penchant for masquerades ..." (p. 24). Had he not freely participated in a masquerade at the time of the Incarnation, when he dwelt on earth as a man among men? The truth, Miss Malin contends, is both unnecessary and undesirable. This ripe wisdom leads her to treasure the uses of the imagination

[12] Isak Dinesen, *Seven Gothic Tales* (New York: The Modern Library, 1961), p. 10.

and to recognize the need for the ingenious disguises truth must wear if it is to be welcomed by humankind. When the naked truth finally becomes known, "that is the end of the game" (p. 25). For then the absurdity of the masquerade is no longer to be borne.

The Cardinal in the story, who wears a disguise (since he is not the Cardinal but his servant), declares that the mask, after all, does reveal something of the character of the man who wears it. In the end, death strips off the mask, but what lies beneath? "A poor little doll stuffed with sawdust, a caricature of a skull" (p. 49). The servant masquerading as the Cardinal points out that he is an actor and therefore impersonating a role. Again, in "The Monkey," the character Boris felt that "the theater was real life" (p. 140). When he could not play a part, the world puzzled him. Only as an actor did his true self emerge. Like the Cardinal's servant, he acted his part with skill. "He had laid his mask with great care in front of the mirror..." (p. 141). Dinesen plays striking variations on the theme of *theatrum mundi* and, like Pirandello, on the related theme of the self, the image of which is reflected in different ways by different mirrors. Thus the living self that is ours is reflected, as in a mirror, within the minds of the people we meet, but this reflection is only a caricature of our inner self, though it pretends to uncover the truth about us. "Even a flattering picture is a caricature and a lie" (p. 166). The witch in a marionette play, when asked what is really the truth, replies: "The truth...is that we are all of us, acting in a marionette comedy" (p. 199).

3. THE NIHILISTIC HERITAGE OF THE THIRD REICH

Like the previous war, the Second World War was attended with disastrous consequences, many of them unforeseen. The honorific values of the past were blown to bits and could not be reinstated on the old terms. Conditions during the period of the aftermath were ripe for the outbreak of nihilism. *The Outsider,* by Wolfgang Borchert, evokes a sense of horror so extreme that it shakes loose all faith in man. A crippled soldier returns home to discover that he is unwanted. His house has been razed to the ground. Tired of life, he jumps into the Elbe. The fat man who observes what has just happened is not at all put out. It goes on all the time in Germany after the war, with returned soldiers who are without work, without hope, and without roots. The fat man, who has waxed prosperous, is an undertaker; his establishment does a flourishing business. Then an old man comes on the scene, the senile, impotent God whom mankind has forgotten. The two confront each other: the obsolete God, an utter failure on earth, and the undertaker, who symbolizes Death, a decided success.

Using Expressionistic techniques, Borchert shows that Beckmann, the returned soldier, is rejected by the spirit of the Elbe. She will not allow him to run away from life. The action now focuses on Beckmann's despairing efforts to find out where he belongs; his search is fruitless. All those to whom he turns for recognition, especially God, fail him. Like Kragler, the returned soldier in *Drums in the Night* (1918), by Bertolt Brecht, Beckmann gives expression to the mood of nihilistic disillusionment that swept over the younger generation in Germany after the defeat of Hitler.

They had been wantonly betrayed by their erstwhile leaders: Germany is now a land of graveyards and ruins. God weeps because he is helpless to change things. When the Undertaker asks the Old Man who he is, he replies: "The God in whom no one believes any more."[13] He can do nothing to stop the epidemic of suicides. When the Undertaker identifies himself, the Old Man says: "You're the new God. They believe in you. They love you. They fear you. You can't be deposed" (p. 55). In all modesty, the Undertaker, who represents the new God, Death, admits that business has been uncommonly good.

When Beckmann, who has been away at the front for three years, comes back home, he finds his wife estranged. She has chosen another man as her mate. His son lies dead beneath the mountain-high piles of rubble and debris. Beckmann cannot forget the horror of the war in which he had fought—the agonized cries

---

[13] *Postwar German Theatre,* ed. Michael Benedikt and George E. Wellwarth (New York: E. P. Dutton & Co., 1967), p. 54.

of the wounded, the look in the eyes of the dying, the traumatic memory of killing. He is haunted by ghastly apparitions; his dreams are nightmares from which he wakes up screaming. But the civilian world to which he has returned is heedless of his spiritual suffering. The people who have survived are hardened; they are able to bear up under the worst blows of adversity; they scarcely react, no matter how bad the news is. The authorities feed the populace with a stupefying diet of statistics, but Beckmann is not fooled by the numbers racket. He knows that each number stands for a wounded or starved or drowned or killed soldier.

He meets the old man, who looks like God. He has no pity on this senile, weeping creature. Where was God when his little son was smashed to fragments by falling bombs? Where was God when men were being slaughtered en masse by falling bombs? Pointblank he asks: "When have you ever bothered yourself about us, God?" (p. 96). God sadly acknowledges the fact that no one believes in him any longer. But why, Beckmann wants to know, should people be concerned about him? He tells God bluntly that he is old-fashioned:

> you can't just cope with our long lists of the dead, with our agonies now. We really don't know you any more, you're a fairy tale God. Today we need a new one. One for our own misery and our particular fear. A completely new one. Oh, we've searched for you, God, believe me, in every shell hole, during every passing night. (p. 97)

The search was all in vain. God never replied, God never appeared. God is dead. Beckmann bids this caricature of God to go away— and God takes himself off. Whereas *Baal* and *Drums in the Night* voiced the amorality and nihilistic cynicism of a defeated Germany after the First World War, *The Outsider* releases a heart-rending cry from the depths.

4. ALAIN ROBBE-GRILLET: THE END OF TRAGEDY

> In tragedy the terrible side of life is presented to us, the wail of humanity, the reign of chance and error, the fall of the just, the triumph of the wicked; thus the aspect of the world which directly strives against our

will is brought before our eyes. At this sight we feel ourselves challenged to turn away our will from life, no longer to will it or love it. But just in this way we become conscious that there still remains something over us, which we absolutely cannot know positively, but only negatively, as that which does not will life.[14]

The notion most alien, most antipathetic to Robbe-Grillet's art is doubtless the notion of tragedy, for in Robbe-Grillet nothing of man is offered as a spectacle, not even his abandonment. . . . Tragedy is but a means of recovering human misery, of subsuming it, hence of justifying it in the form of a necessity, a wisdom, or a purification.[15]

What Robbe-Grillet calls for is a new method of observation that will revolutionize the art of the novel—a method that is strictly "objective," free of anthromorphic projections, a method that views the universe without humanistic preconceptions. Such a method, if it keeps faith with its strictly neutral premises, would even refrain from designating as absurd or tragic the world that man inhabits. Such an aesthetic outlook, Robbe-Grillet contends, is bound to have a decisive bearing on the future of the novel. The new fiction will emphasize the phenomenological perspective, the thereness of things that possess no hidden signification, no intrinsic core of meaning. The objects man perceives will henceforth be divested of their aura of mystery. The art of the new fiction will dedicate itself to the task of showing how utterly alien objects are to man. Robbe-Grillet rejoices now that the metaphysics of transcendence has been disposed of. Its elimination thrusts upon the novelist the responsibility for forging a radically changed technique, a narrative order that reflects a world in process, contingent, alogical, unstable; the new fiction rejects the pre-Einsteinian principle of cause and effect.

In "Nature, Humanism, Tragedy," Robbe-Grillet formulates his aesthetic philosophy, which stresses the alienation of man from things. Nature is not man and has nothing in common with him.

---

[14] Arthur Schopenhauer, *The World as Will and Idea,* trans. R. B. Haldane and J. Kemp (London: Routledge & Kegan Paul, 1948), 3:212.

[15] Roland Barthes, *Critical Essays,* trans. Richard Howard (Evanston, Ill.: Northwestern University Press, 1972), p. 92.

Nor does it respond to his gaze. The protagonist in Robbe-Grillet's novels does not question things, since he knows they are incapable of giving any answer. In discarding the metaphysical myths of the past, man affirms his freedom; he has no further use for the concept of tragedy. Robbe-Grillet is attacking the mystique of a Beyond: a secret power in the universe that somehow justifies the suffering man endures on earth and presides over his destiny. Robbe-Grillet urges twentieth-century man to refuse the consolations offered by tragedy; he must not become reconciled to his fate. He calls upon man to shape his world and impose his values upon it.

Robbe-Grillet declares that he is not presuming to speak as the founder or prophet of the New Novel; the expression, the New Novel, he remarks, "is merely a convenient label applicable to those seeking new forms for the novel," by those who have "determined to invent the novel, in other words, to invent man."[16] He is resolved to put an end to the wearisome repetition of exhausted forms, the facile imitation of the models of the past. The novel, if it is to be a genuine creation, must be born anew. Each writer of fiction must design the form to suit his needs. "For the function of art is never to illustrate a truth . . . but to bring into the world certain interrogations (and also, perhaps, in time, certain answers) not yet known as such to themselves."[17]

If we regard Robbe-Grillet as the initiator and theorist of the movement associated with *le nouveau roman,* we can see that the transvaluation of values he has attempted to bring about in the aesthetics of fiction rests squarely on a nihilist base. It is not the experimental innovations he has introduced but the philosophical presuppositions and implications of his work that have called forth a fierce critical debate. His fiction embodies his "negative" outlook, his dehumanized metaphysics. Like the existentialist hero in Sartre's novels, he feels alienated from the world of things. He questions the nature of reality, and like Valéry he is not sure that it can be apprehended by the mind of man. Like Kant, he sus-

[16] Alain Robbe-Grillet, *For a New Novel,* trans. Richard Howard (New York: Grove Press, 1965), p. 9.
[17] *Ibid.,* p. 14.

pects that the mind stamps its own interpretation upon the universe. He does not copy a preexisting reality; he creates it, and he devises new techniques for handling this material. He reduces the importance of the plot:

> The absence of plot in most New Novels no doubt expresses the author's skepticism about the possibility of establishing, with any degree of certainty, the causes of any particular event—or indeed of isolating such events at all from the continuum of experience.[18]

In his first novel, *The Erasers* (1953), Robbe-Grillet endeavored to portray a world of objects undistorted by moral or intellectual intuitions. The novelist must not humanize the world but describe its phenomenological surface so that metaphysical quiddities or transcendental meanings are excluded. The so-called "higher" essence of being disappears; it was never there in the first place. It was only a semantic phantom, a ghost conjured up by the mind of the observer, who injects human traits into the neutral economy of nature. Robbe-Grillet's technique necessitates the liquidation of the humanized metaphor. He wishes to get rid of the pathetic fallacy. If it is unwarranted, if not downright foolish, to see the world in the manner of Carlyle's persona, Teufelsdrökh, as the symbolic vestment of God, it is equally unwarranted to regard it as irremediably absurd.

But this hostility to anthropomorphism or humanism lands Robbe-Grillet in the nihilist camp. He avoids tragic crises and confrontations. His anti-tragic position is coupled with the belief that the metaphor is responsible for the falsification of reality and leads to the formation of the ultimate metaphor: the hypostatization of the divine. Robbe-Grillet reformulates and reaffirms the view that God, the supreme example of the pathetic fallacy, is a projection of the human sense of the numinous, a *sub rosa* attempt to find an answer to the riddle of the universe.

Man is the spectator, the observer, the witness. Nature does not respond to his overtures, his appeals. In an eloquent passage

---

[18] Vivian Mercier, *The New Novel: From Queneau to Pinget* (New York: Farrar, Straus and Giroux, 1971), p. 7.

Robbe-Grillet sums up the predicament of illusionless man in a God-abandoned world.

> I call out. No one answers me. Instead of concluding that there is no one there . . . I decide to act as if there *were* someone there, but someone who . . . will not answer. . . . I try once again. . . . Very quickly I realize that no one will answer.[19]

Robbe-Grillet is not only an atheist who opposes the effort to smuggle in the contraband notion of God; he is the nihilist who, like Samuel Beckett, is convinced that the human cry will receive no answer. There can be no reply to the questions man asks of the universe. "Does reality have a meaning? The contemporary artist cannot answer this question: he knows nothing about it" (p. 141). Nature is neither benevolent nor malevolent, neither good nor evil, neither meaningful nor absurd. As Robbe-Grillet phrases it, the world simply *is*. "That . . . is the most remarkable thing about it" (p. 19).

In discarding the human element from the act of perception, in reducing the world of phenomena to brute sense-data, and particularly in arbitrarily discarding the idea of tragedy, Robbe-Grillet is undermining the art of the novel that he is supposed to be defending. The rationale that directs his straitened method of narration fails to achieve its purpose. Without man, the novel is denuded of vital content. By attenuating the human significance of the action, Robbe-Grillet mystifies the reader. In *The Voyeur,* the mystery of the murder is hinted at, dwelt upon by indirection, but never cleared up. The author, in keeping with his intentions, betrays no concern with moral or human values. The same technique of allusiveness is present in *Jealousy.* We cannot make out whether the adultery was committed or whether it was all imagined by the jealous husband, who is without name or face. In the novel *In the Labyrinth,* the author's concentration on objects in a room or the geometry of a street becomes a mannerism. Past and present are inextricably confounded, so that it is difficult to make out what is perceived in immediacy and what is recalled or imagined. The

---

[19] Robbe-Grillet, *For a New Novel*, p. 60.

260 THE LITERATURE OF NIHILISM

point of view is retained; at least there is a recognizable "I," never otherwise named, who opens the story: "I am alone here now, under cover. Outside it is raining, outside you walk through the rain with your head down. . . ."[20]

It takes some time before we can identify or become interested in the nameless, shadowy protagonist, a taciturn soldier wearing a faded military overcoat, his face grayish in color from fatigue. He remains mysterious in his search; he is carrying a package under his left arm, which looks like a shoe box tied with a white string. His object, apparently, is to deliver the box as he had promised. The street is covered with unmelted snow; the doors of the houses are closed. This soldier is on a journey he does not comprehend, the destination of which he knows only dimly. It costs him great effort to speak and when he does speak it is usually in monosyllables. He walks and talks like one who is drugged, unobservant of what is going on around him. He is reluctant to answer questions; he is tempted at times to surrender the box he is carrying. But he persists in his search, looking for the street whose name he cannot remember. When he is asked whether the street he is looking for is important, he replies: "Yes . . . No . . . Probably."[21] He spends the night at the barracks in the town. He has no identification papers, and he vouchsafes no information as to the contents of the box he is carrying. He leaves the barracks with his box. He remembers that he was supposed to meet someone at a crossroads and surrender the box to him, but now he is confused. He cannot explain the arrangement he had made. He cannot talk coherently. How will he recognize the man he is looking for? Is this a metaphysical novel, a symbolic novel? The total meaning eludes our grasp.

In his essay on Robbe-Grillet, John Weightman mentions the two major intellectual contradictions on which his work rests. Robbe-Grillet seeks to "cleanse the external world of the pathetic fallacy and show us things as they are, independently of human

---

[20] Alain Robbe-Grillet, *In the Labyrinth,* trans. Richard Howard (New York: Grove Press, 1960), p. 7.

[21] *Ibid.,* p. 57.

emotions."[22] In his fiction Robbe-Grillet contrasts the indifference of the world with the subjective distortion man imposes on his environment. He stresses the alienation of man, the incomprehensibility of the world, and the meaninglessness of the illusion of purpose to which man clings. The absurd in his nihilistic vision ceases to be a metaphysic and becomes an oppressive fact.

5. PERPLEXITIES AND PARADOXES OF CONTEMPORARY NIHILISM

Of the writers discussed so far, not one, with the exception of Nietzsche, would have acknowledged his linkage, at some point in his career, to the nihilistic outlook. And they are perfectly sincere in disclaiming their affiliation with the *nihil*. Their exploration of this negative vision was tentative, the expression of a transient mood, a Wertherian *Weltschmertz*. It seems misleading and decidedly unfair to accuse such dedicated writers as Malraux, Valéry, Camus, and Sartre as smutched with the nihilistic taint. Their work as well as their life is sufficient refutation of such a reckless charge. Such spirited denials are caused by the fact that the term *nihilism* resonates with a pejorative ring. Actually, no stigma should be attached to this descriptive label. There are many different forms and degrees of nihilism as it makes itself felt in the body of modern literature. The leading symptoms of the nihilist syndrome can be readily identified: the acknowledgment, mournful or defiant, of the death of God, the realization that the life of man serves no ultimate purpose, that man is the sole author and architect of value, that there are no absolute moral standards, that death is utter annihilation, that all that the human race has labored to create may go down in a global disaster and leave not a wrack behind.

But those symptoms, abstractly stated, fail to do justice to the inner dialectic of literary nihilism. The Everlasting No the modern nihilist utters springs out of his existential devotion to "the truth"

---

[22] John Weightman, "Alain Robbe-Grillet," in John Cruickshank, ed., *The Novelist as Philosopher* (London and New York: Oxford University Press, 1962), p. 251.

of being, his courageous resolve to confront the reality of chaos without opiate illusions. What he beholds is not the ineffable radiance of God but the blackness of nothingness[23], the negation represented by the diabolical principle. Nihilists suffer from "the dread" that this experience of nothingness induces. "These whom this blackness has almost blinded do not believe that nature is good, man noble, progress natural, or the godhead a good God."[24] Testifying to this loss of faith is the progressive disintegration of form, so that the art of the modern world is anarchic, dehumanized. "We must acknowledge," Erich Neumann declares, "the evil, the blackness, the disintegration which cry to us so desperately from the art of our time, and whose presence it so desperately affirms."[25]

Despite his radical pessimism, the creative nihilist does not give up his writing career. Beckett went on with his work even though he felt that his commitment to literature was useless and absurd. Gottfried Benn, who openly proclaimed his nihilistic beliefs, distinguished nihilism from resignation. The latter carries "its philosophical implications to the brink of darkness, but upholds its standards of dignity even in the face of the darkness."[26] Then he composes this revealing statement about the emotional condition of the creative nihilist:

[23] What is Nothing? The question, as Heidegger points out, immediately implies that Nothing is something that somehow "is." But that is not so. Though Nothing represents the negation of all that is, Heidegger states that Nothing is anterior to the Not and the process of negation. How and where can Nothing be found? Heidegger defines Nothing as "the complete negation of the totality of what-is." (Martin Heidegger, *Existence and Being* [Chicago: H. Regnery Co., 1949], p. 363.) He draws a distinction between the imaginary and the authentic Nothing. Heidegger makes an important contribution to existential analysis in his close examination of the state of "dread," which is to be distinguished from both anxiety and fear, that one experiences in the presence of Nothingness. Whereas the man who is stricken with fear is afraid of "something" in his environment, the one who is overcome by dread knows not what it is he dreads. "'Nothing' is revealed in dread, but not as something that 'is.' Neither can it be taken as an object." (*Ibid.*, p. 368.) "Only in the clear night of dread's Nothingness is what-is as such revealed in all its original overtness *(Offenheit)*: that it 'is' and is not Nothing." (*Ibid.*, p. 369.)
[24] Erich Neumann, *Art and the Unconscious,* trans. Ralph Manheim (New York: Pantheon Books, 1959), p. 113.
[25] *Ibid.*, p. 122.
[26] Gottfried Benn, *Primal Vision,* trans. E. B. Ashton (Norfolk, Conn.: New Directions, 1960), p. 209.

it seems to me self-evident that such a man, even if personally and privately afflicted with the deepest pessimism, would rise from the abyss by the mere fact that he works. The accomplished work itself is a denial of decay and doom. Even if creative man realizes that cycles of culture must end, including the one to which he belongs—one cycle ends, another reaches its zenith, and above everything floats infinity whose essence is probably not accessible to human comprehension— creative man faces all this and says to himself: weighing on me in this hour is the unknown and deadly law which I must follow; in this situation I must assert myself, confront this hour with my work and thereby give it articulate expression.[27]

It speaks well for the nihilists of our time that they still wish to communicate with their fellow men, even as they reaffirm the nothingness of being. In *Beyond Existentialism,* J. Von Rintelen sharply condemns the nihilistic malaise of his contemporaries:

The question of the nothing and the appeal to it is a fundamental concern of our burdened time.... For our contemporaries love the ever dangerous situation, which affects them very powerfully: in a pathological confusion they actually enjoy this leap into the nothing as a titanic attitude. Thus everything becomes questionable, and finally they say a radical no to everything and are utterly lost.[28]

Though it is doubtful if the nihilists actually enjoy this leap into the nothing, it is certainly true that they are prophets of negation. Having abandoned the Absolute as a relic of the outlived past, they are forced to dwell in the realm of the finite and the relative. Yet nihilism, as Von Rintelen points out,

does not mean malicious and chaotic denial. It rather includes the ability to discard, if necessary, all ties and repressions in an attitude that is beyond good and evil. Nihilism is perfectly compatible with a strict daily discipline (even in a modern concentration camp) and with a natural joie de vivre. Fundamentally, however, its only possible content is an empty gesture that seeks release in dynamism.[29]

---

[27] *Ibid.,* p. 210.
[28] J. Von Rintelen, *Beyond Existentialism,* trans. Hilda Graef (London: George Allen & Unwin, 1961), p. 43.
[29] *Ibid.,* p. 45.

The sense of the ubiquitous nothing is confirmed by man's awareness of the inevitability of death, the bourne of nothingness toward which he is being relentlessly swept by the swift current of time.

Though not all rebels are nihilists, the nihilist is often a rebel at heart. Sisyphus takes on at times the traits of Prometheus. Unlike the socially committed rebel, he does not believe that the establishment of Kingdom Come on earth would make any difference in his outlook. "Even in Utopia, man will still be faced with death, with boredom, with absurdity. . . ."[30] The nihilist is no crusader. Some rebels come close to nihilism in their rejection of the values of culture, the criterion of truth, the importance attributed to literature.[31]

Examples of a thoroughgoing nihilism on the contemporary literary scene are hard to find. *The Flood,* by J. M. G. LeClézio, voices a despairing nihilism. Under the penetrating gaze of the young protagonist, the seemingly solid world falls apart, revealing its internal rottenness. He is haunted by this vision of universal decay. "Today I, Francis Besson, see death everywhere."[32] Everything around him appears dead; the people passing him in the street are walking ghosts. The victim of ultimate meaninglessness, he feels like one lost in a vast cemetery. "Today the world is finished. Nothing lives any more" (p. 16). Life is a ghastly mockery. Destruction is going on all the time, everywhere, even within the human body. Once man

> possessed a halo of mystery, the product of his collisions with the real world; then a dream, a premonitory vision of ruin and destruction enters the picture, and this man at once becomes united with his true self. The gods are sent packing, the void spins around him, and the earth becomes, in his eyes, a deserted planet, a complex place full of signs and booby-traps. (p. 35)

[30] Richard N. Coe, *Eugène Ionesco* (New York: Grove Press, 1961), p. 99.
[31] The consistent rebel, Widmer declares, "must even mock rebellion and truth—his appropriate claim to esoteric power; many do, with an ultimate (though hardly attainable) nihilism which provides the rebel's unique terror and strength." Kingsley Widmer, *The Literary Rebel* (Carbondale and Edwardsville, Southern Illinois University Press, 1965), p. 30.
[32] J. M. G. LeClézio, *The Flood,* trans. Peter Green (New York: Atheneum, 1968), p. 16.

Death—that is the doom which confronts Besson on every side. His dreams are nightmares filled with the horror of dissolution. This is the fate that befalls all men, without exception. Like Roquentin in *Nausea,* Besson suffers from the compulsion to indulge in endless bouts of introspection. He is forever watching himself think, act, write. "I am writing, I am writing that I am writing. I am writing that I am writing that I am writing" (p. 130). That way madness lies. Besson enters a confessional and tells the priest of his grievous sins: his evil thoughts, his evil acts, his infernal doubts that God exists. He has fallen into a state of despair, he has contemplated taking his own life. "I have blasphemed on many occasions. I have said that God is dead" (p. 216). He has lost not only his faith but the very meaning of his life.

In his review of LeClézio's novel, John Wain quotes from an article by André Malraux that underlines the ultimate powerlessness of man, the knowledge that he is slated to grow old and infirm and finally to die. Malraux contends that the human race cannot face this appalling prospect indefinitely. Then John Wain concludes his review with this passage:

> There speaks the modern mind, the mind that has finally accepted a life set against a background of death rather than against a background of eternity. If your basic feeling about life is that it is temporary, a stage on the way to something else, then you can quite easily face "going on like this indefinitely." If you even allow for a reverberating agnosticism, a series of question-marks receding into infinity, then human life remains, at least, an interesting mystery. If, on the other hand, you belong to a generation that has grown up with atheism and never known anything else, even imaginatively, then you will be with Besson, facing the fact of death with "a soft and agonized whimpering, the hoarse unhappy cry of a gibbon, screaming without rhyme or reason at the onset of darkness.[33]

6. NIHILISM AMERICAN STYLE

Another good example of nihilistic fiction is *The Illusionless Man* by Allen Wheelis, an American analyst. This collection of short

[33] *The New Republic,* January 27, 1968, p. 32.

stories reveals that many people in affluent America suffer from anomie, though they may not be aware of precisely what ails them and would certainly not regard themselves as nihilists. The author speaks not as an analyst using the specialized terminology of his profession but as a man, himself fallible, suffering from chronic seizures of doubt, dread, and despair as he confronts his mortal fate. He does not don the mantle of scientific omniscience nor offer clinically tested pearls of therapeutic wisdom. In everything he says, even in his fictional fantasies, it is as if he were thinking aloud, as if he were communing with himself in the privacy of his study. *The Illusionless Man* is one of the few attempts in American literature[34] to grapple with the problem of meaninglessness and the existential anxiety it generates.

His psychoanalytic orientation undoubtedly helped to prepare him for the difficult creative task of writing *The Illusionless Man.* In his first book, *The Quest for Identity,* Wheelis analyzes the conditions that reduce man to a cipher, a nonentity. Gone is the old reliance on the integral self. The individual is no longer guided by an inner light, and he knows not the direction in which he should move toward the consummation of his life's purpose. Institutional props have increasingly taken the place of the nineteenth-century ethic of self-reliance. Experts are now hired who administer diagnostic aptitude and personality tests. Public opinion polls are conducted to determine what the public believes and wants. Everything is decided by anonymous but all-powerful collective persuaders. Subject to these formidable pressures, the individual forfeits his autonomy; he does not know where to turn or what to do. Shall he identify himself with some huge organization? Shall he consult a psychoanalyst and thus perhaps be cured of his traumatic loss of identity? It does not dawn on him that while analysis can serve to clarify his personal problem, it has "no answer to the confusions of the age. It does not reveal what is worth struggling for or how much."[35]

---

[34] It is preceded by Melville's "Bartleby the Scrivener," which foreshadows the comedy of the Absurd.

[35] Allen Wheelis, *The Quest for Identity* (New York: W. W. Norton & Company, 1958), p. 50.

The individual is today beginning to realize that he cannot find a remedy for his ills apart from society. Yet he continues to struggle on his own; he bears his painful burden of alienation and fitfully pursues the ideal of personal growth. He supports no world-shaking causes; he has completely given up his utopian aspirations. He has ceased to believe that he can, single-handed or in association with others, reconstruct the world nearer the heart's desire. Wheelis contends that values make themselves felt, always, in a social context; society provides the only soil in which they can take root and grow.

The alienated man, cut off from his nourishing social roots, feels confused, lost. The life he leads is deprived of significance. He has no vital incentive to go on living. He must rely on his own spiritual resources to create the values that will make his life meaningful. But how can he achieve this second birth, this self-renewal, when he knows that death will defeat all his projects?

> From a cosmic point of view—a hypothetical consciousness which takes all of space and time as its referent—the entire life of man on this planet is meaningless, being but as a season of locusts; the social point of view appears to have been invalidated by the fall of institutional absolutes, and from an individual point of view life is absurd. There is no meaning beyond mere existence, and even the abstention from suicide is difficult to justify. One may commit one's life to passion or violence or conquest, but this too is absurd; and even the dignity and courage with which one may face death is absurd.[36]

This passage has been quoted not only because it defines so well the condition of nihilistic alienation and despair but also because it captures the feeling of the inescapable absurdity of existence. This constitutes the underlying theme of *The Illusionless Man*. In the fantasy "The Illusionless Man and the Visionary Maid," Wheelis portrays the life of a man who has lost all his illusions. Even as a child he gave up his belief in fairies and Santa Claus. By the time he could read he ceased to believe in magic. One by one, he divested himself of all his illusions. He stopped his prayers. He began to comprehend that it was the pres-

[36] *Ibid.,* pp. 191–92.

sure of self-interest that motivated the most altruistic acts, that words can lie, that art is no refuge against the onset of despair. "For beauty passes and deathless art is quite mortal."[37] What, he asks, is he to do? How is he to live?

He meets a woman who falls in love with him. He tells her he is incapable of love; he regards it as nothing more than a chemical process set off by glandular secretions in the body. But he is fond of this woman and for her sake he agrees to marry her in church, though personally he has no use for such ritualistic nonsense. The religious ceremony is only "a primitive and preposterous attempt to invest copulation with dignity and permanence..." (p. 17). His wife, unlike him, is full of enthusiasm and high ideals. She cannot win him over. He will not lie to please her by saying that he loves her. Love is the worst of all the illusions by which man can be trapped. He will not divorce her. She falls in love with a number of other men but each proves unworthy. In her distress she goes to an analyst and begins to idealize him, but he gives her no encouragement. After five years the husband refuses to pay for these sessions, and that is the end of the matter for the wife. Her capacity for illusions remains undiminished. She tries Catholicism, Christian Science, yoga, hypnotism, technocracy, what not. Though she grows older she manages to stay young, while the husband turns prematurely gray. Finally he confesses that he loves her. It is an illusion but it is nonetheless precious for all that. There is nothing else.

In another fantasy Wheelis describes the career of a psychoanalyst who becomes disillusioned with his profession. He suffers from excruciating attacks of boredom. His heart is not in his work. What is the remedy for his spiritual condition? He must recognize that death is the ineluctable fate of man. He turns to the study of death and forms the American Thanatotherapy Association. He has a patient who threatens to shoot him, and these sessions with him are alive, filled with tension. He soon realizes that an awareness of the closeness of death is not enough;

---

[37] Allen Wheelis, *The Illusionless Man* (New York: W. W. Norton & Company, 1966), p. 14.

the reality of death must be faced. He concludes that "the risk of death must be intrinsic to the pursuit of value. Whatever you find in life of meaning or desire you must strive for so hard . . . as to increase the likelihood of death" (p. 97). The American Thanato-therapy Association succeeds in banishing boredom. The analyst at the end discovers that he is in love with death; he sleeps with his gun as if it were a woman he passionately loved.

If we were to assume that the author is closely identified with these illusionless, dead-end characters we would be badly mis-taken, for in two recent books, *The End of the Modern Age* and *The Moralist,* Allen Wheelis launches a fierce attack on the nihilist outlook. In *The End of the Modern Age,* he fulminates against not only the materialist mania of Western civilization but also the hegemony of science and its hubristic assumption of omni-science. His jeremiad ends on this urgent, cautionary note:

> We have lived a delusion, we cannot know the world. Aided or un-aided, we stumble through an endless night, locked in a range of ex-perience the limits of which are given by what we are and where we live. . . . Our eyes have seen the glory, but only within a narrow range, while by us, through us, flow visions for other eyes, music we shall never hear. . . . May we see but well enough to lay aside the weapons with which we are about to destroy, along with the little we do see, a potential of experience we know not of.[38]

In *The Moralist,* Wheelis is more militant in his condemnation of nihilism. In the first chapter, which hears the title "Nihilism," he diagnoses the reasons for the spiritual demoralization and impotence of modern man.

> The anguished cry of the moralist announcing nihilism has become the dictum of our age: everything is permitted. If God is dead our standards are necessarily manmade, are therefore arbitrary in that no such standard can be endowed with the right to disallow opposing standards.[39]

---

[38] Allen Wheelis, *The End of the Modern Age* (New York and London: Harper & Row, 1971), p. 115.
[39] Allen Wheelis, *The Moralist* (New York: Basic Books, 1973), p. 3.

Power is enthroned as the ruling principle of the world. Even those who do not know what nihilism means agree with Ivan Karamazov that everything is permitted. In rebuttal, Wheelis argues that

> some things are not permitted, that there are immanent standards, of man's making but not of man's design, that they are therefore to be discovered but not created, that though not absolute they change but slowly, that to live by them is what is meant by being human. (p. 4)

Unfortunately man is today puffed up with pride and boasts that he has mastered the secrets of nature and is in full control of his environment. Intellectual arrogance—that, Wheelis charges, is his cardinal sin and constitutes his gravest danger. He has toppled God from His throne and rashly usurped His place. Wheelis reminds us that we still inhabit a universe that is beyond our finite comprehension. The Age of the Enlightenment with its confident faith in the triumph of reason has been discredited. Wheelis affirms that life is the source of value. "What enlarges and enriches life is good; what diminishes and endangers life is evil" (p. 8), even though we are aware that the moral truths we abide by in our time may later be invalidated. But if absolute certainty is beyond our reach, does this mean, Wheelis asks, that we must become nihilists? Our nihilism is fed by this sickly craving for the lost certainties of the past. Then Wheelis unleashes a furious frontal assault on nihilism:

> Nihilism is a fraud. Beneath the mournful trappings lies a base heart. . . . The world it sees is without meaning, without purpose, without point. (p. 13)

Wheelis rejects nihilism on the ground that it culminates in a mood of quietism. Though theoretically motivated by its insistence on disclosing the truth of the human condition, nihilism finally results in a feeling of utter helplessness born of resigned despair. For nihilism is convinced that nothing can be done to avert this ultimate fate of meaninglessness. It declares that no distinction can be drawn between good and evil and that all is vanity. Wheelis questions the sincerity of the nihilist in his dedication to the quest for truth. This articulate critic proposes to subject the *bona fide* nihilist to this test: let him earn the right, in the form of a license, to teach mankind "his vision of life as meaningless" (p. 14).

PART IV:
Dionysian Nihilism

15

Kazantzakis: Dionysian Nihilism

Art . . . fights to convert the ephemeral into the eternal and to transubstantiate man's suffering into beauty.[1]

1. THE MAN AND HIS WORK

The writer, once he is suspected of nihilism, suffers a serious loss of reputation. He is without moral stamina. Deprived of faith, the seed of hope for the future dead within him, the nihilist in his despair turns to alcohol or drugs, indulges in orgiastic sex, experiments with vice, or commits suicide. Having ceased to believe in the essential meaningfulness and worth of life, he becomes obsessed with the thought of death. His existence lacks nourishing roots. He is without a goal toward which to strive. Though he may on occasion rebel against his wretched condition, he soon relapses into his wonted state of acedia. His creativity is blighted and he finally falls silent.

This portrait is not only badly overdrawn but basically false. Does the writer—a Samuel Beckett, for example—necessarily fall silent when he has lost faith not only in life but in literature as well? Certainly not. He struggles to communicate his encounter with nothingness. Despite his dominant feeling of hopelessness, he searches for a way out of his predicament. He is human and therefore often contradicts himself. He will not keep silent. He refuses to enjoy the ephemeral pleasures of the earth and thus

---

[1] Nikos Kazantzakis, *Report to Greco,* trans. P. A. Bien (New York: Simon and Schuster, 1965), p. 392.

blind himself to the truth that tomorrow we die. Frequently he persists in his search for God even as he denies the possibility of ever finding him.

What of the creative nihilist who catches no hint of ultimate meaning in the universe? What effect does his nihilism, though he may not use that invidious term, have on his life and work? Is he a sufferer from ennui like Baudelaire? Or does his unmitigated pessimism spur him on by way of compensation to prodigies of achievement? If one knew nothing of Kazantzakis's negative beliefs and his open espousal of nihilism, one would be inclined to hail him as a religious visionary engaged in a lifelong quest for God. He is a mystic who habors no illusions. As he wrote in a letter dated July 20, 1924: "I have no illusion, and that is why I am struggling untiringly, desperate and free. I know that when this miserable, faded social class falls, the proletariat will come. They will give whatever thought, whatever beauty they are capable of, and then they too will become stingy."[2] He is not taken in by Marxist ideology or the mystique of the proletariat. Everything in the universe is subject to endless change and cycles of transformation, and this process will go on until the earth is no more.

Here, then, is an avowed nihilist who is not misanthropically withdrawn from his fellow men. He aims to awaken those who are content with their lot and infect them with the virus of divine dissatisfaction. "And why? So that the world will not rot in tranquillity and stagnation...."[3] Far from being a melancholiac, sicklied o'er with the pale cast of thought, he is, like Camus, glad to be alive, grateful for the unique privilege of being a man. Never in love with easeful death, he strives constantly to perfect himself. Throughout his active and fruitful career, he prized life above art.

Kazantzakis is a fitting example of the secular saint. A religious atheist, he never gave up the quest for the innermost secret of life even after he became convinced that there was no ultimate meaning to be found. In the course of his search for sanctity, he passed through a number of stages: he venerated the figure of Christ,

[2] Helen Kazantzakis, *Nikos Kazantzakis,* trans. Amy Mims (New York: Simon and Schuster, 1968), p. 27.
[3] *Ibid.,* p. 28.

KAZANTZAKIS: DIONYSIAN NIHILISM

later he embraced the gospel of Buddha, then for a time he was converted to the evangel of Communism. His autobiography, *Report to Greco,* records the history of his spiritual pilgrimage. Even the onset of old age could not break his will and induce in him a feeling of resignation. He knew the dark night was coming but he would not give in to despair. "The light . . . knows there is no salvation."[4] All his life he sought salvation, and salvation for him meant climbing steadily upward to reach the sanctuary of God, who did not exist. He was driven by the dire necessity of creating God in his own image, of building a temple of faith over the abyss of darkness. Without this labor God would perish and man without God would perish too. Kazantzakis was resolved to use up his spirit to the full before death could claim him as its own. That was his driving ambition: to cheat death by creatively consuming his fund of vital energy and thus leave nothing for the grave "but a few bones" (p. 28). He held up Don Quixote as the perfect model of the metaphysical hero in quest of the essence, which is hidden by the beguiling veil of appearance. What was that essence? Later he learned the answer. Man is spurred on by an inner necessity to defeat the world of matter and to strive steadily toward a goal that transcends the limits of the individual self, even if that goal is only a figment of the imagination. "When the heart believes and loves, nothing chimerical exists . . ." (p. 79).

Kazantzakis is the picaresque saint who unites in his soul the heritage of Christ and Lenin, St. Francis of Assisi and Nietzsche, Buddha and Odysseus. He leads an ascetic life. He devotes himself to his literary tasks but does not overestimate the importance of the work of art. Like Kafka and Beckett, he knows the impotence of the Word as it confronts time and death, but he will not silence his cry in the night, a cry that is both a lament and a protest. The key metaphors in his work that best sum up his life are "the abyss" and "the ascent," both of which resonate with religious connotations. Everyone, Kazantzakis believed, who has earned the right to be called a son of man, must hear his own cross and climb the steep path to his Golgotha. Many of the pilgrims are

---

[4] Kazantzakis, *Report to Greco,* p. 17.

faint-hearted; they grow weary and do not finish their journey. They "do not know that the cross is the only path to resurrection" (p. 15).

Kazantzakis voiced the faith that all of Nature is instinct with the spirit of upward striving. Man, above all other creatures in the world, is chosen to carry on God's work. Kazantzakis articulates an idealism that is all the more impressive in that it puts on record the indwelling faith of a nihilist. This ennobling faith he never abandoned despite his awareness of the nothingness that in the end wipes out all traces of human achievement. The saint without God is the man who, despite his nihilistic convictions, strives to reach the highest ideal the human mind is capable of conceiving. He expects no rewards for his pains. If he is judged by his life and work rather than his negations, it can be seen that he represents an exemplary figure, one who wished "to stare straight into the Nada and to have a burning love of life (of the path leading to the Nada). . . ."[5]

All Gods, Kazantzakis maintained, imaged the face of one God —the indomitable spirit of human striving. He had recovered from the ontological wound inflicted by science; the knowledge that the earth was not the center of the universe and that man, far from being a special creation, the son of God, was descended from lower forms of life. He was tormented by the thought that all things die, that all flesh turns to dust, that beauty lasts but a brief season in the sun. Even as a youth he rebelled against a God who, instead of insuring the immortality of beautiful bodies or heroic souls, decrees that death must always triumph. What kind of God is this who hurls the brave and the cowardly, the virtuous and the wicked, the ugly and the beautiful, the wise man and the fool, into oblivion? "Either He is not just or not omnipotent—or else He simply does not understand!"[6]

Kazantzakis rebelled against such a cruel and senseless fate. How could he decide what to make of his life before solving the monstrous riddle of death? If the earth was but a speck of mud

[5] Helen Kazantzakis, *Nikos Kazantzakis,* p. 256. Written by Kazantzakis in Madrid in November 1932.
[6] Kazantzakis, *Report to Greco,* p. 17.

revolving in empty space, if man is the end-product of an evolutionary development from the amoeba, then life was a worthless gift, a miserable farce, "since everything was ephemeral and raced into the abyss, incited ... by some merciless, invisible hand" (p. 133). Like Tolstoy and Unamuno, he questioned the invisible powers that had sentenced man to death, but unlike the Russian and the Spaniard, he could not accept a religious solution.

He could not rest until he had found an answer to the haunting and timeless question of the meaning of life, and then perhaps he would be able to discover the purpose his precarious existence was supposed to serve.

> I was not interested in finding what life's purpose was objectively ... but simply what purpose I, of my own free will, could give it in accord with my intellectual and spiritual needs. (p. 189)

In groping for a purpose and a faith that would liberate his spirit, he realized that he needed help. He decided to visit Mount Athos. There he listened to the monks who found in Christ the answer to all the questions the restless heart of man might ask. "Questions are asked only by those without faith ..." (p. 199). When he traveled to the Holy Land, he stopped at the famous monastery of Mount Sinai; he told the abbot he wanted to hear God's voice so that he could decide which road to follow. The abbot in turn asked him what it was he sought so obstinately. Why did he shake off belief as soon as it lay within his grasp? Why did he not give "a contemporary form to the age-old passions of God and man" (p. 275)? Kazantzakis walked in the desert that surrounds the monastery and heard the voice of the Lord in a cry that has been taken over by man whose body is wracked by the yearning of the spirit to triumph over time and death.

Kazantzakis, the modern Odysseus, has passed through various stages of mysticism, sainthood, messianic radicalism, but no one stage could long retain his allegiance. He could give unconditional fealty to nothing outside of himself; the creative urge alone could hold him, though it was coupled with an insatiable lust for life, a hunger for experience of all kinds that the years allotted to him were not enough to satisfy. He lived his life with verve and zest and continued his amazing productivity to the last while inwardly convinced that there was no solution to the mystery of existence. Out of his dark, negative vision he wrought what is virtually a "religion," an ethic of commitment born of his capacity to say yes to life and to explore new fields of thought and expression. He marched resolutely onward to the buoyant drumbeat of his own heart and persisted in his effort to climb ever upward, not deterred by the passing of the gods and the ubiquitous threat of death. He knew only when the eager spirit of man has sunk below the nadir of despair can it behold the redeeming vision of absolute hope. Those who are unable to conquer this feeling of absolute despair remain, Kazantzakis observes with tautological emphasis, "incurably despairing."[7]

If Unamuno's work is a symbolic expression of faith achieved through the deliberate humiliation of the intellect and the stern suppression of the infidelity of doubt, Kazantzakis is the nihilist who, tormented by the absence or death of God, proceeds to fashion his own God. Poet, novelist, philosopher, prophet, journalist, quasi-saint, he labored earnestly at his creative task for no redeeming purpose that he could make out. When despair assailed him as to the ultimate fate of the harvest he was gleaning, he applied himself more furiously to his writing. He is not animated by the Goethean belief that the man who persistently strives to save himself from error is thereby redeemed. Nor does he, in the spirit that informs the Second Part of *Faust,* counsel his fellow men to abandon their restless questioning and find salvation in work. All struggles, he contends, are in vain; nevertheless he marches on, seeking to make real the God he aspires to reach. The single passion that sustains him through all the trials of doubt and denial is the conviction that man must never pause in his journey toward the City of God. He may, like Ibsen's Brand, not be able to descry the light that beacons at the peak of the holy mountain, darkness may swirl all around him as he climbs the

---

[7] Nikos Kazantzakis, *The Odyssey: A Modern Sequel,* trans. Kimon Friar (New York: Simon and Schuster, 1958), p. xxi.

perilous cliffs, so that he can hardly distinguish where he is going or what progress, if any, he is making; storms and avalanches may hurl him from his precarious footing and smash him to bits in the gulf below; but he will not turn aside from his search for God. Like Carlyle, he affirmed that the Shekinah is man.[8]

But what kind of God is this that Kazantzakis aspired to reach? He is unmistakably a God of the West, dynamic, cruel, unmerciful, demanding the extreme sacrifice that will ensure a higher degree of perfection. He is an ascetic God who looks with scorn upon all those who, in their besetting fear of life, pamper the body and indulge in sensuality. He is a God who needs man if He is to remain not only alive but free to grow out of brutishness into pure spirit. God is man's supreme creation. It is man who has given birth to God in order to make himself God.

A man is known by the nature of his obsessions, by the heroes he worships and earnestly tries to emulate. There were times when the writing of books seemed to Kazantzakis an affectation, an evasion of social responsibility, but he was, after all, essentially a writer, not a man of action. His creative work was the testament of his lifelong quest for salvation. He remarked that his purpose in life was not to create beauty but to achieve "deliverance."[9] At the end of every road he traveled he faced "the abyss," his favorite symbol of the *nihil*. He rejoiced in the knowledge that the whole world is "a deep inscrutable mystery...."[10] His Dionysian nihilism was uncompromising in its nay-saying.[11]

---

[8] Carlyle quotes St. Chrysotom's saying: "The true Shekinah is Man!" (Thomas Carlyle, *Sartor Resartus* and *Heroes and Hero Worship* [London: J. M. Dent Sons, 1948], p. 247). Carlyle declares that "the Highest Being reveals himself in man." (*Ibid.*, p. 248).

[9] Kazantzakis, *Report to Greco*, p. 452.

[10] *Ibid.*, p. 275.

[11] Kimon Friar is impressed not by Kazantzakis's Dionysian nihilism but "by the heroic affirmation of life which he shouted into the maw of the obliterating void. What I recall most is the great Yes, and not the great No. Kazantzakis gives value and dignity to the human condition by asserting that man himself, with passionate affirmation, may create the structure of his life and work on the abyss itself. This work and this life become more precious and more worthy than any other comparable structure built on illusion, hope and dream, whether of heavenly recompense or personal or earthly immortality." (Pandelis Prevalakis, *Nikos Kazantzakis and*

In Berlin during the early twenties he began *The Saviors of God.*
In a Germany rendered desperate after its defeat in the First World
War, he heard Communism preached and adopted the faith
promulgated by Marx and Lenin, a faith that spoke the language
of logic, materialism, and class warfare. He planned to go to
Russia, where he would practice the craft of carpentry and earn his
bread by doing useful work. By identifying himself with some communal movement, he hoped to find an outlet in socially constructive
action. He wrote at this time: "Oh, to lose oneself suddenly in
the service of a purpose! What purpose? Have this earth, this
starlight, a purpose? What does it concern us? Do not ask. Simply
fight!"[12]

If he was driven by this need to participate in an ideal community, he was impelled by the countervailing need to be alone,
to record the voices of his vision, to devote himself wholly to his
creative daimon. He went to Russia in 1925, but by that time
his mission was limited in scope. He saw the naked realities that
no utopian dream of collectivization could conceal or disguise:
the spirit of the Revolution perverted by the necessities of indus-
trial production and the imposition of brutal bureaucratic control.

It was while he was in Russia that he was overcome by an oppressive feeling of nihilistic futility. Only the flux of energy exists,
the rest is but a mirage. That is the way the cosmic purpose,
whatever it be, fulfills itself, through cycles of energy perpetually
renewed. The traumatic loss of his faith in Communism made
him attach all the greater importance to his creativity, but this
in itself was no solution. He could not rid himself of the guilt
that weighed him down while writing and revising his epic poem,
The Odyssey, which rejects everything men had formerly believed in: their values, their hopes and ideals, their gods. The
faith that the modern Odysseus affirms, the new myth he would
bestow on mankind, is heroic in temper but nihilistic in content.
For Kazantzakis, death is the ultimate reality, but because death

His Odyssey [New York: Simon and Schuster, 1961], p. 10). Whether we discover
affirmation or negation in Kazantzakis and his work depends on what we mean by
nihilism.
[12] *Ibid.,* p. 19.

is, he insists that life must be lived to the full. Though the journey ends in failure, in the shipwreck of all human aspirations, Kazantzakis holds that the struggle is worth waging for its own sake.

Far from resigning himself to despair, Kazantzakis preached a pessimism that is Promethean in its celebration of life. The prophet of gratuitous striving, Kazantzakis balked at swallowing the dogmatic philosophy of materialism. From Bergson he derived his anti-rationalist and anti-mechanistic conception of life. The will of man is free. Only through the mediation of the creative spirit can man shape his own destiny and keep God alive. Kazantzakis himself set an example of the "heroic pessimism"[13] presented in *The Odyssey,* which rejoiced in the courage of man to bear whatever fate may have in store for him.

Kazantzakis tackled the theme of Dionysian nihilism. He would show that civilizations are born, endure for a time, and then perish. The unique feature of Western civilization is that it anticipates its own demise. If that is so, if everything in the world is doomed to perish, then the moral issue is no longer in question. Like Nietzsche, whom he venerated, Kazantzakis cries out that God is dead. In Nietzsche he found a kindred spirit; here was a tragic philosopher who taught him to leave all religious consolations behind him. From this confessed murderer of God, this iconoclast who lyrically praised life as suffering, he learned the basic truths of nihilism: that the belief in progress is based on illusion, that human destiny is not ruled by reason, and that only cowards and fools are nourished and consoled by the empty myths of religion or the God-supported cult of morality. Knowing all this, the superior man "confronts the world's purposeless phantasmagoria with tranquility. . . ."[14] He acknowledged the same God Nietzsche worshiped—Dionysus.

He studied the work of the German philosopher and wrote a monograph entitled *Friedrich Nietzsche and the Philosophy of Right.* He even visited the places associated with the name of

---

[13] Prevalakis correctly designates Kazantzakis's view of the world as heroic pessimism. "All his works without exception could furnish material for the development of this theme." *Ibid.,* p. 38.

[14] Kazantzakis, *Report to Greco,* p. 322.

Nietzsche, his birthplace in Röcken, in the Prussian province of Saxony, the university town in which he served as professor, the Engadine, the Riviera, Turin. From the master he garnered the insights that make up the foundation of nihilism. The disciple of Zarathustra must live dangerously. The moments of Dionysian illumination and ecstasy are only fleeting moments, evanescent epiphanies, flickers of light that are soon swallowed by sempiternal darkness. Nietzsche confirmed the truth of Kazantzakis's own discovery that the pilgrim of the absolute has no assurance of finally arriving at certainty. The highest deliverance is not to believe in hope and to deny the reality of salvation. Tragedy is man's fate.

Kazantzakis endeavored to reconcile such antinomies as Nietzsche and Buddha, self and society, nihilism and art. Life and death, spirit and flesh, the Occident and the Orient, the ego and the extinction of the personality: out of these conflicts he sought to create a myth that would enable him to overcome chaos.[15] Man, in short, must give up all illusions and go beyond tears, beyond despair, beyond the tragic vision, so that he can respond to the world in a spirit of Dionysian laughter, the laughter of the liberated nihilist.[16] Kazantzakis recommends a tragic form of laughter.[17]

The Odyssey was meant to be a summing up of all that Kazantzakis had experienced in the course of his life—the temptations and the transgressions, the failures and frustrations and triumphs, the suffering and the despair, the Dionysian joy and laughter, the power of affirmation, the miracle of transcendence. He was

---

[15] "Basic to all of Kazantzakis's vision . . . has been the attempt to synthesize what seem to be contraries, antitheses, antinomies." Translator Kimon Friar's Introduction to Kazantzakis, *The Odyssey,* p. xviii.

[16] Kimon Friar insists that it is wrong to call Kazantzakis a nihilist, but his defense of the writer on this score is not convincing.

[17] Kazantzakis, in commenting on the laughter of the Japanese, has this to say: "Laughter has always been for me one of the greatest, most revealing gods. . . . Only the spontaneous, purest laughter can neutralize (not, of course, overcome, because it is never overcome) the horror of life, as long as we live. Tragedy could not have been born (it would have been unbearable for man) had not comedy been born at the same moment. They are twin sisters. Only he who feels the tragedy of life can feel the redeeming power of laughter." Nikos Kazantzakis, *Japan/China,* trans. George C. Pappageotes (New York: Simon and Schuster, 1963), p. 47.

determined to release his anguished cry of protest before the night of nescience covers the earth. Every man, Kazantzakis proclaimed, must let loose his personal cry before death overtakes him. Like Robbe-Grillet, Kazantzakis realizes that this piercing cry may not be answered, that perhaps there is no one to hear it, but it is nevertheless the duty of man to utter his cry. "Well then— shout!"[18] Odysseus, the persona of the poet, is a rebel by temperament, stricken with disbelief but courageous enough to face the vision of the Absurd. The nihilistic quester of the twentieth century, he is no longer national in origin but belongs to the entire Western world.

> His shadow haunts the works of contemporary writers: of Malraux, Sartre, Hermann Hesse, Ernst Jünger, T. S. Eliot. The desperado has something of Don Quixote, but lacks his credulity. He is an open-eyed lover of chimeras, a megalomaniac without any consecrated material for his mania, a hero with contempt for the rewards. . . . His own heroism is nihilistic: he lays no foundations, he does not build, he contributes nothing to the common fund.[19]

How different in character and outlook is Kazantzakis's Odysseus from Goethe's Faust! The twentieth-century desperado signs no compact with the Devil. He knows there is no Heaven and no Hell, no God and therefore no Devil. If, like Faust, he strives toward the goal of Godhood, he is not dependent on God. God is dependent on man's efforts to transform matter into spirit, dust into divinity. God is the spirit of striving, the force that transmutes nothingness into being. Odysseus does not look for redemption to come from God; he must redeem himself. Not only is God man's creation but the world, too, is a reflection of human consciousness. The act of creation counters the dismaying sense of futility called forth by the vision of the absurd. Like Odysseus, Kazantzakis was driven by an inexhaustible lust for life. In his seventies, though suffering from leukemia at the time, he traveled to China. Neither age nor sickness could daunt his hunger for more of life. Like his hero, he disciplined his body

---

[18] Kazantzakis, *Report to Greco*, p. 478.
[19] Pandelis Prevalakis, *Nikos Kazantzakis and His Odyssey*, pp. 58–59.

to obey his soul, and therefore never grew tired. He died as the result of this trip.

2. THE SAVIORS OF GOD

Kazantzakis announced that the theme of the spiritual quest was ended; it could be carried no further. The universe turns an uncomprehending and indifferent gaze on the metaphysical manias of the modern hero. Aeons of evolution have given birth to this flash of consciousness and to this frail, vulnerable body that yearns to enter the realm of spirit, but the flesh is imprisoned in its finitude. Nature grants no exception to any of its creatures; all are destroyed. Kazantzakis knows the nature of his madness, his search for the Absolute, and yet he gives in to it. He is serving a lost cause, but this does not discourage him. He will follow the *via negativa* as far as it will lead him, but even as darkness covers him he will cry out against his incomprehensible fate.[20]

The irrational but irrepressible need for salvation raged like a fever in his blood as he wrote *The Saviors of God* (1927), which describes his desperate struggle to find the God that lies beyond selfhood. To his wife he confessed the difficulties he encountered, the doubts that assailed his mind. He wondered when this search would end. Perhaps there would never be an end to it. Perhaps his purpose was rooted in the search itself, and it may be that this characterizes the progression of God, who is the supreme symbol of human aspiration. "The search itself—upward and with coherence—perhaps this is the purpose of the Universe."[21] He hoped to deliver the message that would free mankind from the trammels of illusion. He would reveal to them that the meaning of life is to be found in life itself. The journey is always toward

[20] Kazantzakis is prophetic in his development of the theme of nihilism and the moral dilemma it creates for the unheroic heroes of our age. Beckett's novels, for all their nihilistic pessimism, portray anti-heroes who, however badly wounded and overcome by infirmities of the flesh, persist in their hopeless quest for ultimate meaning. See *Heroes and Anti-Heroes,* ed. Harold Lubin (San Francisco, Calif.: Chandler Publishing Company, 1968).

[21] Nikos Kazantzakis, *The Saviors of God,* trans. Kimon Friar (New York: Simon and Schuster, 1960), p. 13.

the interior self. God is everywhere, in man, in the work and deeds of daily life, but God stands perpetually in peril. After finishing *The Saviors of God,* Kazantzakis wrote: "His [God's] salvation depends upon us. And only if he is saved may we be saved" (p. 19). He exalts the Immanent Will that Schopenhauer described with loathing. Like Nietzsche, he strives to affirm a transcendent purpose when he is convinced there is none to be found. He declares:

> Where are we going? No one knows. Don't ask, mount higher! Perhaps we are going nowhere. (p. 24)

The Saviors of God gives utterance to a dynamic, affirmative nihilism. Kazantzakis describes the struggle each one must wage to transcend the vision of nada. His beatitude sounds like a demonic chant of blasphemy. He believes that those are thrice blessed who can bear the terrifying and sublime secret that even God does not exist—a leitmotif that is woven into the thematic structure of *The Odyssey.* On Kazantzakis's tombstone are engraved the words: "I do not hope for anything. I do not fear anything. I am free" (p. 36).

Kazantzakis rejected all belief in the supernatural, but like Nietzsche, whose works *The Birth of Tragedy* and *Thus Spake Zarathustra* he had translated into Greek, he longed passionately for the hidden or absent or dead or nonexistent God. He could not follow the example of Unamuno and affirm God's existence in the face of all reasons and proofs to the contrary, but as a poet and mystic he responded to the inexplicable strangeness and mystery of life—the mystery there all around him—the darkness from which he emerged and the darkness of the common earth to which he, like all men, must return. As soon as we are born, each breath brings us nearer to the end: "we die in every moment" (p. 43). But if death seems to be the goal of life, it is combated by the urge to create new life. Two impulses are in irreconcilable conflict: Eros and Thanatos, life and death, creativity and annihilation. Kazantzakis resembles Unamuno in his unceasing effort to fathom the dread mystery of death that baffles the comprehension of reason, but he parts company with him in his insistence that faith in the supernatural is based on illusion.

Kazantzakis has worked out his own philosophy of being. The world is his idea. He created the forms of Nature he beholds, the stars and sun and moon and earth. "Only I exist!" (p. 47). The mind, leaping across all epistemological gulfs, masters the phenomena it creates, establishes "laws," and thus imposes order upon the primordial chaos. Kazantzakis, however, is no Platonic idealist striving to grasp the noumenal reality; the world, which is the creation of man, provides the only reality man can apprehend and dwell in. Yet the mind continues to protest: "Nothing beyond me exists" (p. 48). Kazantzakis accepts the insuperable limitations of the mind that, as Kant demonstrated, can deal with appearances only and the relationship between them. True, it is the mind that perceives these relationships, yet Kazantzakis cannot banish the disturbing thought that perhaps all this is an elaborate game of make-believe, a stupendous hoax. Then the mind sets such foolish notions aside and reasserts its sovereignty: the universe springs to life once more, and man, the explorer in time and space, resumes his struggle and his striving.

This does not, of course, dispose of the matter. Reason, as Kazantzakis well knew, is not the ruler of life; if it prevented him from taking the headlong leap into the sea of faith, it was nonetheless a fallible and absurdly limited instrument of thought. Countering the rational decision to remain within the bounds of the finite was the "mad" metaphysical compulsion to go beyond it. Why labor at science, why seek to conquer space and fight against the fatality of time, if we cannot penetrate the heart of the mystery? Like all romantic rebels, like Melville and Malraux, he was determined to lift the veil of Isis, to track down the secret of the mysterious force which drags us into life and then destroys us, "to discover if behind the visible and unceasing stream of the world an invisible and immutable presence is hiding" (p. 51). Like Nietzsche, he desired to capture the ultimate secret of existence, find out what, if anything, lay beyond the confines of his own mind.

If his mind cried out against this quixotic pursuit of the unknowable, his heart refused to acknowledge the all-too-human limitations that hemmed him in. No, he would deny the report of his senses and the reality of death. The mind, recognizing that life is but "a game, a performance given by the five actors" (p. 53) of the body, bade the heart cease to wage this useless battle, but the heart will not be counseled by the voice of reason. Though he is a creature composed of mud and dreams, man concentrates within himself all the powers of the universe. Like Tolstoy, Kazantzakis wanted to find a single principle of justification which would enable him to endure "this dreadful daily spectacle of disease, of ugliness, of injustice, of death" (p. 54). What is the purpose of this wayfaring from birth to death, from womb to tomb? Kazantzakis knew that Nature is not at all concerned about the fate of man or the perpetuation of the species; it will live on even after the human race is wiped out. Man must be prepared to face the anguish of the nihilistic disclosure that the world of Nature is without heart or mind, meaning or purpose.

Kazantzakis displays existential courage as he confronts this epiphany of the void. It is useless, he concludes, to seek for the reality behind appearances. He repeats his stern injunction that it is the duty of man to relinquish the anchor of hope so that he will be free to strive and to create without thought of reward. The free man must do so even though he is aware that nothing lasts, that all things, however beautiful, he brings to birth will turn to dust. This marks the triumph of the human spirit, that it alone can lend meaning to the cosmic process, that it can affirm life in all its tragic vicissitudes and contradictions.

Numerous contradictions also crop up in Kazantzakis's work. He employs religious terms—faith, striving, God, perfection, spirit, transcendence—to embody his symbolic version of the quest. He finds it enormously difficult to reconcile this religious terminology with his professed atheism and his nihilistic *Weltanschauung*. He emphasizes that nothing can hold back the dreamer in pursuit of the Absolute, neither despair nor the illusion of happiness. For all his intransigent skepticism, Kazantzakis chooses to climb steadily upward. Why does he do so? He can give no reason for his action, and there is no certainty that sustain him during this perilous and exhausting climb.

Through him countless generations speak; the hosts of the dead are now incarnate in him, future generations are alive in his being. He must carry on the work started by his ancestors and play his part in the evolution of human destiny. Catastrophes occur, tragic misfortunes, but the marchers have the courage to face the abyss "without illusion or . . . fear" (p. 78). Man is but an infinitesimal fraction of an unimaginable Whole, a single note in a universal symphony. While the flame of life courses through him, his imperative duty is to voyage toward his goal. God is the force that compels man to strive ever upward from the beast in an ascent that never ends. Man might just as well not have emerged on the terrestrial scene, but now that he has lifted himself above his animal origins he must struggle to go beyond the human. Thus Kazantzakis affirms the "passion" of his commitment to the spiritual quest without ever subscribing to a justificatory purpose or a redemptive faith.

He celebrates the power and the glory of the God who elevates man above the plane of transient joy and sorrow. It is a God who grows out of the pulsating blood and fecund mire of biological evolution, a God who distils light out of darkness, a God of paradoxical incarnations who encompasses all that is and was and shall be. Each one must strive with all his heart to merge with God, who is to be found everywhere, in the most unlikely places. God wears a multitude of masks and semantic disguises. He can be named, says Kazantzakis, "Abyss, Mystery, Absolute Darkness, Absolute Light, Matter, Spirit, Ultimate Hope, Ultimate Despair, Silence" (p. 101). God changes his features and character as well as his name. He grows, but He is now one with the Abyss. This is "the new, contemporary face of God" (p. 103). Kazantzakis beholds, not the God of logic or mathematics, but a God who is born from a dialectic of contradictions, from the incessant conflict between dung and spirit, death and life. He is a God who must, like man, struggle without the support of certainty. He knows not in advance whether he will be victorious or be defeated. In a contingent universe "he gambles all his destiny at every moment" (p. 104). So does man.

The final section of *The Saviors of God,* called "Silence," resounds with Kazantzakis's bitter cry of triumph. The time comes

when the striving spirit ceases to strive, when the warrior no longer
hurls his rhetoric of defiance at the heedless skies, when the mind
merges with the flowering Silence. Each one, Kazantzakis reiterates,
must free himself in his own way: there are no guides, no *vade
mecum*. Indeed, "no Savior exists to open up the road. No road
exists to be opened" (p. 129). In the Silence the pilgrim tears off,
one by one, the innumerable masks God puts on, and comes to
understand the meaning of the Abyss. Kazantzakis blesses those
who believe that only God and they exist; he also blesses those
who feel they are made one with the Lord of Hosts; but he blesses
thrice those who have grasped the truth of the secret: "THAT
EVEN THIS ONE DOES NOT EXIST!" (p. 131).

3. THE ODYSSEUS MYTH

Kazantzakis departs from the traditional framework of the myth
by taking up the adventures of Odysseus, the far-wandering hero
whose spirit cannot be confined by hearth and home, wife and
son, after he slays the suitors in the palace. Thus he is able to
range far afield, to give his imagination ample freedom to invent
new versions of the motif of the quest. Odysseus is portrayed as
the representative of modern man living in a civilization on the
verge of collapse. He seeks God, but the kind of God he seeks we
can by this time readily surmise. In exploring the various roads
that lead to freedom, Kazantzakis rejects the Oriental ideal of
contemplation and renunciation[22] and tries to defeat the forces
of chaos and old night.

The Prologue sounds the motif that will be embodied in the
narrative proper: the perilous yet joyous quest that is not to be
restrained by the dictates of prudence or the realization that the

---

[22] As Kazantzakis says: "The supreme ideal of the Orient is to unite the I with the
infinite.... Passive contemplation, the bliss of renunciation, an utterly trustful
self-abandonment to mysterious and impersonal forces: such is the essence of the
Orient." Quoted in W. B. Stanford, *The Ulysses Theme* (Oxford: Basil Blackwell,
1954), p. 238.

universe is born of the fiat of the human mind. The central theme focuses on the process whereby all earthly things are transformed into spirit. For that to be achieved, freedom must break out of the chains of necessity.

At the very beginning of the epic, Odysseus strikes a note of revolt. Having inherited the qualities of the three Fates—Tantalus, Prometheus, and Herakles—who hovered over his cradle, he refuses to settle down. He will not submit to the iron law that decrees that since death is inevitable, man must perforce yield to the command of the earth. To Odysseus this is anathema. Though he knows that in the end the earth triumphs, he will not be deflected from his goal by the weakness of the body. He recounts how he had been tempted by each of the various disguises Death wears: the Circean enchantment of sensual love that turns man into beast and the temptation, personified by Nausicaa, of following the placid routine of domestic life. He will leave his home and set out on this voyage of exploration with a few congenial comrades: Captain Clam; Hardihood, the bronzesmith; Kentaur, the Falstaffian trencherman who is no coward; Orpheus, the minstrel; and finally, Granite, a wanderer from his native land.

Kazantzakis weaves his own philosophical speculation into the warp and woof of his narrative. Odysseus relates the parable of how the battle of the worm (man) against the might of God ended: man's ingenuity and indomitable will forged a sword of iron and slew God in Heaven. This worm is capable of defying even unto death the tyrannical God who seeks to exercise absolute dominion over the earth and its creatures. Odysseus feels that the sword of the worm that killed God has fallen into his hands.

Odysseus, who welcomes the call of danger, cares not where the journey takes him. He has entered upon this quest together with his followers, knowing that none would return. The earth, which will last until the end of time, is unmoved by this singular human craving to taste all of experience before death supervenes. Odysseus reveals the metaphysical madness that has him in its grasp, the urge to be utterly consumed in the flame of life. The resurrection takes place hourly, the world strives unceasingly upward, and the mind, too, risen from the grave of despair, gives

KAZANTZAKIS: DIONYSIAN NIHILISM

birth to nobler thoughts until finally the ultimate thought breaks through: "Death."[23]

It is these insights that make Odysseus a free man. A skeptic, a born rebel, he carries on the tradition represented by such heroes as Manfred, Ahab, Ivan Karamazov, and Maldoror. Whereas Menelaus believes that defiance is blasphemy, that it is incumbent on man to accept calmly whatever fate ordains, Odysseus asserts that it is man's highest duty to combat his fate. The spirit must dominate the body and leave nothing undone that is within its power to do. That is why Odysseus welcomes the invasion of the barbarians, those who will conquer the countries inhabited by an exhausted people.

Odysseus is a desperado who cannot be broken on the wheel of fortune. Since life is a dream, he will not allow himself to be crushed by the dead weight of the past, for the past, too, is a mirage. A disillusioned fighter, Odysseus will not permit even the gods to curb his freedom; the gods are but the children of his mind; fathered in darkness by the magic of dreams, they come chiefly at night and vanish like ghosts at break of day. When he calls on God for help and finds that the God who answers his call (a God who takes on the likeness of Odysseus) is frightened, he repudiates this craven God. Odysseus knows that if he dies, then God dies with him.

Having overcome the fear of death, Odysseus does not fear God. But he is forever dogged by the shadow of Death. No hero of our time has been more tenaciously pursued by the hound of Death. It keeps on sending him messages, reminders, but he is not frightened. God endeavors to cow mankind with the weapon of terror, but man resists by affirming the freedom of his mind. It is then that Odysseus announces his discovery that God is shaped by man. It is man whose ten fingers mold the clay into the figure of God.

When the wanderers reach Egypt and sail down the Nile, visiting along the way a ghost town peopled by tombs and ruins and gods bearing the heads of animals, Odysseus recognizes the symbolic enactment of what he had long known: the gods struggle to over-

[23] Nikos Kazantzakis, *The Odyssey: A Modern Sequel,* trans. Kimon Friar (New York: Simon and Schuster, 1958), 4:263.

come the beast in man. He is surprised by none of life's vicissitudes. Hunger, suffering, plagues, disaster, devastation, sudden death—all these serve a higher, if still obscure, purpose. If he agrees to participate in the revolutionary struggle, he is not deluded by millennial expectations; he is not interested in abstract questions of justice or right; he simply obeys the mandates of his heart. The revolutionaries agree to accept him on his terms: they will fight for freedom and bread and justice while he pursues his quest for God. He tells the revolutionaries the nature of the faith that spurs him on: he will not allow hope to hold him captive. He will persist in his search for God to the end of the world.

When Odysseus leaves Egypt with his rabble of an army, the dregs of society, he bids these outlaws, in the name of the God whose fearful mask he displays, to choose between creaturely comforts and the hazards of the quest. His followers, sustained by their longing for freedom, must be prepared to endure the worst blows of adversity for the sake of building the ideal city. He tells them he is under the command of a God who grants no mercy, a God who grows as man grows. There is to be no yielding to weakness or despair. The nature of his "religious" madness is evident in his declaration that the more boldly man extends the horizon of his journey and explores new roads, the more does God manifest himself on earth.

Thus God assumes the character man invests him with: barbaric or tame, Dionysian or Apollonian, civilized or savage. God needs man because the two are one. This is the faith that animates Odysseus as he goes ahead with his plan of building the ideal city. His God is a God of transformation, the worm bursting its entrails to become a bright-winged butterfly, but this God is also cruel, effecting his cosmic purpose, whatever it may be, without the bestowal of love. Orpheus, the gullible poet, may fall to the ground and worship the idol his own hands have fashioned, but not Odysseus. In his dreams at night, when he is merged with all of Nature, Odysseus perceives that the distinction between life and death rests on illusion; they are one and the same. God stirs within man, striving through the force of blood and the eruption of violence to rise above the earth and beyond man. The spirit must be released from its tenement of clay. That is how man emulates and finally becomes God.

When catastrophe overtakes the ideal city he has built and everything is destroyed, Odysseus is put to the test. He turns his mind inward and beholds the tragic vision, which teaches that all experience, even the worst, is to be accepted. He preserves his faith in the power of the mind, its capacity to create its own gods. In facing the challenge of Death, Odysseus reaffirms his Promethean belief that man must not give up the endless struggle to transform flesh into spirit and darkness into light.

It is at this juncture that Kazantzakis gives expression to his nihilistic *Weltanschauung*. Odysseus grasps the relativistic truth that the universe is conceived differently by each mind. When consciousness is extinguished, phenomena disappear. Man is the creator of phantasmagorias that temporarily hold the howling legions of darkness at bay. This insight sets Odysseus free. His freedom consists of the knowledge that there is nothing beyond the veil. Now, like Zarathustra, he can dance joyously as he embraces life in all its intractable contradictions. He has no need to be saved. He shapes some clay into an image of God and then crushes it in the dirt. Once God is slain, his mind is released from its thralldom. Odysseus celebrates the beauty and plenitude of life without purpose, as if echoing the Dionysian theme Nietzsche formulated in *The Birth of Tragedy*: "that this world can be justified only as an esthetic phenomenon."[24]

Having beheld this vision of the universe as an aesthetic spectacle, Odysseus is able to reconcile the contradictions of existence and bless everything that *is,* the evil as well as the good. His quest for beauty and virtue and truth was a mistake, though it, too, was part of an overall plan. Odysseus, like Kazantzakis, praises the creative power of the mind to impose cosmos on chaos.

Having climbed the tower beyond tragedy, Odysseus looks upon death as the challenge that adds zest to life. As he tells the prostitute, nothing exists, neither the you nor the I; it is all a dream.

[24] Friedrich Nietzsche, *The Birth of Tragedy* and *The Genealogy of Morals,* trans. Francis Golffing (Garden City, N.Y.: Doubleday & Company, 1956), p. 143.

He proclaims a nihilism that is fundamentally joyous. He is buoyed up by the knowledge that man is alone in the world, that human life lasts but for a brief flash of time; the mind must conquer the terror of death. While the flame of life still burns in his blood, he will praise the universe of being, the miracle of life that springs out of death. Hence, when the Tempter bids him enter the state of nonbeing, since he is purged of hope and desire, he repeates the truth that has set him free: the knowledge that he is the savior, though there is no salvation for mortal man.

Toward the end of *The Odyssey* the thematic intention becomes more clearly defined: the quest has turned into a battle against Death. The search for ultimate meaning is essentially a struggle to conquer Death. With no God to help him, Odysseus marches on toward his final adventure. He is consistent in his espousal of the nihilistic vision. He knows that no intelligent Power watches over mankind or even stoops to mock human aspirations, failures, and defeats. All he knows is the Nemesis that destroys us. Today the soul of man is free, not governed by God or fate, capable of directing its own destiny. When Odysseus reaches the world's end, he reflects on the meaning of life and the nature of God. He suddenly perceives that God is a projection of the human mind, "a labyrinthine quest deep in our heads."[25] Kazantzakis reaffirms the reality and the glory of the Quest.

The end of the epic describes how Odysseus dies his own death. Odysseus dies, all his faculties are darkened, like the light of a lamp that goes out; his mind breaks free and enters the kingdom of freedom, no longer subject to the dominion of death. He dies with laughter on his lips, but it is not the mocking laughter of Caligula in Camus's play of the Absurd. It is Dionysian laughter, the laughter of a nihilistic Prometheus who knows that life and death are songs and the mind "the singing bird" (XXIV:1383). His last cry is "Forward."

4. CONCLUSION

Here is an epic that describes the difficult quest of a modern hero in search of God, in the course of which he raises the age-

[25] Kazantzakis, *The Odyssey*, XXII, 414.

old questions and answers them in his own iconoclastic way. He is determined to experience all forms of life, to fulfill every potentiality of his being. Like Faust, he is filled with the spirit of infinite striving. Despite his nihilism, Kazantzakis did not share the general feeling that in this age of crisis and catastrophe, the nuclear material for the construction of epics had been exhausted. Precisely in such an age, he argued, are epics born. As he wrote:

> For me, the *Odyssey* is a new epical-dramatic attempt of the modern man to find deliverance by passing through all the stages of contemporary anxieties and by pursuing the most daring hopes. What deliverance? He does not know as he starts, but he creates it constantly with his joys and sorrows, with his successes and failures, with his disappointments, fighting always. This, I am certain, is the anguished struggle, whether conscious or subconscious, of the modern man (p. xii).

Kazantzakis's hero may never find deliverance, but it is characteristic of him, as it is of the author, that he always fights on. What makes Odysseus so representative a figure of our time is that even as he realizes that the mind of man is incapable of ever penetrating to the heart of things, he presses further ahead in his need to find some object of ultimate concern.[26]

It is this Promethean evangel, both nihilistic and heroic in content, that the poet promulgates in his work. God needs man— this is one of the leitmotifs of the poem—because man embodies His highest manifestation.[27] We have seen that Kazantzakis's pantheon includes such diverse figures as Buddha and Christ,

[26] The most oppressive problem modern man has to face is that of handling the anxiety generated by his encounter with the specter of meaninglessness. The self cannot bear up under the mounting pressure of spiritual emptiness, the enervating sense of utter purposelessness. The human spirit breaks down when it is not sustained by a feeling that its life is basically meaningful. The absence of meaning must be courageously confronted and then transcended so that the self that is not can come into being. A decision must be made even though the outcome of that decision cannot be assured. Man must gamble by leaping into the problematical future. "We create our values." Herbert Fingarette, *The Self in Transformation* (New York and London: Basic Books, 1963), p. 101.

[27] For Jung, too, the gods are the personification of psychic forces. Whatever God may be, He cannot be endowed with the quality of existence. See Raymond Hostie, *Religion and the Psychology of Jung,* trans. G. R. Lamb (New York: Sheed and Ward, 1957). See also C. G. Jung, *Answer to Job,* trans. R. F. C. Hull (London: Routledge & Kegan Paul, 1954).

Lenin and St. Francis, Nietzsche and Greco. Though he is repeatedly drawn to the Christ theme, he treats it, as one might expect, in
an unorthodox fashion. *The Last Temptation of Christ* includes
no resurrection. Observe how Jesus, in the novel, reflects on the
fruitful relation between God and man.

> Without man, God would have no mind on this earth. . . .
>   But man, without God, would have been obliterated by hunger, fear
> and cold: and if he survived these, he would have crawled like a slug
> midway between the lions and the lice: and if with incessant struggle
> he managed to stand on his hind legs, he would never have been able
> to escape the tight, warm, tender embrace of his mother the monkey. . . .
> Reflecting on this, Jesus felt more deeply than he had ever felt before
> that God and man could become one.[28]

If Kazantzakis found a kindred spirit in Odysseus, he was also
able to identify himself with Jesus, the man who would fain
become God. Like Gide, Kazantzakis was fascinated by the duality
of the sacrificial son of God, essentially human in his aspirations
and yet yearning to become God. The life of Christ demonstrates,
only in a more extreme form, the battle all men must wage between
flesh and spirit, the Devil and God. In the Prologue Kazantzakis
remarks: "I have fought to reconcile these two primordial forces
which are so contrary to each other, to make them realize that
they are not enemies but, rather, fellow workers . . ." (p. 1). His
interpretation of the Christ mythos is closely bound up with his
belief that all men partake of the divine, not only in the spirit but
also in the flesh. "That is why the mystery of Christ is not simply
a mystery for a particular creed: it is universal. The struggle between
God and man breaks out in everyone, together with the longing
for reconciliation." (pp. 1–2). Christ, like Odysseus, offers a perfect
model "to the man who struggles . . ." (p. 4).

Whether Christ or Odysseus is his hero, Kazantzakis transforms
Schopenhauer's Will into a Dionysian love of life. Kazantzakis
says yes to the life-force, yes to ugliness, evil, violence, terror,
yes to the snake and the ant and the worm as well as the eagle and

[28] Nikos Kazantzakis, *The Last Temptation of Christ,* trans. P. A. Bien (New
York: Simon and Schuster, 1960), p. 281.

butterfly and nightingale. It is when he attempts to affirm the principle of endless striving that he falls into a quagmire of contradictions. He cannot, like Odysseus, determine what purpose this passion of the quest is meant to serve.

Thus Kazantzakis presents a tragic yet not disheartening version of the quest. God is a flame lit by the spirit of man. Death is final, but the earth is both creator and destroyer. There is no cause for despair. The tragic hero, released from the bondage of hope and fear, can respond to the beauty of existence and observe with equanimity how life feeds on life. Whereas Nietzsche in *Thus Spake Zarathustra* unfolds the demented dream of eternal recurrence, Kazantzakis in *The Odyssey* communicates his Dionysian vision of cosmic ecstasy, a pantheistic vitalism that requires no rational justification. The Schopenhauerian Will is blind, but Kazantzakis attempts to make it see; it is cruel, but the cruelty gives rise to incredible beauty; it breeds death, but it is also the source of life everlastingly renewed.

PART V:
Conclusion

16

Conclusion

To write is to affirm at the very least the superiority of *this* order over *that* order. But superiority according to what code of values? Any answer will necessarily contradict complete nihilism. For the complete nihilist, suicide, not the creation of significant forms, is the only consistent gesture.[1]

What threatens contemporary man is that which I call "the existential vacuum" within him. What we have to deal with, then, is, as it were, a "living" nihilism, characterized, as is each sort of nihilism, by the denial that Being has meaning.[2]

I believe that neither life nor history has an ultimate meaning which in turn imparts meaning to the life of the individual or justifies his suffering. . . . Only man can find a goal for life and the means for the realization of this goal. He cannot find a saving ultimate answer but he can strive for a degree of intensity, depth and clarity of experience which gives him the strength to live without illusions, and to be free.[3]

The great task of humanity, now that "God is dead," is, as Nietzsche was the first to realize, the conquest of nihilism. The world has not made much progress in that direction since his famous announcement. God has not risen again from the dead, and the ideal of the Superman that was to replace him has been vulgarized by barbarians like Mussolini and Hitler. Nihilism—nothingness, despair, and the nervous hilarity that goes with them—remains the universal state of mind. From such an abyss the soul of man does not rise in a decade or two. If a human

[1] Wayne C. Booth, *The Rhetoric of Fiction* (Chicago: The University of Chicago Press, 1961), p. 298.
[2] Victor E. Frankl, *From Death-Camp to Existentialism,* trans. Ilse Lasch (Boston: Beacon Press, 1959), p. 99.
[3] Erich Fromm, *Beyond the Chains of Illusion* (New York: Simon and Schuster, 1962), pp. 175–76.

world survives the atomic holocaust—and it is now difficult to see how such a holocaust is to be avoided—it will only be because man has first overcome his Nihilism.[4]

An intelligent and sensitive man who genuinely believed that life was entirely without meaning and purpose, an idiotic accident, would never take pains not only to write but also to negotiate and argue with agents, publishers, theatre managers, and the rest.[5]

Pure chance, absolutely free but blind, at the very root of the stupendous edifice of evolution: this central concept of modern biology is no longer one among other possible or even conceivable hypotheses. It is today the *sole* conceivable hypothesis, the only one that squares with observed and tested fact.[6]

Most of the writers I have discussed repudiate the invidious label of nihilism. If they entertained nihilist beliefs in the past, they subsequently outgrew them and cast them off. Since nihilism is commonly used as a pejorative term, few writers are willing to call themselves nihilists. Those who do—a Gottfried Benn, a Kazant-zakis—are again and again faced with the embarrassing question of why they continue to practice their art. The mind, however governed by instinct and the power of the irrational, strives to achieve some measure of consistency in the conduct of life. When the light of meaning is totally eclipsed and the darkness of despair shrouds the soul, the *complete* nihilist would be, as Wayne C. Booth contends, logically driven to take his own life. But the *complete* nihilist does not exist. His nihilism is a matter of degree; he revises his outlook as he grows older. Nor is he the slave of logic. He uses logic for his own ends. Like Camus in *The Myth of*

---

[4] Herbert Read, *The Contrary Experience* (New York: Horizon Press, 1963), p. 69.
[5] J. B. Priestley, *Man's Time* (Garden City, N.Y.: Doubleday & Company, 1964), pp. 180–81. This is the substance of the charge commonly hurled at the literary nihilist. If he truly believed in the nihilism he preaches, he would give up his creative calling and lapse into silence. When Nietzsche was asked why he wrote, he replied tersely that he had hitherto "found no other means of *getting rid of* my thoughts." Friedrich Nietzsche, *Joyful Wisdom,* trans. Thomas Common (New York: Fredrick Ungar Publishing Co., 1960), p. 127.
[6] Jacques Monod, *Chance and Necessity,* trans. Austryn Wainhouse (New York: Alfred A. Knopf, 1971), pp. 112–13.

Sisyphus, he is quick to realize that suicide fails to solve his problem. It is difficult to picture a writer who would fit the model, whatever that might be, of a *complete* nihilist. The literary art of the confirmed nihilist consists of a symbolic interrogation of the universe, perhaps a way of shedding his metaphysical sickness; often it represents a struggle against the very nihilism he voices in his work. Booth points out

> that though we may find lost characters in hopeless situations, characters whose only discovery is that there is nothing to discover, or whose final action is suicide or some other gesture of despair, the works in which they appear can be called nihilistic only in a loose, conventional sense.[7]

In fact, "most so-called nihilistic works are ... really works of active protest or even of affirmation. ..."[8] The writer who beholds the epiphany of the void struggles hard to cure himself of his ontological wound.

The nihilist may be utterly wrong in his judgments, but he will not abandon them simply because they are brought under attack. His declared bankruptcy of faith not only in God but in life itself, his awareness that the experiment in civilization is but a transient episode in the spectacular profusion of energy in space, his suspicion that the goals men set for themselves are less substantial than the stuff of dreams, his knowledge of the ineluctable and absurd fate of death—these insights are not born of a perverse intellect or a morbid mood. They indicate, rather, that the writer in question is wrestling with problems of ultimate concern. They reflect his uncompromising fidelity to what he regards as the truth of being.

He is not satisfied with this dismal conclusion and therefore seeks a way out. He is a divided personality, at war with himself, burdened with contradictions he cannot resolve. He may, like Andreyev or Céline, vent his rage in furibund negations; like Artzybashef, he may project a philosophy of universal suicide.

---

[7] Booth, *The Rhetoric of Fiction,* p. 298.
[8] *Ibid.,* p. 299.

Or, in the manner of Anatole France, he may embrace a hedonistic and cynical form of nihilism. If life is meaningless and tomorrow we die, then there is no reason why man should not live solely for the sake of pleasure. Unamuno used his powerful intellect to attack rationalism in order to satisfy his longing for immortality and overcome his dread of nada. Those who refused to take this irrational leap into faith tended to accept their role in history. Camus joined the Resistance movement and published his ethic of revolt in *The Rebel*. Sartre became a militant Marxist. As we have seen, Kazantzakis, though haunted by his perception of the vanity of all earthly effort, affirmed the beauty of paganism, sought to become a saint, supported the Communist cause, even though he knew that all his aspirations served no purpose. "I believe that there is no religion more in accord with man's deepest hardihood than the cultivation of purposeless heroism."[9]

If the universe is absurd, it is the consciousness of man that perceives the absurdity and either becomes resigned to it or decides to revolt against it. If the vision of nothingness is the source of the anomie that afflicts the intelligentsia today, then the act of writing about it, the effort to understand it and deal with it somehow in terms of art, is not in itself absurd. If God does not exist, then man is responsible for creating his own values, values that are relative and true for him at this hour and this place, even though the mysterious universe lends no support to his affirmations. Nature drives home the lesson that nothing endures. All men are the victims of time and death; it is the specter of death that overshadows every moment of human existence. As William James observes: "The fact that we *can* die ... is what perplexes us; the fact that we now for a moment live and are well is irrelevant to that perplexity. We need a life not correlated with death. ..."[10]

It is the craving for a moral order that justifies existence and demonstrates that evil, suffering, and death are not meaningless, that makes itself strongly felt in the work of such nineteenth-century

[9] Peter Bien, "Nikos Kazantzakis (1883–1957)," in George A. Panichas, ed., *The Politics of the Twentieth-Century Novel* (New York: Hawthorn Books, 1971), p. 154.
[10] William James, *The Varieties of Religious Experience* (New York: Longmans, Green & Co., 1902), p. 137.

prophets as Dostoevski, Kierkegaard, and Nietzsche. Dostoevski, speaking through the mask of Ivan Karamazov, asserts that he cannot live according to scientific principles of causation; he must have justice and he wants it now. How can the suffering of children on earth be justified? Kierkegaard found a cure for the sickness unto death by surrendering the self to the Absolute of the Absurd that is God—an experience that cannot be directly communicated. Nietzsche welcomed the challenge of chaos and responded to it by affirming the sovereignty of art. The mark of the free spirit is its superabundance of creative energy. Values are the result of man's unremitting efforts to enhance life.[11]

It was Nietzsche who explored the full range of possibilities of art as salvation. He derived from Schopenhauer the idea of aesthetically validating the universe. He grappled with the problem that lies at the heart of nihilism: whether existence could be invested with significance. Life, as Nietzsche saw it, was an enigma, a magnificent but fortuitous display of energy. He posed the crucial question of our time: if there is no overriding pattern of significance in the world, then what is to be done? His reply was that life must be embraced despite the worst ordeals of suffering to which man is exposed. What characterizes the uniqueness of man is his ability to introject the knowledge that there are no absolute goals. It is man who confers meaning and value on the world. By acting on his nihilistic premises, man is able to construct his own universe. Rejoicing in the death of God, the superman is free to exert the full force of his will and to live without the prop of certainty.

Nihilism denies that total and true assertions about existence are possible, since it believes, among other things, that existence is basically irrational. The writer as nihilist, however, is often guilty of making a total assertion, one beyond the reach of proof, that life is incomprehensible and therefore, as far as he is concerned, irremediably absurd. He continues to view this allegedly hopeless situation from different viewpoints as if by dwelling on it obsessively he can perhaps discover some convincing reason for

[11] William Earle, "The Paradox and Death of God," in William Earle, James M. Edie, and John Wild, *Christianity and Existentialism* (Evanston, Ill.: Northwestern University Press, 1963), p. 85.

existence, though he assumes beforehand that none is to be found. Nevertheless, he does not fall into silence and, consequently, does not utterly despair. He is, after all, not bound to keep faith with the spirit of nihilism. He is, in fact, prepared at a moment's notice to abandon his position and go beyond it. He examines his nihilism skeptically from opposing angles of vision, at times laughing at himself and his predicament. He fights nihilism in this and in other ways because he will not allow himself to become a victim of his own thoughts. He decides to live for a relative ideal, to devote his energies to some social or political cause. The universe may be devoid of meaning, but it offers a stage on which he is free to work out the drama of his life.[12]

The literary nihilist does not reason his way into this metaphysical cul-de-sac, nor as a rule is he able to reason his way out of it. He hails contradiction as the law of life. In any event, the writer who transmutes his nihilistic vision into the form of art is, in effect, rebelling against it. He is not by any means resigned to things as they are. The myth of Sisyphus exposes the absurd trap in which mankind is caught, but the artistic embodiment of this myth is in itself a symbolic act of revolt. A creature of paradox, the nihilist adopts the role of metaphysical rebel. While continuing to live, he vents his rage against the curse or farce of life. The creative nihilist is guilty of *hubris* in condemning all of existence as futile and he strains the resources of his art to communicate his message of cosmic futility.[13] He professes to seek no converts and

---

[12] "Yet this life, so demonstrably worthless, remains for every man of unique value, and everything else depends on it. With its loss all reality vanishes for him, the whole world collapses. He has to reconcile himself to the fact of natural death, and he is able to develop a faith in values which transcend life, so that he can give a meaning to death." Paul Roubiczek, *Thinking in Opposites* (London: Routledge and Kegan Paul, 1952), p. 4.

[13] In "Never *Nothing,*" George P. Elliot attacks the dangerous presumptions of literary nihilists, their hubristic aspiration toward "nothing." Nihilism he defines as "a philosophy of rage, for it can never attain what it wants, can be neither fulfilled nor permanently relieved. Its fulfillment would be to have all things cease to exist, the Void...." (George P. Elliot, *Conversions* [New York: E. P. Dutton & Co., 1971], p. 212). Nihilism, he holds, "is an ethical impulse: it is fed by, expresses, justifies the rage of some whom rationalism has unchristianed. It is the dark side

yet he strives to make his fellow men, his potential readers, realize the enormity of the fraud that has been perpetrated upon them.

In every generation appear men of vision who refuse the world as it is while remaining in it. They ask all over again the age-old questions: What am I living for? What is life worth? Since death is bound sooner or later to overtake all those who are now alive, what is the ultimate meaning and purpose of life? These are the very questions that, from the beginning of recorded time, man has attempted to answer. What was the purpose of the ancient myths if not to affirm the continuity of life and to assume the rebirth of the dying God. What is the underlying dynamic of the tragic vision if not to redeem the order of the world from the empire of chaos and the oblivion of old night? The heart of man is so constituted that it cannot reconcile itself to a universe that is completely indifferent to the fate of the human race.[14] As Dostoevski wrote: "Without some goal and some effort to reach it no man can live. When he has lost all hope, all object in life, man often becomes a monster in his misery."[15]

Nihilism frequently culminates in a form of secular humanism, which shares many of the beliefs of nihilism, though it arrives at conclusions that distinguish it from the philosophy of nihilism. Humanists are in search of the truth of the human condition, whatever that truth happens to be:

> if in fact it is gloomy, and they have to build on despair or on the other side of despair, so be it; at least they can build and do not have to turn bored and indolent or violent and destructive. Nihilism does not follow logically from humanist premises.[16]

of the Enlightenment." (*Ibid.,* p. 214). He accuses nihilists of forming a militant sect. "Believing in nothing, doubting everything except their own doubts, they also want you to believe in nothing, at least to doubt everything." (*Ibid.,* p. 220).
[14] According to Walter Kaufmann, the realization that the universe is not governed by some transcendental purpose should prove exhilarating. "Life ceases to be so oppressive: we are free to give our own lives meaning and purpose, free to redeem our suffering by making something of it." Walter Kaufmann, *The Faith of a Heretic* (Garden City, N.Y.: Doubleday & Company, 1961), p. 178.
[15] Fyodor Dostoevski, *The House of the Dead,* trans. Constance Garnett (New York: The Macmillan Company, 1917), p. 240.
[16] H. J. Blackham, "The Pointlessness of It All," in H. J. Blackham, ed., *Objections to Humanism* (London: Constable, 1963), p. 107.

Both humanism and nihilism acknowledge that the ultimate end of life is death. "On humanist assumptions, life leads to nothing, and every pretense that it does not is a deceit."[17] Humanism departs from nihilism in its insistence that though death marks the end of all endeavor, it does not follow that human life cannot pursue a meaningful and rewarding, even if man-made, purpose.[18]

Humanism, for all its limitations of vision, provides the writer with a framework of viable values. E. M. Forster, for example, believes in the sanctity of personal relations. The sound of "Boum" reverberates through *A Passage to India* as a reminder that all religious faiths—Buddhism, Mohammedanism, Hinduism, Christianity—are not only ineffectual in piercing the mystery of existence but actually absurd. Yet this pervasive symbol of the ineffable Absurd does not diminish the force of Forster's insistence on the sacredness of friendship and love in the life of man. Forster acknowledges the ultimate victory of the void, but he does not let this knowledge affect his humane values.

> The people I respect most behave as if they were immortal and as if society was eternal. Both assumptions are false: both of them must be accepted as true if we are to go on eating and working and loving, and are to keep open a few breathing holes for the human spirit. No millennium seems likely to descend upon humanity . . . no form of Christianity and no alternative to Christianity will bring peace to the world or integrity to the individual; no 'change of heart' will occur.[19]

---

[17] *Ibid.,* p. 119.

[18] Leonard Woolf, when at the age of eighty-eight he was writing the last volume of his autobiography, asked himself what all his conscientious labor had achieved. Looking back over the past, he felt that his work was utterly useless, yet he was not disheartened by the objective evidence of the futility of his efforts. He knew that in the light of eternity the human adventure mattered not at all; "but in one's own personal life, in terms of humanity and human society, certain things are of immense importance: human relations, happiness, truth, beauty or art, justice and mercy. . . . And in a wider context, though all that I tried to do politically was completely futile and ineffective and unimportant, for me personally it was right and important that I should do it, even though at the back of my mind I was well aware that it was ineffective and unimportant." Leonard Woolf, *The Journey Not the Arrival Matters* (New York: Harcourt, Brace & World, 1969), p. 172.

[19] E. M. Forster, *Two Cheers for Democracy* (New York: Harcourt, Brace and Company, 1951), p. 71.

Joseph Conrad also communicated in his fiction his awareness of the futility of human aspiration in the cosmic scheme of things, but he balanced the nihilistic vision by exalting the human qualities of courage, fidelity, and endurance in the face of hardship, danger, and death. If he pictured the dark, the tragic side of existence, he did not fail to celebrate the greatness of the human spirit.

The outbreak of the First World War unleashed a movement called Dada, which rejected *in toto* not only Christianity but humanism as well. It exposed the meaninglessness of Western culture, it marked the apotheosis of the Absurd. Carrying skepticism to a violent extreme, Dada culminated in a nihilism that spat upon the vaunted ideals of the race. Nothing mattered. Art was a pointless activity. Many of the gifted artists affiliated with the Dada group questioned the value of art because they did not believe that life had any meaning. Picabia, like Marcel Duchamp, was a nihilist of this stamp.

> Picabia confronted us with a radical belief in unbelief, a total contempt for art. . . . I could see that there was more in him than the anti-art impulse incessantly belied by his works. Over and above this, there was an urge to deny that there is any sense or meaning in life as such, a rejection of art in so far as it constitutes an affirmation of life.[20]

Alfred Jarry went even further than the devotees of Dada in turning against everything the world of man stood for. He condemned not only the society of his time but the cosmos as a whole. Convinced that death reduced all human striving to nothingness, he threw his life away as a thing of no worth. Antonin Artaud saw enormous possibilities in Jarry's nihilistic aesthetic: it could support his use of the drama as a protest against the intolerable condition of human life.[21]

---

[20] Hans Richter, *Dada: Art and Anti-art* (New York and Toronto: McGraw-Hill Book Company, n.d.), p. 72.
[21] "For him [Artaud] all drama was an action that emanated from a perception of man's helplessness in a universe of which he could comprehend that it was implacably hostile. On a cosmic level man's cry of defiance is only that of a mote whirled around in a trackless void; but on a microcosmic level of the drama, man's protest attains the significance granted to it by its more restricted context." George E. Wellwarth, *The Theater of Protest and Paradox* (New York: New York University Press, 1964), p. 13.

The literary nihilist continues to write and thus tries to conquer the pessimism that oppresses him. As Gottfried Benn points out:

> The accomplished work itself is a denial of decay and doom. Even if creative man realizes that the cycles of culture must end, including the one to which he belongs—one cycle ends, another reaches its zenith, above everything floats infinity whose essence is probably not accessible to human comprehension—creative man faces all this and says to himself: weighing on me in this hour is the unknown and deadly law which I must follow: in this situation I must assert myself, confront this hour with my work and thereby give it articulate expression.[22]

Nihilism, Benn maintains, is inevitable. Nothing can avert the catastrophe that will soon overtake civilization. This is the ineluctable law of life: "Nothing is, if anything ever was; nothing will be."[23] The twilight of history announces the end of man.[24] The world has not come to an end, and creative man today is faced with the stupendous task of shaping his destiny in the future despite the knowledge he has gleaned of his own insignificance in the universe.[25] Biologist Jacques Monod ends his book *Chance and Necessity* on this inspiriting note: "The ancient covenant is in pieces; man knows at last that he is alone in the universe's unfeeling immensity, out of which he emerged only by chance. His destiny is nowhere spelled out, nor is his duty. The kingdom above or the darkness below: it is for him to choose."[26]

The only way to transcend nihilism is not by vehemently denying that it exists, as if by incantation the specter of absolute pessimism

---

[22] Gottfried Benn, *Primal Vision,* ed. E. B. Ashton (Norfolk, Conn.: New Directions, n.d.), p. 210.

[23] *Ibid.,* p. 82.

[24] "Benn believed that nihilism is the inevitable frame of mind of every contemporary European whose mind is highly developed; but, in later years especially, he also speaks of 'transcending nihilism,' and this is done by setting up new values to take the place of those no longer tenable. . . ." Michael Hamburger, *Contraries* (New York: E. P. Dutton & Co., 1970), p. 326.

[25] "A man who looks through the historical parade of cultures and civilizations, styles and isms which provide most of us with a glorious and yet miserably fragile sense of immortal identity, defined status, and collective grandeur faces the central truth of our nothingness—and, *mirabile dictu,* gains power from it." Erik H. Erikson, *Gandhi's Truth* (New York: W. W. Norton & Company, 1969), p. 397.

[26] Monod, *Chance and Necessity,* p. 180.

can be exorcised. It is comparatively easy to mouth the platitude that this is the best of all possible worlds. It is even easier to point out that undue emphasis on the dark side of existence tends to weaken the fibre of a people and undermine their instinctive attachment to life. This charge is based on the assumption that it is an unqualified good to remain in a state of idyllic illusion. This is the argument Plato presents in *The Republic,* when he recommends that in the ideal commonwealth the multitude be proffered consolatory myths as objects of belief while the ruler, the philosopher-king, would know that these myths were nothing more than fictions. This is basically the reason that prompts the Grand Inquisitor to reject Christ when he returns to earth: he disturbs the temporal order.

If nihilism is to be transcended, the transcendence must be rooted in truth, not in the avoidance of it. Evil exists; let it be acknowledged. Only then can it be combated. Horror exists; let it be faced. The beast in man periodically leaps forth to tear down the walls of the City and proclaim the supremacy of force. The Nazi superman believes that laws, like moral categories, are but human inventions and need not be obeyed. Might creates its own categorical imperative. Since man dies no matter what he does, there is no absolute justice to which he can appeal. This is the modern plague that writers like Malraux, Camus, and Ionesco sought to extirpate.

The nihilist is at heart unreconciled to his knowledge that the world has no ultimate meaning; his humanity labors to impose meaning on the universe. He is the creator of value; without him no values would exist. He is the author of God, the Ten Commandments, the Sermon on the Mount. He is responsible for the preservation of whatever values distinguish him from the animal kingdom.[27] He cherishes the consciousness by means of which he obtains authentic knowledge, and relies on the power of reason,

---

[27] "Man transcends all other forms of life because he is, for the first time, *life aware of itself.* Man is *in* nature, subject to its dictates and accidents, yet he *transcends* nature because he lacks the unawareness which makes the animal a part of nature. . . ." Erich Fromm, *The Heart of Man* (New York and London: Harper & Row, 1964), p. 117.

which leads him to rebel against all that is "unjust" in existence. He rejects the Absolute, but resolves to keep faith with his fellow men, companions in misery, bound prisoners of time, victims-to-be of the fatality of death. He seeks, as far as lies in his power, to prevent or remove the man-made evils and oppressions of history, though he realizes that there is no cure for the tragicomic absurdity of the human condition.

Nihilism is an ambivalent concept. It can result in the barbarism of the Nazi regime and the death-factories that were the product of its fiendish amorality, or it can give birth to a humanistic ethic of responsibility and compassion. It is not necessary to invoke the image of God or to brandish the threat of eternal damnation in order to keep the feral instincts in man under control. Was Nietzsche, for all his anathemas hurled against Christianity, an enemy of mankind? Was Sigmund Freud, an uncompromising foe of religion, hostile or indifferent to the welfare of the human race? Are men like Kafka, Eugene O'Neill, Camus, and Samuel Beckett to be regarded as a menace to humanity?

If there is the possibility of achieving a faith that can transform the nihilist into a humanist, it is faith in the liberating power of truth. Science does not tell men what values they are to choose, but it can save them at least from the folly of pursuing the will-o'-the-wisp of illusion. Nihilism, which begins in categorical negation, rejects the fictions born of the heart's desire for order and unity in the universe, the craving of the mind for a transcendental pattern of meaning and purpose. The nihilist, once he comes to terms with the insuperable limitations imposed by the human condition, stands ready to affirm that which can be rationally affirmed. Man, as Sartre has insisted, is invested with the freedom to choose his values and shape the course of his life. With what measure of courage, born of the hope that he never completely abandons even in the worst of times, will man today bear this burden of freedom?[28] The moral commitment of Camus after he had

---

[28] This is the heartening message the anthropologist Loren Eiseley addressed to his fellow Americans on the day before the Presidential election:

> Hope and risk, are they too great to expect of man? I do not believe it. They constitute his shadow. They have followed him for a million years. They stood

published *The Myth of Sisyphus,* the tragic humanism of Malraux, the shift in Sartre's allegiance to the Communist evangel, the Dionysian cry of Kazantzakis, Nietzsche's cult of the superman and his doctrine of eternal recurrence—these are, as we have seen, some of the ways in which modern writers have struggled to rise above the nihilism of their age.

with him at the Hot Gates of Thermopylae. They shared the cross at Calvary. I think it was really there that the great wave began to gather when all else seemed lost. We are again threatened with the insidious Elizabethan malady of weariness. But a voice spoke then of hope, and of great reversals, of impending tides. May this too be such an age. May Francis Bacon's voice still speak of hope, not for man only, but of the survival of the planetary life without which our own lives are as nothing. The risk is there but the indomitable human spirit will cry "assume the risk." By it alone has man survived. ("The Hope of Man," *The New York Times,* November 6, 1972).

Appendix A
Two Philosophers and Nihilism

Nietzsche died in 1900. He had alerted later generations to the danger of nihilism. If nihilism was, as many intellectuals assumed, the ineluctable fate of modern man, nevertheless the ways in which the mind reacted to this fate were strikingly different. For example, Bertrand Russell's scientifically grounded nihilism, while it offered no scintilla of hope, did not fall into despair. His essay "A Free Man's Worship," first published in 1903, is a blast of Promethean defiance, a heartening affirmation of the courage to be. Russell, like Nietzsche, is not the type of man to say that the struggle avails nothing. After acknowledging the insuperable powers against which the puny strength of man is pitted, he refuses to admit defeat. He overcame nihilism by settling down to his life's work, engaging in the noblest exercise of the mind, the philosophical search for true knowledge.

"A Free Man's Worship" interprets the world as science sees it; it is a world that has no room in it for human values, and yet it is in this world that man must build his home and discover his life-purpose. Unlike Nietzsche, Russell assumes that the findings of science must be accepted as true, even though its conclusions inflict a mortal wound on human pride. Russell declares:

> That Man is the product of causes which had no prevision of the end they were achieving; that his origin, his growth, his hopes and fears, his loves and beliefs, are but the outcome of accidental collocations of atoms; that no fire, no heroism, no intensity of thought and feeling, can preserve an individual beyond the grave; that all the labours of the ages, all the devotion, all the inspiration, all the noonday brightness of human genius, are destined to extinction in the vast death of the solar

system, and that the whole temple of Man's achievement must inevitably be buried beneath the debris of a universe in ruins—all these things, if not quite beyond dispute, are yet so nearly certain, that no philosophy which rejects them can hope to stand. Only within the scaffolding of these truths, only on the firm foundation of unyielding despair, can the soul's habitation be built.[1]

This was the heritage bequeathed to twentieth-century man by the scientific truths that biologists like Darwin and Thomas Henry Huxley earnestly promulgated; this was the foundation of despair —in Russell's as in Nietzsche's case an *unyielding* despair—on which the modern writer had to build his creative vision. Russell, like Nietzsche, is voicing the pandemic obsession of an age. He examines the formidable difficulties that stand in the way of man's implementing his aspirations in an indifferent and therefore hostile universe of atoms and electrons, but these difficulties, he believes, can be overcome. Russell, like most of the literary nihilists whose work I have analyzed, had no intention of yielding to the infection of nihilism. For Nature, strangely enough, has given birth to a creature who, though subject to her laws, is yet capable of tracking them down, judging them, and affirming his own charter of freedom —freedom to seek out knowledge and freedom to create. It is this endowment of freedom that makes man superior to the physical forces that control him. Though the world is not designed to satisfy the heart's desire, man must not become a fearful and abject slave. Russell calls upon him to resist the tyranny of non-human power. Man must resign himself to the governance of fate in the physical universe, but outside of it he is free to put his imagination to work and assert his mastery over the brute energy coursing through Nature. Russell concludes his essay with a confession of faith that, though nihilistic in content, is essentially humanistic in its affirmations:

Brief and powerless is Man's life; on him and all his race the slow, sure doom falls pitiless and dark. Blind to good and evil, reckless of destruction, omnipotent matter rolls on its relentless way: for Man,

[1] Bertrand Russell, *Mysticism and Logic* (New York: W. W. Norton & Company, 1929), pp. 47–48.

condemned to-day to lose his dearest, to-morrow himself to pass through the gates of darkness, it remains only to cherish, ere yet the blow falls, the lofty thoughts that ennoble his little day ... proudly defiant of the irresistible forces that tolerate for a moment, his knowledge and his condemnation, to sustain alone, a weary but unyielding Atlas, the world that his own ideals have fashioned despite the trampling march of unconscious power.[2]

Bertrand Russell offers the classic example of a philosopher who, far from being crushed by his nihilistic insights, transformed them into an altruistic evangel of social betterment. He begins his autobiography with a statement of what he has lived for. "Three passions, simple but overwhelmingly strong, have governed my life: the longing for love, the search for knowledge, and unbearable pity for the suffering of mankind."[3] Early in life he became an atheist. His life convincingly demonstrates that it is not necessary to be a religious believer in order to devote one's energies to the task of benefiting mankind. Even more to the point, it is perfectly possible to believe that life on earth, including the life of man, serves no ultimate purpose, and yet work unweariedly for the sake of improving the lot of man. Philosophical nihilism is not incompatible with commitment to a humanistic ethic. In the First World War Russell was a militant pacifist and gladly went to prison rather than agree to stop broadcasting his unpopular views. He acted on his conviction that this war entailed a needless slaughter of the young and should be brought to an end. He confesses that he is governed by his intellect.

From adolescence until the completion of *Principia Mathematica*, my fundamental preoccupation has been intellectual. I wanted to understand and to make others understand; also I wished to raise a monument by which I might be remembered, and on account of which I might feel that I had not lived in vain.[4]

---

[2] *Ibid.*, pp. 56–57.
[3] Bertrand Russell, *The Autobiography of Bertrand Russell* (Boston and Toronto: Little, Brown and Company, 1967), p. 3.
[4] Bertrand Russell, *The Autobiography of Bertrand Russell: 1914–1944* (Boston and Toronto: Little, Brown and Company, 1968), p. 219.

Even if the universe was to perish and all that men have built through the ages sink into the everlasting night of nothingness, he would not give up the mental struggle.

Few men, and fewer philosophers, have given more generously of their time to causes that would profit mankind. Soon after the bombing of Hiroshima and Nagasaki, he spoke in the House of Lords warning of the universal catastrophe that would occur if nuclear warfare broke out. During the sixties, at an age when most men would seek rest and retirement, he was active in the campaign to Ban the Bomb. It is interesting to note that he never repudiated the beliefs he voiced in "A Free Man's Worship": "my outlook on the cosmos and on human life is substantially unchanged."[5] Yet, on his eightieth birthday he could declare that he retained his optimistic faith. He believed that the man-made evils that afflict the race can be overcome.

> I may have thought the road to a world of free and happy human beings shorter than it is proving to be, but I was not wrong in thinking that such a world is possible, and that it is worth while to live with a view to bringing it nearer. I have lived in the pursuit of a vision, both personal and social. Personal: to care for what is noble, for what is beautiful, for what is gentle.... Social: to see in imagination the society that is to be created, where individuals grow freely, and where hate and greed and envy die because there is nothing to nourish them.[6]

Another philosopher who gave expression to the nihilistic vision and whose work had a considerable influence on a number of modern German writers is Martin Heidegger.[7] Like Nietzsche, he shows that once man became aware that God is dead, he could not escape the realization that he is the source of ontological meaning and the generator of value. Heideggerian metaphysics, which goes beyond the historical and the socioeconomic sphere and beyond the plane of the finite and the conditioned, voices the

---

[5] Bertrand Russell, *The Autobiography of Bertrand Russell: 1944–1969* (New York: Simon and Schuster, 1969), p. 248.
[6] *Ibid.,* p. 330.
[7] For a documented study of Heidegger's influence on a number of modern German writers, see Hans Jaeger, "Heidegger's Existential and Modern German Literature," *Publications of the Modern Language Association* 67 (1962): 655–83.

nihilistic anguish of twentieth-century man. Nihilism, as Heidegger points out, reigns everywhere; the movement is irresistible. "No one with any insight," he declares, "will still deny that nihilism is in the most varied and hidden forms 'the normal state' of man."[8] The reaction it has called forth, the frenetic attempts to abolish it and return to what has been, confirm its importance. No salvation is to be found in psychology or sociology or metaphysics. The deadly truth that nihilism reveals must be grappled with and its implications for the life of man honestly elucidated.

[8] Martin Heidegger, *The Question of Being,* trans. William Kluback and Jean T. Wilde (New York: Twayne Publishers, 1958), p. 47.

Appendix B
Intimations of the
Absurd in the Nineteenth Century

The theatre of revolt ... is the temple of a priest without God, without a God, without an orthodoxy, without even much of a congregation, who conducts his services within the hideous architecture of the absurd. A missionary of discord, he spreads a gospel of insurrection, trying to substitute his inspired vision for traditional values, trying to improvise a ritual out of anguish and frustration.[1]

Our own age should by now have learned to distinguish between varieties of nihilism, for we have had genuine nihilists breathing down our very backs. Nonetheless, a modern critic calls Büchner "the most uncompromising nihilist of the nineteenth century."[2]

The vision of order, justice, and mercy is a tenacious one and not easily eradicated; the alternative is too fearsome to contemplate. Yet order, regularity, law, and the like are not inherent in nature; they are imposed on it by the frantic fears of man. They are read, not out of nature, but into it, and not by mathematics and physics and chemistry, but by mathematicians, physicists, and chemists, who have their illusions, too.... If it takes faith to believe, it takes courage not to, and who is to say which is the deeper and more truthful.[3]

Far from being crushed by his vision of the absurd, the creative nihilist produces work that is often an expression of revolt. An

---

[1] Robert Brustein, *The Theatre of Revolt* (Boston and Toronto: Little, Brown and Company, 1964), p. 16.
[2] Max Spalter, *Brecht's Tradition* (Baltimore, Ind.: The Johns Hopkins Press, 1967), pp. 77–78. The modern critic is August Closs.
[3] Herbert Weisinger, *The Agony and the Triumph* (East Lansing, Mich.: Michigan State University Press, 1964), pp. 239–40.

imaginative outburst of defiance, it articulates no evangel of redemption. The literary nihilist has cast aside as delusions the hopes of the humanist, the faith of the revolutionary in Marxist-Leninist solutions, the eschatological dream of Christianity. An inconoclastic and rebellious novelist like Robbe-Grillet is a nihilist (he does not call himself that) who feels no twinge of regret for what he has given up, no yearning for the God he has dismissed as the supreme example of the pathetic fallacy. He is the proud bearer of the spirit of denial, not in the least afraid to face the consequences of his revolt.

No two nihilists, of course, draw the same conclusions from their metaphysical premises. Complex and characteristically human is the nihilism born of the myth of the absurd and yet (in the case of writers like Camus, Malraux, and Sartre) it is outraged by the spectacle of injustice or oppression and takes up the fight to reduce the sum total of man-made suffering. Büchner, an early nineteenth-century figure, offers an excellent example of a dramatist in whom two sharply conflicting impulses coexisted: that of the revolutionary saint and that of the fatalist who saw the vanity of human ambition.

Büchner, a forerunner of the modern spirit, exemplifies this strange mixture of nihilism and a passionate commitment to the cause of social justice. Büchner represented a special kind of nihilist, a type whose portrait would be drawn a century later in *The Conquerors, The Royal Way,* and *Man's Fate*: he was a revolutionist who realized that the revolution would accomplish very little in changing human nature or the condition of life man must of necessity put up with. *Danton's Death* gives expression in part to a nihilistic *Weltanschauung*. For Büchner, history is a trap, a temporal process without meaningful direction or purpose. Human beings are marionettes pulled by invisible wires, governed by incognizable powers. Blind necessity shapes the course of events. All human ambition and endeavor is in the end a senseless outpouring of energy. The "repetition of the idea that man suffers in a meaningless world is integral to *Danton's Death* as to *Woyzek*."[4] Büchner's materialist interpretation of history singled out hunger

[4] Spalter, *Brecht's Tradition,* p. 85.

as the prime mover in effecting social change. With the exception
of religious fanaticism, nothing could so rouse the masses to action
as the pressure of hunger. Though Büchner participated in a
revolutionary movement, he believed that men are at the mercy
of circumstances beyond their control. He was a fatalist.[5] He felt,
as he said, crushed down

> under the ghastly fatality of history. I find a horrible sameness in all
> human nature, and in men's relationships one inevitable power lent
> to all and to none. Individuals are so much surf on a wave, greatness
> the sheerest accident, the strength of genius a puppet play—a child's
> struggle against an iron law—the greatest of us can only recognize it,
> to control it is impossible. "Must" is the cursed word to which all
> human beings are born.[6]

Büchner is essentially modern in his dramatic portrayal of the
fatalism of history. *Danton's Death* pictures the way in which
the Revolution—in this case the French Revolution—devours
its children. The dedicated revolutionists become the sacrificial
victims of the cause they championed; the fanatics assume command since they are willing to satisfy the demand of the masses
for blood and more blood. Büchner, though he engaged in underground political agitation in his native land, did not believe in
the lofty humanitarian sentiments mouthed by the liberals of his

[5] We cannot *prove* that our conduct is free, and yet our reactions seem to indicate
that we blame ourselves for the wrong decisions made in the past. That is to say,
we take it for granted that we are responsible for our actions. Can we then assume
that the responsibility is fully ours? But if we are thus responsible, then it means
that we are free to choose, to act or not to act in a given way. Necessity does not
hem us in. But then the counterargument raises the formidable objection: are
we not the end-product of all the forces—heredity, the environment, the unconscious
—brought to bear on us? In grappling with the problem of free will versus determinism, Büchner opts for the philosophy of absolute necessity, though he obviously
had little relish for it emotionally. Büchner's obsession with the absurd is evident
in his intent "to point to the perpetual, poignant, horrifying contrast between
men, so hopelessly involved in a universe not made by them and hostile to their
interests and efforts, and that universe itself, as it mechanically functions in the
manifestations of external nature, so indifferent and so beautiful, such a perfect
spectacle, especially to the eye of the trained scientific observer." A. H. J. Knight,
Georg Büchner (Oxford: Basil Blackwell, 1951), p. 147.
[6] Georg Büchner, *The Plays of Georg Büchner,* trans. Geoffrey Dunlop (New York:
The Viking Press, 1928), p. 37.

day. The masses, he insisted, would have to achieve their own liberation. Though in *Danton's Death* he made use of historical material, he succeeded in imbuing it with the breath of life; he created complex characters to carry his meaning, he attempts to do justice to both Danton and Robespierre.

If he paints a sympathetic and insightful portrait of Danton, he does not gloss over his marked weaknesses of character. Danton is depicted as a lover of freedom, whereas Robespierre, the revolutionary fanatic, is inflexible, merciless, motivated in his behavior by abstract principles and moral maxims. If Büchner refrains from taking sides, it is because he knows that Robespierre is as much the pawn of the irresistible forces active in the history of his time as is his adversary. Danton, however, is shown to be a sensitive and introspective figure. In his talk with Julie, his wife, he reveals his awareness of how difficult is the process of communication, how lonely each person feels, how impossible it is to reach the inner self of the other. All he knows is that the grave will finally bring peace to suffering mortals.

These character traits inevitably affect his role during the reign of terror in France. Büchner informs the audience of the toll the guillotine takes each day; the Revolution is steeped in rivers of blood. The ignorant citizens want nothing more than to destroy aristocrats and kill off all the enemies of the Revolution. Yet they continue to suffer as much as they did in the past; their hunger is real. The only remedy they can devise for their economic distress is to make the guillotine work overtime. Robespierre, their demagogic leader, is determined to show no mercy; he invokes the Terror as the supreme weapon to be employed in defense of the Revolution. All traces of disaffection and rottenness must be ruthlessly purged from the body politic. Thus will the cause of Virtue be vindicated. As Robespierre says righteously: "The Revolutionary Government is the dictatorship of freedom against tyranny."[7]

Danton, heedless of consequences, refuses to heed the warning

---

[7] Georg Büchner, *Danton's Death,* trans. Stephen Spender and Goronwy Rees (London: Faber & Faber, 1939), p. 38.

of his friends that his life is in danger. He knows that "the Revolution is like Saturn and devours her children" (p. 48), but he thinks that the Committee of Public Safety will not dare to strike at him. He is a moderate, however, and "the people" construe that as a sign of ideological weakness. Besides, Robespierre, the austere Puritan, is revolted by Danton's libertinage; he hates those who pursue a life of pleasure. In the confrontation scene between Danton and Robespierre, Büchner reveals the differences that separate the two men. The latter, a political fanatic, firmly believes that he who is not for him and the cause he represents is against him, whereas Danton deplores the casuistry that glorifies mass murder. For Robespierre, like the Communist spokesmen in Brecht's *The Measures Taken,* the end justifies the means. Danton bids him consider whether his conscience does not whisper to him that he is in the wrong. Why should he play the wicked role of God's policeman? Danton denies that virtue and vice are factors that influence the behavior of human beings. "All men are hedonists, some crude and some sensitive ... that is the only difference between men I've been able to discover. Every one acts according to his nature; that is, he does what does him good" (pp. 52–53). Though Robespierre has been affected by Danton's words, he is all the more resolved to dispose of this man.

Danton, as disaster is about to strike home, betrays a curious indifference as to the outcome. He is tired of life's fixed routine, the settled habits into which one falls, the sameness of the pattern that fate weaves, the unrelieved tedium of existence. He will not adopt measures that will safeguard his life. He is resigned to his fate. The Revolution has taken a turn that no one could have prevented: it must have its hecatombs of victims. As he declares: "We haven't made the Revolution, the Revolution made us" (p. 63). Why should he resist? He would rather die by the guillotine than resort to the tactics of the killers. Why, he wonders bitterly, must there be this bloody strife? There is something woefully wrong in the make-up of man. Humanity is a monster bent on destroying its own kind.

But if nothing is done at this critical juncture, then, as Danton's friends point out, France is left at the mercy of its hangmen.

Danton, a passive, nihilistic hero,[8] remarks that the people enjoy this saturnalia of slaughter. "Does it matter," he asks, "whether they die on the guillotine or from fever or from old age?"[9] The guillotine at least makes it possible for them to make their exit in a spectacular manner on the stage of history. "It's quite right," Danton adds, "that the length of life should be reduced a little . . ." (p. 64). Danton has reached the end of his resources; he will not put up a fight to preserve his life; the effort would be too much for him right now; besides, "life is not worth the trouble one takes to hold on to it" (p. 64).

Profoundly pessimistic in his outlook, Danton is indifferent to the fate that is in store for him. Tired of living, he will not bother to defend himself before his accusers. If the guardians of the Republic want his life, he is prepared to let them have it. "I'll know how to die with courage; it's easier than living" (p. 71). However, he keeps on trying to reassure himself that his enemies would never dare deprive him of his life. He explains to his wife that when the Revolution first broke out, he, too, was guilty of killing, but then civil war was raging in France at the time; he had acted in self-defense. What intensifies his sense of the ineradicable absurdity of existence is the necessity, "the must," that governs events, though he is not blind to the beast that dwells in man and drives him to lie, steal, and murder. He tells his wife: "We're puppets drawn by unknown powers on wire . . ." (p. 78).

Danton defends his course of action, but his enemies are too cunning for him. His doom is sealed. He expects no reward for his sacrifices, for the part he played in the Revolution. An atheist, he looks forward to the Nirvana of nothingness that death will bring him. He broods on the paradox: how can something be transformed into nothing? "If one could believe in annihilation!" (p. 118). A creature of contradictions like all nihilistic heroes, he is not at all eager to die, though he will meet his end bravely. He knows what

---

[8] In his review of *Danton's Death,* as adapted by Herbert Blau and produced at the Repertory Theatre of Lincoln Center, Brustein says: "Danton himself is a thoroughly passive hero, 'lazy,' inert, nihilistic." Robert Brustein, *The Third Theatre* (New York: Alfred A. Knopf, 1969), p. 161.

[9] Büchner, *Danton's Death,* p. 64.

will happen to the Revolution under Robespierre: the spirit of liberty will be perverted and betrayed, but the victor will suffer too. His last words, just before the carriage arrives to take him and others to the guillotine, are: "The world is chaos. The Nothing is its too fertile Deity" (p. 136).

What is remarkable about Büchner is that his chief works— *Danton's Death, Woyzeck,* and *Lenz*—were completed in a period of two years, before he died at the age of twenty-three. *Danton's Death* came out in 1835. In 1836 he was granted the degree of Doctor of Philosophy by the University of Zurich. In composing *Danton's Death* he sought to avoid the error of idealizing and therefore distorting the true character of the leaders of that time; he would delineate them as they were, with all their faults and vices: their licentiousness, their indulgence in obscenities, their love of power, their sadism, their atheism. He is seeking to mirror the realities of life, however repellent they prove to be. Why should he strive to interpret the world as being better than God actually made it? In *Danton's Death,* a play of uncompromising pessimism, the protagonist has reached a point of nihilistic detachment where nothing matters. In this extraordinary tragedy, Büchner anticipated the appearance of Hardy's Will in *The Dynasts*: the blind force of history that sweeps everything before it. Like Hardy, Büchner shows that men are helpless as they face disaster, despite their display of courage, fortitude, and dignity before they go down to ultimate defeat. Men, societies, and nations are overcome by forces that are without moral aim. The Juggernaut of history spares none of its predestined victims, regardless of their worth or eminence. Blind chance enters into the warp and woof of life, and each individual, as in Kafka's fictive universe, stands condemned, without the benefit of a trial. The world that Büchner holds up for our contemplation is indeed the theater of the absurd, a nihilistic chaos. "There is no sense, no purpose, no God behind it all, and we can do absolutely nothing about it."[10]

[10] Knight, *Georg Büchner,* p. 174.

Selective Bibliography

Adams, Robert Martin. *Strains of Discord.* Ithaca: Cornell University Press, 1958.

———. *Nil.* New York: Oxford University Press, 1966.

Albérès, R. M., and Boisdeffre, Pierre de. *Kafka.* Translated by Wade Baskin. New York: Philosophical Library, 1968.

Allsop, Kenneth. *The Angry Decade.* New York: British Book Center, 1958.

Altizer, Thomas J. J. *The Gospel of Christian Atheism.* Philadelphia: Westminster Press, 1966.

Alvarez, A. *The Savage God.* New York: Random House, 1972.

Anders, Gunther. *Franz Kafka.* Translated by A. Steer and A. K. Thorlby. London: Bowes & Bowes, 1960.

Andreyev, Leonid. *Plays.* Translated by Clarence L. Meader and Fred Newton Scott. New York: Charles Scribner's Sons, 1925.

———. *Letters of Gorky and Andreev.* Translated by Lydia Weston. New York and London: Columbia University Press, 1958.

———. *Seven Who Were Hanged.* In *Ten Modern Short Novels.* Edited by Leo Hamalian and Edmond L. Volpe. New York: G. P. Putnam's Sons, 1958.

———. *Professor Storitsyn.* Translated by Isaiah Minkoff, George Rapall Noyes, and Alexander Kaun. In *Masterpieces of the Russian Drama.* New York: Dover Publications, 1960.

Arendt, Hannah. *The Human Condition.* Chicago and London: University of Chicago Press, 1959.

Artzybashef, Michael. *Breaking-Point.* New York: B. W. Huebsch, 1917.

Barnard, G. C. *Samuel Beckett.* New York: Dodd, Mead & Company, 1970.

Barnes, Hazel E. *An Existentialist Ethics.* New York: Alfred A. Knopf, 1968.

Barrett, William. *Irrational Man.* Garden City, N.Y.: Doubleday & Company, 1958.

Barthes, Roland. *Critical Essays.* Translated by Richard Howard. Evanston, Ill.: Northwestern University Press, 1972.

Beckett, Samuel. *Watt.* New York: Grove Press, 1959.

Benedikt, Michael, and Wellwarth, George E. eds. *Postwar German Theatre.* New York: E. P. Dutton & Company, 1967.

Benn, Gottfried. *Primal Vision.* Norfolk, Conn.: New Directions, 1960.

Berdyaev, Nicolas. *Dream and Reality.* Translated by Katherine Lampert. New York: The Macmillan Company, 1957.

Bevan, Edwyn. *Symbolism and Belief.* Boston: Beacon Press, 1957.

Biasin, Gian Paolo. *The Smile of the Gods.* Translated by Yvonne Freccero. Ithaca: Cornell University Press, 1968.

Blackham, H. J., ed. *Objections to Humanism.* London: Constable, 1963.

Blixen, Karen [Isak Dinesen]. *Seven Gothic Tales.* New York: Modern Library, 1961.

Bloch, Ernst. *Atheism in Christianity.* Translated by J. T. Swann. New York: Herder and Herder, 1972.

Bobbio, Norberto. *Decadentism.* Translated by David Moore. Oxford: Basil Blackwell, 1948.

Bogard, Travis, and Oliver, William E., eds. *Modern Drama.* New York: Oxford University Press, 1965.

Bonnefoy, Claude. *Conversations with Ionesco.* Translated by Jan Dawson. New York and Chicago: Holt, Rinehart and Winston, 1971.

Booth, Wayne C. *The Rhetoric of Fiction.* Chicago: University of Chicago Press, 1961.

Borges, José Luis. *Labyrinths.* Translated by Donald A. Yates and James E. Irby. Norfolk, Conn.: New Directions, 1962.

Borras, F. M. *Maxim Gorky.* Oxford: Clarendon Press, 1967.

Brustein, Robert. *The Theatre of Revolt*. Boston and Toronto: Little, Brown and Company, 1964.

———. *The Third Theatre*. New York: Alfred A. Knopf, 1969.

Büchner, Georg. *The Plays of Georg Büchner*. Translated by Geoffrey Dunlop. New York: Viking Press, 1928.

Burke, Kenneth. *The Rhetoric of Religion*. Boston: Beacon Press, 1961.

Camus, Albert. *The Plague*. Translated by Stuart Gilbert. New York: Modern Library, 1948.

———. *The Stranger*. Translated by Stuart Gilbert. New York: Vintage Books, 1954.

———. *The Rebel*. Translated by Anthony Bower. New York: Alfred A. Knopf, 1954.

———. *The Myth of Sisyphus*. Translated by Justin O'Brien. New York: Vintage Books, 1955.

———. *Resistance, Rebellion and Death*. Translated by Justin O'Brien. New York: Alfred A. Knopf, 1961.

———. *Lyrical and Critical Essays*. Translated by Ellen Conroy Kennedy. New York: Alfred A. Knopf, 1961.

———. *Notebooks, 1935–1943*. Translated by Philip Thody. New York: Alfred A. Knopf, 1963.

Canetti, Elias. *Crowds and Power*. Translated by Carol Stewart. New York: Viking Press, 1962.

Carlyle, Thomas. *Sartor Resartus*. London: J. M. Dent & Sons, 1948.

Chernyshevski, N. G. *Selected Philosophical Essays*. Moscow: Foreign Language Publishing House, 1953.

Closs, August. *Medusa's Mirror*. London: Cresset Press, 1957.

Coe, Richard N. *Ionesco*. Edinburgh and London: Oliver and Boyd, 1961.

Cohn, Ruby. *Samuel Beckett*. New Brunswick, N.J.: Rutgers University Press, 1962.

Crow, Christine. *Paul Valéry*. Cambridge: University Press, 1972.

Cruickshank, John. *Albert Camus and the Literature of Revolt*. London and New York: Oxford University Press, 1950.

Desan, Wilfred. *The Tragic Finale*. Cambridge, Mass.: Harvard University Press, 1954.

Donato, Arthur C. *Nietzsche as Philosopher*. New York: Macmillan Company, 1965.

Dostoevski, Fyodor. *The House of the Dead*. Translated by Constance Garnett. New York: Macmillan Company, 1917.

Dubos, René. *The Dreams of Reason*. New York and London: Columbia University Press, 1961.

Duckworth, Colin. *Angels of Darkness*. New York: Barnes & Noble, 1972.

Dumitriu, Petru. *Incognito*. Translated by Norman Denny. New York: Macmillan Company, 1964.

Durkheim, Emile. *Suicide*. Translated by John Spaulding and George Simpson. Glencoe, Ill.: Free Press, 1951.

Dürrenmatt, Friedrich. *Four Plays*. London: Jonathan Cape, 1964.
————. "Problems of the Theatre." In *The Modern Theatre*. Edited by Robert W. Corrigan. New York: Macmillan Company, 1965.

Earle, William; Edie, James M.; and Wild, John. *Christianity and Existentialism*. Evanston: Northwestern University Press, 1963.

Eliade, Mircea. *The Myth of the Eternal Return*. Translated by Willard Trask. New York: Pantheon Books, 1954.

Elliot, George P. *Conversions*. New York: E. P. Dutton & Company, 1971.

Eoff, Sherman H. *The Modern Spanish Novel*. New York: New York University Press, 1964.

Erikson, Erik H. *Gandhi's Truth*. New York: W. W. Norton & Company, 1969.

Fallico, Arturo B. *Art and Existentialism*. Englewood Cliffs, N.J.: Prentice-Hall, 1962.

Farber, Leslie H. *The Ways of the Will*. New York and London: Basic Books, 1966.

Farberow, Norman I., and Shneidman, Edwin S., eds. *The Cry for Help*. New York and London: McGraw-Hill, 1961.

Federman, Raymond. *Journey to Chaos*. Berkeley and Los Angeles: University of California Press, 1965.

Fingarette, Herman. *The Self in Transformation*. New York and London: Basic Books, 1963.

Fletcher, John. *Samuel Beckett's Art.* New York: Barnes & Noble, 1967.

Flores, Angel, and Swander, Homer. *Franz Kafka Today.* Madison: University of Wisconsin Press, 1958.

Forster, E. M. *Two Cheers for Democracy.* New York: Harcourt, Brace and Company, 1951.

Foulkes, A. P. *The Reluctant Pessimist.* The Hague and Paris: Mouton, 1967.

Fowlie, Wallace. *Dionysus in Paris.* New York: Meridian Books, 1960.

Frankl, Viktor E. *From Death-Camp to Existentialism.* Translated by Ilse Lasch. Boston: Beacon Press, 1959.

Frazer, James G. *The Golden Bough.* New York: Macmillan Company, 1958.

Freeborn, Richard. *Turgenev.* London: Oxford University Press, 1960.

Friedman, Maurice. *Problematic Rebel.* New York: Random House, 1963.

Friedman, Melvin J., ed. *Samuel Beckett Now.* Chicago and London: University of Chicago Press, 1970.

Fromm, Erich. *Beyond the Chains of Illusion.* New York: Simon and Schuster, 1962.

———. *The Heart of Man.* New York and London: Harper & Row, 1964.

Glicksberg, Charles I. *The Tragic Vision in Twentieth-Century Literature.* Carbondale, Ill.: Southern Illinois University Press, 1963.

———. *The Self in Modern Literature.* University Park, Pa.: Pennsylvania State University Press, 1963.

———. *Modern Literature and the Death of God.* The Hague: Martinus Nijhoff, 1966.

———. *Modern Literary Perspectivism.* Dallas, Texas: Southern Methodist University Press, 1970.

Goldberger, Avriel. *Visions of a New Hero.* Paris: M. J. Minard, 1965.

Goldmann, Lucien. *The Hidden God.* Translated by Philip Thody. New York: Humanities Press, 1964.

Gorky, Maxim. *Letters of Gorky and Andreev.* Translated by Lydia Weston. New York and London: Columbia University Press, 1958.

Gourfinkel, Nina. *Gorky.* Translated by Ann Feshbach. New York: Grove, 1960.

Greenberg, Martin. *The Terror of Art.* New York and London: Basic Books, 1968.

Greene, Norman N. *Jean-Paul Sartre.* Ann Arbor: University of Michigan Press, 1960.

Grene, Marjorie. *Martin Heidegger.* London: Bowes and Bowes, 1957.

Hamburger, Michael. *The Truth of Poetry.* New York: Harcourt, Brace & World, 1969.

———. *Contraries.* New York: E. P. Dutton & Co., 1970.

Hanna, Thomas. *Bodies in Revolt.* New York and Chicago: Holt, Rinehart and Winston, 1960.

Hannah, Donald. *"Isak Dinesen" and Karen Blixen.* New York: Random House, 1971.

Harrington, Alan. *The Immortalist.* New York: Random House, 1969.

Hartman, Geoffrey. *André Malraux.* London: Bowes and Bowes, 1960.

Hartmann, Eduard von. *Philosophy of the Unconscious.* Translated by William Chatterton Coupland. New York: Harcourt, Brace and Company, 1931.

Hartnack, Justus. *Wittgenstein and Modern Philosophy.* Translated by Maurice Cranston. New York: New York University Press, 1965.

Hassan, Ihab. *The Literature of Silence.* New York: Alfred A. Knopf, 1967.

Heidegger, Martin. *Existence and Being.* Chicago: Henry Regnery Co., 1949.

———. *The Question of Being.* Translated by William Kluback and Jean T. Wilde. New York: Twayne Publishers, 1958.

———. *An Introduction to Metaphysics.* Translated by Ralph Manheim. New Haven: Yale University Press, 1959.

Heller, Peter. *Dialectics and Nihilism.* Amherst, Mass.: University of Massachusetts Press, 1967.

Helsa, David H. *The Shape of Chaos.* Minneapolis, Minn.: University of Minnesota Press, 1971.

Heppenstall, Rayner. *The Fourfold Tradition.* London: Barie and Rockliff, 1961.

Hinchliffe, Arnold. *The Absurd.* London: Methuen & Co., 1969.

Hingley, Ronald. *Nihilism.* New York: Delacorte Press, 1969.

Hoffman, Frederick J. *The Mortal No.* Princeton, N.J.: Princeton University Press, 1964.

Hofmannsthal, Hugo von. *Selected Prose.* New York: Pantheon Books, 1952.

Hollingdale, R. J. *Nietzsche.* London: Routledge & Kegan Paul, 1965.

Huertas-Jourda, José. *The Existentialism of Miguel de Unamuno.* Gainesville, Fla.: University of Florida Press, 1963.

Husserl, Edmund. *Cartesian Meditations.* Translated by Dorion Cairns. The Hague: Martinus Nijhoff, 1960.

Ilie, Paul. *Unamuno.* Madison (Wis.) and London: University of Wisconsin, 1967.

Ionesco, Eugène. *Exit the King.* Translated by Donald Watson. New York: Grove Press, 1963.

———. *Fragments of a Journal.* Translated by Jean Stewart. New York: Grove Press, 1964.

———. *Notes and Counter Notes.* Translated by Donald Watson. New York: Grove Press, 1964.

———. *The Colonel's Photograph and Other Stories.* Translated by Jean Stewart. New York: Grove Press, 1969.

Jaeger, Hans. "Heidegger's Existential Philosophy and Modern German Literature." *Publications of the Modern Language Association* 67 (1952): 655–83.

James, William. *Varieties of Religious Experience.* New York: Longmans, Green & Co., 1902.

Jaspers, Karl. *Nietzsche and Christianity.* Translated by E. B. Ashton. Chicago: Henry Regnery Company, 1961.

———. *Nietzsche.* Translated by Charles F. Wallraff and Frederick J. Schmitz. Tucson, Ariz.: University of Arizona Press, 1965.

Jenkins, Cecil. "André Malraux." In *The Novelist as Philosopher,* edited by John Cruickshank. London: Oxford University Press, 1962.

Johannesson, Eric O. *The World of Isak Dinesen.* Seattle, Wash.:
University of Washington Press, 1961.

Johnson, Howard, and Thurlstrup, Niels, eds. *A Kierkegaard
Anthology.* New York: Harper & Brothers, 1962.

Jonas, Hans. *The Gnostic Religion.* Boston: Beacon Press,
1958.

Jones, Ernest. *The Life and Work of Sigmund Freud.* vol. 3. New
York: Basic Books, 1957.

Jones, Robert Emmet. *The Alienated Heroes in Modern French
Drama.* Athens, Ga.: University of Georgia Press, 1962.

Jung, C. G. *Answer to Job.* Translated by R. F. C. Hull. London:
Routledge & Paul, 1954.

―――. *Memories, Dreams, Reflections.* Translated by Clara and
Richard Winston. New York: Pantheon Books, 1963.

Kafka, Franz. *Diaries of Franz Kafka.* Translated by Joseph
Kersh. New York: Schocken Books, 1948.

―――. *Dearest Father.* Translated by Ernst Kaiser and Eithne
Wilkins. New York: Schocken Books, 1954.

―――. *Letters to Milena.* Translated by Tania and James Stern.
New York: Schocken Books, 1953.

―――. *Description of a Struggle.* Translated by Tania and James
Stern. New York: Schocken Books, 1958.

―――. *The Trial.* Translated by Willa and Edwin Muir. New
York: Modern Library, 1956.

―――. *The Castle.* New York: Alfred A. Knopf, 1965.

Kallen, Horace M. *Freedom, Tragedy, and Comedy.* De Kalb, Ill.:
Northern Illinois University Press, 1963.

Kaufmann, Walter. *Critique of Religion and Philosophy.* New
York: Harper & Brothers, 1958.

―――. *The Faith of a Heretic.* Garden City, N.Y.: Doubleday &
Company, 1961.

Kaun, Alexander. *Leonid Andreyev.* New York: B. W. Hubsch,
1924.

―――. *Maxim Gorky and His Russia.* New York: Jonathan Cape
& Harrison Smith, 1931.

Kayser, Wolfgang. *The Grotesque in Art and Literature.* Translated by Ulrich Weisstein. Bloomington, Ind.: Indiana University Press, 1963.

Kazantzakis, Nikos. *The Odyssey.* Translated by Kimon Friar. New York: Simon and Schuster, 1958.

———. *The Saviors of God.* Translated by Kimon Friar. New York: Simon and Schuster, 1960.

———. *The Last Temptation of Christ.* Translated by P. A. Bien. New York: Simon and Schuster, 1960.

———. *Report to Greco.* Translated by P. A. Bien: New York: Simon and Schuster, 1965.

Kazantzakis, Helen. *Nikos Kazantzakis.* Translated by Amy Mims. New York: Simon and Schuster, 1968.

Kierkegaard, Søren. *Concluding Unscientific Postscript.* Translated by David F. Swenson. Princeton, N.J.: Princeton University Press, 1941.

———. *The Journals of Søren Kierkegaard.* Translated by Alexander Dru. London and New York: Oxford University Press, 1951.

———. *Philosophical Fragments.* Translated by David F. Swenson. Princeton, N.J.: Princeton University, 1962.

Killinger, John. *Hemingway and the Dead Gods.* Lexington, Ky.: University of Kentucky Press, 1960.

———. *The Failure of Theology in Modern Literature.* New York and Nashville (Tenn.): Abingdon Press, 1963.

Knight, Everett W. *Literature Considered as Philosophy.* London: Routledge & Kegan Paul, 1957.

Knight, George. *Georg Büchner.* Oxford: Basil Blackwell, 1957.

Kolakowski, Leszek. *The Alienation of Reason.* Translated by Norbert Guterman. Garden City, N.Y.: Doubleday & Company.

Kurz, Paul Konrad. *On Modern German Literature.* Translated by Sister Mary Frances McCarthy. University, Ala.: University of Alabama, 1967.

Landsberg, Paul-Louis. *The Experience of Death.* Translated by Cynthia Rowland. New York: Philosophical Library, 1953.

Langbaum, Robert. *The Gayety of Vision.* New York: Random House, 1964.

Lapp, Ignace. *Atheism in Our Time.* Translated by Bernard Murchland. New York: Macmillan Company, 1963.

Lavrin, Janko. *Tolstoy.* London: W. Collins Sons & Co., 1924.

LeClézio, J. M. G. *The Flood.* Translated by Peter Green. New York: Atheneum, 1968.

Lester, John A., Jr. *Journey Through Despair 1880–1914.* Princeton, N.J.: Princeton University Press, 1968.

Levy, G. R. *The Sword from the Rock.* London: Faber and Faber, 1953.

Lewis, R. W. B. *The Picaresque Saint.* Philadelphia and New York: J. B. Lippincott, 1959.

Luijpen, William A. *Phenomenology of Atheism.* Pittsburgh, Pa.: Duquesne University Press, 1964.

Lukács, Georg. *Realism in Our Time.* Translated by Necke Mander. New York and Evanston: Harper & Row, 1964.

Malraux, André. *The Walnut Trees of Altenburg.* Translated by A. W. Fielding. London: John Lehmann, 1952.

———. *Anti-Memoirs.* Translated by Terence Kilmartin. New York and Chicago: Holt, Rinehart and Winston, 1968.

———. *Felled Oaks.* Translated by Irene Clephane. New York: Holt, Rinehart and Winston, 1971.

Mangy, Claude-Edmonde. "The Duplicity of Being." In *Sartre,* edited by Edith Stern. Englewood Cliffs, N.J.: Prentice-Hall, 1962.

Mann, Thomas. *The Magic Mountain.* Translated by H. T. Lowe-Porter. New York: Alfred A. Knopf, 1952.

Manser, Anthony. *Sartre.* London: Athlone Press, 1966.

Magarshack, David. *Turgenev.* New York: Grove Press, 1954.

Maritain, Raissa. *We Have Been Friends Together.* New York and London: Longmans, Green and Co., 1942.

Marty, Martin E. *Varieties of Unbelief.* New York: Holt, Rinehart and Winston, 1964.

Masaryk, T. G. *The Spirit of Russia.* 2 vols. Translated by Eden and Cedar Paul. London: George Allen & Unwin, 1919.

———. *The Spirit of Russia.* Translated by Robert Bass. vol. 3. New York: Barnes & Noble, 1967.

Maugham, Somerset. *Of Human Bondage.* New York: George H. Doran Company, 1915.

Mauriac, François. *Words of Faith.* Translated by Edward H. Flannery. New York: Philosophical Library, 1955.

Mayer, Hans. *Steppenwolf and Everyman.* Translated by Jack D. Zipes. New York: Thomas Y. Crowell Company, 1971.

Meier-Graefe, Julius. *Dostoevsky.* Translated by Herbert H. Marks. London: George Routledge and Sons, 1928.

Mercier, Vivian. *The New Novel.* New York: Farrar, Straus and Giroux, 1971.

Miller, J. Hillis. *The Disappearance of God.* Cambridge, Mass.: Harvard University Press, 1963.

———. *Poets of Reality.* Cambridge, Mass.: Harvard University Press, 1965.

Molina, Fernando. *Existentialism as Philosophy.* Englewood Cliffs, N.J.: Prentice-Hall, 1962.

Money-Kyrle, R. E. *Man's Picture of His World.* New York: International Universities Press, 1961.

Monod, Jacques. *Chance and Necessity.* Translated by Austryn Wainhouse. New York: Alfred A. Knopf, 1971.

Montherlant, Henry de. *Selected Essays.* Translated by John Weightman. New York: Macmillan Company, 1961.

———. *Chaos and Night.* Translated by Terence Kilmartin. New York: Macmillan Company, 1964.

Mora, José Ferrater. *Unamuno.* Translated by Philip Silver. Berkeley and Los Angeles (Calif.): University of California Press, 1962.

Moser, Charles A. *Antinihilism in the Russian Novel of the 1860's.* The Hague: Mouton & Co., 1964.

Mossop, D. J. *Pure Poetry.* Oxford: Clarendon Press, 1971.

Mounier, Emmanuel. *Existentialist Philosophies.* Translated by Eric Blow. London: Rockliff, 1948.

Mumford, Lewis. *The Conduct of Life.* New York: Harcourt, Brace and Company, 1951.

Murdoch, Iris. *Sartre.* New Haven: Yale University Press, 1953.

Naess, Arne. *Four Modern Philosophers.* Translated by Alastair Hannay. Chicago and London: University of Chicago Press, 1968.

Neumann, Erich. *Art and the Unconscious.* Translated by Ralph Manheim. New York: Pantheon Books, 1959.

Nietzsche, Friedrich. *The Will to Power.* Translated by Anthony

M. Ludovici. Edinburgh and London: T. N. Foulis, 1910.
———. *The Birth of Tragedy.* Translated by Francis Golffing.
   Garden City, N.Y.: Doubleday & Company, 1956.
———. *Joyful Wisdom.* Translated by Thomas Common. New
   York: Ungar Publishing Co., 1960.
———. *The Will to Power.* Translated by Walter Kaufmann and
   R. J. Hollingdale. New York: Random House, 1967.
———. *Thus Spake Zarathustra.* Translated by Thomas Common.
   New York: Boni and Liveright, n.d.
Nott, Kathleen. *Philosophy and Human Nature.* New York: New
   York University Press, 1971.
Odajnyk, Walter. *Marxism and Existentialism.* Garden City, N.Y.:
   Doubleday & Company, 1965.
Olson, Robert G. *An Introduction to Existentialism.* New York:
   Dover Publications, 1962.
Ortega, José y Gasset. *Man and Crisis.* Translated by Mildred
   Adams. New York: W. W. Norton & Company, 1958.
———. *History as a System.* Translated by Helene Weyl. New
   York: W. W. Norton & Company, 1961.
Panichas, George A., ed. *The Politics of the Twentieth-Century
   Novel.* New York: Hawthorn Books, 1971.
Parker, Emmet. *Albert Camus.* Madison, Wis.: University of
   Wisconsin Press, 1965.
Pater, Walter. *The Renaissance.* London: Macmillan and Co.,
   1924.
Pavese, Cesare. *This Business of Living.* Translated by A. E.
   Murch. London: Peter Owen, 1961.
Peckham, Morse. *Beyond the Tragic Vision.* New York: George
   Braziller, 1962.
———. *Art and Pornography.* New York and London: Basic
   Books, 1969.
Peyre, Henri. *Literature and Sincerity.* New Haven (Conn.) and
   London: Yale University Press, 1963.
Pitcher, George. *The Philosophy of Wittgenstein.* Englewood
   Cliffs, N.J.: Prentice-Hall, 1964.
Polanyi, Michael. *Personal Knowledge.* Chicago: University of
   Chicago Press, 1958.

Prevalakis, Pandelis. *Nikos Kazantzakis and His Odyssey*. Translated by Philip Sherard. New York: Simon and Schuster, 1961.

Priestley, J. B. *Man's Time*. Garden City, N.Y.: Doubleday & Company, 1964.

Pronko, Leonard Cabell. *Avant-Garde*. Berkeley and Los Angeles (Calif.): University of California Press, 1962.

Quilliot, Roger. *The Sea and Prisons*. Translated by Emmet Parker. University, Ala.: University of Alabama Press, 1970.

Rank, Otto. *Art and Artist*. Translated by C. Atkinson. New York: Alfred A. Knopf, 1932.

Raymond, Marcel. *From Baudelaire to Surrealism*. Translated by G. M. New York: Wittenborn, Schultz, 1950.

Read, Herbert. *Anarchy and Order*. London: Faber and Faber, 1954.

———. *The Contrary Experience*. New York: Horizon Press, 1963.

Richter, Hans. *Dada*. New York and Toronto: McGraw-Hill Book Company, n.d.

Righter, William. *The Rhetorical Hero*. London: Routledge & Kegan Paul, 1964.

Rintelen, J. von. *Beyond Existentialism*. Translated by Hilda Graef. London: George Allen & Unwin, 1961.

Rivière, Jacques. *The Ideal Reader*. Translated by Blanche A. Price. New York: Meridian Books, 1960.

Robbe-Grillet, Alain. *The Voyeur*. Translated by Richard Howard. New York: Grove Press, 1958.

———. *Jealousy*. Translated by Richard Howard. New York: Grove Press, 1959.

———. *In the Labyrinth*. Translated by Richard Howard. New York: Grove Press, 1960.

———. *For a New Novel*. Translated by Richard Howard. New York: Grove Press, 1965.

Robinson, Michael. *The Long Sonata of the Dead*. New York: Grove Press, 1969.

Rosen, Stanley. *Nihilism*. New Haven (Conn.) and London: Yale University Press, 1969.

Rosenberg, Harold. *The Tradition of the New.* New York: Horizon Press, 1959.

Rostand, Jean. *The Substance of Man.* Translated by Irma Brandeis. Garden City, N.Y.: Doubleday & Company, 1962.

Roubiczek, Paul. *Thinking in Opposites.* London: Routledge & Kegan Paul, 1942.

Rubenstein, Richard L. *After Auschwitz.* Indianapolis (Ind.) and New York: Bobbs-Merrill Company, 1966.

Rudd, Margaret Thomas. *The Lone Heretic.* Austin, Tex.: University of Texas Press, 1963.

Ruggiero, Guido de. *Existentialism.* Translated by E. M. Cocks. London: Secker & Warburg, 1946.

Russell, Bertrand. *Mysticism and Logic.* New York: W. W. Norton & Company, 1929.

———. *The Autobiography of Bertrand Russell.* Boston and Toronto: Little, Brown and Company, 1967.

———. *The Autobiography of Bertrand Russell: 1914-1944.* Boston and Toronto: Little, Brown and Company, 1968.

———. *The Autobiography of Bertrand Russell: 1944-1969.* New York: Simon and Schuster, 1969.

Santayana, George. *My Host the World.* New York: Charles Scribner's Sons, 1953.

Sartre, Jean-Paul. *Nausea.* Translated by Lloyd Alexander. New York: New Directions, 1964.

———. *Being and Nothingness.* Translated by Hazel E. Barnes. New York: Philosophical Library, 1956.

———. *Existentialism and Humanism.* Translated by Philip Mairet. London: Methuen & Co., 1949.

———. *What is Literature?* Translated by Bernard Frechtman. New York: Philosophical Library, 1949.

———. *Existentialism.* Translated by Bernard Frechtman. New York: Philosophical Library, 1947.

———. *Saint-Genet.* Translated by Bernard Frechtman. New York: George Braziller, 1963.

———. *The Words.* Translated by Bernard Frechtman. New York: George Braziller, 1964.

Sartre. Edited by Edith Stern. Englewood Cliffs, N.J.: Prentice-Hall, 1962.

Scarfe, Francis. *The Art of Paul Valéry.* London and New York: William Heinemann, 1954.

Schaff, Adam. *A Philosophy of Man.* New York: Monthly Review Press, 1963.

Schilpp, Paul, ed. *The Philosophy of Karl Jaspers.* New York: Tudor Publishing Co., 1957.

Scholes, Robert. *The Fabulators.* New York: Oxford University Press, 1967.

Schopenhauer, Arthur. *The World as Will and Idea.* Translated by R. B. Haldane and J. Kemp, vol. 1. London: Kegan Paul, Trench, Trübner & Co., 1906.

Scott, Nathan A. *Samuel Beckett.* London: Bowes and Bowes, 1965.

Sellin, Eric. *The Dramatic Concepts of Antonin Artaud.* Chicago and London: University of Chicago Press, 1968.

Smart, Ninian. *Reasons and Faiths.* London: Routledge & Kegan Paul, 1958.

Spalter, Max. *Brecht's Tradition.* Baltimore, Md.: Johns Hopkins Press, 1967.

Spiegelberg, Herbert. *The Phenomenological Movement.* The Hague: Martinus Nijhoff, 1960.

Stanford, W. B. *The Ulysses Theme.* Oxford: Basil Blackwell, 1954.

Steiner, George. *In Bluebeard's Castle.* New Haven, Conn.: Yale University Press, 1971.

Stern, Alfred. *Sartre.* New York: Dell Publishing Co., 1967.

Stoltzfus, Ben F. *Alain Robbe-Grillet and the New French Novel.* Carbondale, Ill.: Southern Illinois University Press, 1964.

Suckling, Norman. *Paul Valéry and the Civilized Mind.* London and New York: Oxford University Press, 1954.

Suhl, Benjamin. *Jean-Paul Sartre.* New York: Columbia University Press, 1970.

Sypher, Wylie. *Loss of the Self in Modern Literature and Art.* New York: Random House, 1962.

Thielicke, Helmut. *Nihilism.* Translated by John W. Doberstein. New York: Harper & Brothers, 1961.

Thiher, Allen. *Céline*. New Brunswick, N.J.: Rutgers University Press, 1972.

Tillich, Paul. *The Protestant Era*. Chicago: University of Chicago Press, 1948.

———. *Theology of Culture*. New York: Oxford University Press, 1959.

Turgenev, Ivan. *Literary Reminiscences and Autobiographical Fragments*. Translated by David Magarshack. New York: Farrar, Straus and Cudahy, 1958.

Unamuno, Miguel de. *The Tragic Sense of Life*. Translated by J. E. Crawford Flitch. London: Macmillan Company, 1926.

———. *Perplexities and Paradoxes*. Translated by Stuart Gross. New York: Philosophical Library, 1945.

———. *Poems*. Translated by Eleanor L. Trumbull. Baltimore, Md.: Johns Hopkins Press, 1951.

———. *The Agony of Christianity*. Translated by Kurt F. Reinhardt. New York: Ungar Publishing Co., 1960.

Urzidil, Johannes. *There Goes Kafka*. Translated by Harold A. Basilius. Detroit, Mich.: Wayne State University Press, 1969.

Usher, Arland. *Journey Through Dread*. London: Bowes and Bowes, 1955.

Valdes, Marie J. *Death in the Literature of Unamuno*. Urbana, Ill.: University of Illinois Press, 1964.

Vaihinger, H. *The Philosophy of "As if"*. Translated by C. K. Ogden. New York: Harcourt, Brace and Company, 1925.

Valéry, Paul. *Monsieur Teste*. Translated by Jackson Mathews. Princeton, N.J.: Princeton University Press, 1973.

———. *Reflections on the World Today*. Translated by Francis Scarfe. New York: Pantheon, 1948.

———. *Dialogues*. Translated by William McCausland Stewart. New York: Pantheon Books, 1956.

———. *The Art of Poetry*. Translated by Denise Folliot. New York: Pantheon Books, 1959.

———. *Masters and Friends*. Translated by Martin Turnell. Princeton, N.J.: Princeton University Press, 1968.

———. *Idée Fixe*. Translated by David Paul. New York: Pantheon Books, 1965.

Vivas, Eliseo. *The Artistic Transaction.* Columbus, Ohio: Ohio State University Press, 1963.

Waidson, Margaret M. *The Victorian Vision.* New York: Sheed & Ward, 1961.

Webb, Eugene. *Beckett.* Seattle, Wash.: University of Washington Press, n.d.

Weber, Alfred. *Farewell to European History.* Translated by R. F. C. Hull. New Haven, Conn.: Yale University Press, 1948.

Weisinger, Herbert. *Tragedy and the Paradox of the Fortunate Fall.* East Lansing, Mich.: Michigan State University Press, 1953.

———. *The Agony and the Triumph.* East Lansing, Mich.: Michigan State University Press, 1964.

Wellwarth, George E. *The Theater of Protest and Paradox.* New York: New York University Press, 1964.

West, Rebecca. *The Court and the Castle.* New Haven, Conn.: Yale University Press, 1957.

Wheelis, Allen. *The Quest for Identity.* New York: W. W. Norton & Company, 1958.

———. *The Illusionless Man.* New York: W. W. Norton & Company, 1966.

———. *The End of the Modern Age.* New York and London: Harper & Brothers, 1971.

———. *The Moralist.* New York: Basic Books, 1973.

Widmer, Kingsley. *The Literary Rebel.* Carbondale and Edwardsville, Ill.: Southern Illinois University Press, 1965.

Wilder, Amos N. *Modern Poetry and the Christian Tradition.* New York: Charles Scribner's Sons, 1952.

———. *Theology and Modern Literature.* Cambridge, Mass.: Harvard University Press, 1958.

Wilkinson, David. *Malraux.* Cambridge, Mass.: Harvard University Press, 1967.

Wilson, Colin. *Beyond the Outsider.* Boston: Houghton Mifflin Company, 1965.

Wittgenstein, Ludwig. *Tractatus Logico-Philosophicus.* London: Routledge & Kegan Paul, 1922.

———. *The Blue and Brown Books.* Oxford: Basil Blackwell, 1960.

Woolf, Leonard. *The Journey Not the Arrival Matters.* New York:
 Harcourt, Brace & World, 1969.
Yarmolinsky, Avraham. *Turgenev.* New York: Orion Press, 1959.
Ziolkowski, Theodore. *Dimensions of the Novel.* Princeton, N.J.:
 Princeton University Press, 1969.

Index

Abel Sanchez (Unamuno), 65
Absurd, The, 222; in Beckett, 143, 238;
    in Camus, 49, 98, 142, 143, 198–99,
    200, 202–3, 204; and Dada, 311;
    in Ionesco, 142–43, 223, 224, 225,
    226–28; in Kafka, 124, 126, 139–40,
    141; in Kierkegaard, 122–23, 143,
    180; myth of, 122; and nihilism,
    143, 155, 247; in Robbe-Grillet,
    261; in Sartre, 218, 219; and suicide,
    200; in Unamuno, 143; and Valery,
    149–50; vision of, 246
Adamov, Arthur, 203
Adams, Robert Martin: *Nil*, 27; *Strains
    of Discord*, 29, 30, 95
Alice in Wonderland (Carroll), 29
Altizer, Thomas J. J., 43
Alvarez, A.: motivation for suicide,
    99; *The Savage God*, 98, 99
Anders, Gunther, 127
Andreyev, Leonid, 83, 86, 93, 94, 103,
    305; *The Black Maskers*, 90; on
    death, 84, 86; *The Life of Man*,
    86–90, 229; Nietzsche's influence
    on, 86; and nihilism, 82–85, 86;
    Professor Storitsyn, 91–92; and the
    psychological theater, 87; Schopen-
    hauer's influence on, 86, 92; *Seven
    Who Were Hanged*, 86–87; on sui-
    cide, 85, 99, 100
Archetypes, 15; fear of death, 53–57,
    58; and nihilism, 60; and the tragic
    vision, 19

Arendt, Hannah, 95, 98–99
Art and Artist (Rank), 69
Art and Pornography (Peckham), 121
Artaud, Antonin, 311; and psycho-
    pathology, 94
Artzybashef, Michael, 94, 305; *Break-
    ing-Point*, 14, 103–15; Christianity,
    rejection of, 104; on death, 14, 106,
    107, 108, 109, 110, 111, 112; and
    Nietzsche, 104; nihilism, 103, 104,
    106; *Sanine*, 103; and Schopenhauer,
    104; and suicide, 103–15
Atheism, 46; Christian, 42–43; in
    Sartre, 210, 211

Baal (Brecht), 255
Barrett, William: *Irrational Man*, 47
Barthes, Roland, 128; "Kafka's An-
    swer," 126
Baudelaire, Charles, 43, 89
Beckett, Samuel, 30, 61, 120, 203,
    249, 259, 262, 275, 277, 314; and
    the Absurd, 143, 238; *Endgame*,
    239; on God, 235, 236, 237; *Malone
    Dies*, 235, 237; *Molloy*, 235, 237;
    Murphy, 235; and nihilism, 94, 235,
    237; *The Unnamable*, 235, 237; *Wait-
    ing for Godot*, 239, 244; *Watt*, 235,
    237–44
Beddoes, Thomas Lovell, 99, 228
Belinsky, Vissarion Grigorievich, 30–31
Benn, Gottfried, 57, 262–63, 304; on
    nihilism, 179, 182, 312

JAN 1 4 1977

DATE DUE			

79 80   04   96
88 90 92
    93 08

South Huntington Public Library
Huntington Station, New York
11746

005